Understanding the Great Recession

The Great Recession, including the preceding events and the subsequent recovery period, has been the dominant feature of US capitalism in the 21st century. But what can we learn about economic behavior, policies, and relationships by studying this period of marked general decline? *Understanding the Great Recession* seeks to answer this question by facilitating an advanced theoretical and practical understanding of the Great Recession, using multiple approaches to economic analysis.

This textbook uses the Great Recession as a case study for understanding economic concepts, the conduct of policymaking, and competing schools of economic thought. It introduces readers to multiple perspectives on the crisis, including feminist, institutionalist, Marxian, monetarist, neoclassical, post-Keynesian, and stratification economics, among others. Divided into four parts, the textbook begins by introducing readers to the headline events of the crisis, and the major differences between neoclassical and heterodox economics. The second part investigates the lead-up to the crisis, beginning with the long-term restructuring of capitalism following the Great Depression, the housing market bubble, and the transmission of the 2008 financial crisis. The third part investigates the policy responses to the crisis, such as financial reform, monetary policy, and fiscal policy. In the final part, economic performance, the shift toward populism, and policy developments during the recovery are all analyzed.

Providing the basis for understanding the long-term trajectory of capitalism today, this book is an invaluable resource for students of economics, public policy, and other related fields.

Jared M. Ragusett, Associate Professor of Economics, Central Connecticut State University, United States.

Understanding the Great Recession

A Pluralist Approach to US Capitalism in the 21st Century

Jared M. Ragusett

LONDON AND NEW YORK

Cover image: © Getty Images

First published 2024
by Routledge
4 Park Square, Milton Park, Abingdon, Oxon OX14 4RN

and by Routledge
605 Third Avenue, New York, NY 10158

Routledge is an imprint of the Taylor & Francis Group, an informa business

British Library Cataloguing-in-Publication Data
A catalogue record for this book is available from the British Library

Library of Congress Cataloging-in-Publication Data
Names: Ragusett, Jared, author.
Title: Understanding the Great Recession : a pluralist approach to US capitalism in the 21st century / Jared Ragusett.
Description: Abingdon, Oxon ; New York, NY : Routledge, 2024. | Includes bibliographical references and index. | Identifiers: LCCN 2023021668 | ISBN 9781138618176 (hardback) | ISBN 9781138618183 (paperback) | ISBN 9780429461316 (ebook)
Subjects: LCSH: Recessions--United States--History--21st century. | Capitalism--United States--History--21st century. | United States--Economic conditions--2001-2009. | United States--Economic conditions--2009- | United States--Economic policy.
Classification: LCC HC106.84 .R336 2024 | DDC 330.973--dc23/eng/20230504
LC record available at https://lccn.loc.gov/2023021668

ISBN: 978-1-138-61817-6 (hbk)
ISBN: 978-1-138-61818-3 (pbk)
ISBN: 978-0-429-46131-6 (ebk)

DOI: 10.4324/9780429461316

Typeset in Times New Roman
by SPi Technologies India Pvt Ltd (Straive)

For Chet.

CONTENTS

FIGURES

TABLES

PREFACE

This book uses the 2008 financial crisis and the Great Recession as a case study for exploring economic concepts and principles, the conduct of economic policies, and competing schools of economic thought. It is the primary textbook for my upper-level course on the Great Recession at Central Connecticut State University (CCSU), which I have taught since 2014. When I completed my doctoral dissertation in 2012, I never expected that my teaching and research interests would focus on the Great Recession. Looking back, however, those interests (and this book) clearly evolved with the crisis itself.

My interests in this subject area began during the summer of 2006, when I was developing a dissertation prospectus at the University of Massachusetts—Amherst (UMass—Amherst). My dissertation critiqued a body of research within mainstream economics on the relationship between metropolitan land use patterns and various facets of racial inequality, principally housing consumption and residential segregation. I was also teaching a course on money and banking. By the end of the summer, the first trembling of the crisis began to emerge. Housing prices were dropping, uncertainty was spreading across Wall Street, and two words kept appearing in the press: "subprime mortgages." As the crisis unfolded, I quickly realized that it intersected with my dissertation in fundamental ways. I began exploring the connections between my research question and the provision of subprime mortgage products, securitization by financial institutions, and the stability of global financial markets.

As I was completing my dissertation, I accepted a full-time position at CCSU during the fall of 2010. By that point, the US government and the Federal Reserve had enacted the major policy responses to the crisis, including the bailouts, Dodd-Frank, quantitative easing, and the American Recovery and Reinvestment Act. The National Bureau of Economic Research also determined that the trough of the recession occurred in June 2009. However, I was fascinated by the growing opposition toward the policy responses and the shift toward austerity, which set the stage for the Tea Party wave during the midterm elections.

As I was working my way through the tenure-track process, I decided that there was enough content in this subject area to warrant a new economics course. I appreciated (and continue to appreciate) the open curriculum process at CCSU, which allows faculty to test-run special topics courses before adding them to the course catalog. I had a significant volume of resources and information from my dissertation to cover the housing market and financial structure. Between financial reform, the monetary policy measures, and the fiscal policy measures, there was certainly enough information for a policy unit. The recovery itself brought about some very compelling debates about austerity versus stimulus, inequality, labor rights, legal accountability for Wall Street, and the role of government. Most importantly, I could draw upon the theoretical and historical analysis from my graduate courses at UMass—Amherst to offer students different tools of economic inquiry to understand this crisis, how it arose, and its aftermath.

For the first few iterations of this course, I used original articles, chapters, publicly available data, technical reports, and a limited number of course readers that were on the market. Although students appreciated working with primary resources that were current, the syllabus was very piecemeal. Furthermore, those resources quickly became outdated, especially following the 2010 midterm elections. I decided that the course—and the market—needed something more comprehensive and cohesive.

Once I was promoted to associate professor in 2017, I began pursuing this project, but had no idea how (or where) to start. In order to organize my own process, and also to collaborate with my fellow heterodox economists, I organized a panel on Teaching the Great Recession Using Radical Economics for the Union for Radical Political Economics Program at the Allied Social Sciences Association (ASSA) Annual Meeting. Just before the ASSA, I received an email from Andy Humphries at Routledge, who saw the session on the program, and wanted to meet to discuss potential book projects. From there, we began developing the proposal.

One point in that conversation still resonates with me. I explained to Andy that I wanted the book to be chronological. It would trace the lead-up to the crisis, the policy responses during the crisis, and then the recovery from the crisis. My biggest concern was the third phase: the recovery. At that point, the recovery from the crisis was still underway. The most important question was: where would this book end? I jokingly said, "I hope the economy tanks sometime in 2020, so I can have an official end date to the recovery before the book is published …" That end date turned out to be February 2020, with the onset of the Covid-19 pandemic recession. While the pandemic made writing this book much more challenging, it provided a suitable conclusion to this work. Or perhaps the beginning of another work …

ACKNOWLEDGMENTS

I would like to thank the following people for their encouragement, feedback, and support during this process. Writing a solo-authored textbook while managing a heavy teaching load is a challenging endeavor, but it is even more challenging during a global pandemic. Whether it was through an encouraging word, an informal conversation, or a formal review of a draft manuscript, I appreciate everyone who contributed in some way to this work.

I would first like to thank Andy Humphries, senior editor at Routledge, for helping get this project off the ground. In 2017, I organized a panel session on Teaching the Great Recession using Radical Economics, as part of the Union for Radical Political Economics Program (URPE) at the Allied Social Science Associations Annual Meeting. While at the meetings in Chicago, Andy reached out to discuss potential book projects and I, in fact, had a potential book project. Over the next several months, we worked together on a proposal that proved to be very successful, as the final version of this book is largely consistent with that proposal. I would also like to thank the editorial assistants at Routledge for their assistance, communication, and patience throughout this process; as well as four anonymous reviewers for their comments and suggestions.

I would like to thank several friends and colleagues for taking the time to review chapter manuscripts: Anita Dancs (Western New England University), Paramita Dhar (Central Connecticut State University), Nina Eichacker (University of Rhode Island), Michael Meeropol (Western New England University), Özgür Orhangazi (Kadir Has University), and Carolyne Soper (Central Connecticut State University). Perhaps inadvertently, a number of informal conversations proved to be very helpful in the development of this work. Jerry Epstein (University of Massachusetts—Amherst) gave me excellent advice on how to frame the structure and purpose of this book, when I developed the initial proposal for Routledge. Carlos Liard-Muriente (Central Connecticut State University) provided significant guidance on how to present monetary policy; as did Alfredo Rosete (Central Connecticut State University) on the topic of populism. I am also grateful for the feedback that I received on presentations of this work at the 2021 Eastern Economic Association Annual Meeting and the 2022 Western Social Science Association Annual Conference.

I am grateful to my students and colleagues at Central Connecticut State University (CCSU) for their support. I have offered my course on the Great Recession four times at CCSU, and I continue to be impressed by the interesting and compelling research projects that students have completed in this subject area. I am also grateful to my colleagues for supporting this project through several semesters of research-reassigned time, and a one-semester sabbatical leave during the spring of 2020.

I would like to express my gratitude to my friends and family for their encouragement and motivation, especially at the most difficult stages of this project during Covid-19. I would also like to dedicate this work to the people who forged my interest in heterodox economics, including the economics graduate students and faculty of the University of Massachusetts—Amherst, my colleagues on the Steering Committee of URPE, as well as my undergraduate mentor Louis-Philippe Rochon, who first introduced me to the work of Hyman Minsky in 1999.

Lastly, the deepest appreciation is owed to my husband, Chet Jordan, who supported me from nearly the beginning of this project. Chet read every single chapter of this book. But most importantly, I could not have completed this project without his patience and encouragement, both on the good writing days and the bad writing days.

To everyone, thank you.

We learn geology the morning after the earthquake …

Ralph Waldo Emerson

PART I

Understanding the Crisis

CHAPTER 1

Introduction to the Great Recession

With the onset of the Covid-19 pandemic recession in February 2020, US capitalism has now experienced 12 official recessions since the end of World War II. It is likely that policymakers have celebrated the economic expansions that preceded those recessions and diminished the prospects of future downturns—despite the regularity at which such downturns occur. According to the National Bureau of Economic Research (NBER), the organization that determines the official dates of the US business cycle, the average expansion lasts only about five years. The 2001–07 expansion is no different in this regard. On August 1, 2006, US Treasury Secretary Hank Paulson was asked on CNBC: "Do you think the U.S. economy is facing a recession?" His answer: "Absolutely not." In the summer of 2007, President George W. Bush tried to calm increasing financial and economic instability by maintaining that: "The fundamentals of our economy are strong." And at the height of the financial crisis in September 2008, Republican senator and presidential candidate John McCain famously stated: "Our economy, I think, still the fundamentals of our economy are strong."

It is also likely that most of the 12 postwar downturns do not warrant an entire textbook devoted to understanding their underlying causes, the transmission of their effects on the economic system, the policies crafted in response to them, and their lasting historical legacy. However, the Great Recession—the severe downturn that officially occurred between December 2007 and June 2009—is unique in both regards. It is notable not only for its historical severity and complexity, but also for the misguided and at times fraudulent assessments of the economic system that preceded the downturn.

Why then does the Great Recession—more commonly referred to as the "crisis"—warrant an entire textbook devoted to it? After all, according to Table 1.1, the recovery from the crisis now exceeds the long and celebrated expansions of the 1960s, 1980s, and 1990s. The purpose of this book is to use the Great Recession as a case study in order to understand economic concepts and principles, the conduct of economic policies, and competing schools of economic thought. Despite the duration of the post-crisis recovery, the Great Recession was

DOI: 10.4324/9780429461316-2

TABLE 1.1 US Expansions and Recessions since World War II

	Duration (Months)	
November 1945–November 1948	Expansion	37
December 1948–October 1949	*Recession*	*11*
November 1949–July 1953	Expansion	45
August 1953–May 1954	*Recession*	*10*
June 1954–August 1957	Expansion	39
September 1957–April 1958	*Recession*	*8*
May 1958–April 1960	Expansion	24
May 1960–February 1961	*Recession*	*10*
March 1961–December 1969	Expansion	106
January 1970–November 1970	*Recession*	*11*
December 1970–November 1973	Expansion	36
December 1973–March 1975	*Recession*	*16*
April 1975–January 1980	Expansion	58
February 1980–July 1980	*Recession*	*6*
August 1980–July 1981	Expansion	12
August 1981–November 1982	*Recession*	*16*
December 1982–July 1990	Expansion	92
August 1990–March 1991	*Recession*	*8*
April 1991–March 2001	Expansion	120
April 2001–November 2001	*Recession*	*8*
December 2001–December 2007	Expansion	73
January 2008–June 2009	*Recession*	*18*
July 2009–February 2020	Expansion	128
March 2020–April 2020	*Recession*	*2*
	Average Expansion	64.2
	Average Recession	10.3

Source: Business Cycle Dating Committee of the National Bureau of Economic Research, "US Business Cycle Expansions and Contractions:" https://www.nber.org/research/data/us-business-cycle-expansions-and-contractions

the longest contraction of the postwar period. Just as earthquake fissures allow geologists to study the structure and evolution of the Earth's interior, crises allow economists to study the structure and evolution of the capitalist economic system. The fundamental question that this textbook asks is: what can economists learn about economic behavior, policies, and relationships by studying the Great Recession? This question connects the major events and headline stories—before, during, and after the Great Recession—with the concepts that are the central focus of this book. To be clear, studying an economic system through its failures is an approach that is rare in the economics discipline. For example, studying economic history prior to the crisis facilitates a deeper understanding of the evolutionary nature of capitalism and the US class structure. Studying the housing market bubble and the ensuing foreclosure crisis facilitates a deeper understanding of racial inequalities in mortgage lending and home ownership, which have persisted for decades. Learning about the 2008 financial crisis is a lens for investigating the complexity of financial structure, regulation, and reform. Similarly, the fiscal policies of the W. Bush and Obama administrations, as well as the monetary policies of the US Federal Reserve under Ben Bernanke and Janet Yellen, are vehicles for understanding the conduct, effectiveness, and limitations of government policies. As this textbook will show, the forces that culminated in the Great Recession were present long before the recovery that preceded it, just as the effects of the Great Recession continue to shape the long-term trajectory of capitalism in the twenty-first century. In many ways—especially for workers and historically under-represented groups—the Great Recession began well before December 2007 and did not simply end in June 2009.

This chapter introduces readers to the Great Recession and the ways that this textbook will approach it. The first section summarizes the major events, policy responses, and economic changes related to the Great Recession. This overview will either remind or introduce readers to the headline stories of the crisis. However, this textbook is not simply a recounting of those events. Its primary goal is to facilitate an advanced theoretical and practical understanding of the Great Recession using multiple approaches to economic analysis. The second section therefore surveys competing perspectives in economics—in particular, the key distinctions between orthodox and heterodox approaches to the appropriate unit of analysis, economic behavior, the structure and operation of the economic system, the relevance of history, the role of government, and the method of investigation. The third section explains the plan and purpose of the book for both students and instructors.

Box 1.1 Determining Booms and Busts: The National Bureau of Economic Research

The NBER is responsible for determining the official dates of the US business cycle. The NBER is a non-partisan, non-profit, private research organization. The Business Cycle Dating Committee of the NBER defines an "expansion"—or "recovery"—as a sustained period of rising economic activity. Although the Committee considers multiple economic indicators in its assessments, real gross domestic product—the market value of goods and services produced within US borders, adjusted for inflation—is the primary measure. A "peak" occurs when an expansion ends. Conversely, the Committee defines a "recession"—or contraction—as a period of declining economic activity. A "trough" occurs when a recession ends. A trough simply marks when a contraction is over. It does not mark a full return to the level of economic activity prior to the contraction. Therefore, an expansion is a period when the economic system moves from trough to peak; whereas a recession is a period when the economic system moves from peak to trough.

Box 1.2 The Capitalist Economic System

This textbook frequently uses the term "economic system," as opposed to the traditional term "economy." Whereas mainstream economists typically use the term "economy" to describe the organization of markets—in which the exchange of goods, services, and resources occurs—heterodox economists use the term "economic system" to describe the organization of production. Although heterodox economists also analyze the nature of market exchange, they ask deeper questions about the process of production. For example, who performs labor and produces output? Who controls and organizes the production process? What property rights do producers and controllers have? How do their roles in the production process determine their compensation? The answers to these questions vary across human societies and historical contexts.

Capitalism is one such economic system. In a capitalist system, the capitalist class privately owns means of production (capital goods, infrastructure, raw materials, etc.), and therefore organizes and controls the production process. Since it controls the output of the production process, the capitalist class earns profit. The working class, which does not own means of production, performs labor and produces output in exchange for a wage or salary.

THE GREAT RECESSION: A CHRONOLOGY

This chronology outlines the major events surrounding the Great Recession. For some readers, it will serve as a refresher. For others, it will serve as an introduction. In either case, it includes references to economic concepts, policies, practices, and terms, with brief explanations. The primary chapters of the book then develop a full analysis of those concepts and their relationship to the crisis. Table 1.2 presents a timeline of these events between 2006 and 2020.

The Rise and Fall of the 2001–07 Expansion

The pre-Great Recession expansion began in December 2001 following an eight-month contraction of economic activity. That recession, principally brought about by the bursting of the dot-com bubble, ended the lengthy 1991–2001 expansion. By historical standards, the 2001 recession was short and relatively mild. With the exception of corporate profitability, however, the recovery that followed was the weakest of the postwar period according to a study conducted by the Economic Policy Institute. This was especially the case in the labor market. For individuals who derive income from labor, the 2001–07 expansion continued a pattern of jobless recovery that arose in the 1990s. A jobless recovery occurs when an economic system experiences growth but without substantial gains in employment and wages, despite rising labor productivity. The United States also carried a larger trade deficit during this period, whereby foreign imports exceeded exports to the rest of the world.

The obvious question becomes: how did US capitalism expand without significant job creation, without rising real incomes for workers, and with relatively greater consumption of foreign goods and services? There are two major reasons.

TABLE 1.2 The Great Recession: A Timeline

April 2006	US home prices reach their pre-crisis peak
August 2007	The Federal Reserve begins lowering interest rates
December 2007	The US officially enters a recession (2001–07 expansion ends)
February 2008	President Bush signs the Economic Stimulus Act
March 2008	Collapse of Bear Stearns and sale to JPMorgan Chase
June 2008	Oil prices surge to $133.93 per barrel
July 2008	President Bush signs the Housing and Economic Recovery Act (HERA)
September 2008	Federal government takes over Fannie Mae and Freddie Mac; Collapse of Lehman Brothers; Bailout of American International Group (AIG); Stock market crashes
October 2008	President Bush signs the Emergency Economic Stabilization Act, initiating the Troubled Assets Relief Program (TARP); FDIC raises deposit insurance coverage and guarantees bank debt
November 2008	Bailout of Citigroup
December 2008	President Bush initiates bailout of the US auto industry
January 2009	Bailout of Bank of America; US consumer prices begin to rise following months of deflation
February 2009	President Obama signs the American Recovery and Reinvestment Act (ARRA); Oil prices bottom out at $39.16 per barrel
June 2009	The recession officially ends (The recovery begins)
October 2009	US unemployment reaches its recession peak of 10%
July 2010	President Obama signs the Dodd-Frank Wall Street Reform and Consumer Protection Act
December 2010	President Obama signs the Tax Relief, Unemployment Insurance Reauthorization, and Job Creation Act
January 2011	Propelled by the Tea Party wave, Republicans regain control of the US House of Representatives
August 2011	Debt ceiling crisis; President Obama signs the Budget Control Act; Standard & Poor's reduces its rating on long-term US debt
September 2011	Occupy Wall Street Movement begins in New York City
March 2012	US home prices reach their post-crisis low
September 2015	US unemployment returns to its pre-crisis low of 5%
December 2015	The Federal Reserve raises interest rates
January 2018	US home prices return to their pre-crisis peak
May 2018	President Trump signs partial repeal of Dodd-Frank
February 2020	The US officially enters a recession (2009–20 expansion ends)

First, the W. Bush administration ran budget deficits. A deficit occurs when government expenditures exceed tax revenues. However, both policy decisions and weak economic performance can contribute to a deficit, meaning a deficit can be structural or cyclical in nature. On the one hand, the W. Bush administration eliminated the budget surpluses of the Clinton era through deliberate policy changes, such as a series of tax cuts that heavily favored the rich, a significant expansion of Medicare, and the wars in Afghanistan and Iraq. On the other hand, the sluggish economic growth that characterized this period also contributed to the deficit. Tax revenues decreased, as it was more difficult for the government to collect taxes from middle-income earners, whose incomes were stagnant. Tax cuts for top-income earners in particular, whose incomes indeed grew substantially during this period, exacerbated the drop in federal tax receipts. Expenditures also increased as more people qualified for social welfare programs, such as food stamps and unemployment insurance.

But the second and most important reason is that consumption increased significantly. The deeper question then becomes: how did US workers spend more without actually earning more? The simple answer is: they *borrowed* more. Beginning in the late 1990s, US capitalism experienced a significant home price appreciation that developed into a housing market bubble. Workers financed greater consumption, despite stagnant earnings, by borrowing against the only asset that they typically own: their home. Historically low interest rates, as a result of the Federal Reserve's expansionary monetary policy, combined with greater access to credit through subprime mortgage lending, enabled a sharp increase in household debt. A subprime mortgage product is a loan for riskier borrowers who do not qualify for a traditional 30-year, fixed-rate mortgage due to poor credit, low or irregular income, or lack of a down payment.

In the spring of 2006, the rapid home price appreciation ended and the bubble began to burst. As home prices fell, workers no longer had access to a significant source of credit. This had several dire consequences that slowed economic performance over the next year. First, they could no longer sustain their level of consumption, which was (and still is) the largest source of overall spending. Second, they could no longer refinance their already high level of debt, which led to a surge in mortgage defaults and foreclosures. Third, as economic uncertainty rose with the implosion of the subprime mortgage market, business investment collapsed. In an effort to stem the increasingly inevitable slide into recession and boost spending, the Federal Reserve lowered benchmark interest rates in the summer of 2007. It was nowhere near enough. By December, the inherently weak fundamentals following the 2001 downturn were no longer sustainable, and US capitalism slipped back into recession.

The 2008 Financial Crisis and the Policy Responses of the W. Bush Administration

In an attempt to jumpstart economic growth, President Bush signed the Economic Stimulus Act in February 2008. The Economic Stimulus Act included tax rebates for individuals in an effort to boost consumption, as well as tax incentives for businesses in a bid to boost investment. However, it proved largely ineffective, as the overriding drag on economic activity was a lack of confidence due to the accelerating housing market bust and subprime mortgage meltdown.

In March, the collapse of Bear Stearns set in motion the transition from a mortgage default crisis to a full-blown financial crisis. Bear Stearns was a Wall Street investment bank that engaged in mortgage securitization. Securitization is a process whereby an investment bank purchases mortgages from a commercial bank using borrowed funds, pools the mortgages, and sells the income flow from the underlying pool as a security. As long as borrowers paid their mortgages, investors in mortgage-backed securities held financial assets with solid market value and Bear Stearns in turn made a profit. The perception at the time was that mortgage-backed securities were high-quality, low-default risk investments because commercial banks primarily lent to low-default risk borrowers. With the subprime crisis, however, investors began to question Bear's exposure to subprime mortgages, and a lack of confidence in the quality and risk of Bear's mortgage pools set in. The problem for Wall Street was this: if Bear had invested heavily in subprime mortgages, and those borrowers defaulted on their payments, then Bear would no longer have access to the income flows from the mortgages. If Bear ran out of money, and the underlying value of its mortgage pools collapsed, it would be unable to transfer income to mortgage-backed security investors. Bear would also be unable to repay its own creditors. This sentiment heightened the default risk of mortgage-backed securities and led to a collapse in their market value throughout global financial markets. With their rebranding as "toxic assets," Bear could no longer engage in profitable securitization. Furthermore, institutional investors in mortgage-backed securities throughout the financial system now held an asset with almost zero market value, which they could no longer liquidate, resulting in a loss of net worth for them. To be clear, it did not matter whether Bear had *actually* run out of money (in fact, analysts continue to debate this question to this day). Once confidence in Bear Stearns deteriorated, a self-fulfilling prophecy ensued, and the process unwound. When investors perceived that Bear was at risk of default, they took actions that culminated in the very outcome they sought to avoid. Unable to raise capital due to a high degree of uncertainty, the Federal Reserve Bank of New York arranged the sale of Bear Stearns to JPMorgan Chase. What started as a housing market bust led to a mortgage default crisis, the failure of an investment bank, and now a crisis in securities markets.

By the summer of 2008, it was clear that uncertainty in the financial system had extended beyond the failure of Bear Stearns. A surge in oil prices to over $130 per barrel placed further stress on economic activity. It was also clear that traditional expansionary fiscal and monetary policies would not be enough to boost economic growth. The federal government therefore decided to take more direct action against the subprime mortgage meltdown and passed the Housing and Economic Recovery Act (HERA) in July. HERA featured the following provisions: a tax credit for new homeowners, in order to stimulate housing demand and stem the collapse of housing prices; funding to refinance subprime loans to traditional 30-year, fixed-rate loans; and capital injections for Fannie Mae and Freddie Mac, which set the stage for their eventual takeover by the federal government in the fall of that year.

Fannie Mae and Freddie Mac are government-chartered, publicly traded home mortgage companies. At the time of the 2008 financial crisis, they owned or guaranteed half of all US mortgages. Fannie and Freddie are unique corporations in that they serve both public interests and private interests. On the one hand, as government-chartered firms, they must fulfill a public interest by expanding access to home ownership. On the other hand, as publicly traded firms, they must fulfill a private interest by earning a profit for their shareholders. Like Bear Stearns, Fannie and Freddie engaged in mortgage securitization. But unlike the "private-label" securities created by investment banks, their primary motivation was to free up access to credit in the private mortgage industry in order to increase home ownership. This process is how Fannie and Freddie fulfilled their dual interests: they purchased mortgages in order to fulfill their public interest of increasing middle-class wealth, and sold mortgage-backed securities in order to fulfill their private interest of earning a profit. However, given their exposure to the mortgage default crisis *and* the mortgage-backed security crisis, confidence in their ability to fulfill *both* missions fell, and uncertainty grew. If Fannie and Freddie collapsed, the consequences would be even more far-reaching than Bear Stearns and would almost assuredly lead to a credit crisis unseen in generations.

Few economists would disagree that the fall of 2008 was the most disastrous period for US capitalism to date since the Great Depression of the 1930s. The uncertainty and lack of confidence that continued to spread throughout the financial sector stemmed from two sentiments: (1) investors held severely negative expectations because the government did not seem to have a concerted plan to intervene and resolve the crisis; and (2) investors held severely negative expectations because the government *was* intervening or would further intervene. The events of September only further intensified both of those fears. The federal government took over Fannie Mae and Freddie Mac, acting on the provisions of HERA. Lehman Brothers, which did not receive a Bear Stearns-style rescue package, filed for bankruptcy. American International Group, on the other hand, which insured mortgage-backed securities against default, received a bailout from the Federal Reserve. And after the failure of an initial bill to bail out the financial industry, due to a revolt by Congressional Republicans, the stock market crashed. The financial meltdown was, in part, the result of an instilled belief that the financial system itself protected the economic system from instability. In 2002, then-Governor Ben Bernanke stated the following before the National Economists Club:

> Over the years, the U.S. economy has shown a remarkable ability to absorb shocks of all kinds, to recover, and to continue to grow. Flexible and efficient markets for labor and capital, an entrepreneurial tradition, and a general willingness to tolerate and even embrace technological and economic change all contribute to this resiliency. A particularly important protective factor in the current environment is the strength of our financial system ...

Contrary to Bernanke's statements, the financial system was not a protective factor but rather a threat to economic stability.

The second attempt at passing a comprehensive bailout bill was successful, if not controversial. In October, President Bush signed the Emergency Economic Stabilization Act. The Act initiated the infamous Troubled Asset Relief Program, which allowed the federal government to purchase mortgage-backed securities and other toxic assets, and provided direct capital injections to distressed banks. In fact, capital injections would become the principal mechanism of the government's response to the financial meltdown. The Federal Deposit Insurance Corporation also increased deposit insurance coverage and guaranteed bank debt. Separate government bailouts of Citigroup and Bank of America would follow, as would a bailout of the US auto industry.

The Policy Responses of the Obama Administration and the End of the Crisis

During the 2008 US presidential election, Barack Obama ran on a largely liberal policy platform. In the end, he would essentially have two years to implement his domestic economic agenda. By early 2009, US capitalism reached the point where private sector spending alone was simply unable to jumpstart economic growth. Consumption remained weak in light of high unemployment and sluggish hiring. Investment remained weak in light of significant uncertainty in the direction of the economic system. Housing was not the only sector that experienced a crash in market prices; oil prices, wages, and market interest rates fell as well. The tax credits and incentives of the previous administration, as well as a massive increase in the money supply through quantitative easing, were also unable to resuscitate spending. In order to counteract a severe shortfall in private sector spending, Congress enacted a $787 billion fiscal stimulus package. The American Recovery and Reinvestment Act (ARRA) carried three major provisions:

- a series of tax cuts—by far the largest provision—which included individual, business, infrastructure, and energy tax cuts;
- an increase in government spending on goods and services directed towards infrastructure, education, and health research; and
- an increase in funding for social welfare programs, such as Medicaid, food stamps, and unemployment insurance; as well as funding for states to balance education budgets and prevent cuts.

While the effectiveness of the ARRA and other fiscal and financial policies remains heavily debated, the Great Recession came to an end in June 2009. This only means that the economic system reached a "trough," and that the contraction was over. It does not mean that the economic system reached a full recovery. President Obama signed two more major pieces of legislation from a Democratic Congress in order to encourage further recovery. First, in July 2010, he signed the Dodd-Frank Wall Street Reform and Consumer Protection Act. The broad purpose of Dodd-Frank was to reform the financial structures and regulatory oversights that culminated in the 2008 financial crisis. Among other things, the Act called for the establishment of a Financial Stability Oversight Council in order to identify systemic risks in the financial sector that threaten economic stability; a process of liquidating failing financial firms in order to avoid taxpayer-funded bailouts; greater enforcement of regulations already in place; the elimination of regulatory loopholes in financial markets; increased transparency and accountability of the credit rating agencies; executive compensation reform; the establishment of a Bureau of Consumer Financial Protection; Federal Reserve reform; mortgage lending reform; and measures to combat the foreclosure crisis. Second, at the end of 2010, Obama signed the Tax Relief, Unemployment Insurance Reauthorization, and Job Creation Act. On the tax side, it included an extension of the middle-income Bush-era tax cuts, as well as a temporary reduction in payroll taxes. On the spending side, it included an extension of certain provisions of the ARRA and a one-year extension of unemployment insurance.

The Uneven Recovery and the Shift towards Populism

For the remainder of his time in office, however, Obama's domestic economic agenda stalled. Propelled by the conservative Tea Party wave, Republicans regained control of the US House of Representatives in 2010 and the US Senate in 2014. The GOP also regained control of several governorships and state houses, which are the incubators of public policy in the United States, leading to drastic cuts in taxes, austerity budgets, and attacks on public sector collective bargaining rights. A series of bitter political stalemates over fiscal policy and the federal budget process began with the debt ceiling crisis of 2011. Congressional Republicans called for greater fiscal restraint and deficit reduction in exchange for raising the debt ceiling, which previously carried without concessions, controversy, or even debate. Had it not raised the debt ceiling, the federal government would have assuredly defaulted and triggered yet another financial crisis. Although Congress and the White House reached an agreement, resulting in the Budget Control Act, further stalemates throughout Obama's tenure would ensue. As a result of the political brinksmanship surrounding the debt ceiling crisis, Standard & Poor's downgraded its credit rating on long-term US government debt.

The inadequate and sluggish policy process of the remaining Obama-Tea Party years reflected an inadequate and sluggish recovery. In retrospect, this statement by Ben Bernanke in 2004 regarding the long-term decline in macroeconomic volatility is still technically true:

> One of the most striking features of the economic landscape over the past twenty years or so has been a substantial decline in macroeconomic volatility ... The reduction in the volatility of output is also closely associated with the fact that recessions have become less frequent and less severe.

Since the Great Recession, recessions have not become more frequent, and output has not become more volatile. The greater concern is the persistence of secular stagnation. Secular stagnation occurs when an economic system experiences sluggish growth—just enough to avoid recession, but not enough to constitute a substantive expansion. Moreover, owners of capital almost exclusively receive the benefits of any new growth—a trend that has persisted for several decades. For individuals who derive income from capital, the latter six years of the Obama administration featured a rebound in corporate profits, a surge in cash reserves, a stock market recovery, and a Wall Street comeback. But for individuals who derive income from labor, those years featured stagnant wages, underemployment, and shrinking labor force participation. Housing prices, which recovered slightly after bottoming out in May 2009, would continue to slip until early 2012. Unemployment, which continued to rise until October 2009, would not return to its pre-crisis level until late 2015. In fact, the initial years of the recovery were so weak that many analysts feared a "double-dip" recession.

Beyond the inequality in the distribution of wealth and income, the strength of the recovery varied within the United States and around the world. States, cities, and even counties had different experiences with the crisis and have therefore had different experiences with the recovery. Some metropolitan areas were hit particularly hard by the housing bust and subprime meltdown, while others were not. Some states and regions struggled to fully recover, while others prospered following the crisis. Around the world, instability has also marked the period since the Great Recession. The European Monetary Union faced a sovereign debt crisis starting in 2009, while Brazil fell into crisis in 2014.

Although the Federal Reserve began raising interest rates at the end of 2015, signaling that the national recovery was firmly on track, unresolved economic anxieties from the Great Recession fueled populist movements on both the Left and the Right. Once again, contrary to the expectations of Bernanke and other policymakers, workers expressed hostility—not resilience—toward economic, technological, and cultural change. On the Left, grassroots activists organized against inequality, corruption, and corporate influence in government through the Occupy Wall Street movement. Fight for $15, which began after fast-food workers in New York City demanded higher wages and union rights, became a global campaign for low-wage service workers. At the state level, activists have mounted successful campaigns for minimum wage increases, stronger environmental protections, criminal justice reform, and legalization of recreational marijuana. Bernie Sanders mounted two serious bids for president on a democratic socialist platform—a movement that continues to push the Democratic policy platform in a more progressive direction. As a result, Democrats have developed serious proposals for a Green New Deal, Medicare-for-All, and student loan forgiveness. Social movements against racial and gender stratification, and greater attention to issues of intersectionality, have also pushed the party to the left. On the Right, of course, Donald Trump ran a successful presidential campaign on his own populist platform that combined anti-trade and anti-immigrant sentiments with a pledge to challenge established power structures in government and the economic system. Trump departed from Republican orthodoxy by repositioning the United States away from its postwar alliances and position of global leadership. Despite his election loss in 2020, his legacy of a Republican Party pervaded by anti-intellectualism, conspiracy theories, domestic terrorists, and White nationalism persists. Elsewhere in the world, Great Britain voted to withdraw from the European Union; while Jeremy Corbyn—another democratic socialist—became leader of the British Labour Party. Far-right candidates and political parties have also grown in influence in Brazil, Germany, Hungary, Poland, Turkey, India, and the Philippines.

In the policy arena, President Trump and Congressional Republicans reversed, or attempted to reverse, the legacy of Obama's economic agenda using both legislative and non-legislative measures. On the legislative side, Trump signed a partial repeal of Dodd-Frank in May 2018. On the non-legislative side, the administration appointed heads of regulatory bodies who are hostile toward regulation; rescinded regulations by executive order; appointed federal judges and Supreme Court justices who are hostile toward consumer protection, financial regulation, and labor; or simply did not enforce regulations already on the books. Regardless of how successful the Biden administration is in steering US capitalism through the aftermath of the Covid-19 pandemic, Trump's policies and judicial appointees will continue to shape the trajectory of US capitalism in still untold ways.

The purpose of this chronology was to present the foremost events and observations related to the Great Recession. At a practical level, there is widespread agreement in the field of economics as to what those events are. There is widespread agreement, for example, on the information presented in Table 1.2. The more challenging exercise for economists is to develop theories that explain *why* the specific events related to the crisis happened. Unlike natural scientists, economists and social scientists cannot conduct controlled experiments in order to trace causes and effects, especially when examining national or global economic systems. They must therefore make assumptions about human behavior and the nature of economic relationships. They must use logic and deduction to develop models of complex events like the Great Recession. At a theoretical level, there is disagreement in economics on how to build such models. The next section of this chapter introduces the nature of those disagreements between competing perspectives.

COMPETING PERSPECTIVES IN ECONOMICS

In 1924, John Maynard Keynes published a tribute to the late Alfred Marshall in *The Economic Journal*. In this memoir, Keynes discusses the attributes of the 'master economist:'

> The study of economics does not seem to require any specialised gifts of an unusually high order. Is it not, intellectually regarded, a very easy subject compared with the higher branches of philosophy or pure science? Yet good, or even competent, economists are the rarest of birds. An easy subject, at which very few excel! The paradox finds its explanation, perhaps, in that the master-economist must possess a rare *combination* of gifts. He must reach a high standard in several different directions and must combine talents not often found together. He must be mathematician, historian, statesman, philosopher—in some degree. He must understand symbols and speak in words. He must contemplate the particular in terms of the general, and touch abstract and concrete in the same flight of thought. He must study the present in the light of the past for the purposes of the future. No part of man's nature or his institutions must lie entirely outside his regard. He must be purposeful and disinterested in a simultaneous mood; as aloof and incorruptible as an artist, yet sometimes as near the earth as a politician.

One of the compelling points raised by Keynes in this passage is the inherent difficulty in formulating theories of the economic system that are both rigorous and intelligible. This challenge applies no less to the Great Recession. Although other fields face similar challenges in developing theories of their respective subjects, the focus of the economist *appears* to be easier. It seems as though the subject of the economist (the structure and operation of the economic system) is easier than that of the natural scientist (the structure and operation of the natural and physical world), as well as the philosopher (the nature of ethics, existence, knowledge, and logic). Economists, however, must consider and weigh multiple dimensions of analysis that are mathematical, historical, political, and philosophical in nature. They face further challenges in developing scientific techniques that are also understandable; in determining an appropriate scale of analysis; in weighing reality versus the abstract; in considering time; and in accounting for the complexity of human nature and institutions. Like other social sciences, competing perspectives exist within economics due to disagreements over the balance and relevance of these different roles and issues. Unlike most social sciences, however, economics is unique in that one school of thought dominates the profession throughout academia, government, international institutions, the private sector, and think tanks.

This section explains the theoretical differences between neoclassical economics—regarded as the mainstream or orthodox approach to economic analysis—and a body of alternative schools of thought known as heterodox economics. It does so by comparing their approaches to the appropriate unit of analysis, economic behavior, the structure and operation of an economic system, the relevance of history, the role of government, and the method of investigation. The purpose of this discussion is twofold. First, it lays the basis for future units and chapters, which explore economic principles in more detail and in more specific contexts. Second, it establishes the pluralist approach to economic analysis taken by this book. Pluralism is a tradition that emphasizes diversity in economic thought by elevating the rich contributions of heterodox perspectives and their critiques of neoclassical theory. This is another aspect of this book's method that is rare in the economics discipline: counterbalancing the dominance of orthodoxy in the dissemination of economic principles.

Why are these distinctions important for understanding the Great Recession? In the spirit of Keynes, the Great Recession is an easy subject that is difficult to explain. It is easy in the sense that most readers will be familiar with the major events and broad issues related to the crisis. Moreover, the crisis may have personally affected many readers. The difficulty lies in constructing a logical and accurate explanation of the Great Recession. For example, the Great Recession raises ethical questions about the business practices of financial institutions. It raises philosophical questions about the role of government when the economic system fails. Economists can analyze the Great Recession using mathematical and statistical models (or not). They can analyze it in historical context (or not). Economists must make critical assumptions about economic behavior, and the decision making of individuals and organizations, across multiple facets of the crisis. Orthodox and heterodox theories differ according to which of these roles and elements of economic analysis they consider, and the weight they assign to each of them. The goal of this section is not just to acknowledge these differences, but also to evaluate and critique their contributions to understanding how economic systems function, and at times fail. Table 1.3 summarizes these differences across six major points of comparison.

TABLE 1.3 Competing Perspectives in Economics

	Neoclassical Economics	*Heterodox Economics*
Unit of Analysis	Individual agents or organizations.	Classes, institutions, group affiliations, the national economic system, or the global economic system.
Economic Behavior	Self-interest exclusively motivates behavior. Individuals have full information and optimize subject to monetary and technological constraints.	Self-interest motivates behavior as does the desire to improve, or worsen, the well-being of others. Individuals lack full information and must learn through adaptation. Behavior may reflect enabling myths. Individuals make decisions under uncertainty.

(*Continued*)

TABLE 1.3 (Continued)

	Neoclassical Economics	*Heterodox Economics*
Structure and Operation of the Economic System	Scarcity is the core economic dilemma. Capitalism is a system of competitive markets that naturally gravitate towards equilibrium. Economic decisions are voluntary.	Capitalism is a system of production carried out by labor processes. Labor processes include commodity production, social reproduction, and non-capitalist economic systems. Analysis of production emphasizes power relations. Core issues include capital accumulation, surplus production, unemployment, and excess capacity.
History	Economic analysis is ahistorical. The operation of the economic system preserves the status quo. Cultural, environmental, historical, and social changes are exogenous.	Economic analysis is historical. The operation of the economic system generates change and interacts with social systems, culture, and the environment.
Role of Government	Policy should maintain little to no government intervention in the economic system. Analysis of government intervention largely focuses on barriers to entry.	Policy can change the structure and direction of the economic system. The government's relationship with the economic system reflects power relations within production.
Method of Investigation	Mathematical and statistical modelling is the predominant form of economic investigation.	Economic investigation includes mathematical and statistical tools, but should be realistic, pragmatic, and conscious of the influence of social values, gender biases, and racial biases.

Neoclassical Economics

Although it presents itself today as a uniform body of thought, the work of several British and continental European economists during the latter half of the nineteenth century—principally William Jevons, Carl Menger, Léon Walras, and Alfred Marshall—comprises the body of neoclassical theory. Neoclassical economics formulates theories of economic activities, interactions, and relationships from the perspective of the individual—a doctrine known as methodological individualism. The individual can refer to an economic agent or organization, such as consumers and firms, savers and investors, as well as employers and employees. Although they appear distinct, neoclassical theory reduces each of these roles to either an activity related to demand (the ability and willingness to buy) or an activity related to supply (the ability and willingness to sell).

With regard to human behavior, neoclassical theory adopts a strict and narrow assumption: self-interest exclusively motivates the economic decisions and interactions of individuals, in that they only seek to improve the wellbeing of the individual. With full information, economic agents and organizations are also optimizers, meaning they pursue maximum outcomes and individual wellbeing under constraints. Consumers maximize utility—the satisfaction derived from consumption—subject to budget constraints. Firms maximize profits, subject to cost and technological constraints. This understanding of human behavior—commonly referred to as "Homo Economicus" or "Economic Man"—is one of the most important foundational principles of neoclassical theory.

With regard to the operation of the economic system, the constraints and dilemmas of a scarcity-based economic system inform the structure of neoclassical thought. Given their preferences and technological endowments, individuals must allocate, maintain, or manage a limited amount of resources in a world of unlimited wants, needs, or goals. Neoclassical theory regards capitalism as a system of free markets—more specifically, a system of competitive markets that naturally gravitate toward equilibrium. The interactions of supply and demand determine socially optimal prices and quantities for goods, services, and scarce resources. Economic decisions are therefore voluntary in that they are expressions of individual choices.

Moreover, neoclassical analysis is ahistorical. Ahistorical means that the operation of the economic system and the motivations for economic behavior do not fundamentally change or evolve with history, social forces, culture, or changes in the natural environment. The operation of the economic system therefore preserves the status quo. Neoclassical economics regards historical, social, cultural, and environmental changes as exogenous, or external, to the economic system. Neither the operation of the economic system itself, nor changes within it, influence the non-economic spheres of capitalist societies. The idea that the economic system follows a pre-determined path also has important policy implications.

What role does government play in such an economic system? In a world where individuals pursue their self-interest; where they seek maximum outcomes with full information; where resources are scarce but wants are not; where competitive markets efficiently price and allocate output; where economic decisions are voluntary; and where the economic system operates independently of historical, social, cultural, or environmental context, the role of government is clear: the conduct of policymaking should maintain little to no government intervention in economic activities and relationships. If capitalism already follows a pre-determined path, then government can do little to alter its direction. Where it does occur, neoclassical analysis of government intervention largely centers on the effects of barriers to entry and price manipulations that prevent otherwise competitive markets from reaching equilibrium. Barriers to entry prevent competition and consolidate market power, resulting in higher prices, constrained output, and limited incentives to improve quality and innovate. For example, unions, minimum wage laws, and social welfare programs set artificially high wages, create voluntary unemployment, and prevent equilibrium in the labor market. Financial regulations have similar effects in the financial sector. Heavy progressive income taxation, business regulation, and public investments create the same distortions in markets for capital goods and raw materials, reducing incentives to invest.

Lastly, one of the most important features of neoclassical economics is the use of mathematical and statistical modelling. During the late nineteenth century, neoclassical economists were conscious in their efforts to emulate the scientific techniques of the time from mathematics and the natural sciences, especially physics. Although neoclassical economics is not alone in its use of mathematical models, it is unique in its near-universal commitment to such techniques by its adherents. For example, macroeconomists vary in their use of mathematical models; many do, but others do not. This variation essentially does not exist among neoclassical economists. It is extremely rare to find a neoclassical economist who does *not* use mathematical models to engage neoclassical principles.

Returning to the quote by Keynes at the beginning of this section: what are the "specialised gifts" of the neoclassical economist? Which talents, according to Keynes's conception of the master economist, does the neoclassical economist possess? Which elements of economic analysis does he or she give weight to (or not) in building theories? In sum, the neoclassical economist occupies the mathematician role to a much greater extent than that of the statesman and philosopher, but especially the historian. He or she gives greater weight to understanding symbols over speaking in words; to contemplating the particular over the general; and to considering the abstract over the concrete. Moreover, although self-interest and optimization are certainly elements of human nature and institutions, the neoclassical economist investigates those elements to the exclusion of many others.

The principles of neoclassical economics discussed in this section have deeper implications than the assumptions and approaches that characterize a school of thought. These principles also have very important professional implications. The economics profession is not neutral in its consideration of viewpoints that either counter or affirm neoclassical theory. The field of economics today regards neoclassical theory as the orthodox or mainstream school of thought. What does this mean in practice? It informs the theoretical positions of those who serve on the editorial boards of top academic journals and publishing houses, as well as the steering committees of professional associations and learned societies in economics. It informs the positions of those who serve as advisors to industry leaders in the private sector, government agencies and policymakers, as well as international institutions. Neoclassical economics is the foundation of the curriculum of most graduate programs in the United States, which produce nearly all of the candidates for these occupations and appointments. Although the Royal Swedish Academy of Sciences has awarded the Nobel Prize in Economics to those whose work does not affirm neoclassical theory, textbooks continue to present mainstream principles with very few exceptions, alternatives, or critiques.

In relation to the Great Recession, neoclassical economics serves as the predominant lens for understanding the crisis. It is the primary explanatory mechanism offered by the economics profession for the underlying causes of the housing market bubble and financial crisis, the transmission of the 2008 financial crisis throughout the financial sector and the economic system, the effects of the policy responses to the Great Recession, as well as the nature and direction of the recovery. Although neoclassical economics is the prevailing mainstream school of thought, it does not stand alone in the economics profession. The next section discusses a group of critical alternative schools of thought known as heterodox economics. These theories differ not only in their assumptions about economic activities, interactions, and relationships, but also in their conscious efforts to critique the core principles, methods, and policy recommendations of neoclassical economics.

Heterodox Economics

The term "heterodox economics" refers to a set of theories that are not just alternatives, but critical alternatives, to neoclassical economics. In most cases, heterodox theories explicitly reject the assumptions, methods, or policy positions held by the mainstream. However, they also include approaches, subjects, or theories rejected by the mainstream itself. Heterodoxy refers to a wide range of economic theories that often intersect, and share similar values, but differ in their approaches to economic analysis and critiques of orthodoxy. These critiques center on one or more of the fundamentals of neoclassical economics discussed in the previous section. What follows is a collective critique of neoclassical economics that draws key elements from several schools of thought, including ecological, evolutionary, feminist, institutionalist, Marxist, post-Keynesian, social, and stratification economics.

First, albeit in differing ways, heterodox economists generally reject methodological individualism. They do so by analyzing economic behavior and phenomena using larger units of analysis, such as classes, institutions, group affiliations, national economic systems, or global economic systems. For example, Marxists utilize the concept of class and emphasize class struggle as the driving force behind economic, social, and historical change. Evolutionary and institutional economists study the formation of institutions and the nature of institutional change, such as individual habits and routines related to group dynamics. Feminist and stratification economists investigate not only the differing economic experiences of women and racial minorities, but also the reproduction of intergroup exclusion and inequality. Post-Keynesians promote the use of policy levers to manage aggregate demand in order to reach full employment.

Second, heterodoxy offers a more complex understanding of behavior than Economic Man. For example, post-Keynesians argue that economic agents make decisions, especially those related to investment, under fundamental uncertainty. Ecological economists hold a similar position regarding the uncertain effects of economic activities on the environment. Institutionalists maintain that agents make decisions based upon enabling myths. Enabling myths—such as classism, racism, and sexism—are conventions that reinforce existing economic and social power structures. Evolutionary economists posit that agents lack full information about choices. Rather than optimize, they must learn what choices they face through adaptation. Furthermore, a wide range of heterodox schools examine the presence of other-regarding behavior, the desire to improve or worsen the wellbeing of others, in economic decision making. Ecological economists promote a greater sense of community in order to achieve sustainability. Feminists contend that both altruism and self-interest motivate behavior not only within the household, but also in the market. Institutionalists point to worker-owned firms as examples of the productive capacity of cooperation and self-management within the workplace. Although they often seek to improve the wellbeing of others, and certainly themselves, agents may also pursue negative outcomes for others through discrimination and exclusion. The fields of feminist and stratification economics investigate how deliberate collective actions by majority groups, and structural barriers to intergroup equality, constrain the choices of women and minorities. These constraints include discrimination in labor and credit markets, divide and conquer strategies in the workplace, and conflict over resources within the household.

Third, while they also formulate theories of market competition, understanding the process of production is a distinguishing feature of heterodox economics. Marxism, among other schools, uses the organization of the labor process as its entry point to analyzing the operation of economic systems. A labor process involves not only the production of commodities (goods and services exchanged in the market for money) but also activities of social reproduction within the household (biological reproduction, childcare, education, household maintenance and sustenance, etc.). Furthermore, heterodox economists study the internal dynamics of both capitalist and non-capitalist economic systems. Across these variations in the purpose and organization of work, they seek to understand the social relations between people that exist in production—especially relations that involve power and exploitation along the lines of class, gender, nationality, and race. In this sense, "class" refers to divisions over who owns the means of production, who performs labor, and who organizes and controls the product of the labor process. Understanding economic inequality in this sense requires an understanding of the inequality that exists with respect to property rights and authority within the realm of production. Scarcity of resources is not the core economic dilemma. Rather, the drive to accumulate capital and the production of a surplus product—the portion of output that exceeds what is necessary to maintain all inputs in a labor process—are core issues within heterodox economics. Post-Keynesians also reject the neoclassical entry point of scarcity by arguing that unemployment and excess capacity are the norm in capitalist societies, which implies that effective demand determines aggregate output and employment. Post-Keynesians advance monetary theories of production that emphasize the fundamental role of time, and the centrality of money and credit, in the process of production.

Fourth, heterodox economic analysis is historical. Historical analysis does not simply entail a narrative or recounting of past events. It is a principle that asserts that the operation of the economic system itself generates change and evolves over time. The economic sphere therefore fundamentally interacts with the non-economic spheres of society. While heterodox analysis in general integrates this dynamic feature, debate exists over the nature and direction of those interactions. For example, ecological economists emphasize the ecological limits to economic activities, and contend that both economic and ecological systems evolve together. Institutionalists embed economic systems within broader social and cultural systems. Marxists argue that the historical evolution of different economic systems tends toward greater equality. Although the non-economic spheres of society may affect the operation of the economic sphere, the structure of the economic system ultimately determines the character of culture, ideology, laws, politics, religion, and social consciousness, etc.

Fifth, heterodox economics advances an understanding of government that goes beyond intervention in competitive markets. The government's relationship with the economic system is not exogenous, or separate, from the operation of the economic system. The historical and evolutionary character of capitalism implies that it does not necessarily follow a pre-determined path. The future is not set: it can be changed. Heterodox schools often hold a positive view of government, arguing that policy can alter the structure and direction of the economic system. Others, however, contend that the government's relationship with the economic system reflects power structures within production, which themselves are exploitative and oppressive. The broad heterodox policy platform includes, among many others: cultural reform of class, gendered, and racial power structures; establishment of worker-owned enterprises; institutional reforms that expand citizen oversight and participation in corporate behavior and decisions; national and global regulation of financial markets and capital flows; national economic planning; and significant expansion of social welfare and income security programs.

Finally, heterodox economists employ a variety of methods in economic analysis, including mathematical and statistical modelling. However, they generally reject the purported scientific approach of neoclassical economics, and are more conscious of the political nature of theoretical and empirical investigation. Marxists notably critique economic theory in order to critique capitalism and establish a scientific basis for socialism or communism. Not unlike mainstream economists, who develop a scientific theory that celebrates and defends capitalism, Marxists construct an argument based upon an already determined conclusion—just as all theory does. Institutionalists take a pragmatic approach to economic analysis, and share an emphasis on realism with post-Keynesians. The field of social economics examines the ways in which social values influence economic activities and economic theory. Social economists also reject the lack of attention to social values within mainstream economics. Feminist and stratification economists draw attention to, and critique, the gender and racial biases that exist within both neoclassical and heterodox schools of thought.

There are many cases in which heterodox economics agrees with or confirms aspects of neoclassical theory. The distinctive feature of heterodox economics is that it continuously investigates *why* things are as they are. For example, even if they accept the neoclassical understanding of the labor market, heterodox economists ask: *why* does wage labor exist? Even if they accept the mainstream premise of a scarcity-based economic system, heterodox economists ask: *why* is the vast majority of capital owned by a privileged minority? Neoclassical and heterodox economists may also share similar interests and subject areas, such as race, gender, and the environment. By contrast, heterodox economists are conscious in their efforts to improve the wellbeing of the disadvantaged, excluded, or exploited; and to achieve ecologically sustainable development. The primary chapters of this book apply these distinguishing principles to the chronology of the Great Recession, not only to present the alternative perspectives of the crisis offered by heterodoxy, but also to critique the limited and ineffectual perspectives offered by neoclassical orthodoxy.

PLAN AND PURPOSE OF THE BOOK

This textbook is comprised of three main parts, organized on a largely chronological basis. Each part corresponds to the period before, during, and after the crisis. Although it covers the major economic, historical, and political events associated with the Great Recession, it does not investigate every aspect or event by design. The primary goal of this textbook is to use the crisis as a way to engage economic concepts and principles from multiple perspectives. Successful students will develop the tools to be independent learners in this subject area beyond the reading of the book and the courses which utilize it. For example, they will be able to develop and investigate independent research questions of topics not necessarily covered in great detail.

Students in courses in which the Great Recession is either the primary or a substantial focus are the intended audience of this textbook. Although it reviews core concepts as necessary, readers should be familiar with macroeconomic and microeconomic theory at the principles level. Familiarity with principles of economics at the intermediate level is not a requirement, however. This textbook is suitable for upper-level undergraduate audiences, as well as students in applied master's programs in economics, public policy, or other related fields. It is versatile enough to serve either as a primary textbook for a full-semester course, or as a supplementary resource for specific units in multiple courses.

Part II, entitled "The Road to the Great Recession," examines the history and structure of US capitalism prior to the crisis. Four chapters in this part focus on the lead-up to, and transmission of, the 2008 financial crisis and Great Recession. Chapter 2 sets the stage with a comprehensive analysis of the long-term evolution of US capitalism from the 1930s to 2008. This chapter examines the explicit policy decisions and conflicts that gradually transformed capitalist institutions in profit making and investment. It explains the strategies that governed profit making and investment following World War II; the disruption of those strategies during the 1970s; and the reconfiguration of those strategies during the three expansions that preceded the Great Recession. Chapter 3 then investigates a critical aspect of US capitalism prior to the crisis: the housing market bubble (and bust). Chapter 3 delves into the costs and benefits of home ownership; the history of mortgage redlining; the analysis and measurement of market bubbles; the various explanations of the housing market bubble; and the federal government's responses to the foreclosure crisis. In arguably the most important chapter in this part, Chapter 4 analyzes the complex components and relationships of financial structure leading up to the 2008 financial crisis; the transmission of the financial meltdown; the transmission of the economic crisis across the real sector; and the conduct of the Wall Street bailouts. Chapter 5 concludes Part II with a presentation of competing explanations of the crisis from multiple schools of economic thought, including neoclassical, post-Keynesian, institutionalist, feminist, and Marxian economics, among others.

Part III investigates the policy responses to the Great Recession. Two presidential administrations, Congress, the Federal Reserve, and multiple agencies of the federal government implemented three sets of policies during and after the Great Recession: financial reform, monetary policy, and fiscal policy. Each set of policies focused on either the financial crisis, the economic crisis, or both. Financial reform (Chapter 6) addressed the financial relationships and transmission mechanisms that facilitated the 2008 financial crisis, as presented in Chapter 4. Dodd-Frank introduced mechanisms that monitor systemic risk; created a federal agency devoted to consumer financial protection; and closed financial regulatory gaps and inefficiencies, among other new measures. Monetary policy (Chapter 7) addressed both the financial crisis and the economic crisis. The Federal Reserve conducted traditional monetary stimulus in order to boost economic growth in the real sector. However, it also enacted extraordinary measures that stabilized financial markets, directly assisted individual financial institutions, and expanded access to credit. In doing so, the Federal Reserve was forced to develop several new tools of monetary policy during the recovery. Finally, fiscal policy (Chapter 8) addressed the economic crisis in the real sector. Between 2008 and 2012, the federal government enacted a multitude of measures that increased government spending, expanded the provision of income transfers, and lowered taxes. This chapter also presents the results of empirical studies that assessed the effectiveness of expansionary fiscal policies, as well as the other comprehensive policy responses, on US macroeconomic performance following the Great Recession.

Finally, Part IV investigates the debates and controversies surrounding the recovery from the Great Recession. Following the official trough of the Great Recession in June 2009, US capitalism expanded until February 2020, making the recovery the longest economic expansion to date. However, the 2009–20 recovery has been marked by lingering economic and cultural anxieties following the Great Recession, ongoing structural imbalances in the economic system, and animosity toward the policy responses to the crisis. Chapter 9 therefore examines several aspects of the 2009–20 recovery and their ongoing effects on the trajectory of US capitalism. It compares the performance of US capitalism during the 2009–20 recovery to previous recoveries. It discusses the relationship between the Great Recession and the growth of populism. Lastly, it examines the major economic policies during the recovery prior to the Covid-19 pandemic recession in 2020.

Sources

Bernanke, B.S. (2002, November 21). Deflation: Making sure "it" doesn't happen here [Transcript]. Remarks by Governor Ben S. Bernanke before the National Economists Club, Washington, DC. Retrieved from https://www.federalreserve.gov.

Bernanke, B.S. (2004, February 20). The Great Moderation [Transcript]. Remarks by Governor Ben S. Bernanke at the meetings of the Eastern Economic Association, Washington, DC. Retrieved from https://www.federalreserve.gov.

Bivens, J. & Irons, J. (2008). *A feeble recovery: the fundamental weaknesses of the 2001-07 expansion* (Briefing Paper #214). Washington, DC: Economic Policy Institute.

Bush seeks to reassure amid market turbulence. (2007, August 9). *The New York Times*. Retrieved from https://www.nytimes.com.

Federal Reserve Bank of St. Louis. (n.d.). *FRED economic data* [Data file and codebook]. Retrieved from https://fred.stlouisfed.org.

Gross, D. (2008, September 17). "The fundamentals of our economy are strong." *Slate*. Retrieved from http://www.slate.com.

Keynes, J.M. (1924). Alfred Marshall, 1842–924. *The Economic Journal, 34*(135), 311–72. doi: 10.2307/2223058

Mishel, L., Bivens, J., Gould, E., & Shierholz, H. (2012). *The state of working America*. Ithaca, NY: Cornell University Press.

National Bureau of Economic Research. (n.d.). US business cycle expansions and contractions. Retrieved from http://www.nber.org.

O'Hara, P. (ed.). (1999). *Encyclopedia of political economy*. London, UK: Routledge.

Stewart, J.B. (2008). Stratification economics. In *The international encyclopedia of the social sciences*. Farmington Hills, MI: Cengage.

Transcript of Treasury Secretary Henry Paulson on CNBC. (2006, August 1). *The Wall Street Journal*. Retrieved from https://www.wsj.com.

Further Reading

Baiman, R., Boushey, H., & Saunders, D. (2000). *Political economy and contemporary capitalism: radical perspectives on economic theory and policy*. Armonk, NY: M.E. Sharpe.

Bowles, S., Edwards, R., Roosevelt, F., & Larudee, M. (2018). *Understanding capitalism: competition, command, and change*. New York, NY: Oxford University Press.

Sackrey, C., Schneider, G., & Knoedler, J. (2016). *Introduction to political economy*. Boston, MA: Economic Affairs Bureau.

Sherman, H.J., Hunt, E.K., Nesiba, R.F., O'Hara, P.A., & Wiens-Tuers, B. (2008). *Economics: an introduction to traditional and progressive views*. Armonk, NY: M.E. Sharpe.

PART II

The Road to the Great Recession

CHAPTER 2

US Capitalism Prior to 2008

Having explored some essential background information on the Great Recession, and the theoretical concepts that this book will apply to it, we now turn toward a comprehensive investigation of the crisis itself. Part II of this textbook explores "The Road to the Great Recession." This part encompasses a series of four chapters that develop a theoretical and practical understanding of the lead-up to the crisis. The first step, taken in this chapter, is to examine US economic history prior to the Great Recession.

Although the Great Recession officially began in December 2007, the story does not start there. Beginning an analysis at the end of 2007 would limit the exploration of any precipitating factors and causes of the crisis. So where does this story start? One possibility is to begin with the 2001 recession—the last US downturn to precede the crisis. While plausible, doing so would exclude an examination of the long-term restructuring of capitalism that facilitated the Great Recession. Another possibility is to begin with the 1980s or 1990s, during which such structural changes originated. However, those changes evolved from another economic crisis that occurred in the 1970s, which had its own causes and historical roots. In order to trace the incremental economic, historical, and institutional changes that culminated in the Great Recession, this analysis begins with the US government's responses to the Great Depression of the 1930s, and the restructuring of global capitalism following World War II.

This chapter investigates the history of US capitalism prior to 2008 from a heterodox perspective. The first section introduces the key concept of accumulation, and how it differs from mainstream expositions of economic history. Accumulation is a distinctly heterodox principle that emphasizes the evolutionary character of capitalist institutions in profit making and investment. The remainder of the chapter divides the period between the 1930s and 2008 into the following five segments:

- Established in the aftermath of the Great Depression and World War II, the "regulated" stage of US capitalism lasted from the late 1940s until the early 1970s. Regulated capitalism was the product of a particular set of policy

DOI: 10.4324/9780429461316-4

decisions and struggles at the time. Regulated capitalism featured a significant expansion of government intervention in the income and wealth security of the working class, the operations of industrial and financial capitalists, as well as international flows of goods and money. The purpose of these policies was to generate high demand for goods and services in order to maintain a high level of output and employment.

- During the 1970s, however, regulated capitalism faced a series of crises that disrupted longstanding institutions that facilitated profit making and investment. The end of the Vietnam War, multiple energy crises, growing international competition, and speculative attacks on the postwar international financial system created "stagflation"—a rare combination of high unemployment and high inflation.
- By the early 1980s, a "neoliberal" stage of US capitalism shifted the balance of power from government to free markets, and from labor to capital. Policies such as lower taxes, deregulation, de-unionization, cuts to social welfare programs, Cold War militarization, and monetary restraint underscored a conservative pushback that prioritized production over spending. Like regulated capitalism, neoliberal capitalism was the outcome of a specific structure of policies and struggles, which reconfigured the institutional setting of profit making and investment.
- During the 1990s, neoliberalism flourished as a result of a technological revolution, globalization, and financial deregulation. Fiscal surpluses and low interest rates also extended the neoliberal agenda. The "financialization" of capitalism—the growing influence of finance in economic production, politics, culture, and society—became clear and apparent during this period.
- The War on Terror, tax cuts for the rich, and a vision of an "ownership society" were fiscal priorities during the early 2000s. Low interest rates and a housing market bubble produced a surge in consumer spending that sustained economic growth. Despite notions of a "Great Moderation" between the 1980s and the early 2000s, the neoliberal period featured greater inequality, jobless recoveries, higher debt burdens, and financial instability. These structural imbalances became unsustainable with the collapse of the housing market bubble and the onset of the Great Recession in 2007.

UNDERSTANDING ACCUMULATION

Chapter 1 introduced several critical distinctions between neoclassical and heterodox economic analysis, particularly regarding historical change and economic behavior. The ahistorical nature of neoclassical economics means that change is considered an exogenous, or external, process that does not result from the operation of capitalism. By contrast, the historical nature of heterodox economics means that change is considered an endogenous, or internal, process that results from the operation of capitalism, which fundamentally interacts with the non-economic spheres of capitalist societies. Moreover, neoclassical economists argue that profit making results from the entrepreneurial ability of the individual firm, and that self-interest exclusively motivates investment decisions regardless of context. Heterodox economists, on the other hand, argue that social forces condition profit making, and that investment behavior evolves over time. This chapter introduces a theoretical concept that distinguishes heterodox economics in this regard.

This chapter applies a heterodox framework known as social structure of accumulation theory (SSA) to US capitalism from the 1930s until 2008. The term "accumulation" refers to the generation and reinvestment of profits by capitalist enterprises. The principal motivation of capitalists is to earn profit, but they must reinvest in order to continue earning profit over time. If not, they will be unable to remain capitalists due to competitive market forces. The accumulation process involves the continuous pursuit of new ways to deploy inputs and organize the production of output. SSA theorists argue that distinct configurations of institutions (i.e., customs or strategies) over long periods of time govern the acquisition and eventual reinvestment of profits. These institutions can be economic in nature, but also have cultural, social, and political dimensions. Examples include the composition of human capital, the demographics of the labor force, unionization, the distribution of income and wealth, consumerism, technological advancement, property rights, market structure, the sectoral composition of the economic system, government intervention, social and cultural norms, as well as global integration of resource, labor, financial, and consumer markets.

SSA theorists define a social structure of accumulation—or stage of capitalism—as a distinct historical configuration of these institutions. Although the profit motive itself does not change, the institutional context of profit making and investment evolves, albeit slowly, over long periods of time. Each SSA includes a period of growth and development during which the institutional setting generates substantial profits and opportunities for reinvestment. However, each SSA eventually includes a period during which the same social structure limits profits and discourages investment. The oscillation between these two periods occurs over a much lengthier period of time than a short-run business cycle, usually several decades. Under certain historical conditions, a conflict may emerge between new opportunities for profitable investment and the existing social structure of accumulation. A period of economic and social upheaval known as a crisis occurs, as capitalism transitions to new institutions that facilitate a favorable process of accumulation. While not inevitable, the realignment of institutions may then give way to a new stage of capitalism. SSA theorists argue that US capitalism has featured four stages since the mid-nineteenth century. This chapter analyzes the two stages that preceded the Great Recession.

THE ESTABLISHMENT OF REGULATED CAPITALISM: 1945–73

The late 1940s was a period of significant transition and uncertainty for both US and global capitalism. The economic devastation brought about by the Great Depression was still fresh in the minds of workers, capitalists, and policymakers across the major industrialized economic systems. Following World War II, US capitalism restructured away from military mobilization and toward the resumption of peacetime economic production. For perspective, the war effort constituted such a substantial share of US output that demobilization itself led to a recession in 1945. The war devastated economic systems across Africa, Asia, and Europe, including those aligned with the Allied and Axis powers. Eviscerated resource bases either limited, or halted altogether, economic production. Arable land, civilian labor forces, factories, financial institutions, and infrastructure all began a long period of rebuilding. As the major imperial powers recovered and receded from global influence, independence movements and decolonization spread throughout Africa, Asia, and the Middle East. Given the power vacuum left by the rebuilding of the previous empires, and the establishment of newly independent governments, the division of the global economic system into blocs dominated by the United States and Soviet Union took hold in the postwar era. It was clear that capitalism would operate under a new social structure of accumulation; but what kind of capitalism would emerge?

The "regulated" stage of US capitalism refers to the period between the late 1940s and early 1970s. Regulated capitalism marked a significant shift in the role of government, both in economic thought and in its relationship with capitalism. In the aftermath of the Great Depression, a new consensus emerged that rejected the nineteenth century-oriented principles of neoclassical economics, and embraced the principles set forth by John Maynard Keynes. Keynes and his contemporaries argued that unregulated capitalism is inherently unstable. Although free markets may reach stable points of equilibrium that minimize unemployment and maximize economic capacity, such outcomes are only a special case and not the general case—hence the title of his most famous work, *The General Theory of Employment, Interest, and Money*. Keynes expresses this sentiment in Chapter 1 of *The General Theory*, where he states:

> I shall argue that the postulates of the classical theory are applicable to a special case only and not to the general case, the situation which it assumes being a limiting point of the possible positions of equilibrium. Moreover, the characteristics of the special case assumed by the classical theory happen not to be those of the economic society which we actually live, with the result that its teaching is misleading and disastrous if we attempt to apply it to the facts of experience.

Although many of Keynes's ideas were radical at the time, he did not embrace Marxism or Soviet-style state socialism. He believed in capitalism—but in a demand-driven capitalism that minimized economic and political instability through government intervention. Governments actively used policies, programs, and regulations to support a high level of aggregate spending in order to achieve a level of aggregate output and employment that would eliminate cyclical unemployment—a condition known as "full employment." Heavy progressive taxation generated government revenues that financed public investments in infrastructure, the modern welfare state, regulation and oversight of industry and finance, Cold War militarization, as well as fiscal and monetary policies to correct volatility in the business cycle. A well-organized labor movement and the genuine threat of socialism can also not be discounted as contributing factors to the rise of regulated capitalism. This expanded role of government extended to all sectors of the national economic system and the US-dominated bloc of the global economic system. It conditioned the consumption and incomes of workers, the process of accumulation by capitalists, and the structure of international economic relationships.

The Working Class During Regulated Capitalism

For the working class as a whole, regulated capitalism resulted in a significant expansion of incomes and living standards. Consumption, which constitutes over two-thirds of US output, is by far the largest source of spending. Securing a high level of consumption for workers was essential to securing stability in aggregate demand. This historical expansion of income for those engaged in wage labor was purposeful in order to increase consumer spending. Beginning in the 1930s, the US government actively regulated labor markets through labor laws, the promotion of industrial unions, and the provision of social welfare programs. The National Labor Relations Act established, and continues to enforce, labor rights in the private sector. It protects the rights of workers to join unions and engage in collective bargaining. It prohibits capitalists from pursuing unfair labor practices. The Act also established the National Labor Relations Board, a federal agency that enforces the rights of workers. The Fair Labor Standards Act instituted a federal minimum wage, overtime pay, and the prohibition of child labor. The Social Security Act set forth the provision of retirement benefits, disability insurance, and unemployment insurance, as well as the power of the federal government to collect taxes in order to fund such benefits.

The federal government also took direct action to protect household wealth. The purpose of the Home Owners' Loan Act was to alleviate a foreclosure crisis during the Great Depression. The law created the Home Owners' Loan Corporation, which refinanced residential mortgages that were in, or at risk of, foreclosure. One of the most important outcomes was the implementation of the self-amortizing loan for mortgage contracts. In such cases, borrowers make a fixed monthly payment of principal and interest to a lending institution, at a fixed interest rate, for a term of 15 to 30 years. Prior to the Act, the typical mortgage featured higher interest rates, much shorter terms, and "balloon" payment structures. Under such contracts, borrowers made interest-only payments during the term of the loan, and paid the entire principal at maturity. Borrowers who were unable to pay off the principal would typically take out another mortgage, or default, thus keeping them in perpetual debt.

In the decades following World War II, administrations from both parties built upon the policies and programs established during the 1930s. The G.I. Bill created an array of veterans' benefits, including unemployment insurance, assistance for education and job training, as well as home and business loans. The Food Stamp Act initiated the Food Stamp Program, which provides food and nutrition assistance to the underprivileged. The Medicare and Medicaid programs provide health insurance for the elderly and the poor respectively. The Occupational Safety and Health Act regulates workplace safety and environmental hazards.

Regulated capitalism therefore facilitated greater bargaining power for workers against capitalists, both within the workplace and in the realm of public policy. Policymakers believed that equalizing workplace bargaining power would minimize the forces that exacerbated the Great Depression by reducing the likelihood of strikes and inhibiting wage suppression. By 1964, the national union membership rate reached 29.3%. Several state-level union membership rates in the Midwest, Northeast, and West were either close to or exceeded 40%. As a result, workers secured real wage increases in line with productivity increases throughout this period. According to Figure 2.1, real hourly compensation increased 91% between 1948 and 1973, while labor productivity increased 97%. This increase in labor income led to an increase in consumption that stabilized economic fluctuations and reduced income inequality. The significance of this shift in income distribution is clear when one compares this period to the pre-Great Depression era, as shown in Table 2.1. Between 1917 and 1929, real average incomes in the United States grew by $935. During that time, all growth went to the richest 10%, while the incomes of the bottom 90% declined. By contrast, between 1945 and 1973, real average incomes grew by *$21,526*. Although 32% of new income growth went to the richest 10%—which was still unequal—the bottom 90% received 68%.

FIGURE 2.1 Real Hourly Compensation vs. Total Economy Productivity 1948–73

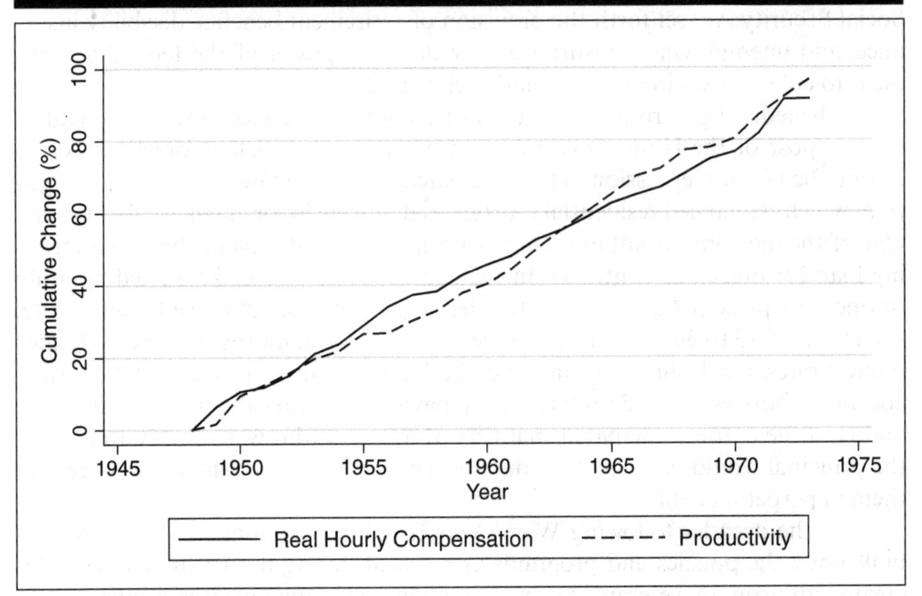

Source: The Economic Policy Institute's The State of Working America: http://www.stateofworkingamerica.org.

TABLE 2.1 Long-Run Shifts in Income Distribution

	Change in Real Average Income	*The Top 10%...*	*The Bottom 90%...*
1917–1929	+ $935	Claimed 100%	Saw Lower Incomes
1929–1939	− $2,534	Absorbed 54%	Absorbed 46%
1945–1973	+ $21,526	Claimed 32%	Claimed 68%
1973–1982	− $3,663	Absorbed 11%	Absorbed 89%
1982–2007	+ $18,901	Claimed 81%	Claimed 19%

Source: The Economic Policy Institute's *The State of Working America*, "When income grows, who gains?" http://www.stateofworkingamerica.org/index.html%3Fp=764.html.

The Capitalist Class During Regulated Capitalism

For the capitalist class, the institutions of regulated capitalism fostered profit making and investment. In this sense, "investment" refers to non-financial investment, meaning spending on capital goods, raw materials, inventories, and other forms of physical assets. Investment is a much smaller source of aggregate demand than consumption, contributing less than 20% to US output. However, it is much more volatile. Keynesian economists argue that "animal spirits" are the reason for this volatility. "Animal spirits" refers to the degree of confidence in the future direction of the economic system. Although investment may be sensitive to traditional cost factors—such as prices for capital goods, interest rates, taxes, and wages—psychological forces are the primary motivating factor. For example, low interest rates may not be enough to stimulate business investment during a slump if investors are pessimistic and hold negative expectations of future economic conditions. Conversely, high investment costs may not act as deterrents during a boom if investors are optimistic and hold positive expectations of future conditions. When the future is fundamentally uncertain, confidence, emotions, and norms ultimately determine investor sentiment. However, that sentiment can shift unexpectedly when investors revise profit expectations. The implication is that investor behavior is subject to change and may not follow the stable, rational construct of Economic Man.

The basis for the heavy tax and regulatory environment during regulated capitalism lies in the Keynesian theory of investment. Although industrial capitalists paid high wages and benefits to workers, and faced high taxes and regulations from the government, they were still able to secure record profits during this period, for three reasons. First, large corporations continued to dominate the production of goods and services, which found cost efficiencies through expansion and mass production. Second, given the recovery of the industrial powers of Europe and Asia following World War II, and the economic isolation of the Soviet bloc from the West, US industry dominated global trade in goods. Third, strong demand from the working class as well as the government supported corporate profitability. The robust demand from the working class resulted from the sustained increase in real incomes and living standards; while the robust demand from the government resulted from the expansion of government services and contracts, especially in the area of national defense.

Financial capitalists also faced substantial regulation and restructuring during this stage of capitalism. The most important piece of legislation to that effect was the Glass-Steagall Act. The purpose of Glass-Steagall was to prevent the complex and unstable financial forces that contributed to the stock market crash and banking panic during the Great Depression. Two provisions of Glass-Steagall directly addressed such forces. First, it established federal deposit insurance. Second, it defined and separated the businesses of commercial banking and investment banking. Glass-Steagall defined "commercial banks" as financial institutions that raise financial capital from deposits and use those funds to create loans. Although it permitted commercial banks to invest in government bonds, it forbade them from investing in, or underwriting, stocks and other types of securities. Glass-Steagall defined "investment banks" as financial institutions that trade in securities. Although it permitted investment banks to speculate in the stock market, it forbade them from raising financial capital from depositors. Moreover, Glass-Steagall dissolved ownership stakes between commercial banks and investment banks. The Securities Exchange Act implemented further government oversight and regulation of financial markets by creating the Securities and Exchange Commission. The practical effect of these laws was that they created a financial sector that channeled financial capital to industry and manufacturing. The purpose of finance was to support investment in production and employment, and the primary source of financing for such purposes was commercial bank capital.

The Global Economic System During Regulated Capitalism

In the aftermath of World War II, national policymakers coordinated the restructuring of international economic relationships between capitalist systems. The goal was to develop a system that avoided the isolationism and lack of policy cooperation during the Great Depression, while also avoiding unrestrained free market globalization. During the Great Depression, national economies erected significant barriers against import competition, and engaged in competitive devaluations of their own currencies in order to boost exports. Both strategies, however, ended up limiting their own exports and exacerbating the contraction. The new system of trade and finance therefore promoted, but managed, international flows of goods and money.

In the realm of international trade, the General Agreement on Tariffs and Trade (GATT) facilitated cooperation and coordination between member countries on tariffs, quotas, and other forms of trade barriers. The purpose was to expand international trade in the postwar era and reduce the use of such barriers over time. Although GATT increased economic interdependence, members rejected the creation of a formal international trade organization for several decades.

In the realm of international finance, the Bretton Woods Agreement established a system of fixed exchange rates and created two international financial institutions. The goal of this new international monetary system was to prevent speculative attacks on currencies that destabilized exchange rates, disrupted international trade, and contributed to the adoption of protectionist policies during the Great Depression. The exchange rate system, known as the gold exchange standard, featured two key pillars. Member countries agreed to maintain a fixed exchange rate between their domestic currency and the US dollar. The United States then agreed to maintain a fixed exchange rate between the dollar and gold at $35 per ounce. Member countries held reserves in either dollars or gold, and could exchange their dollars for gold at the fixed price. Member central banks were responsible for intervening in currency markets in order to maintain their fixed exchange rate with the dollar. The US Federal Reserve was responsible for maintaining the fixed dollar price for gold, and redeeming dollars for gold. The first international financial institution created at Bretton Woods—the International Monetary Fund (IMF)—lent money to countries that encountered difficulties maintaining their fixed exchange rate with the dollar. The second institution—the International Bank for Reconstruction and Development, or World Bank—assisted World War II combatants with financial and physical reconstruction.

THE DEMISE OF REGULATED CAPITALISM: 1973–82

Due to its expansion of prosperity and strong economic performance, economic historians often refer to the postwar era as the "Golden Age" of US capitalism. Although the institutions that supported capital accumulation were generational, they were not permanent. By the early 1970s, the institutions that facilitated profit making during regulated capitalism were no longer sustainable. A new crisis emerged, with constraints on capital accumulation that led to the restructuring of capitalism, just as the Great Depression had done a generation earlier. There are four major elements of the crisis of the 1970s: the end of the Vietnam War; a series of energy crises; increasing global competition; and speculative attacks on the Bretton Woods system.

Barriers to Accumulation During the 1970s

The winding down of the Vietnam War during the early 1970s affected quality of life issues in two important ways. First, unemployment began to rise. As a result of troop withdrawals, millions of active military members re-entered the civilian labor market searching for jobs. Unemployment also rose in the private defense industry in response to diminished demand from the war effort. Second, the war effort itself created excess demand for goods and services, and especially resources, which contributed to an increase in the cost of living. Consequently, the real wage increases that workers had enjoyed for a generation began to disappear.

However, the defining factor that produced double-digit rates of inflation was the energy crises. At two points during the 1970s, the United States faced severe oil shortages caused by embargoes. These crises created a new institutional constraint on capital accumulation that did not exist under regulated capitalism: energy independence. The first oil crisis occurred in 1973. In retaliation for supporting Israel during the Yom Kippur War, the Organization of Arab Petroleum Exporting Countries declared an embargo on the United States and several other industrialized countries. Cutting off a critical source of oil supply created a shortage, since domestic demand for oil increasingly relied on foreign sources as postwar capitalism expanded. Prices for gas and heating oil skyrocketed. Disruptions in the price of oil, and in access to oil, also led to spikes in prices for goods and services. A second oil crisis followed in 1979 when the production and export of oil from Iran ceased during the Iranian Revolution, with similar effects on energy prices.

A third factor that limited profit making during this period was increasing global competition. For the first few decades after World War II, US industry dominated global markets for goods as industrialized economies in Asia and Europe rebuilt. By the early 1970s, however, the recovery of countries like Japan and West Germany, as well as the emergence of newly industrialized countries like South Korea and Taiwan, significantly challenged US dominance of the global economic system. Demand for US exports dropped in the face of growing competition, while US spending shifted toward cheaper imports from the rest of the world. As a result, the trade balance shifted from a surplus, which the United States carried for most of the postwar period, to a consistent deficit.

A fourth factor which disrupted postwar institutions designed to maintain stability in the global economic system was a series of speculative attacks against the US dollar. During the late 1960s and early 1970s, international financial investors began to contest the value of the dollar—that is, the fixed price of the dollar in terms of gold that was the foundation of the Bretton Woods system of fixed exchange rates. Investors perceived that the demand-driven orientation of US capitalism pushed more and more dollars into circulation, and contributed to an overvaluation of the dollar. They therefore began to sell dollars in foreign exchange markets in the belief that the United States did not have sufficient gold reserves to maintain its price of $35 per ounce, and would eventually have to devalue. Other participant countries in the Bretton Woods system, which had agreed to fix the value of their currency against the dollar, also faced difficulties adjusting to the new reality of higher oil and energy prices under fixed exchange rates.

Why Did Regulated Capitalism Falter?

Taken together, the conditions that arose in the 1970s constrained the process of capital accumulation that prevailed under regulated capitalism. The chief principle of regulated capitalism—using government intervention to stimulate aggregate demand and achieve full employment—was no longer sustainable. It was not just that aggregate demand weakened during the 1970s. There were certainly periods during the postwar era when aggregate demand became unstable, and recessions emerged, as they did in 1948, 1953, 1957, 1960, and 1969. The problem was that demand-side stimulus itself became the barrier, and not the solution, to economic stability. Under regulated capitalism, the purpose of increasing real wages was to secure a strong level of aggregate demand with a strong level of consumption from the working class. During the 1970s, however, higher unemployment and a higher cost of living cut into real wages and weakened consumption. Despite heavy regulations designed to minimize volatility, investment by industrial capitalists collapsed with the spike in energy prices and the uncertainty surrounding the diminished position of the United States in the global economic system. International competition shifted the longstanding US trade surplus into a deficit, further weakening aggregate demand. Speculative runs on the Bretton Woods system disrupted foreign exchange stability and international trade—the very outcomes the system was designed to prevent.

The combination of economic stagnation and rising inflation, commonly referred to as "stagflation," posed a conundrum for policymakers who followed Keynesian prescriptions for stabilizing the economic system. Stagflation was a historical exception to the behavior of the postwar US business cycle. On the one hand, economic expansions normally reduced unemployment by increasing the demand for labor. Lower unemployment then expanded incomes and thereby demand for goods and services, leading to an increase in inflation. On the other hand, recessions normally led to higher unemployment, since labor demand fell. Stagnant or falling incomes then suppressed demand for goods and services, resulting in lower rates of inflation, or in some cases deflation. Economists and policymakers therefore perceived an *inverse* relationship between unemployment and inflation. Stagflation, however, presented an unusual case of high unemployment *and* high inflation. When unemployment was high, and the economic system stagnated, inflation was typically low (not high). When inflation was high, and the economic system grew, unemployment was typically low (not high). This situation created a dilemma for policymakers, since correcting one outcome would only exacerbate the other. Further stimulus to the demand-side of the economic system could reduce unemployment but would put further upward pressure on inflation. Cutting aggregate demand through policy restraints could reduce inflation but would worsen output and unemployment.

While the pillars of Richard Nixon's domestic and foreign policy agendas were decisively conservative, Keynesian principles largely informed his economic policies. In the summer of 1971, as regulated capitalism began to weaken, he addressed the nation on "The Challenge of Peace":

> Prosperity without war requires action on three fronts: We must create more and better jobs; we must stop the rise in the cost of living; we must protect the dollar from the attacks of international money speculators ... As the threat of war recedes, the challenge of peaceful competition in the world will greatly increase.

As unemployment, the cost of living, and international speculation against the dollar all increased, Nixon proposed a set of policies that continued to pursue full employment. The purpose of this agenda was to protect workers and wage earners, and impede the destabilizing influences of bankers and financial speculators. First, he called for expansionary fiscal policies to stimulate spending and job creation—for example, new tax reductions and credits designed to increase investment and consumption. Second, he called for price and wage controls in order to limit inflation. Third, he suspended the foundation of the Bretton Woods system: the convertibility of the US dollar into gold. The practical effect of this third provision was that it freed the conduct of monetary policy from the gold exchange standard. Thereafter, the United States adopted a floating exchange rate, whereby the value of the US dollar relative to other currencies fluctuated according to changes in supply and demand. Finally, in the wake of the first oil crisis in 1973, Nixon declared that the economic independence of the United States would thereafter be tied to energy independence: "In the last third of this century, our independence will depend on maintaining and achieving self-sufficiency in energy."

Although the intention of Nixon's economic policy was to stabilize regulated capitalism, it ultimately contributed to its demise. Between 1973 and 1982, notwithstanding periods of expansion, US capitalism suffered a series of severe recessions: November 1973 to March 1975, January 1980 to July 1980, and July 1981 to November 1982. At the depth of these recessions, real gross domestic product (GDP) contracted by 4.8% during the first quarter of 1975, 8% during the second quarter of 1980, and 6.1% during the first quarter of 1982. Unemployment reached 9% in May 1975 and 10.8% in November 1982—the highest it had been since the end of World War II. Annual rates of inflation also reached postwar records of 11% in 1974 and 13.5% in 1980.

The significance of the crisis of the 1970s lies not just in its historical severity. It was not just that capitalism faced its biggest crisis to date since the Great Depression. The crisis marked another period of transition, both in the structure of capitalism and in the social sentiment surrounding it. People began to question social progress and resist social change, especially the pace at which it was occurring. Ohio national guardsmen killed four students at Kent State University during a protest against the US bombing campaign in Cambodia. Less than two weeks later, the Mississippi Highway Patrol opened fire on a demonstration by Black students at Jackson State University. The conservative trajectory of the Nixon administration and its domestic policy agenda was a pointed shift from the Kennedy and Johnson administrations on civil rights. Resistance to school desegregation at the local and national levels continued into the 1970s, sometimes culminating in violence, as it did during the Boston Busing Crisis. Nixon became the first US president to resign in the wake of the Watergate scandal. The Equal Rights Amendment to the US Constitution, which would have guaranteed equal rights on the basis of sex, failed ratification by the states. By the late 1970s, a general lack of confidence in economic, government, and social institutions set in. President Jimmy Carter, in what became known as "The Malaise Speech," famously summarized the erosion of these institutions, and the seeming unwinding of society in the wake of the economic and energy crises:

> Human identity is no longer defined by what one does, but by what one owns. But we've discovered that owning things and consuming things does not satisfy our longing for meaning. We've learned that piling up material goods cannot fill the emptiness of lives which have no confidence or purpose.

While the full scale of the new institutional context of US capitalism would not be apparent until the early 1980s, it was clear that workers were bearing the brunt of the restructuring. According to Table 2.1, an entirely new structure of income distribution emerged. This shift against wage earners was historically unique, even in comparison to the Great Depression. Between 1929 and 1939, real average incomes in the United States decreased by $2,534, with the rich bearing over half of that loss. Whereas the top 10% absorbed 54% of the income lost during the Depression, the bottom 90% absorbed 46%. Between 1973 and 1982, however, real average incomes declined by $3,663—a significant reversal of the growth that occurred under regulated capitalism. Although the top 10% absorbed 11% of the income lost, the bottom 90% absorbed an astounding 89%.

THE ESTABLISHMENT OF NEOLIBERAL CAPITALISM: 1982–91

Just as the late 1940s had been a generation earlier, the early 1980s was a critical period of capitalist restructuring. Whereas regulated capitalism emerged from the aftermath of the Great Depression and World War II, a new social structure of accumulation emerged from the crisis of the 1970s. The "neoliberal" stage of US capitalism refers to the institutional setting of capital accumulation that followed the 1970s (and has been in place since then). Albeit in a fundamentally different direction from regulated capitalism, neoliberal capitalism marked a significant redefinition of the role of government, both in the process of accumulation and in economic theory. Neoliberalism represents a conservative pushback against the big-government, pro-labor orientation of the regulated era, and its theoretical foundations in Keynesian economics. By contrast, the principles of neoclassical economics returned to inform the free-market, pro-capitalist orientation of the neoliberal era.

The transition to neoliberalism conditioned fundamental changes in the system of economic production, as well as the domains of politics, intellect, and social thought. In the realm of politics, the elections of British Prime Minister Margaret Thatcher in 1979 and US President Ronald Reagan in 1980 denote the advent of the neoliberal era. Both leaders, who were close on an intellectual and a personal level, aggressively pursued conservative policies that celebrated individual freedom and liberty—for example, lower taxes, fiscal and monetary restraint, deregulation of financial markets and labor markets, as well as privatization of state industries. In stark contrast to his postwar predecessors, Democratic and Republican alike, Reagan famously stated in his first inaugural address: "In this present crisis, government is not the solution to our problem; government is the problem."

In the realm of academia and economic theory, a new consensus emerged that embraced the work of Milton Friedman and Friedrich von Hayek, and spurned the work of John Maynard Keynes. Friedman and his contemporaries—a school of thought known as monetarism—countered that free-market capitalism is inherently stable. Monetarists critique the use of active fiscal and monetary policies to stimulate aggregate demand and pursue full employment. Instead, they believe that the government's sole intervention in the economic system should be to maintain steady growth in the money supply. Hayek's championing of individualism, and vehement critique of socialist central planning as a form of tyranny, also became popular with the Thatcher government and the Reagan administration. In the social realm, the growing influence of conservative media (e.g., William F. Buckley's *National Review*) and conservative think tanks (e.g., the Cato Institute and the Heritage Foundation) materialized during this period.

But the most significant document that ignited the conservative pushback was the infamous Powell Memorandum. In 1971, Lewis F. Powell, Jr., a prominent corporate attorney, sent a confidential memorandum to Eugene B. Sydnor, Jr., chair of the Education Committee of the US Chamber of Commerce. In the memo, entitled "Attack on American Free Enterprise System," Powell assails the anti-capitalist views of college faculty, consumer advocates, environmentalists, the media, organized labor, and politicians, among others. He also assails the appeasing attitude and lack of political influence of corporations:

> The traditional role of business executives has been to manage, to produce, to sell, to create jobs, to make profits, to improve the standard of living, to be community leaders, to serve on charitable and educational boards, and generally to be good citizens … But they have shown little stomach for hard-nose contest with their critics, and little skill in effective intellectual and philosophical debate.

Powell therefore calls for more aggressive and coordinated actions by corporations to expand their influence in education, the media, politics and lobbying, and the courts:

> Business must learn the lesson, long ago learned by Labor and other self-interest groups. This is the lesson that political power is necessary; that such power must be assidously [sic] cultivated; and that when necessary, it must be used aggressively and with determination – without embarrassment and without the reluctance which has been so characteristic of American business.

Two months later, Powell was nominated by President Nixon to the US Supreme Court, on which he served until 1987. The critical point here is that the emergence of neoliberal capitalism was by no means inevitable. Just like regulated capitalism, it was the product of a unique set of conflicts, strategies, and policy decisions at the time.

Instruments of Accumulation During the 1980s: Monetary Restraint and the Reagan Revolution

Turning now to the system of economic production, what types of institutions facilitated accumulation under neoliberal capitalism? Following the disintegration of the Bretton Woods fixed exchange rate system, the Federal Reserve pursued an aggressive monetary restraint in order to contain double-digit rates of inflation. Central bankers accepted that workers would bear the burden of ending high inflation, as it would likely result in higher unemployment. Indeed, they were right. In 1979, President Carter appointed Paul Volcker as chair of the Federal Reserve Board of Governors. Following his appointment, the federal funds rate—the interest rate on a loan between commercial banks—reached 19% by early 1981. The discount rate—the interest rate on a loan from the Federal Reserve to a commercial bank—reached 14% by mid-1981. Raising these benchmark interest rates—which are the basis for lending and borrowing rates across the economic system—led to a credit crunch for workers, capitalists, and the government. By significantly raising the price that banks pay for reserves, banks had fewer funds with which to create loans. As happens in any market facing a shortage, borrowers had to compete for a smaller amount of funds available, resulting in significantly higher borrowing costs. This spike in market interest rates had several important consequences. It led to a contraction in consumption, especially of housing and other long-term durable goods. It led to a contraction in investment in plant and equipment. It also led to higher debt burdens for both the private sector and the public sector—and by consequence, to a significant redistribution of income from borrowers to lenders. Although the policy was successful in that high inflation and inflationary expectations ended by 1983, the United States experienced two severe downturns in the process.

However, contractionary monetary policy was not the only proposed solution to stagflation. Under the Reagan administration, the federal government implemented a number of policies informed by supply-side economics. Supply-side theory is a direct critique of Keynesian theory. On the one hand, Keynesian economists argued that stimulating aggregate demand was the key to economic growth. Demand-side policies encourage spending, especially by workers, since consumption is the largest source of aggregate spending. Supply-side economists, on the other hand, argued that increasing supply was necessary to jumpstart the type of growth necessary to end stagflation. Supply-side policies incentivize production by capitalists, since private firms are responsible for the vast majority of output in a capitalist system. By stimulating the supply side of the economic system, production and employment would expand, thereby resolving the recessionary aspect of stagflation. Unlike demand-side policies, however, flushing markets with more output would create market surpluses, and put downward pressure on prices, thereby resolving the inflationary aspect of stagflation.

Supply-siders contended that the heavy tax and regulatory environment of the postwar era discouraged entrepreneurship and production. While the Reagan administration certainly implemented significant deregulation and tax cuts during the early 1980s, Congress actually began reducing the capital gains tax during the Carter administration in 1978. The long title of the Economic Recovery Tax Act of 1981, which slashed capital gains, corporate, estate, and income taxes, states:

> To amend the Internal Revenue Code of 1954 to encourage economic growth through reduction of the tax rates for individual taxpayers, acceleration of capital cost recovery of investment in plant, equipment, and real property, and incentives for savings, and for other purposes.

Notice the new emphasis on using the tax code to encourage saving and production as compared to consumption and spending. Similarly, the Tax Reform Act of 1986 cut taxes and simplified the federal tax code.

Furthermore, the deregulatory, pro-capitalist agenda of the administration extended to the labor market. In 1981, Reagan famously fired over 11,000 federal air traffic controllers who were on strike. The failure of the strike undoubtedly weakened the bargaining power of public sector workers, especially federal workers. It likewise shifted the balance of power against labor within the private sector workplace, as capitalists were less willing to grant concessions to workers. Thereafter, the national union membership rate in the United States began a steady decline—a hallmark of neoliberal capitalism illustrated in Figure 2.2. The early budgets of the Reagan years also fundamentally altered government intervention in the labor market through cuts to social welfare programs directed at the

FIGURE 2.2 Union Membership Among all Wage and Salary Workers 1973–2018

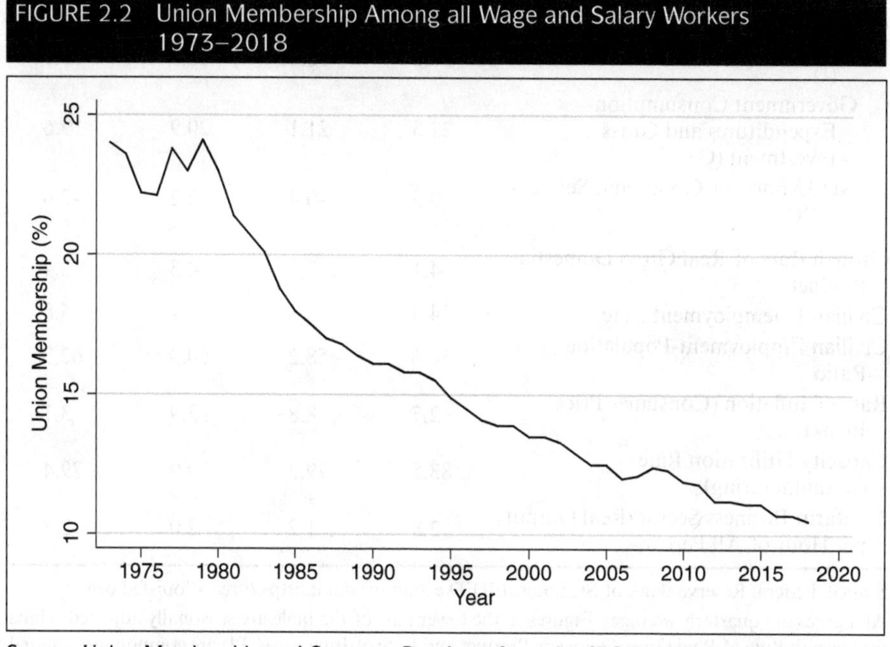

Source: Union Membership and Coverage Database from the CPS (http://unionstats.com).

working poor—in particular, Aid to Families with Dependent Children (AFDC), a cash assistance program for low-income families created during the Great Depression. However, those budgets still generated fiscal deficits, as they expanded a key aspect of postwar capital accumulation: Cold War-era national defense spending.

The Transition to Neoliberal Capitalism in Perspective

The effect of this policy agenda was to shift the institutional context of accumulation from one oriented toward workers to one oriented toward capitalists. Instead of increasing real wages in order to incentivize consumption and spending by workers, the purpose of government policy was to expand after-tax profits in order to encourage saving and production by capitalists. The transition to neoliberal capitalism consequently altered the composition and performance of the US economic system, as well as the distribution of income. Table 2.2 compares four historical phases in the restructuring of US capitalism during the latter half of the twentieth century. Column 1 covers the regulated stage of capitalism until the onset of the first oil crisis and the 1973–75 recession. Column 2 covers the crisis of

TABLE 2.2 Long-Run Shifts in US Economic Performance

	[1]	*[2]*	*[3]*	*[4]*
	1948(I)–1973(IV)	*1973(IV)–1982(IV)*	*1982(IV)–1990(III)*	*1982(IV)–2007(IV)*
Shares of Gross Domestic Product (%)				
Personal Consumption Expenditures (C)	60.6	60.9	63.0	64.9
Gross Private Domestic Investment (I)	16.6	18.4	18.3	18.1
Government Consumption Expenditures and Gross Investment (G)	22.3	21.1	20.9	19.6
Net Exports of Goods and Services (NX)	0.5	-0.4	-2.2	-2.6
Growth Rate of Real Gross Domestic Product	4.1	2.0	4.3	3.4
Civilian Unemployment Rate	4.8	7.3	6.7	5.8
Civilian Employment-Population Ratio	56.6	58.2	60.9	62.3
Rate of Inflation (Consumer Price Index)	2.7	8.8	3.9	3.1
Capacity Utilization Rate (Manufacturing)	83.5	79.3	79.9	79.4
Nonfarm Business Sector: Real Output per Hour of All Persons	2.8	1.2	2.0	2.3

Source: Federal Reserve Bank of St. Louis, FRED economic data: https://fred.stlouisfed.org.

All figures are quarterly averages. Figures in the lower half of the table are seasonally adjusted. Units for Growth Rate of Real Gross Domestic Product and Rate of Inflation (CPI) are compounded annual rates of change. Unit for Real Output per Hour of All Persons is percent change at annual rate.

the 1970s, including the 1973–75 recession, the second oil crisis in 1979, the monetary restraint by the Federal Reserve, and the "double-dip" recession of the early 1980s. Columns 3 and 4 then examine two periods during the neoliberal stage of capitalism. Column 3 presents the recovery of the 1980s until the 1990–91 recession. Column 4 presents the span of the neoliberal era until the Great Recession in 2007. All figures in the table are the quarterly averages for each period.

Three major observations are evident in this table. First, the transition to neoliberalism brought about a clear shift in the composition of US output. While net exports and government spending on goods and services became smaller contributors to GDP, consumption and investment became much larger contributors. When comparing the 1948–73 and 1982–2007 periods, government spending and net exports combined decreased from 22.8% to 17% of output. At the same time, consumption and investment increased from 77.2% to 83% of output. The key point here is that the US private sector increasingly claims a larger share of output as the government and foreign sectors claim less. Second, just as economic performance unambiguously weakened between 1973 and 1982, it re-stabilized during the 1982–90 recovery. This is especially the case for real GDP growth, inflation, and productivity growth. Third, the economic performance of the neoliberal period was largely weaker than the regulated period—in particular, the quarterly averages for real GDP growth (0.7 percentage points lower), unemployment (1 percentage point higher), capacity utilization in manufacturing (4.1 percentage points lower), and productivity growth (0.5 percentage points lower).

Furthermore, the pushback against government regulation and labor fundamentally changed who the beneficiaries of new income growth would be. Under regulated capitalism, labor secured real wage increases in line with productivity increases. Since 1973, however, real wages no longer increased in line with labor productivity increases. According to Figure 2.3, although productivity continued to rise, real wages were largely stagnant under neoliberal capitalism. Figure 2.4 illustrates the full scope of the decoupling of real wages from labor productivity after 1973. Unsurprisingly, the top 10% of the income distribution now claims the vast majority of new income growth. Returning to Table 2.1, between 1982 and 2007, real average incomes increased by $18,901—not an insignificant increase, but still $2,625 lower than the increase between 1948 and 1973. The critical change is that the top 10% claimed 81% of new income growth, while the bottom 90% claimed a mere 19%.

Several events during the 1980s underscored the growing complexity and instability associated with the evolution of global market integration, especially in finance. For example, while many economists celebrate the decade as a period of recovery and expansion for US capitalism, Latin America experienced a foreign debt crisis. During the 1970s, the oil crises resulted in large trade deficits for oil-importing countries in Latin America, which financed such deficits by borrowing from US commercial banks. In the early 1980s, however, higher interest rates and a global recession led to unsustainably high debt burdens, triggering a near decade-long default crisis. In the US, regulators also faced new challenges of financial instability. In 1984, Continental Illinois Bank and Trust Company became the largest US bank failure prior to the 2008 financial crisis. Instead of liquidating Continental, the federal government chose to protect its depositors and creditors, out of concern that the failure of a large bank would spread to

FIGURE 2.3 Real Hourly Compensation vs. Total Economy Productivity 1973–2015

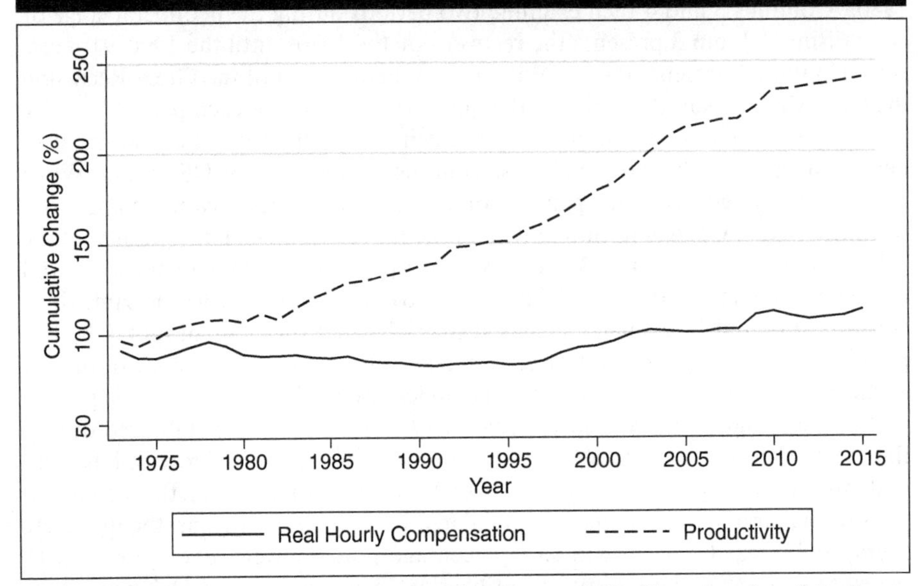

Source: The Economic Policy Institute's The State of Working America (http://www.stateofworkingamerica.org).

FIGURE 2.4 Real Hourly Compensation vs. Total Economy Productivity 1948–2015

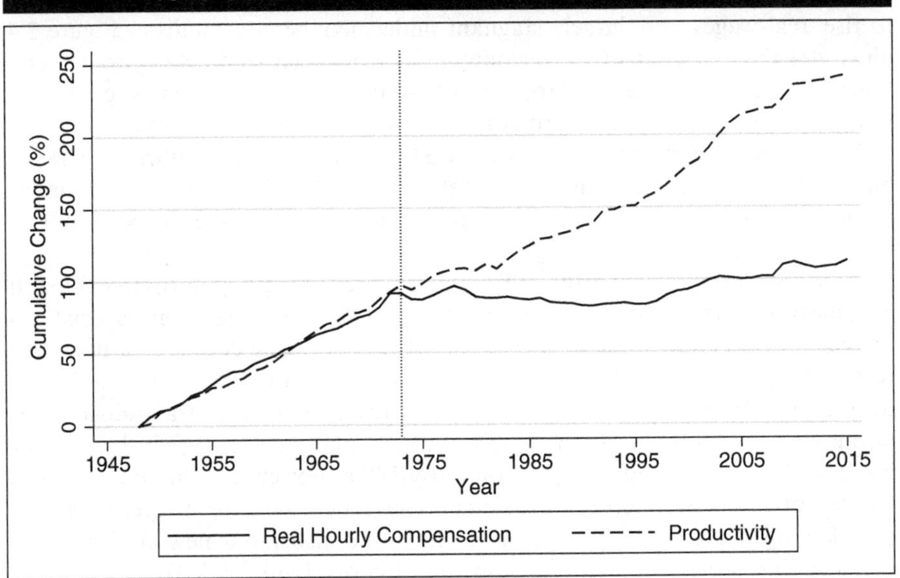

Source: The Economic Policy Institute's The State of Working America (http://www.stateofworkingamerica.org).

other banks and disrupt the economic system—an exceptional move at the time. In doing so, the government initiated the principle of "too big to fail," whereby it would prevent large bank failures that threatened the stability of both the financial system and the economic system. Elsewhere in the financial sector, federal regulators addressed a crisis in the savings and loan industry. Savings and loan associations (or "thrifts") were smaller financial institutions that raised capital from savings deposits and issued consumer loans, especially home mortgages. Prior to the crisis, thrifts were an important source of financing for US workers. The high interest rates of the late 1970s and early 1980s led to a significant loss of net worth, for two reasons. On the one hand, savings and loans had to offer higher deposit rates, or else depositors would withdraw funds, thus raising costs on the liability side of their balance sheets. On the other hand, rates of return on the asset side of their balance sheets were fixed, since they primarily issued long-term mortgages at fixed interest rates, which were much lower than market rates at the time. In an effort to allow associations to recover their losses, the Depository Institutions Act deregulated the industry in order to stabilize mortgage lending—another shift away from the regulatory responses to financial instability that were characteristic of postwar policymaking. However, risk-taking only increased, culminating in an industry-wide government bailout of approximately one-third of all savings and loan associations. Lastly, the stock market experienced its worst crash since 1929 on October 19, 1987—commonly referred to as "Black Monday"—following a build-up of stock prices that year.

After 92 months of expansion, US capitalism entered a recession in the summer of 1990, concluding what was the second-longest postwar expansion at the time. The 1990–91 recession proved to be minor compared to the downturns of the 1970s and early 1980s. In fact, by the time the US economic system recovered in March 1991, the neoliberal structure of accumulation would not only hold, but flourish, through the following decade.

THE EXTENSION OF NEOLIBERAL CAPITALISM: 1991–2001

The 1992 US presidential election featured a three-way race that centered on economic issues, especially the 1990–91 recession. Incumbent President George H.W. Bush, a Republican, promoted globalization and foreign policy achievements while defending the neoliberal status quo. Arkansas Governor Bill Clinton, a Democrat, carved out a "third way" between his party's historical roots in Keynesianism and conservative free-market fundamentalism. H. Ross Perot, an independent billionaire, railed against free trade, the federal deficit, and the major-party establishments, all of which he argued had failed the middle class. Despite calls for change and voter fatigue toward the 12-year Reagan-Bush era, Clinton's victory did not significantly alter the social structure of economic production set forth during the expansion of the 1980s; in fact, it enhanced it. In 1993, Clinton famously stated: "We stand for lower deficits and free trade and the bond market. Isn't that great?"

Similar to what transpired during the regulated stage of capitalism, neoliberalism evolved into a consensus that informed administrations of both parties, and other domestic and international institutions.

The Clinton-Greenspan Policy Mix

Clinton's policy proposals during the 1992 election included a number of liberal mainstays: a national healthcare plan; gay rights in the military; higher taxes for the rich; lower taxes for the middle class; environmental protection; and public investments in education, training, and infrastructure. In practice, however, he moved the needle on government intervention toward the center, if not the center-right—away from the *laissez-faire* inaction of the Reagan-Bush period, but not back to the active demand-side management of the regulated period. During his first two years in office, efforts at healthcare reform failed. On gay rights, Clinton agreed to the purported compromise policy of "Don't Ask, Don't Tell," which allowed the military to discharge gay and lesbian service members, but barred recruitment on the basis of sexual orientation. He later signed the Defense of Marriage Act, which prohibited federal recognition of same-sex marriages, and allowed states to prohibit recognition of such marriages performed in other states. Instead of lowering middle-class taxes and increasing federal investments in education and infrastructure, the 1993 budget included spending cuts and across-the-board tax increases in order to reduce the deficit overhang of the Reagan-Bush years. A 1994 crime bill banned assault weapons, but expanded the federal death penalty statute, discontinued education funding for incarcerated individuals, and funded the construction of new prisons. One of the most controversial provisions of the crime bill was the "Three Strikes" law, which contributed to the subsequent wave of mass incarceration, especially of racial and ethnic minorities. Republicans regained control of both houses of Congress in the 1994 midterm elections by highlighting Clinton's policy setbacks and committing to the "Contract with America," a package of conservative Reagan-inspired policy changes. In 1996, Clinton compromised on a centerpiece of the Contract with America by signing the Personal Responsibility and Work Opportunity Reconciliation Act, fulfilling his promise during his State of the Union address that "the era of big government is over." The Act fundamentally reformed the welfare system by replacing the AFDC program with Temporary Assistance for Needy Families. Welfare benefits were now temporary (not entitlements) and carried work requirements under a lifetime limit. The Act also granted more leverage to states to administer welfare and pursue welfare reform. By the end of the decade, the combination of strong economic growth, the 1993 budget act, and welfare reform contributed to fiscal surpluses, which neither party had achieved in decades.

In the realm of monetary policy, Alan Greenspan presided over a historic reduction in interest rates that eased access to credit. Although Reagan originally appointed Greenspan as chair of the Federal Reserve in 1987, he became a close advisor to Clinton on domestic and international economic matters following his reappointment. In the aftermath of the 1987 stock market crash, Greenspan used monetary stimulus to expand liquidity to the financial sector and economic system. The purpose of that liquidity was to increase demand for consumer goods and services, capital goods and infrastructure, as well as financial assets. Figure 2.5 illustrates the shift in interest rates for long-term US government bonds beginning in the 1980s. Although considerable debate remains over the effectiveness of expansionary monetary policy on market interest rates in real terms—for example, corporate bond rates, mortgage rates, etc.—the figure demonstrates the long-term reduction in nominal interest rates initiated by Federal Reserve policy.

FIGURE 2.5 Long-Term US Government Bond Rates 1948–2007

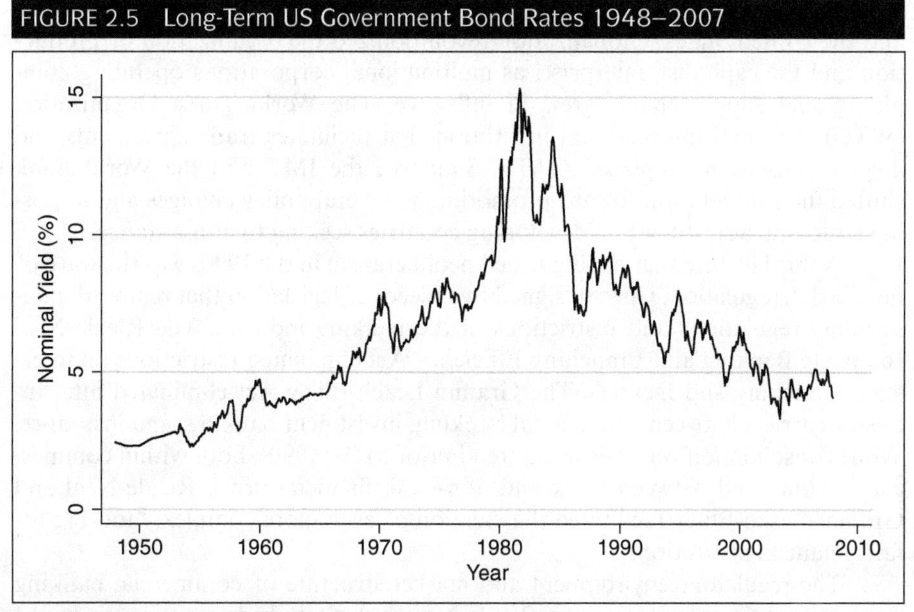

Source: Online data maintained by Robert Shiller (http://www.econ.yale.edu/~shiller/data.htm).

Engines of Accumulation During the 1990s: Technology, Globalization, and Financialization

Three further economic and policy changes fostered capital accumulation during the 1990s. First, although it had been building for several decades, a technological revolution swept global capitalism. Advances in the Internet, information, communications, computers, cellular phones, robotics, and the sciences transformed the development and allocation of resources, the organization of production, the distribution of goods and services, and their eventual consumption. The technological revolution not only lowered the costs of production and increased labor productivity, but also altered property rights, the nature of competition, decision making by individuals and organizations, and marketing strategies throughout the global economic system.

Second, globalization became a dominant force—especially the globalization of technology, services, intellectual property, information, and finance. International economic relationships certainly existed prior to the 1990s and neoliberal capitalism at large. In fact, one of the most important organizing principles of regulated capitalism was to avoid the economic isolationism of the early twentieth century. However, that system sought to regulate international economic relationships between national economic systems, especially industrialized capitalist countries in light of the Cold War. In contrast, globalization during the neoliberal period involved the reduction of national boundaries through market forces, and the integration of national economic systems into a singular global economic system. Several policies, events, and changes accelerated this process. The end of the Cold War and the collapse of the Soviet Union created new nation states and opened new markets. President Clinton signed the North American Free Trade

Agreement, which eliminated nearly all trade barriers between Canada, Mexico, and the United States. Globalization revolutionized the organization of production and the capitalist enterprise, as multinational corporations operating complex global supply chains grew in influence. The World Trade Organization (WTO), a formal international institution that facilitates trade agreements and dispute resolutions, replaced GATT. Similarly, the IMF and the World Bank shifted their orientation toward promoting neoliberal policy changes and imposing structural adjustment on developing countries seeking their assistance.

A third feature that distinguished neoliberalism in the 1990s was the wave of financial deregulation. Clinton signed two pieces of legislation that removed long-standing regulations and restrictions in the banking industry. The Riegle-Neal Interstate Banking and Branching Efficiency Act eliminated restrictions on inter-state branching and mergers. The Gramm-Leach-Bliley Act eliminated inter-industry barriers between commercial banking, investment banking, and insurance. While consolidation was a growing trend prior to the 1990s, both within commercial banking and between bank and non-bank financial firms, Riegle-Neal and Gramm-Leach-Bliley facilitated the creation of even more complex, "too-big-to-fail" financial institutions.

The regulatory environment and market structure of commercial banking were quite different prior to the Riegle-Neal Act. State banks—meaning banks chartered and regulated by a state government—could not operate branches outside a state. National banks—meaning banks chartered and regulated by the federal government—faced similar geographic restrictions on inter-state branching. Bank mergers and acquisitions across state lines occurred only with the permission of state legislatures. Proponents of this system asserted that it created a banking sector comprised of a large number of small, consumer-friendly, community-oriented firms. For decades, critics argued that the system limited competition by maintaining barriers to entry. They argued that it heightened risk, citing the strong correlation between banking risk and the health of state and regional economic systems, which can vary widely from the national environment. They also argued that it raised costs for consumers, since overhead expenses were more burdensome for banks at a limited scale of operations.

Proponents of Riegle-Neal claimed that allowing banks to operate branches and acquire banks in other states would enable them to offer more services at a lower average cost. Furthermore, deregulation would in fact encourage competition by creating an integrated national market. Banks could then more effectively manage risk by buffering against particular state and regional economic conditions. Detractors then and now contend that Riegle-Neal made the banking industry less competitive, given the smaller number of much larger banks that operate the industry. And although the law removed geographic barriers to entry, it created a new one: large established banks had a cost advantage over potential new competitors. Lastly, the proliferation of large corporate banks that crossed state and regional lines distanced them from local communities and consumers.

Similar arguments informed the debate over the Gramm-Leach-Bliley Act. Gramm-Leach-Bliley essentially repealed the regulatory separation of commercial banking from investment banking and insurance. It did so by allowing firms to create a financial holding company—a larger organization that runs subsidiaries offering different financial services. For example, a commercial bank could be part of a financial holding company that also operates a subsidiary that underwrites securities, or sells insurance. Financial industry advocates claim that consolidation of bank and non-bank activities generates cost efficiencies and convenience for consumers. Both consumers and firms can diversify risk across multiple products and services. Critics claim that the law re-exposed commercial banking to insurance and investment risk—the very outcome that longstanding regulations sought to prevent.

Heterodox economists describe the growing influence of the financial sector in the functioning and performance of capitalism during this period as "financialization." In turn, the expanded influence of the financial sector has extended to politics, culture, and other realms of society. Financialization is a concept rooted in heterodox economic theory, as it emphasizes evolutionary dynamics in the operation of the economic system. The operation of the economic system has historical context, generates change over time, and interacts with non-economic spheres. Financialization first and foremost has shifted relations of power between financial capitalists and industrial capitalists. During the regulated stage of capitalism, finance supported long-term investment in production and job creation. Commercial banks were the primary source of financial capital, which industrial capitalists used to purchase plant, equipment, and infrastructure. In the neoliberal stage of capitalism, however, the distinction between industrial and financial capital is less clear. Commercial banks are no longer the primary source of financial capital. Instead, banks compete with non-bank financial institutions and financial markets as sources of funds. Financial activity is increasingly short term (as opposed to long term) and speculative (as opposed to productive).

Competing Perspectives on the 1990s

Mainstream economists point to several factors that characterize the 1990s as a "Goldilocks economy." Table 2.3 applies the economic performance variables discussed earlier to the first three recoveries during the neoliberal era. Column 1 covers the period from the end of the "double-dip" recession of the early 1980s until the onset of the Great Recession. Columns 2 through 4 then compare the 1982–90, 1991–2001, and 2001–07 recoveries respectively. The 1990s remains one of the longest sustained periods of economic growth in US history, having lasted 120 consecutive months. All of the quarterly averages during the 1991–2001 recovery—for real GDP growth, unemployment, employment relative to population, inflation, capacity utilization, and productivity growth—performed better than during the 1982–2007 period as a whole. In particular, the longstanding tradeoff between unemployment and inflation disappeared, resulting in both lower unemployment and lower inflation. With technological advancements, expanding global markets, and financial innovation, employment in high-end services increased. Most notably, an unprecedented stock market boom increased wealth during the 1990s. Figure 2.6 illustrates the real value of Standard & Poor's Composite Stock Index from 1948 to 2007. Although a stock market boom also occurred during the 1980s, that boom essentially made up for the decline during the 1970s, and pales in comparison to the acceleration of stock prices during the late 1990s.

However, heterodox economists point to a number of structural changes that destabilized capitalism during the 1990s. Despite low rates of unemployment,

TABLE 2.3 Three US Recoveries During Neoliberal Capitalism

	[1]	[2]	[3]	[4]
	1982(IV)–2007(IV)	*1982(IV)–1990(III)*	*1991(I)–2001(I)*	*2001(IV)–2007(IV)*
Shares of Gross Domestic Product (%)				
Personal Consumption Expenditures (C)	64.9	63.0	64.9	67.2
Gross Private Domestic Investment (I)	18.1	18.3	17.7	18.6
Government Consumption Expenditures and Gross Investment (G)	19.6	20.9	18.9	19.1
Net Exports of Goods and Services (NX)	−2.6	−2.2	−1.6	−4.9
Growth Rate of Real Gross Domestic Product	3.4	4.3	3.6	2.9
Civilian Unemployment Rate	5.8	6.7	5.5	5.3
Civilian Employment-Population Ratio	62.3	60.9	63.1	62.7
Rate of Inflation (Consumer Price Index)	3.1	3.9	2.7	2.9
Capacity Utilization Rate (Manufacturing)	79.4	79.9	81.1	76.6
Nonfarm Business Sector: Real Output per Hour of All Persons	2.3	2.0	2.4	2.6

Source: Federal Reserve Bank of St. Louis, FRED economic data: https://fred.stlouisfed.org.
All figures are quarterly averages. Figures in the lower half of the table are seasonally adjusted. Units for Growth Rate of Real Gross Domestic Product and Rate of Inflation (CPI) are compounded annual rates of change. Unit for Real Output per Hour of All Persons is percent change at annual rate.

capitalists consolidated power over workers and suppressed real wages. Although employment in technology and finance increased, so did employment in low-wage services. Many long-term manufacturing jobs became obsolete with deindustrialization and the corresponding growth of the service sector, which lacked the union wages, protections, and benefits that prevailed during regulated capitalism. Technological advancements allowed capitalists to simplify labor processes and outsource component production, reducing the need for high-skilled labor. Globalization allowed them to move production processes partially or fully to countries where wages and non-labor resource costs were cheaper. Welfare reform reduced income security for those unable to transition to stable employment, or who faced long-term structural unemployment. Moreover, the low rates of unemployment during this period did not account for the marked increase in incarceration, as incarcerated individuals are not surveyed by the US Bureau of Labor Statistics.

In this area, the process of financialization was neither a coincidence nor inevitable. It was a purposeful solution to a core issue facing neoliberal capitalism, just as the sustained increase in real wages following World War II was a purposeful solution to a core issue facing regulated capitalism. The situation facing

FIGURE 2.6 Real Standard & Poor's Composite Stock Index 1948–2007

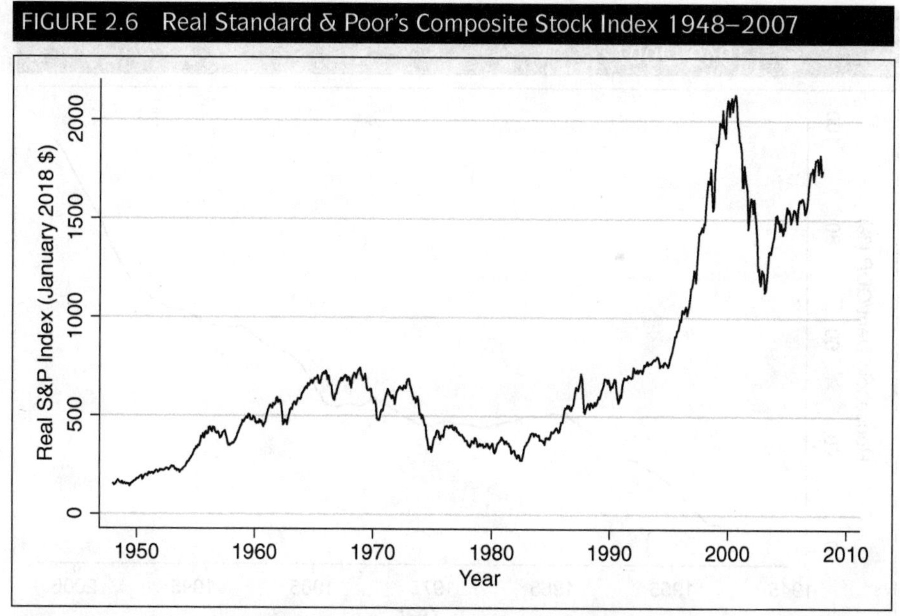

Source: Online data maintained by Robert Shiller (http://www.econ.yale.edu/~shiller/data.htm).

neoliberal capitalism was this: how could consumption increase its share of economic activity while real wages remained stagnant? How could workers spend more while essentially earning the same (or less)? The solution was to increase access to credit. Financialization in a globalized, technologically advanced environment facilitated a significant increase in economic output and living standards. Capitalism was simply able to produce more output with less labor. However, with most new income going to the top and no real expansion of labor income, there had to be a way for workers to purchase that output; otherwise, consumption and living standards would have to decline. Instead of paying workers higher real wages in order to increase consumption, capitalists paid workers the same (or less) to produce goods and services, while financial firms charged them interest in order to consume goods and services. Neoliberal capitalism therefore featured economic growth, but with more inequality and less financial security. Figure 2.7 documents the historical shift in US household debt relative to GDP between 1949 and 2007. For most of the postwar period, the household debt to GDP ratio was stable, and less than 50%. A steady increase began in the 1980s and 1990s, however, as the ratio exceeded 70% by the early 2000s.

Furthermore, while the stock market boom expanded aggregate wealth, wealth concentration increased during the 1990s and early 2000s. Table 2.4 examines changes in wealth inequality for the top 1%, the 90th to 99th percentiles, the 50th to 90th percentiles, and the bottom 50%. "Net worth" in this case refers to total assets minus total liabilities for the household sector. All figures under Columns 1 and 2 are the quarterly averages for each wealth percentile. According to Column 1, the top 1% held 26.7% of aggregate net worth during the 1991–2001 expansion; together with the 90th to 99th percentiles, the top 10% held 61.6%. The bottom 50%, on the other hand, held a mere 3.7% of net worth.

FIGURE 2.7 Household Debt as a Percent of Gross Domestic Product 1949–2007

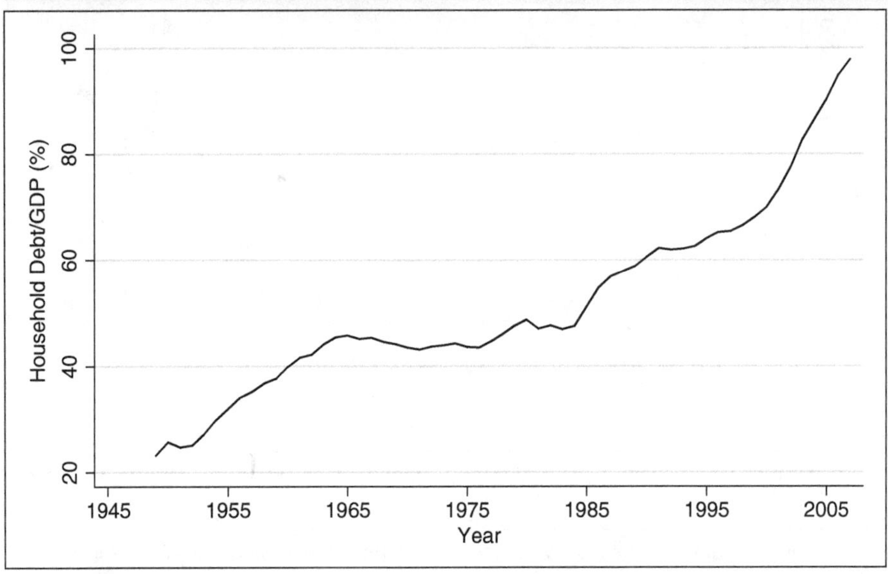

Source: Federal Reserve Bank of St. Louis FRED economic data (https://fred.stlouisfed.org).

TABLE 2.4 Changes in Household Wealth Inequality, 1991–2007

	[1]	*[2]*	*[3]*
	1991(I)–2001(I)	*2001(IV)–2007(IV)*	*Change, 1991(I)–2007(IV)*
Share of Total Net Worth Held by the Top 1%	26.7	27.4	5.5
Share of Total Net Worth Held by the 90th to 99th Percentiles	34.9	36.9	2.2
Share of Total Net Worth Held by the 50th to 90th Percentiles	34.7	33.5	−4.9
Share of Total Net Worth Held by the Bottom 50%	3.7	2.2	−2.8

Source: Federal Reserve Bank of St. Louis, FRED economic data: https://fred.stlouisfed.org.
The unit of measurement is the percentage of aggregate net worth. All figures in Columns [1] and [2] are quarterly averages for each wealth percentile.

However, the deterioration of financial security extended beyond the US working class. Similar to what transpired during the 1980s, increasing global financial integration brought with it increasing instability during the 1990s. The dotcom bubble fueled the iconic stock market boom, as speculative investment flooded into (and eventually retreated from) Internet-based firms. Investor psychology became increasingly complex and volatile by exhibiting patterns of herd behavior, contagion, and other forms of irrational decision making. These patterns affected the stability of the financial sector both in the United States and around the world. In 1997, speculation against the Thai baht diminished foreign exchange reserves and forced Thailand to devalue the baht against the US dollar. Contagion spread the crisis to other trading partners in the region, which suffered from weaker currencies, severe recessions, financial market instability, and banking turmoil. In 1998, the forces that propelled the East Asian financial crisis spread to Latin America, Russia, and eventually Wall Street. Long-Term Capital Management was a prominent hedge fund that had extensive business dealings and relationships throughout the US financial sector. However, financial crises around the world led to a collapse in the value of the firm's fund. Concerned that bankruptcy would destabilize the financial sector and the economic system, the New York Federal Reserve Bank organized a bailout of Long-Term Capital Management using private sector funds.

By the end of the decade, a collapse in market euphoria combined with an increase in interest rates by the Federal Reserve turned the stock market boom into a bust. Mounting pessimism and uncertainty following the dot-com bust led to a slowdown in economic activity that pushed US capitalism into recession in early 2001. Given the bubble mentality, the lack of regulatory oversight, the sustained increase in debt, and the intensification of inequality that fueled capitalism in the 1990s, some economists feared that the correction could trigger a generational crisis akin to the Great Depression. Although it did not, the subsequent recovery indeed laid the foundation for such a crisis, with a new speculative bubble, even less oversight, and an even greater surge in debt and inequality.

THE PRELUDE TO THE GREAT RECESSION: 2001–07

Like the 1990–91 recession, the 2001 downturn officially lasted for eight months. While brief, one of the notable aspects of the recession was a run of corporate accounting scandals, the largest of which was the Enron scandal. At the time, Enron was the largest corporate bankruptcy in US history. Several executives received criminal charges and convictions, investors suffered enormous losses, and in many cases, Enron workers lost a lifetime's worth of savings from their 401(k) retirement plans.

The newly inaugurated George W. Bush administration addressed the 2001 recession in two ways. First, Bush signed the Economic Growth and Tax Relief Reconciliation Act, a package that included disproportionate tax cuts for the rich, and tax rebates to stimulate consumption. The Act was the first piece of what would eventually become the "Bush tax cuts." Despite years of redistribution of income and wealth to the top, Bush believed that the key to jumpstarting growth was to grant even more after-tax earnings to the wealthy. The first column of Table 2.5 presents the shares of the 2001 tax cuts claimed by each income quintile, as well as the share claimed by the top 1%. Whereas the top 40% of the income distribution received approximately two-thirds of the 2001 tax cuts, the bottom 60% received only one-third. Second, in the aftermath of the September 11, 2001 terrorist attacks, Bush called for an increase in consumer spending in order to boost both economic growth and public morale.

Policy Foundations of the 2001–07 Expansion

The fiscal policy agenda of the W. Bush administration prior to the Great Recession focused on three areas. The centerpiece of the president's agenda was the Jobs and Growth Tax Relief Reconciliation Act—the second component of the Bush tax cuts. The Act accelerated many of the 2001 tax cuts, and lowered taxes on capital gains and dividends. These reductions principally benefited the wealthy given the unequal distribution of household net worth noted in the previous section. Bush subsequently signed two pieces of legislation that extended the tax changes of the early 2000s. Table 2.5 illustrates the distribution of these changes during their implementation between 2001 and 2007. Although the top 20% claimed a significant share of the 2001 tax cuts, it claimed an even larger share of the succeeding reductions and extensions. By 2007, the top 20% received nearly three-quarters of the tax cuts. The top 1% eventually received one-third, after claiming 7% of the 2001 cuts. Meanwhile, the quintiles comprising the bottom 80% claimed even smaller shares as the decade progressed. The fourth 20% in particular—a quintile that covers the upper middle class—saw its share nearly cut in half between 2001 and 2007.

On the spending side of Bush's budgets, two factors contributed to an increase in federal expenditures. In the area of social welfare spending, the government expanded Medicare to include a voluntary prescription drug benefit. More significantly, national defense and military spending surged with the wars in Afghanistan and Iraq. Overall, the fiscal policy agenda of the W. Bush era was essentially a redux of the 1980s: tax cuts for the rich in order to incentivize investment and production, an increase in defense spending that enhanced the profits of private defense contractors, and accordingly, a return to fiscal deficits.

The policy agenda of the Federal Reserve was also a continuation of Alan Greenspan's long-term monetary stimulus. Following the dot-com bust and 2001 recession, Greenspan kept benchmark interest rates low until the summer of 2004. The purpose of monetary stimulus was the same as it had been since the late 1980s: to flush the economic system and the financial sector with liquidity as a buffer against instability, and a possible "double-dip" recession. Albeit in different ways, the monetary policies of the Volcker and Greenspan eras both enhanced capital accumulation. Both were essential elements of the operation of neoliberal

TABLE 2.5 Shares of Tax Cuts by Income Group, 2001–07

	2001	*2002*	*2003*	*2004*	*2005*	*2006*	*2007*
Lowest 20%	2%	2%	1%	1%	1%	1%	1%
Second 20%	12%	9%	5%	5%	5%	5%	5%
Middle 20%	18%	14%	10%	9%	9%	8%	8%
Fourth 20%	26%	21%	16%	15%	15%	14%	14%
Top 20%	42%	54%	68%	70%	70%	72%	73%
Top 1%	7%	20%	27%	31%	32%	34%	34%

Source: Wamhoff & Gardner (2018), Institute on Taxation and Economic Policy.

capitalism. During the late 1970s and early 1980s, Volcker's monetary restraint enhanced profit making by increasing unemployment and contributing to real wage suppression. Between the late 1980s and early 2000s, Greenspan's monetary stimulus enhanced profit making by increasing access to credit and supporting demand for goods and services.

Policy Philosophies During the 2001–07 Expansion: The Ownership Society and the Great Moderation

Two visions, each of which advanced neoliberalism, informed the conduct of fiscal and monetary policies during the 2001–07 expansion. The economic policies of the W. Bush administration reflected a conservative conception of an "ownership society." Although the principles of an ownership society center on individual choice and personal responsibility, they essentially represent an even further removal of government from income and wealth security. In an ownership society, individuals exercise more power in education, healthcare, household accommodation, and retirement decisions. The central policy to that effect is lower taxes in order to increase personal savings and expand wealth and property. More specific policies include school vouchers, tax benefits for health savings accounts, and similar incentives for 401(k) retirement funds. A chief goal of the W. Bush administration in this area was to increase home ownership through tax incentives and down-payment assistance, especially for racial and ethnic minorities. In practice, however, these policies were merely mechanisms to justify less public funding for education, housing, and social welfare programs, as well as privatization of Medicare and Social Security. During his second inaugural address in 2005, Bush explained his vision in detail:

> To give every American a stake in the promise and future of our country, we will bring the highest standards to our schools and build an ownership society. We will widen the ownership of homes and businesses, retirement savings, and health insurance, preparing our people for the challenges of life in a free society. By making every citizen an agent of his or her own destiny, we will give our fellow Americans greater freedom from want and fear and make our society more prosperous and just and equal.

At the Federal Reserve, the monetary policies of Greenspan and his successor Ben Bernanke reflected a belief in the "Great Moderation," a term that arose during the early 2000s. Mainstream economists describe the Great Moderation as a period of reduced business cycle volatility, specifically in output and inflation, that began during the 1980s. Since then, US capitalism experienced two lengthy expansions and only two short recessions. Policymakers believed that they had finally found the right mix between allowing efficient market forces to flourish and using minimal government intervention to stabilize and correct imbalances in the economic system. Proponents point to several factors that made expansions longer and contractions briefer, such as expansionary monetary policies, financial innovation, globalization, labor market flexibility, service sector growth, technological progress, and perhaps even good luck.

The Elusive Expansion in Perspective

While mainstream economists and policymakers contend that the Great Moderation continued into the 2000s, even by conventional measures, the 2001–07 expansion was a historically weak recovery within a historically weak stage of capitalism. According to Table 2.3—despite multiple tax cuts, low benchmark interest rates, and two wars—average quarterly output growth was lower than during the 1982–90 expansion (by 1.4 percentage points), the 1991–2001 expansion (by 0.7 percentage points), and the 1982–2007 period as a whole (by 0.5 percentage points). The US trade deficit, which actually decreased from 2.2% to 1.6% of GDP between the 1980s and 1990s, ballooned to nearly 5% of GDP. Capacity utilization in manufacturing was also notably lower by 4.5 percentage points as compared to the 1990s. While the 2001–07 recovery did not continue the "Goldilocks economy" of the 1990s, it did continue the growing structural imbalances that characterize the neoliberal period: stagnant labor earnings, accelerating income and wealth inequality, higher indebtedness, and greater financial instability.

According to Table 2.4, wealth concentration increased even further during the 2000s. While the top 10% saw its share of aggregate net worth increase, the bottom 90% saw its share decline. This is an especially important point to consider: the redistribution of wealth dispossessed not only the share held by the bottom 50%, which was insignificant to begin with, but also the more sizable share held by the 50th to 90th percentiles. Column 3 emphasizes this point further by reporting the change in each percentile's share between the first quarter of 1991 and the fourth quarter of 2007. The top 1% saw the biggest change in its share: a 5.5 percentage point increase over the entire period. The 90th to 99th percentiles also increased their shares by 2.2 percentage points. Although the bottom 50% witnessed a 2.8 percentage point decrease, the 50th to 90th percentiles—a segment that covers a wide span of the middle class—witnessed an even larger 4.9 percentage point decrease.

The most disturbing aspect of the 2001–07 expansion was the persistence of a jobless recovery in the US labor market. Employment recovery following downturns was increasingly sluggish in the neoliberal era, even though official unemployment was relatively low, and recessions were relatively brief. This phenomenon was present following the 1990–91 recession but was even more pronounced following the 2001 recession. For each of the ten recessions that occurred between 1948 and 2001, Table 2.6 documents the official "peak" and "trough" dates; the duration of the recession in months; the number of months it took for total employment to return to its pre-recession level; and the month in which that occurred. Prior to the 1990–91 recession, the average downturn lasted 11 months, while the average period of job recovery lasted 20 months. Depending on the duration of the contraction, employment would reach its pre-recession level within six months to a year from the trough. Although the 1990–91 recession was relatively shorter, it took nearly three years for jobs to recover. Following the similarly brief 2001 recession, it took until January 2005—nearly four years since the March 2001 peak in economic activity—for total employment to recover. The implication is that although the economic system experienced 73 months of official recovery following the 2001 recession, the labor market operated at pre-recession employment levels for about half of that time.

TABLE 2.6 Non-Farm Payroll Employment Recoveries, 1948–2001

Peak	*Trough*	*Duration of Recession (Months)*	*Number of Months to Reach Peak Employment*	*Date of Employment Recovery*
November 1948	October 1949	11	20	July 1950
July 1953	May 1954	10	23	June 1955
August 1957	April 1958	8	20	April 1959
April 1960	February 1961	10	20	December 1961
December 1969	November 1970	11	17	May 1971
November 1973	March 1975	16	25	December 1975
January 1980	July 1980	6	11	December 1980
July 1981	November 1982	16	28	November 1983
July 1990	March 1991	8	31	February 1993
March 2001	November 2001	8	46	January 2005

Source: Federal Reserve Bank of St. Louis, FRED economic data: https://fred.stlouisfed.org.

In the end, the real mechanism that kept the economic system afloat during the 2001–07 recovery, and minimized the 2001 recession, was the housing market bubble. The housing bubble is such an important and complex component to understanding the lead-up to the Great Recession that it warrants an entire chapter. Regarding the 2001–07 expansion, however, the housing bubble largely held up economic growth with a significant increase in consumption. As shown in Table 2.3, personal consumption expenditures reached a historic high of 67.2% of GDP. As has been analyzed throughout this chapter, the increasing share of consumption in economic activity during this period was not due to an increase in real earnings, or even an increase in job creation, but an increase in debt using home equity. This process simply accelerated during the 2000s. Returning to Figure 2.7, the US household debt to GDP ratio first surpassed 50% in 1985 and 60% in 1991. In 2001, it reached 73%. By 2007, household debt reached a staggering 97.9% of GDP. The combination of these factors put US capitalism on an inherently weak foundation that made it difficult to withstand the next contraction in December 2007, when that bubble was no longer sustainable.

FINAL THOUGHTS

Before moving on to the next topic, it is important to note the considerable amount of debate surrounding the concepts and relationships discussed in this chapter, even within heterodox circles. The goal of this chapter is not to settle those debates, but to give readers the tools and direction to explore these ideas further. A particular point of contention is whether capitalism is now entering a new stage, and the nature of the new institutions that may develop. For example, a right-wing populist model of capitalism has emerged in the United States and around the world, which includes attacks on free trade and immigration, a resurgence in ethnic nationalism and white supremacy, the proliferation of religious freedom protections, and the retreat of the United States from global leadership and its post-World War II alliances. On the other hand, a progressive vision has also formulated that addresses income inequality, climate change, and racial and gender stratification; offers debt-free higher education; expands Medicare; and embraces demographic change. Both of these visions have disrupted the neoliberal consensus that has informed major political parties on both the Right and the Left. However, understanding how this debate emerged requires further discussion of the transmission of the crisis, the responses to it, and the recovery. The next step is to examine a particular aspect of the lead-up to the crisis: the housing market bubble.

Sources

Bush, G.W. (2005, January 20). Inaugural address [Transcript]. Retrieved from https://www.presidency.ucsb.edu.

Carter, J. (1979, July 15). Address to the nation on energy and national goals: "The malaise speech" [Transcript]. Retrieved from https://www.presidency.ucsb.edu.

Clinton, W.J. (1996, January 23). Address before a joint session of the Congress on the state of the union [Transcript]. Retrieved from https://www.presidency.ucsb.edu.

Federal Reserve Bank of St. Louis. (n.d.). *FRED economic data* [Data file and codebook]. Retrieved from https://fred.stlouisfed.org.

Hirsch, B. & Macpherson, D. (2018). *Union membership and coverage database from the CPS* [Data file and codebook]. Retrieved from http://www.unionstats.com.

Keynes, J.M. (1964). *The general theory of employment, interest, and money*. New York, NY: Harcourt, Inc.

Mishel, L., Bivens, J., Gould, E., & Shierholz, H. (2012). *The state of working America*. Ithaca, NY: Cornell University Press.

National Bureau of Economic Research. (n.d.). US business cycle expansions and contractions. Retrieved from http://www.nber.org.

Nixon, R.M. (1971, August 15). Address to the nation outlining a new economic policy: "The challenge of peace" [Transcript]. Retrieved from https://www.presidency.ucsb.edu.

Nixon, R.M. (1973, November 25). Address to the nation about national energy policy [Transcript]. Retrieved from https://www.presidency.ucsb.edu.

Powell, L.F. (1971, August 23). *Attack on American free enterprise system* [Memorandum]. Lewis F. Powell, Jr. Archives. Retrieved from https://scholarlycommons.law.wlu.edu.

Reagan, R. (1981, January 20). Inaugural address [Transcript]. Retrieved from https://www.presidency.ucsb.edu.

Shiller, R.J. (n.d.). *Online data – Robert Shiller* [Data file and codebook]. Retrieved from http://www.econ.yale.edu/~shiller/data.htm.

US Bureau of Economic Analysis. (n.d.). *A guide to the National Income and Product Accounts of the United States*. Author.

Wamhoff, S. & Gardner, M. (2018). *Federal tax cuts in the Bush, Obama, and Trump years*. Washington, DC: Institute on Taxation and Economic Policy.

Woodward, B. (1994). *The agenda: Inside the Clinton White House*. New York, NY: Simon & Schuster.

Further Reading

Baker, D., Epstein, G., & Pollin, R. (eds.). (1998). *Globalization and progressive economic policy*. Cambridge, UK: Cambridge University Press.

Blanchard, O. & Simon, J. (2001). The long and large decline in U.S. output volatility. *Brookings Papers on Economic Activity*, *1*, 135–74. doi: 10.2307/30052109

Block, F.L. (1977). *The origins of international economic disorder: A study of United States international monetary policy from World War II to the present*. Berkeley, CA: University of California Press.

Epstein, G.A. (Ed.). (2005). *Financialization and the world economy*. Northampton, MA: Edward Elgar Publishing.

Friedman, M. (1962). *Capitalism and freedom*. Chicago, IL: University of Chicago Press.

Gordon, D.M. (1978). Up and down the long roller coaster. In Union for Radical Political Economics (ed.), *US capitalism in crisis* (pp. 22–34). New York, NY: Union for Radical Political Economics.

Hayek, F.A. (1944). *The road to serfdom*. London, UK: G. Routledge & Sons.

Helleiner, E. (1994). *States and the re-emergence of global finance: From Bretton Woods to the 1990s*. Ithaca, NY: Cornell University Press.

Keynes, J.M. (1933). National self-sufficiency. *The Yale Review*, *22*(4), 755–69.

Meeropol, M. (1998). *Surrender: How the Clinton administration completed the Reagan Revolution*. Ann Arbor, MI: The University of Michigan Press.

McDonough, T., Reich, M., & Kotz, D.M. (eds.). (2010). *Contemporary capitalism and its crises: social structure of accumulation theory for the 21st century*. New York, NY: Cambridge University Press.

Pollin, R. (2003). *Contours of descent: U.S. economic fractures and the landscape of global austerity*. London, UK: Verso.

Shiller, R.J. (2005). *Irrational exuberance*. New York, NY: Currency Books.

CHAPTER 3

The Housing Market Bubble (and Bust)

The extension of private property rights, including the ownership of homes, has long been the subject of intense debate throughout US history—a debate that has evolved considerably since independence. The Founding Fathers believed that property rights promote both economic and political independence. In *Discourses on Davila*, John Adams declared that: "Property must be secured, or liberty cannot exist." Marxists, on the other hand, argue that home ownership in capitalist societies constricts the mobility and collective bargaining power of the working class. In *The Housing Question*, Friedrich Engels discusses the relationship between home ownership and wage suppression in urban areas:

> For our workers in the big cities freedom of movement is the first condition of their existence, and landownership could only be a hindrance to them. Give them their own houses, chain them once again to the soil and you break their power of resistance to the wage cutting of the factory owners.

During the Great Depression of the 1930s, President Franklin Roosevelt expanded the reach of the federal government to protect homeowners and the stability of the economic system from the devastating effects of foreclosures:

> … the broad interests of the Nation require that special safeguards should be thrown around home ownership as a guarantee of social and economic stability, and that to protect home owners from inequitable enforced liquidation in a time of general distress is a proper concern of the Government.

However, the expansion of government intervention in income and wealth security did not extend to all communities and neighborhoods. During the 1960s, civil rights activists organized against residential segregation and racial discrimination in the renting and sale of housing. At the conclusion of the Selma to Montgomery March in 1965, Martin Luther King, Jr. said: "Let us march on segregated

DOI: 10.4324/9780429461316-5

housing until every ghetto or social and economic depression dissolves, and Negroes and whites live side by side in decent, safe, and sanitary housing."

Prior to the Great Recession, Presidents Bill Clinton and George W. Bush sought to ease financial barriers to home ownership. Both presidents heralded the wave of industry consolidation and technological innovation that created new opportunities to secure home financing. The aftermath of the Great Recession, however, has brought forth a new consideration in this debate that challenges the American celebration of home ownership: the prospect that the housing market could trigger a generational economic and financial crisis.

This chapter continues a comprehensive investigation of "The Road to the Great Recession." Chapter 2 traced the long-term evolution of capitalist institutions in profit making and investment, from the Great Depression until 2008, using social structure of accumulation theory. The next step is to analyze the housing market bubble—a more specific and crucial feature of US capitalism during the ten years prior to the Great Recession. In keeping with the theme of this book, the housing bubble serves as a case study in order to understand economic principles, policies, and schools of thought. This chapter not only draws upon the theoretical concepts presented thus far, but also builds upon them by presenting new insights from alternative perspectives—principally the growing field of stratification economics.

Stratification economics offers theoretical and empirical frameworks for understanding the formation and reproduction of intergroup inequality. It investigates both the structural forces and deliberate practices that create hierarchies based upon race, ethnicity, and other group identities, and how such hierarchies sustain income and wealth inequality. Stratification economics occupies a unique space in the economics discipline, as it rejects elements from several schools of thought on the oppression of historically under-represented groups. It rejects both academic and popular narratives that differences in behavior, culture, or personal responsibility explain the underdevelopment of minority communities. Instead, stratification economics examines the social forces and structures of privilege that produce such outcomes. However, it also differs from examinations of race and discrimination across the field of economics, including mainstream and heterodox approaches. For example, neoclassical economics contends that discrimination is an irrational form of behavior, and that market competition will eliminate discriminatory practices. In macroeconomics, conventional measures of the health and performance of the national economic system, such as the National Income and Product Accounts, do not account for intergroup inequality. Heterodox schools of thought have also received criticism for understating race, gender, and other group affiliations in their central focus on class. Given the persistence of discrimination and the transmission of intergroup inequality across generations, stratification economists advocate for the use of government policy in order to redistribute income and wealth.

This chapter develops a framework for investigating the US housing market bubble (and bust) that preceded the Great Recession. In particular, it uses the experiences of racial and ethnic minorities—from the Great Depression through the civil rights era to the subprime mortgage boom and foreclosure crisis—as a lens for understanding the creation and eventual undoing of the bubble. The first two sections set the stage with an examination of the complex relationship between home ownership and the operation of US capitalism. The first section presents several stylized facts about the US home ownership rate, and compares the frequently cited benefits and risks of home ownership. The second section introduces the historical practice of redlining, an intentional barrier to home ownership that arose during the federal government's response to the Great Depression. The next two sections focus on the meaning and empirical measurement of market bubbles: the third section explains the theoretical differences between bubbles and traditional price increases; while the fourth section uses the Case-Shiller Home Price Indexes to place the US housing bubble into historical perspective and compare metropolitan experiences during the bubble and bust. The fifth section applies the principles and concepts presented throughout this chapter to a comprehensive survey of the major explanations of the housing bubble, including those that emphasize market forces, government intervention, and the provision of subprime mortgage loans. The final section concludes the chapter with an analysis of the transmission of the foreclosure crisis and the government's responses to it.

HOME OWNERSHIP AND US CAPITALISM

Home ownership is fundamentally intertwined with the structure, history, and functioning of US capitalism. The housing market is undoubtedly a central element to understanding the Great Recession, but its importance to economic growth and development predates the crisis. While the expansion of home ownership has increased wealth and reduced inequality, it has also intensified social stratification and the dispossession of wealth. The first step in this chapter is to address three questions surrounding the relationship between home ownership and US capitalism:

- How does the US home ownership rate compare to other developed countries?
- What are the benefits and opportunities associated with home ownership?
- What are the drawbacks and risks of home ownership?

The US Home Ownership Rate: A Global Context

The US Census Bureau defines the rate of home ownership as the number of owner-occupied housing units relative to total occupied housing units. In 2018, the national home ownership rate was 64.4%, which means that owners occupied 64.4% of occupied households. According to Figure 3.1, that number is consistent with the average between 1984 and 1994. The recent housing boom, however, pushed it to a high of 69% by 2004. A steady decline then proceeded for more than a decade until the rate of ownership began increasing again in 2017.

Although 64.4% appears high, the United States ranks low among developed countries. Table 3.1 presents national home ownership rates from a study published in the *Journal of Economic Perspectives*. Out of 18 countries, the United States ranked 14th in the study—ahead of the United Kingdom, Denmark, Germany, and Switzerland, but below the sample average of 69.6%. Canada, Japan, and France also ranked higher than the United States. Home ownership rates equaled or exceeded 70% in Spain, the Czech Republic, Slovenia, Italy, Finland, Mexico, Sweden, and Ireland. Bulgaria's ownership rate exceeded 80%; while Singapore topped the list with an ownership rate of 90.8%.

FIGURE 3.1 US Homeownership Rate 1984–2018

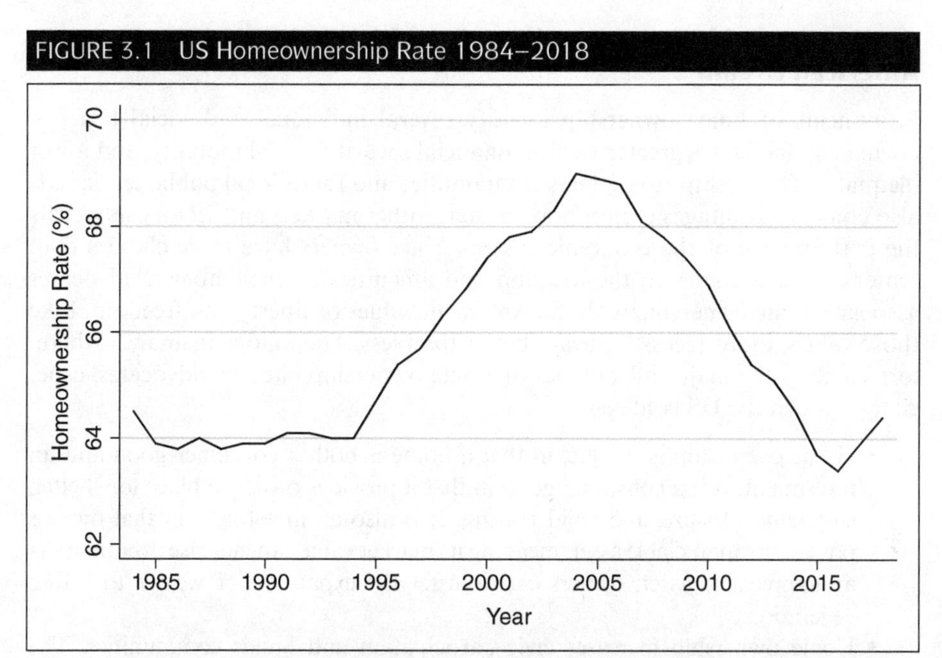

Source: Federal Reserve Bank of St. Louis FRED economic data (https://fred.stlouisfed.org).

TABLE 3.1 Home Ownership Rates by Country in 2015

Country	*Homeownership Rate (%)*
Singapore	90.8
Bulgaria	82.3
Spain	78.2
Czech Republic	78.0
Slovenia	76.2
Italy	72.9
Finland	72.7
Mexico	71.7
Sweden	70.6
Ireland	70.0
Average	**69.6**
Canada	67.0
Japan	64.9
France	64.1
United States	**63.7**
United Kingdom	63.5
Denmark	62.7
Germany	51.9
Switzerland	51.3

Source: Goodman & Mayer (2018).

The reasons for such variations are wide-ranging and complex. Differences in market forces, government policies, politics, as well as social and cultural norms all combine to influence access to home ownership in different ways. While the United States appears unexceptional in these rankings, several factors distinguish the United States from the rest of the world. The longstanding institution that home ownership is almost unambiguously positive is the most important of these factors.

Home Ownership: Opportunities, Benefits, and the American Dream

Proponents of home ownership identify several individual and social benefits. Ownership facilitates greater wealth, financial security, social mobility, and lower inequality. Ownership strengthens communities and funds local public services. It also confers advantages to non-homeowners, other markets and sectors, as well as the performance of the economic system. Since owners have more choices than renters when it comes to the location and amenities of their homes, advocates associate home ownership with the American values of liberty and freedom. Like those values, more access is always better than less. The following analysis therefore catalogs the major advantages of home ownership cited by advocates, especially those in the US context:

- Home ownership is unique, in that a home is both a consumer good and an investment. It is a consumer good in that it provides owners a place for shelter, sustenance, leisure, and child rearing. It is also an investment in that owners possess an appreciable asset, meaning its market value can increase over time. As an appreciable asset, owners can transfer the expansion of wealth to future generations.
- Home ownership increases civic participation and builds communities. The long-term nature of home ownership, along with the positive effect of neighborhood quality on property values, means that owners have a vested interest in the attributes of their neighborhoods. Greater civic engagement enhances the strength and stability of local communities.
- In addition to enhancing social capital, home ownership directly supports the provision of local public services. Owners pay property taxes, which are a significant source of local government revenues in the United States. Local governments in turn finance public schools, infrastructure, public safety, and other direct services to communities. These services benefit all members of the community, not simply homeowners.
- Home ownership facilitates greater access to credit. Owners can secure home equity loans and other lines of credit, which they use to finance more consumer spending, invest in other financial assets, or service other debts.
- The US tax code offers several benefits to homeowners. Homeowners can deduct mortgage interest and up to $10,000 in state and local taxes from their federal income tax. They can also be exempt from paying capital gains tax on any profits made from home sales.
- Home ownership supports the labor market. Home ownership is a source of employment and income in related fields such as real estate, home construction and maintenance, finance, law, as well as government.
- Macroeconomists cite an important relationship between home ownership and the US business cycle. Figure 3.2 presents the annual net change in the home ownership rate between 1985 and 2018. The argument is that the increase in the home ownership rate following the 1990–91 recession, and especially the 2001 recession, provided a critical boost to economic growth during the early years of those expansions. As employment recovered, borrowers took advantage of low interest rates to increase spending on goods and services, which included new homes.

FIGURE 3.2 Change in US Homeownership Rate 1985–2018

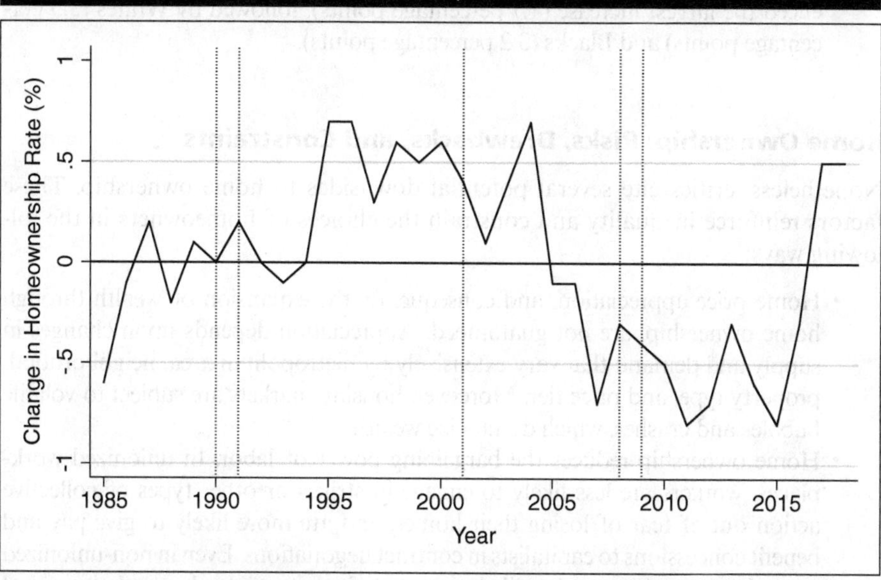

Note: ... indicates recession year.

Source: Federal Reserve Bank of St. Louis FRED economic data (https://fred.stlouisfed.org).

TABLE 3.2 US Home Ownership Rates by Race or Ethnicity, 1994–2019

	[1]	*[2]*	*[3]*	*[4]*	*[5]*
	1994(I)–2001(I)	*2001(IV)–2007(IV)*	*Change*	*2009(II)–2019(III)*	*Change*
Black or African American	44.7	48.0	3.2	43.2	−4.8
Hispanic or Latino	43.8	48.4	4.7	46.5	−1.9
Non-Hispanic White	72.0	75.5	3.5	73.1	−2.4

Source: Federal Reserve Bank of St. Louis, FRED economic data: https://fred.stlouisfed.org. Figures in Columns [1, 2, 4] are quarterly averages for each period.

- Home ownership is a particularly important asset for the wealth building of racial and ethnic minorities. Table 3.2 presents ownership rates for Blacks or African Americans, Hispanics or Latinos, and non-Hispanic Whites during three periods of expansion: 1994 to 2001, the 2001–07 recovery, and the recovery from the Great Recession. Columns 1, 2, and 4 report the average quarterly home ownership rates for each respective period. Columns 3 and 5 report changes in the average home ownership rate from the previous period. The extent of intergroup inequality in this case is quite clear. During each period, there is a sizable Black-White and Latino-White home ownership gap of over 25 percentage points. However, all three groups saw higher home ownership rates during the 2001–07 expansion as compared to the 1994–2001 period. Latinos experienced the largest increase (4.7 percentage points), followed by Whites (3.5 percentage points) and Blacks (3.2 percentage points).

Home Ownership: Risks, Drawbacks, and Constraints

Nonetheless, critics cite several potential downsides to home ownership. These factors reinforce inequality and constrain the choices of homeowners in the following ways:

- Home price appreciation, and consequently the expansion of wealth through home ownership, are not guaranteed. Appreciation depends upon changes in supply and demand that vary extensively by metropolitan area, neighborhood, property type, and price tier. Moreover, housing markets are subject to volatile bubbles and crashes, which destabilize wealth.
- Home ownership reduces the bargaining power of labor. In unionized workplaces, workers are less likely to engage in strikes or other types of collective action out of fear of losing their homes, and are more likely to give pay and benefit concessions to capitalists in contract negotiations. Even in non-unionized workplaces, workers are less likely to search for better jobs due to the time and expense of home sales.
- In metropolitan areas with stagnant property values, lack of home price appreciation limits local government revenues from property tax collections and the provision of public services. The lack of quality public services, especially schooling and public safety, reduces the demand for property in such areas, putting further downward pressure on market values.
- Under similar circumstances, lack of home price appreciation constrains the collateral value necessary to secure new lines of credit from lenders. Credit restrictions make it more difficult for owners to finance consumption, acquire assets, or manage other debts.
- The tax benefits related to home ownership are exclusive to the wealthy. In order to realize such benefits, tax filers must itemize their deductions. For high-income earners, mortgage interest, property tax, and other homeowner deductions typically exceed the federal standard deduction, which reduces their tax burden. For most low-income earners, however, the sum of their deductions is usually lower than the standard deduction, which negates any tax advantage related to ownership.
- Real wage suppression and greater inequality since the 1970s have made it increasingly difficult for workers to afford property taxes, insurance premiums, and unexpected maintenance expenses. Greater financial insecurity restrains investment in home improvements and the ability to realize property appreciation.
- Home ownership no longer provides the buffer to the US business cycle that it once did. In fact, the correction in the home ownership rate is strongly associated with the sluggish recovery for much of the period following the crisis. According to Figure 3.2, the post-Great Recession expansion was notable for the continuous drop in the rate of home ownership, both immediately following the contraction and throughout most of the recovery.

- Finally, the overall decline in home ownership following the Great Recession has intensified intergroup inequality. According to Table 3.2, Blacks experienced the largest decline since 2009 (4.8 percentage points), followed by Whites (2.4 percentage points) and Latinos (1.9 percentage points). In particular, the Black home ownership rate during the recovery is lower than what it was during the 1994–2001 period. As a result, the Black-White ownership disparity has widened. During the 1994–2001 period, the White ownership rate exceeded the Black ownership rate by 27.3 percentage points. Since 2009, the White ownership rate has exceeded the Black ownership rate by 29.9 percentage points.

INTENTIONAL BARRIERS TO HOME OWNERSHIP: REDLINING

An analysis of the benefits and risks of home ownership would be incomplete without an investigation of intentional barriers to home ownership that have existed in the United States. The preceding analysis examined the opportunities and drawbacks of home ownership, particularly for owners in neighborhoods with depressed property values. On a theoretical level, there is a general consensus across the economics discipline as to the nature of those drawbacks. Most economists would agree that owners in such circumstances face greater difficulties transferring wealth to future generations, receiving quality public services, accessing home equity, and managing unexpected expenses. Similarly, most economists would agree that expanding minority home ownership is an important goal, given the well-documented disparities in wealth by race and ethnicity. Heterodox economists differ, however, in that they continuously question *why* things are as they are. In this case, *why* is there such variation in home values by neighborhood? *Why* are there persistent home ownership gaps between Whites and minorities? What are the origins and historical roots of these outcomes?

The term "redlining" refers to a process in which financial institutions deliberately deny mortgages to the residents of particular neighborhoods within a metropolitan area, on the basis of race, ethnicity, or country of origin. Although it commonly involves restrictions on mortgage lending, redlining has also involved restrictions on other financial services, goods, or resources. It is a discriminatory practice, since redlining has overwhelmingly afflicted racial and ethnic minority communities.

The origin of mortgage redlining lies in the federal government's response to the Great Depression. The Home Owners' Loan Act addressed a mortgage default and foreclosure crisis with similarities to that which precipitated the Great Recession. The Act established the Home Owners' Loan Corporation (HOLC), an organization that refinanced residential mortgages and recovered foreclosed properties in order to resuscitate private lending. The new loans featured far more favorable terms than the short-term, interest-only loans that predominated mortgage contracts prior to the 1930s, and kept borrowers in perpetual debt. HOLC mortgages, by contrast, carried fixed interest rates and a self-amortizing payment structure. Borrowers made fixed monthly payments of both principal and interest for 15 years, which actually paid off the debt at the end of the loan term.

The Home Owners' Loan Act called for a property appraisal system that private actors in local real estate used to assess the risk and creditworthiness of neighborhoods. The "Area Description" of each neighborhood reported the physical characteristics of its properties as well as the demographic characteristics of its residents. Information on properties included building type, age, occupancy, rate of home ownership, sales demand and prices, as well as rental demand and prices. Information on residents included class and occupation; income; percentage of foreign-born residents and their nationalities; percentage of Negro residents; infiltration of groups considered subversive; and changes in population. Evaluators assigned a grade (and color) to each neighborhood using both the property and demographic components of the reports, which they demarcated on "Residential Security Maps" of metropolitan areas. Neighborhoods considered "Best" received A (or green) ratings for being the lowest risk to banks. Neighborhoods considered "Still Desirable" received B (or blue) ratings, while those deemed "Definitely Declining" received C (or yellow) ratings. "Hazardous" neighborhoods received D (or red) ratings for being the highest risk to banks. The term "redlining" refers to the delineation of neighborhoods with a D rating—or those marked red—on HOLC maps. Redlined areas were primarily older neighborhoods in inner cities with large shares of workers, immigrants, or racial minorities, especially Blacks. Green areas were largely newer communities in the suburbs, with predominantly White populations working in professional occupations.

For visual reference, the Mapping Inequality project is an interactive website and archive that allows users to view scans of area descriptions, digital versions of residential security maps, and the shares of neighborhoods graded each color. The project not only provides an incredible amount of detail at the metropolitan and neighborhood levels, but also demonstrates the national scope of the HOLC's actions. For reference, Figure 3.3 is an original area description of the Holmesburg neighborhood of Philadelphia, which local evaluators assessed in 1937. Figure 3.4 is the HOLC residential security map for the city of Philadelphia.

The following is a selection of remarks from the HOLC area descriptions about the conditions and populations of neighborhoods. They are often quite specific. For example, the assessment of one neighborhood in San Francisco, which received an A grade, notes that: "This is an exclusive and secluded area, and there is no possibility of invasion by undesirable social elements" (A2).

In New Haven, Connecticut, the explanation of a B rating states:

> This is a newer development of which the architecture is varied and pleasing. The houses are not built too closely together and are well cared for. Were it not for the fact that this area is entirely Jewish, it would command a higher rating.
>
> (B5)

In Los Angeles, the Barnes City area received a C rating due in part to its shifting demographics:

> The Japs in the area operate leased garden tracts, and as development takes place they are being pushed out. There are quite a number of third generation Mexican land owners who leased to Jap gardeners. These are pretty generally staying in district and may prove of sufficient influence to adversely affect area.
>
> (C68)

FIGURE 3.3 HOLC Area Description for the Holmesburg Neighborhood of Philadelphia

NS FORM-8
2-3-37

AREA DESCRIPTION
(For Instructions see Reverse Side)

1. NAME OF CITY Sub. Holmesburg SECURITY GRADE C AREA NO. 11
2. DESCRIPTION OF TERRAIN. Rolling
3. FAVORABLE INFLUENCES. Good transportation - near park
4. DETRIMENTAL INFLUENCES. Negro section in center of section.
5. INHABITANTS:
   a. Type skilled mechanics - clerks ; b. Estimated annual family income $1500. - $3000.
   c. Foreign-born ______ (Nationality) ; ___ %; d. Negro ______ (Yes or No) ; ___ %;
   e. Infiltration of Italian ; f. Relief families nominal except for center ;
   g. Population is increasing ______ ; decreasing ______ ; static.
6. BUILDINGS:
   a. Type or types single detached, twins brick ; b. Type of construction frame - brick ;
   c. Average age 5 to 75 ; d. Repair fair to poor along R. R. trails
7. HISTORY:

YEAR		SALE VALUES RANGE	SALE VALUES PREDOMINATING	%	RENTAL VALUES RANGE	RENTAL VALUES PREDOMINATING	%
1929	level	$5000.-$8500.	$6000.	100%	$40.-$65.	$50.	100%
1933-34	low	$3000.-$5000.	$3500.	60%	$25.-$40.	$30.	60%
June 1937	current	$3500.-$6000.	$4000.	67%	$30.-$45.	$37.50	75%

   Peak sale values occurred in ______ and were ______ % of the 1929 level.
   Peak rental values occurred in ______ and were ______ % of the 1929 level.
8. OCCUPANCY: a. Land 50 %; b. Dwelling units 100 %; c. Home owners 90 %
9. SALES DEMAND: a. poor ; b. ______ ; c. Activity is poor
10. RENTAL DEMAND: a. good ; b. anything ; c. Activity is few available
11. NEW CONSTRUCTION: a. Types none ; b. Amount last year ______
12. AVAILABILITY OF MORTGAGE FUNDS: a. Home purchase very limited ; b. Home building ______
13. TREND OF DESIRABILITY NEXT 10-15 YEARS downward
14. CLARIFYING REMARKS: Italian & negro located along R.R. tracks. Northern part of section not as well built up. Population has been located here for sometime. Negro concentration is affecting values along Welsh Road from Dittman Avenue to Frankford.
15. Information for this form was obtained from Rowland & Banister

Date June 10 193 7

(Over)

Source: Mapping Inequality (https://dsl.richmond.edu/panorama/redlining/).

FIGURE 3.4 HOLC Residential Security Map of Philadelphia

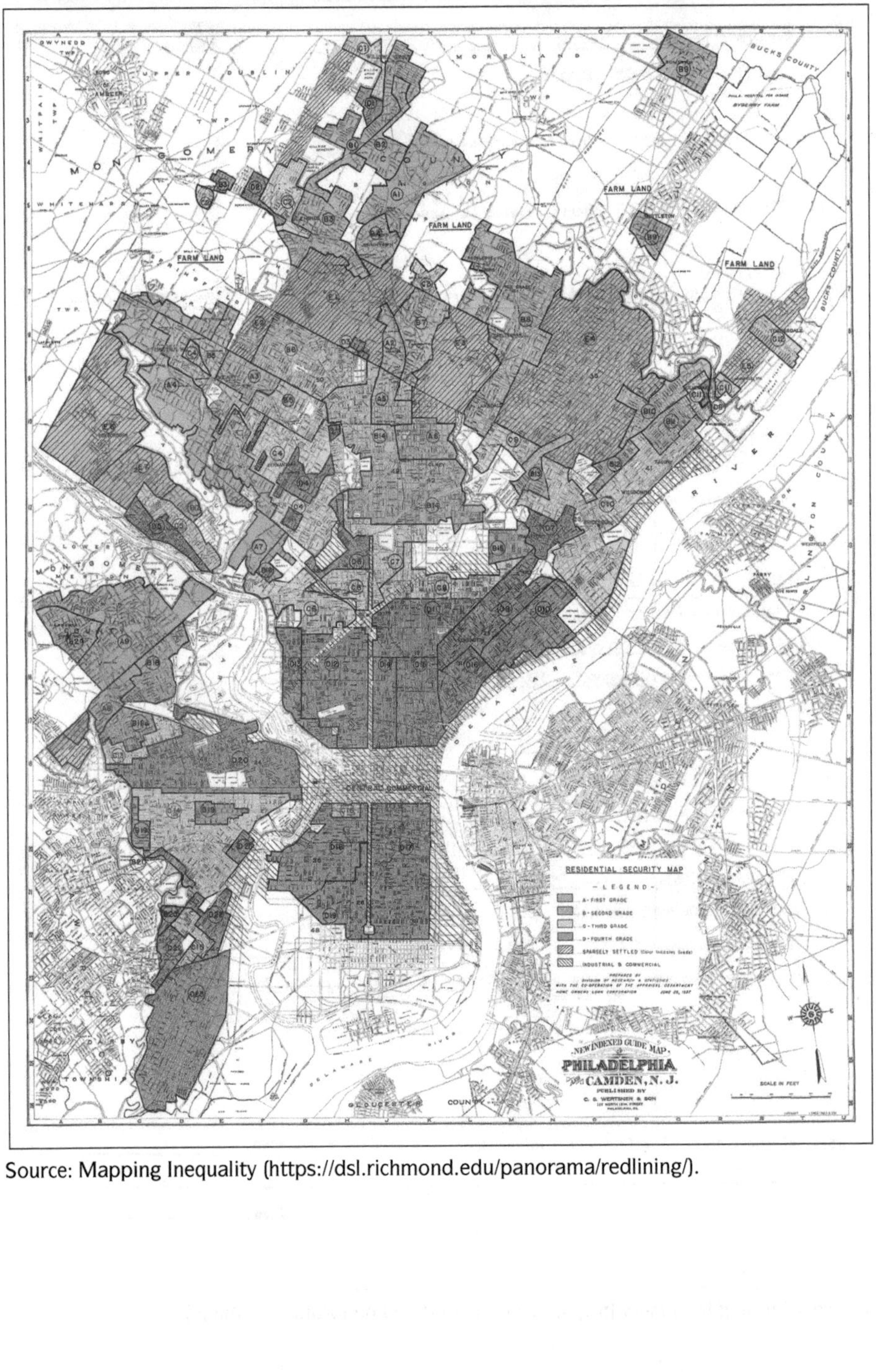

Source: Mapping Inequality (https://dsl.richmond.edu/panorama/redlining/).

Evaluators also assigned C ratings to neighborhoods in New York City whose residents were considered agitators. For example, the West Brownsville neighborhood in Brooklyn allegedly contained: "Comparatively poor type people who have in the past joined together in a rent strike" (C15).

In Chicago, the description of one area near the Chicago Loop concludes with this assessment: "Trend of desirability continues downward as population becomes more and more negro" (D33).

The description of another majority Black neighborhood on the South Side includes this recommendation:

> It is emphasized that one of the most important necessities is to provide a means of financing these colored homes so that they may be rehabilitated; provide a larger turnover of property; and hold these people within the area.
>
> (D74)

Both districts received D grades. The residential security map of greater Atlanta describes the Lakewood Heights area as the "best negro section in Atlanta:" "Property if acquired in this area, should be held for fair value. This is known as best negro area in Atlanta and contains best type of negro residents and highest percentage of negro home ownership" (D17).

It also received a D grade from HOLC evaluators.

These cases are by no means exceptions. Similar examples appear in metropolitan areas across the United States regardless of size or region. To be clear, discriminatory practices in mortgage lending certainly existed before the Great Depression. Racism is clearly evident in the written remarks by evaluators on HOLC forms; but also in the structure of the standardized questionnaires—for example, the use of words like "infiltration" and "invasion" to describe changes in the demographic makeup of neighborhoods, and the desire to contain undesirable or subversive population groups from spreading. Moreover, the HOLC population data clearly indicates a high level of residential segregation given the prevalence of majority Black neighborhoods. The legacy of the Home Owners' Loan Act is its formalization of a process, backed by a federal agency, that reproduced intergroup inequality in mortgage lending and home ownership during the regulated stage of US capitalism. Regulated capitalism was successful according to the standard macroeconomic performance measures, but it exacerbated racial wealth inequalities that persist today. Redlining contributed to the intensification of social stratification and the underdevelopment of minority neighborhoods in multiple ways. On the one hand, it created a structure of privilege in mortgage lending by restricting access to credit in minority neighborhoods and redirecting it to White neighborhoods. On the other hand, HOLC evaluators also *encouraged* lenders to issue mortgages in redlined neighborhoods in order to keep minorities within those communities, which perpetuated residential segregation. In either case, redlining constrained the choices and mobility of future generations. By associating property values with the racial and ethnic composition of neighborhoods, the HOLC made it so that minority homeowners and communities would reap few of the aforementioned benefits of home ownership. Even if private lenders were not explicitly using residential security maps to assess creditworthiness in the years following the Great Depression, the devaluation of property values limited intergenerational transfers of wealth, constrained local government revenues, limited the provision of quality public services, and restrained access to home equity in order to diversify wealth and consumption. Among other things, these outcomes further suppressed property values, and the ability and willingness to acquire property, in such areas. A critical lesson for understanding this subject is that racism is not separate, or exogenous, from the operation of capitalism. It fundamentally interacts, and continues to interact, with the operation and evolution of US capitalism.

WHAT IS A MARKET BUBBLE?

One of the risks of home ownership presented in this chapter—and certainly one with relevance to the transmission of the Great Recession—is that housing markets are subject to bubbles. But what exactly do economists and media analysts mean when they characterize a market trend as a "bubble"? Although rapid price increases often indicate the presence of a bubble, not all price increases necessarily entail a bubble. Likewise, not all price decreases necessarily entail a market crash or bust. Many observers associate bubbles with markets for financial assets, pointing to notable cases like the 1920s stock market boom, Black Monday in 1987, and the 1990s dot-com bubble. However, they can also occur in markets for tangible goods. The Dutch tulip market, for example, famously experienced a bubble during the early seventeenth century. Since real estate is both a tangible good and a financial asset, real estate markets have at times featured bubbles and busts. Before examining the particular aspects of the US housing bubble prior to the Great Recession, this section explains how market bubbles differ from traditional price increases, as well as how market busts differ from price decreases.

According to conventional economic theory, a price increase results from a change in an underlying determinant of supply or demand for a product. In some cases, a higher price occurs when market demand increases—perhaps due to stronger tastes or preferences, an increase in consumer incomes, an increase in the number of buyers, or any other change that expands the ability and willingness to consume. In other cases, a higher price occurs when market supply decreases—perhaps due to an increase in production costs, less access to technology, a decrease in the number of sellers, or any other shift that restricts the ability and willingness to produce. In either scenario, an actual shortage of the product will emerge at the current equilibrium price. A higher price is necessary in order both to incentivize production, by increasing the opportunity to earn profit, and to disincentivize consumption. Conversely, lower prices occur when decreases in demand or increases in supply create an actual surplus in a market. A lower price discourages sellers from holding excess inventories, while also encouraging buyers to increase consumption, until the market reaches equilibrium again.

Bubbles, however, occur when speculation motivates decision making. Under speculation, market participants seek short-term profits in the belief that prices will rise—and only rise. Bandwagon mentality, euphoria, and optimism on the part of buyers and sellers supersede the underlying determinants of market value. During a bubble, there is often no change in any determinants of supply or demand. There is no shortage to speak of that requires a higher price. The product therefore becomes overvalued, as its price will exceed what is expected at equilibrium—meaning the price will be inconsistent with consumer incomes, the number of buyers and sellers, production costs, and so on. The reverse, of course, occurs during market crashes. When panic, contagion, and pessimism motivate decision making, market participants sell in the belief that prices will decrease without correction. There is no surplus to speak of in such cases that requires a lower equilibrium price. The oscillation between these two opposing forces—euphoria versus panic—creates market volatility.

Neoclassical economics has difficulty dealing with the presence of market bubbles, and the complex behavior surrounding them, primarily due to its commitment to Homo Economicus. Homo Economicus is the principle that self-interest exclusively motivates individual behavior and interactions. In general, self-interest means that the desire to improve individual wellbeing is the sole motivating factor in decision making. More specifically, however, it means that the expected return to the individual—and nothing else—informs decision making. Neoclassical theory further assumes that individuals make decisions with full information in an ahistorical context, without regard to culture or changes in psychology. There are indeed elements of Homo Economicus present during speculative bubbles—for example, the self-interested pursuit of profits and wealth is certainly relevant. However, there are several aspects of market bubbles that violate the neoclassical understanding of behavior, especially in the realm of finance. When financial investors exhibit herd behavior, the expected return to others in the market—not just the individual—becomes the motivating factor. When there is inherent uncertainty regarding expected future returns, which is the case for financial assets, complex market psychology, culture, and norms then inform decision making. Even when good information is available, there is significant evidence that financial market participants display confirmation bias. Confirmation bias occurs when investors attach greater weight to information that confirms already established beliefs, and less weight to information that counters their preconceived beliefs. In financial markets, they may disregard information that suggests that an asset is overvalued. When potential losses to their individual profits and wealth no longer deter investors, the market undervalues risk. The result is a severe disconnect between the price of an asset and its underlying risk.

MEASURING THE US HOUSING MARKET BUBBLE

Housing market bubbles (and busts) are not unprecedented in US history. Moreover, dynamics in the national housing market differ substantially from those in metropolitan markets. The wide variety of different property types further complicates the measurement of fluctuations in home values. In order to study long-term changes in housing prices, economists Karl Case and Robert Shiller developed a series of residential real estate price indexes. The Case-Shiller Home Price Index is inarguably the leading measure of housing prices. The index measures the value of existing single-family homes when adjusted for inflation. It does not include the value of new home construction; nor does it include the value of other types of housing units, such as apartments, condominiums, co-ops, multi-family units, etc. Variations in the physical characteristics, quality, size, and type of home are held constant. Different metropolitan areas, property types, and price tiers feature their own market forces and price dynamics, for which there are separate indexes. Despite this complexity, a historically unprecedented spike in the national index is clear and apparent during the latter years of the Great Moderation—the so-called period of reduced macroeconomic volatility celebrated by mainstream economists and policymakers.

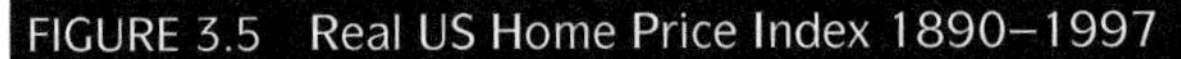

FIGURE 3.5 Real US Home Price Index 1890–1997

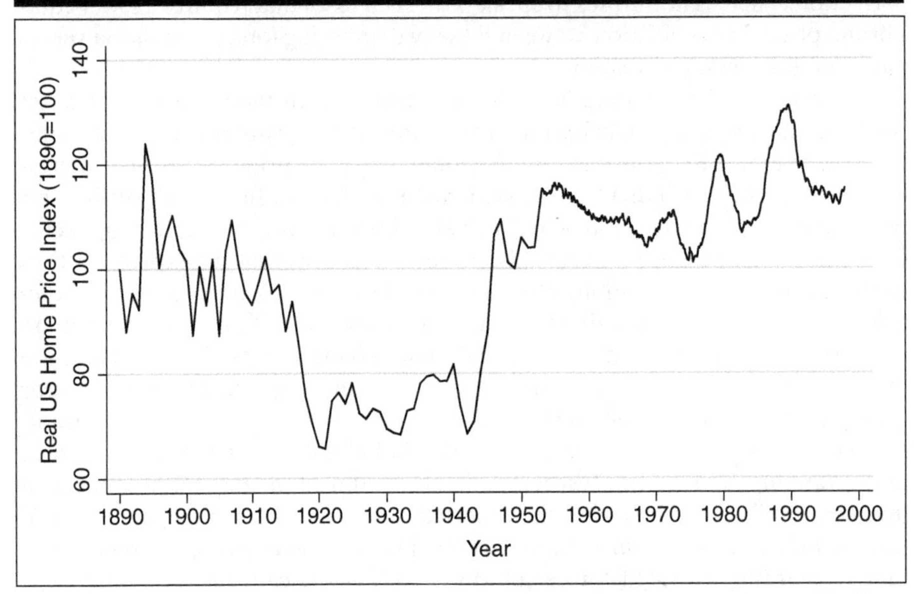

Source: Online data maintained by Robert Shiller (http://www.econ.yale.edu/~shiller/data.htm).

Figure 3.5 first presents movements in the real US Home Price Index between 1890 and 1997, prior to the advent of the recent housing market bubble. The index methodology uses 1890 as a benchmark, which it sets equal to 100. Changes in the index reflect changes over time in the sale price of comparable and existing single-family homes in constant dollars. For example, if the index increases from 100 to 120, a home that initially sold for $100,000 in today's dollars later sold for $120,000, reflecting a 20% increase in market value. Looking more closely at the data, the index shows a more than 30% drop in real housing prices during World War I. Despite two periods of modest recovery, extremely high unemployment and the mortgage default crisis during the Great Depression suppressed home values for the duration of the interwar period. Home prices substantially increased following World War II, and then stabilized throughout the 1950s and 1960s. The postwar recovery of home prices reflects several institutional changes associated with the regulated stage of capitalism. These new social structures enabled an increase in consumer spending on goods and services, including housing—for example, mortgage assistance for veterans, servicemen, and women through the G.I. Bill; the general provision of the 30-year, fixed-rate mortgage contract; and the sustained increase in real incomes through the expansion of collective bargaining rights, labor laws, and social welfare programs. The United States then experienced two housing booms during the 1970s and 1980s, after which housing prices returned to postwar levels. However, those booms differed from the pre-Great Recession housing bubble, for two reasons. First, they were local or regional in nature. Second, they preceded the deregulation of the financial sector during the 1990s. This means that the economic and financial consequences of the regional spike, and then drop, in home prices did not extend across the national banking market, due to longstanding restrictions on inter-state branching and acquisitions.

FIGURE 3.6 Real US Home Price Index 1890–2012

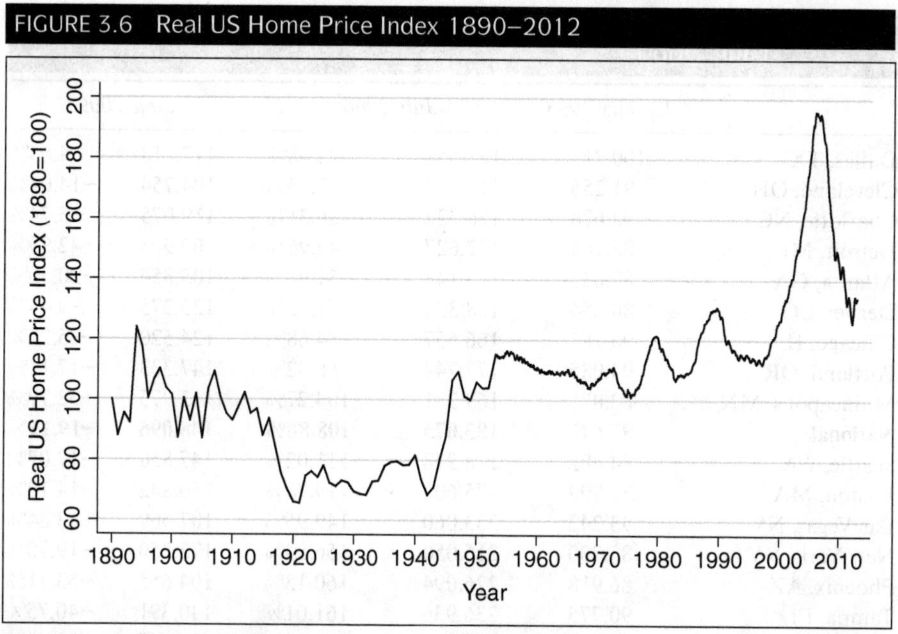

Source: Online data maintained by Robert Shiller (http://www.econ.yale.edu/~shiller/data.htm).

It also means that such consequences did not disrupt other financial services, due to the regulatory barriers between commercial banking, investment banking, and insurance.

Figure 3.6 extends the series through 2012 to include the pre-Great Recession housing market bubble. The rapid increase in real home prices between 1998 and the summer of 2006—the point that most analysts regard as the height of the bubble—surpasses the real estate booms not only of the 1970s and 1980s, but also of the late 1940s. Although the degree of speculation varied across cities and regions, as was the case during previous housing booms, the effects of this bubble extended nationwide and across the financial sector to other financial services. The commercial banking industry was now bigger as a result of the Riegle-Neal Act. It was also more complex and interconnected as a result of the Gramm-Leach-Bliley Act.

In order to put the national trend into perspective, Table 3.3 compares the national index to the 20 metropolitan indexes calculated using the Case-Shiller methodology. The table ranks the series in ascending order according to the percentage change in home prices between January 1998 and July 2006, the period that analysts generally regard as the pre-Great Recession housing market bubble. The last column presents the collapse of home prices between the height of the bubble and the official trough of the Great Recession determined by the National Bureau of Economic Research (June 2009). Two points are important to consider when examining the data. The first is that the national home price index continued to decrease well past the trough of the recession and into the recovery. The second is that the points of variation in the national index often vary from the points of variation in individual metropolitan indexes. In some metropolitan areas, housing prices peaked before (or after) July 2006. Similarly, prices in some metropolitan areas recovered before (or after) June 2009.

TABLE 3.3 S&P/Case-Shiller US National vs. Metropolitan Home Price Indexes, 1998–2009

	January 1998	*July 2006*		*June 2009*	
Dallas, TX*	100.713	123.558	22.68%	117.818	−4.65%
Cleveland, OH	91.255	121.863	33.54%	104.754	−14.04%
Charlotte, NC	92.678	126.332	36.31%	119.075	−5.74%
Detroit, MI	85.184	122.627	43.96%	69.905	−42.99%
Atlanta, GA	87.627	133.143	51.94%	105.854	−20.50%
Denver, CO	80.654	138.338	71.52%	125.275	−9.44%
Chicago, IL	90.187	166.557	84.68%	124.520	−25.24%
Portland, OR	94.085	177.744	88.92%	147.333	−17.11%
Minneapolis, MN	82.871	169.281	104.27%	113.775	−32.79%
National	**87.647**	**183.075**	**108.88%**	**148.096**	**−19.11%**
Seattle, WA	84.482	178.278	111.02%	147.850	−17.07%
Boston, MA	79.899	175.602	119.78%	150.842	−14.10%
Las Vegas, NV	93.242	233.060	149.95%	107.569	−53.84%
New York, NY	83.730	215.050	156.84%	172.250	−19.90%
Phoenix, AZ	86.918	226.094	160.13%	104.655	−53.71%
Tampa, FL	90.775	236.936	161.01%	140.391	−40.75%
Washington, DC	90.108	247.060	174.18%	171.767	−30.48%
San Francisco, CA	77.202	214.984	178.47%	123.342	−42.63%
Miami, FL	90.725	278.469	206.94%	145.945	−47.59%
San Diego, CA	78.977	246.013	211.50%	146.469	−40.46%
Los Angeles, CA	81.035	271.494	235.03%	160.312	−40.95%

Source: Federal Reserve Bank of St. Louis, FRED economic data: https://fred.stlouisfed.org. January 2000=100. All figures are seasonally adjusted.

* Series for Dallas, TX begins in January 2000.

According to the National Home Price Index (presented in bold), US real home values increased by 108.88% between 1998 and 2006, and then decreased by 19.11% between 2006 and 2009. In constant dollars, a home that sold for $100,000 in January 1998 later sold for $208,880 in July 2006, but $168,963 by June 2009. Four distinct groups differentiate metropolitan experiences. As compared to the national trend, some cities—such as Dallas, Cleveland, Charlotte, Denver, and Portland—experienced both shallower booms and shallower busts. However, other cities that experienced shallower booms—such as Detroit, Chicago, Atlanta, and Minneapolis—experienced stronger busts. Most cities that saw booms stronger than the national index also experienced stronger busts. Miami, San Diego, and Los Angeles saw the strongest surge in housing prices between 1998 and 2006. Phoenix and Las Vegas saw the strongest collapse of housing prices between 2006 and 2009. However, there were two exceptions: both Seattle and Boston witnessed stronger housing booms but a weaker decrease in home values after 2006.

EXPLANATIONS FOR THE US HOUSING MARKET BUBBLE

The next step is to examine explanations for the US housing bubble. There is near-universal agreement that a housing bubble occurred between 1998 and 2006.

No credible study has shown that a bubble did not occur. However, there is substantial disagreement, which continues today, on the *causes* of the bubble. What explains the unprecedented spike in US housing prices? What explains the shift in behavior in US housing markets and the severe overvaluation of residential real estate? The economics discipline, other academic fields like public policy and urban planning, the media, the private real estate industry, and multiple government agencies have offered many reasons for the housing bubble. In order to comprehend the complexity of this debate, and evaluate the merits of these arguments, this section organizes the major explanations of the US housing bubble into the following categories: market forces, government intervention, and subprime mortgage lending.

Market Forces

The first class of arguments attributes the housing bubble to market forces. Changes in traditional determinants of the supply and/or demand for housing simply led to substantially higher market prices. Higher housing prices arose from shifts in market sentiment that either strengthened housing demand or constrained housing supply. On the demand side, these shifts include a stronger preference for ownership over renting; an increase in the incomes of prospective home buyers; and an increase in the number of home buyers due to population growth. On the supply side, they include higher costs related to the production and sale of homes; and less access to resources necessary for home construction, maintenance, and renovation (e.g., labor, capital goods, raw materials, and especially land). One or any combination of these factors created a significant level of excess demand for homes, which required higher prices in order to maintain market equilibrium.

Although these arguments are consistent with conventional economic principles, they are inconsistent with the actual market conditions and behavior at the time of the housing market bubble. For example, although preference for home ownership has fluctuated over time, the stronger preference exhibited during the 1990s and early 2000s does not fully explain the spike in housing prices. The economic and social benefits of home ownership were already well-established institutions in the United States. Moreover, the principal advantage to ownership over renting—namely, that a mortgage payment on an equivalent property is cheaper than its rental price—has long been a selling point by real estate brokers. None of this information was new to prospective homebuyers in 1998. There was likewise no unprecedented spike in population growth that exponentially multiplied the number of home buyers. An increase in consumer incomes is an insufficient explanation for two reasons. On the one hand, real wages have been stagnant since the early 1970s and the eventual transition to the neoliberal stage of US capitalism. On the other hand, during the regulated stage of capitalism, which indeed saw substantially higher real wages, real housing prices were stable. Supply-side constraints were also not causal factors. The prices of building materials and equipment were not significantly higher; nor were there new barriers to accessing such resources. In particular, the lack of land available for residential development in metropolitan areas was not new information to real estate developers in 1998.

Although they plausibly explain how higher prices arise from market shortages, these explanations of the housing market bubble suffer from two major problems.

First, no widespread housing shortage occurred between 1998 and 2006, for the simple reason that most prospective home buyers were able to secure a mortgage contract and purchase a home. Second, they do not explain the shift in behavior, and the overvaluation of residential real estate, that characterized market dynamics.

Government Intervention

Another class of theories attributes the housing market bubble to government interventions and regulations related to housing. Government-sponsored enterprises Fannie Mae and Freddie Mac have contributed to the expansion of home ownership since the transition to regulated capitalism. Although they are shareholder-owned companies, both received their charters from the federal government. Fannie Mae and Freddie Mac encourage home ownership by purchasing mortgages from private lenders. Lenders then have a new supply of loanable funds from which to issue new mortgages to borrowers. Federal agencies such as the Federal Housing Administration and the Department of Veterans Affairs guarantee home loans for borrowers in need of financial assistance. The US Federal Reserve contributes to the expansion of credit through expansionary monetary policies that increase the money supply and lower market interest rates. The tax benefits available to both home buyers and real estate developers also encourage the purchase and production of homes.

Housing was a central issue during the civil rights movement. Several federal policies enacted during the 1960s and 1970s address discrimination and the exclusion of minorities from mortgage and housing markets. The Fair Housing Act prohibits discrimination in the buying or renting of housing. In order to combat redlining and identify lending discrimination, the Home Mortgage Disclosure Act mandates that financial institutions disclose mortgage application and lending data. In another attempt to combat redlining, the Community Reinvestment Act evaluates and encourages financial institutions to invest in low-income neighborhoods where they accept, and profit from, local deposits.

All of the explanations in this category share the same problem: they predate the timing of the housing market bubble—that is, the period between 1998 and 2006—in some cases by considerable margins. The federal government originally established Fannie Mae in 1938, privatized Fannie in 1969, and chartered Freddie Mac in 1970. The Federal Reserve conducted expansionary monetary policies beginning in the 1980s. Real estate tax incentives and federal home loan guarantees have been on the books for decades; as have the civil rights laws related to housing and home financing. Furthermore, although they monitored and encouraged the lending practices of banks, none of the civil rights laws in any way mandated that banks issue loans to minority borrowers or neighborhoods, forced banks to issue riskier loan products, or penalized them for not doing so. The still unanswered question is: what changed in the housing market during the late 1990s?

Subprime Mortgage Lending

This final explanation attributes the US housing market bubble to the advent of "subprime" mortgage products. The provision of subprime mortgages is a useful mechanism because it coincides with the timeline of the bubble, the shift in market behavior, as well as federal policy changes during the late 1990s and early 2000s. However, in order to understand the structure of a subprime mortgage, let's first examine the structure of a traditional mortgage.

The traditional mortgage is a long-term loan, ranging between 15 and 30 years. It typically features a fixed interest rate, although in some cases it may carry an adjustable interest rate. In order to qualify, the borrower must have good credit, verify his or her income, and carry a healthy debt load. Once approved by a financial institution, the borrower must make a 10% to 20% down payment. The principal does not change over the life of a traditional mortgage. Each monthly payment gradually reduces the principal balance, which allows the borrower to pay off the debt at the end of the loan. The borrower owes nothing else to the lender and retains any equity earned.

The traditional mortgage emerged as part of the federal government's efforts to provide mortgage relief during the Great Depression, and became the standard product for home financing throughout the regulated stage of capitalism. Traditional mortgages are risky for lenders, for several reasons. First, lenders face default risk. Given the long-term nature of mortgage lending, there is a real probability that borrowers will be unable to pay their mortgages at some point in the future. Over the course of 15 to 30 years, individual financial circumstances can change; as can the overall health of the economic system. Second, traditional mortgages were largely illiquid assets for lenders during regulated capitalism. Once issued, lenders had very few avenues to sell mortgages and convert them into cash. Third, traditional mortgages carry significant information costs due to the time and expense of assessing the creditworthiness of borrowers. The structure of the traditional mortgage loan mitigates these risks. The lender's exposure to default risk, the lack of liquidity, and significant information expenses led to very high lending standards following the Great Depression and World War II.

The evolution of neoliberalism, however, presented a dilemma for financial capitalists. High lending standards limit the market from which lenders earn profit. Two central features of the neoliberal stage of capitalism heightened the riskiness of mortgage applicants: stagnant real incomes and, by consequence, rising debt loads. Restricting access to traditional mortgage lending would have reduced living standards, stifled the benefits of home ownership, and possibly curtailed popular support for neoliberalism. Financial institutions therefore expanded the provision of mortgage products that secure home financing for risky borrowers and increase profitability in mortgage lending: subprime mortgage loans.

Subprime mortgage loans can take many forms, and there is no concrete definition as to what constitutes "subprime." In many cases, the frequency of default during the subprime meltdown is a determining factor. All subprime mortgages, in some way, facilitate access to credit for borrowers who do not qualify for traditional mortgages due to poor credit scores, low or irregular income, or lack of a down payment. The terms of subprime mortgage contracts compensate lenders for taking greater risk and allow borrowers to acquire a home on more affordable terms. Some of the general attributes of subprime mortgages include:

- higher fixed interest rates or, more commonly, adjustable interest rates. The borrower often pays a fixed interest rate for an initial period, after which the interest rate becomes variable. The purpose of an adjustable-rate mortgage is to protect the lender's interest income when market rates fluctuate;

- little to no verification of borrower income, assets, or debts;
- non-traditional down-payment requirements. In some cases, the borrower secures a mortgage with no down-payment or a much smaller down payment. In other cases, the borrower acquires a loan for the down payment;
- higher fees or closing costs; and
- pre-payment penalties, in order to ensure interest income to the lender when the borrower pays down, pays off, or refinances a mortgage.

More specific examples of subprime mortgage products, which Table 3.4 briefly summarizes, include the following:

- Balloon loans: A balloon loan features a short term of five to seven years, during which the borrower makes small monthly payments. At the end of the term, the borrower must then pay off the entire loan balance in one payment.
- Forty to 50-year fixed-rate loans: The borrower makes the same monthly payment, but pays significantly more interest than a traditional mortgage over the life of the loan.

TABLE 3.4 Attributes of Subprime Mortgage Products

	Attributes
Balloon Loan	- Short term - Small monthly payments - Borrower pays off entire loan balance in one payment at the end of the term
Forty- to Fifty-Year Fixed-Rate Loan	- Fixed monthly payments - Borrower pays significantly more interest over the life of the loan
Interest-Only Loan	- Interest-only payments during the initial loan period - Initial monthly payments do not reduce principal - Borrower pays interest and principal after the initial period - Higher monthly payments after the initial period
Negative Amortization Loan	- Initial monthly payments do not cover interest - Principal grows over the life of the loan - Higher monthly payments after the initial loan period
No Income-No Asset Loan	- Lender determines creditworthiness solely using the borrower's credit score - Borrower provides no proof of income
Option Adjustable-Rate Mortgage	- Borrower has monthly payment options during the initial loan period - Full payments cover principal and interest - Interest-only payments do not reduce principal - Minimum payments do not cover interest - Higher monthly payments after the initial period
Shared Appreciation Mortgage	- Low interest rate - Borrower shares portion of home equity earned with the lender

- Interest-only loans: As the name suggests, the borrower makes interest-only payments for the first few years of the loan, which do not reduce the principal balance during that time. After the specified period, however, the borrower has the remainder of the loan term to pay interest and the entire principal, resulting in significantly higher monthly payments.
- Negative amortization loans: The initial monthly payment in this case is so low that it does not cover the interest, which increases the principal balance over the life of the loan. At some point, however, the lender increases the monthly payment in order to recover the entire loan balance.
- No income, no asset loans: The lender determines creditworthiness solely using the borrower's credit score. The borrower provides no proof of income, such as paychecks, bank statements, or tax returns.
- Option adjustable-rate mortgages: For an initial period of the loan, the borrower has the option to make:
  - a full payment of principal and interest;
  - an interest-only payment, which does not reduce the principal balance; or
  - a minimum payment that does not cover the interest, which increases the principal balance.

  After the initial period, the lender increases the monthly payment in order to recover the entire loan balance.
- Shared appreciation mortgages: In return for a lower interest rate, the borrower shares a portion of the home's appreciation with the lender. For example, in the event of a home sale, the borrower pays not only the remaining balance on the loan, but also a percentage of equity earned, to the lender.

Both Democratic and Republican lawmakers celebrated the contribution of subprime mortgage lending to the marked increase in the US home ownership rate during the 1990s and 2000s. For the Clinton administration, the evolution of mortgage lending standards reduced barriers to home ownership for large segments of the Democratic party's historical base with working class voters and Black voters. In 1995, Clinton spearheaded the National Homeownership Strategy, an aggressive plan to increase the rate of home ownership by taking advantage of the wave of technological innovation and financial consolidation. The strategy included several recommendations that lowered traditional mortgage lending standards, such as reduced down payments and closing costs, and expanded access to financing. Interestingly, the administration clearly associated this policy with the wave of financialization and technological innovation during the 1990s:

> There is widespread expectation that the mortgage finance system, and indeed the housing system generally, is on the verge of a period of dramatic change stemming from industry consolidation, redesigned processes, and the application of automation. It is vital that this change in the mortgage finance system be guided by a commitment to increase opportunities for home ownership for more families, particularly for low- and moderate-income and minority families, and to increase the national home ownership rate to an all-time high.

For the W. Bush administration, the surge in mortgage lending complemented its conservative vision of an ownership society, in which individuals exercise more control in their financial decisions through greater ownership of property, and less reliance on social welfare programs. Bush also sought to reduce barriers to minority home ownership as a way of expanding the demographics of the Republican base, especially with Latinos. In 2003, Bush signed the American Dream Downpayment Act, which assisted low-income families with down payments and closing costs:

> Our Government is supporting homeownership because it is good for America; it is good for our families; it is good for our economy. One of the biggest hurdles to homeownership is getting money for a downpayment. This administration has recognized that, and so today I'm honored to be here to sign a law that will help many low-income buyers to overcome that hurdle and to achieve an important part of the American Dream.

Nevertheless, the provision of subprime lending essentially represents a return to the exploitative practices in home financing that predated the Great Depression: short-term loans, interest-only payments, negative amortization, and the appropriation of home equity by financial capitalists. The high interest rates, fees, and especially broker incentives on subprime mortgages led to predatory marketing strategies during the US housing market bubble. Broker commissions in particular were strongly influenced by significant origination fees levied on subprime mortgages. Lenders also contributed to the heavy marketing of subprime loans. In most of the cases noted earlier, the origination of a loan almost always guaranteed a new loan at the end of the initial period. Borrowers who preferred continuing with their lenders could take advantage of the home equity build-up during the bubble through cash-out refinancing. In a cash-out refinance, the lender issues a new loan for more than the balance owed on the original mortgage. The borrower receives a cash payment on the difference, while the lender collects new fees.

Many analysts contend that subprime mortgages were perfectly reasonable products for minority borrowers given that their incomes, credit scores, and neighborhood property values tend to be lower than non-Hispanic White borrowers. However, many minority borrowers who received subprime mortgage products would have qualified for traditional mortgage products. According to a 2006 study conducted by the Center for Responsible Lending, at the height of the housing market bubble, Black borrowers were far more likely than White borrowers to receive higher-rate subprime purchase and refinance loans—even when controlling for income, home location, credit score, and other credit risk variables. In particular, Blacks received a disproportionate share of subprime mortgages with pre-payment penalties. Latino borrowers were also more likely to receive higher-rate subprime purchase loans. What does this mean in practice? Suppose a Black couple and a White couple both submit a mortgage application. Each household has the same income and credit score. Each household is searching for a similar property in the same neighborhood. According to the results of this study, the Black couple was more likely to receive a risky, subprime mortgage product while the White couple was more likely to receive a safer, traditional mortgage product.

This important, and frequently misunderstood, aspect of the US housing market bubble is known as "reverse redlining." Reverse redlining is a process in which financial institutions issue high-cost loans to borrowers from certain communities or neighborhoods, who otherwise qualify for traditional loans, on fraudulent terms. Although the historical context of reverse redlining is different from the traditional form of redlining discussed earlier in this chapter, it is no less discriminatory. Both forms of redlining emerged from concerted attempts to increase access to mortgage lending and home ownership. Both forms also contributed to the dispossession of minority wealth. Under traditional redlining, the provision of traditional mortgage lending during the regulated stage of capitalism led to targeted restrictions on access to home financing for particular groups or neighborhoods. Under reverse redlining, the provision of subprime mortgage lending during the neoliberal stage of capitalism led to targeted expansions of credit to those same groups using predatory practices.

THE FORECLOSURE CRISIS

The rapid home price appreciation was a marketing tactic employed by mortgage brokers in order to convince borrowers to take out subprime loans, especially those with very low initial payments. Many subprime borrowers genuinely believed that they would be able to afford the higher monthly payments built into their mortgage contracts, despite not being eligible for traditional mortgages at the time they purchased their homes. For example, perhaps a borrower expected to rebuild his or her credit during the initial years of the mortgage because of a recent divorce. Likewise, a borrower may have expected a more stable flow of income after the initial loan period, or simply a higher level of income, due to an upcoming promotion or job change. Subprime loans were an important means of accessing home ownership for the self-employed, who typically face challenges in meeting the qualifications for traditional mortgages. It is also plausible that many borrowers faced lingering financial insecurity following the dot-com bust and the weak job market in the wake of the 2001 recession. But even if a borrower was still unable to make the higher monthly payments, he or she could easily refinance the mortgage, or just sell the house. On the other hand, many subprime borrowers were eligible for traditional mortgages but preferred the requirements and payment structures of a subprime loan. For example, a borrower who signed a short-term employment contract, and planned to relocate thereafter, preferred the relaxed down-payment requirements and lower monthly payments associated with a subprime loan, especially since market expectations for profit were strong. The key point is that the expectation that home values would continuously rise was the basis for *all* of these sentiments.

The correction in housing prices beginning at the end of 2006 triggered the worst foreclosure crisis since the Great Depression. The mortgage default crisis in the subprime market was the conduit. Homeowners who could not afford higher mortgage payments were unable to refinance and pay off the remaining balances on their loans. For example, a borrower who received a five-year balloon loan in 2002 could not refinance in 2007 because the collateral behind the loan (the home) was worth far less. A borrower with an interest-only mortgage had not paid down any principal at all. Even worse, a borrower who had only made minimum payments on his or her option adjustable-rate mortgage saw the principal balance grow. A further contributing factor was the gradual, but marked, increase in the federal funds rate during the 2000s, which led to higher mortgage rates and monthly payments on adjustable-rate mortgages. By 2007, those homeowners carried mortgage balances that far exceeded market prices, which were rapidly falling. Unable to make their new monthly payments, refinance their mortgages, or sell their homes, a wave of subprime borrowers defaulted and voluntarily walked away from their properties. A rapid increase in foreclosure rates followed as lenders sought to repossess properties from delinquent borrowers in order to recover what they could of the remaining balances on the mortgages.

It is difficult to ascertain exactly the number of foreclosures completed during the subprime mortgage meltdown. Legal procedures, the involvement of courts, and reporting requirements vary widely by state in the United States. However, a 2010 study by the Center for Responsible Lending estimates a loss of 2.5 million homes to foreclosure between 2007 and 2009 alone, most of which received mortgages between 2005 and 2008. Given the racial and ethnic disparities in subprime mortgage lending, foreclosure rates were substantially higher among Blacks and Latinos. Controlling for differences in income, the percentage of Black borrowers in foreclosure (7.9%) was nearly double the percentage for non-Hispanic White borrowers (4.5%). A similar disparity exists for Latino borrowers, who faced a completed foreclosure rate of 7.7%. However, relative to the total number of mortgages issued, non-Hispanic Whites constitute by far the majority of borrowers who lost their homes to foreclosure (56.1%). These findings debunk yet another misconception about the foreclosure crisis: that most of the families who lost their homes were racial and ethnic minorities.

The federal government's response to the foreclosure crisis, which spanned both the W. Bush and Obama administrations, consisted of two primary mechanisms: mortgage loan workouts and legal settlements. A particular objective of the government's response was to stem the wave of voluntary foreclosures by homeowners. The W. Bush administration established the Hope Now Alliance in 2007 to help homeowners avoid foreclosure. Hope Now is a joint public-private partnership consisting of government agencies, mortgage companies, non-profit foreclosure counseling agencies, and trade associations. It assists homeowners by arranging mortgage loan workouts on a case-by-case basis. Workouts take one of two forms: modified repayment plans or loan modifications. In either form, participation on the part of lenders is voluntary. A loan modification changes the original terms of the mortgage (e.g., the principal, interest rate, or term), resulting in lower monthly payments. A modified repayment plan simply grants the borrower more time to make the regular payments on the balance of the loan, which remains the same. In practice, the vast majority of workouts facilitated by Hope Now resulted in modified repayment plans, not loan modifications. Lenders were very reluctant to adjust the terms of mortgages, especially the principal, which in many cases left borrowers with the same unaffordable monthly payments. Most workouts modified borrower repayment plans by postponing the interest rate or payment resets built into the contracts. Critics frequently cite two flaws in Hope Now: first, the case-by-case processing of workouts could not keep up with escalating rates of foreclosure during the crisis; second, the program did little to curb voluntary foreclosures due to the lack of principal adjustments by lenders. In addition to Hope Now, the Emergency Economic Stabilization Act, which Bush signed in the fall of 2008, created the Home Affordable Modification Program (HAMP). HAMP established guidelines and incentives for loan modifications for at-risk borrowers in the states hit hardest by the recession.

The Obama administration established two foreclosure initiatives in 2009. The Homeowners Affordability and Stability Plan created incentives for lenders to reduce monthly payments to a sustainable share of borrower income. The government also provided funding to share the costs of payment reductions with lenders. The Home Affordable Refinance Program assisted borrowers who were current on their mortgage payments, but unable to refinance due to the collapse in market prices. In the end, the Obama administration largely followed the W. Bush administration's response to the foreclosure crisis. Lender participation was completely voluntary. The programs mostly provided incentives to avoid foreclosures through loan workouts, which they processed on a case-by-case basis. Neither administration took the kind of direct action seen during the Great Depression, when the federal government directly refinanced mortgages, recovered lost properties, and placed responsibility for that foreclosure crisis squarely on banks—not homeowners.

In addition to these anti-foreclosure initiatives, both the federal and state governments filed consumer financial protection lawsuits against mortgage servicers for fraudulent practices related to foreclosure processing and loan servicing. The largest case was the National Mortgage Settlement, which was reached in 2012 with Ally/GMAC, Bank of America, Citi, JPMorgan Chase, and Wells Fargo. The settlement—which was worth over $50 billion—included funding for loan modifications and refinancing, restitution to borrowers who lost their homes to foreclosure, and fines paid to the federal government and states included in the lawsuit.

FINAL THOUGHTS

As devastating as the mortgage meltdown and foreclosure crisis were, their effects spread beyond the borrowers that received subprime loans and the lending institutions that issued them. In fact, instability in mortgage and housing markets evolved into a full-scale financial crisis, as well as a broader economic crisis. The next chapter examines the transmission of the housing market bubble and bust to other segments of the financial sector, such as commercial banks, Fannie Mae and Freddie Mac, financial markets, insurance companies, and investment banks. It examines how the housing market crash led to a severe economic contraction, widespread unemployment, and the rare phenomenon of deflation. It also explores how the federal government's response to Wall Street during the 2008 financial crisis differed markedly from its response to homeowners. Understanding these complex financial and economic processes will facilitate a deeper understanding of the evolution of market behavior during the US housing bubble and the incentives to issue subprime mortgage loans.

Sources

Adams, J. (1805). *Discourses on Davila*. Boston, MA: Russell & Cutler.

Bocian, D.G., Ernst, K.S., & Li, W. (2006). *Unfair lending: The effect of race and ethnicity on the price of subprime mortgages*. Center for Responsible Lending. Retrieved from https://www.responsiblelending.org.

Bocian, D.G., Li, W., & Ernst, K.S. (2010). *Foreclosures by race and ethnicity: The demographics of a crisis*. Center for Responsible Lending. Retrieved from https://www.responsiblelending.org.

Bush, G.W. (2003, December 16). Remarks on signing the American Dream

Downpayment Act [Transcript]. Retrieved from https://www.presidency.ucsb.edu.

Darity, W. (2005). Stratification economics: The role of intergroup inequality. *Journal of Economics and Finance*, *29*(2), 144–53. doi: 10.1007/BF02761550

Darity, W.A., Hamilton, D., & Stewart, J.B. (2015). A tour de force in understanding intergroup inequality: An introduction to stratification economics. *Review of Black Political Economy*, *42*(1–2), 1–6. doi: 10.1007/s12114-015-9212-6

Engels, F. (1935). *The housing question*. New York, NY: International Publishers.

Federal Reserve Bank of St. Louis. (n.d.). *FRED economic data* [Data file and codebook]. Retrieved from https://fred.stlouisfed.org.

Goodman, L.S. & Mayer, C. (2018). Homeownership and the American Dream. *Journal of Economic Perspectives*, *32*(1), 31–58. doi: 10.1257/jep.32.1.31

King, M.L. (1965, March 25). Address at the conclusion of the Selma to Montgomery march [Transcript]. Retrieved from https://kinginstitute.stanford.edu.

Nelson, R.K. & Ayers, E.L. (2020). *Mapping inequality: Redlining in New Deal America* [Data file and codebook]. Retrieved from https://dsl.richmond.edu/panorama/redlining/.

Roosevelt, F.D. (1933, April 13). Message to Congress on small home mortgage foreclosures [Transcript]. Retrieved from https://www.presidency.ucsb.edu.

Shiller, R.J. (n.d.). *Online data – Robert Shiller* [Data file and codebook]. Retrieved from http://www.econ.yale.edu/~shiller/data.htm.

Stewart, J.B. (2008). Stratification economics. In *The international encyclopedia of the social sciences*. Farmington Hills, MI: Cengage.

US Department of Housing and Urban Development. (1995). *The national home ownership strategy: Partners in the American dream*. Author.

Further Reading

Aalbers, M.B. (ed.). (2012). *Subprime cities: The political economy of mortgage markets*. Malden, MA: Wiley-Blackwell.

Aliber, R.Z. & Kindelberger, C.P. (2015). *Manias, panics, and crashes: A history of financial crises*. New York, NY: Palgrave Macmillan.

Darity, W.A., Mason, P.L., & Stewart, J.B. (2006). The economics of identity: The origin and persistence of racial identity norms. *Journal of Economic Behavior and Organization*, *60*(3), 283–305. doi: 10.1016/j.jebo.2004.08.005

Hillier, A.E. (2003). Redlining and the Home Owners' Loan Corporation. *Journal of Urban History*, *29*(4), 394–420. doi: 10.1177/0096144203029004005.

Jackson, K.T. (1985). *Crabgrass frontier: The suburbanization of the United States*. New York, NY: Oxford University Press.

Shiller, R.J. (2005). *Irrational exuberance*. New York, NY: Currency Books.

CHAPTER 4

Financial Structure, Financial Crisis, and the Wall Street Bailouts

In October 2007, the Standard & Poor's Composite Stock Index (S&P) reached a record high of 1539.66. Adjusted for inflation, it went on to lose over half its value by March 2009, including a drop of nearly 20% between September and October 2008 alone. It took until November 2013—over four years after the official trough of the Great Recession—for the S&P to fully recover. Notwithstanding the severity of the stock market crash during the fall of 2008, it was by no means the first instance of financial instability during the neoliberal era. The Latin American debt crisis; the failure of Continental Illinois Bank and Trust Company; the savings and loan debacle; Black Monday; the dot-com bust; the East Asian, Latin American, and Russian financial crises; the failure of Long-Term Capital Management; and multiple corporate accounting scandals all preceded the 2008 financial crisis. What separates the financial crisis is the scale of damage and uncertainty transmitted from home ownership—once considered a bedrock of American capitalism—to the financial sector as well as the economic system. Following the housing market bust and foreclosure crisis, by the end of the crisis in June 2009, capitalism had suffered the failure of some of the largest financial corporations in the world—including investment banks, government-sponsored enterprises, insurance companies, and commercial banks; widespread volatility in securities markets; a comprehensive bailout of the financial industry; and the longest economic contraction since the Great Depression of the 1930s.

This chapter continues our examination of "The Road to the Great Recession" by explaining the complex linkages between the housing market bust, the 2008 financial crisis, the economic crisis, and the conduct of the Wall Street bailouts. This is undoubtedly one of the most important, and likely challenging, topics pertaining to the Great Recession. This analysis accordingly draws upon the concepts and policies presented throughout the first three chapters of this textbook, and traces the complexity of financial structure through several careful steps. Understanding the nature of financial structure prior to the crisis will facilitate a deeper theoretical and practical understanding of the transmission of the financial crisis. Understanding the transmission of the financial crisis will then facilitate an

DOI: 10.4324/9780429461316-6

understanding of the severity of the economic crisis. It will also facilitate an understanding of the conduct of the Wall Street bailouts in 2008 and 2009. By the end of this chapter, readers will have a firm grasp of the contracts, relationships, and securities that enabled the transmission of the financial crisis; how it evolved into a deep economic contraction; and the emergency measures taken by national policymakers to end the crisis of confidence in the financial system.

This chapter develops a detailed model for understanding a wide range of interconnected issues related to the 2008 financial crisis. The opening four sections present the financial structure related to residential real estate and home financing that existed prior to the financial crisis. The first section introduces the practice of asset securitization, a process that is absolutely crucial to understanding this subject. In particular, it explains the process and motivation behind mortgage securitization by government-sponsored enterprises, which first arose during the 1970s. The second section examines the emergence of mortgage securitization by Wall Street investment banks during the 1980s. The third section discusses the credit rating process and the role of the major rating agencies during the financial crisis. The fourth section investigates the provision of credit default swaps—contracts that provide insurance against default on mortgage-related securities. The actions of all three organizations—investment banks, the rating agencies, and insurance companies—contributed greatly to the wave of investment in mortgage-related securities in the lead-up to the crisis. The next section uses the framework of financial structure presented in this chapter to explain, step by step, the transmission of the financial crisis. The penultimate section discusses the forces that brought the financial crisis to the real sector, and the transmission of an economic crisis that resulted in a severe recession, high unemployment, and deflation. The final section examines the conduct of the Wall Street bailouts, how they differed from the government's response to homeowners and the foreclosure crisis, and their enduring controversial legacy.

UNDERSTANDING FINANCIAL STRUCTURE PART I: MORTGAGE SECURITIZATION BY GOVERNMENT-SPONSORED ENTERPRISES

The first step in developing an understanding of financial structure prior to the 2008 financial crisis is to examine the relationship between mortgage lending, home ownership, and financial markets. Chapter 3 explored the relationship between mortgage lending and home ownership, and the evolution of that relationship over time. This section investigates the transmission of those financial relations and income flows, from mortgage markets and housing markets to global securities markets. This analysis will eventually facilitate an understanding of the transmission of the subprime mortgage meltdown and foreclosure crisis to the glut of "toxic assets" during the financial crisis. The first step is to investigate the process of mortgage securitization.

"Securitization" Defined

Let's begin with a general definition of "securitization," as the practice of securitization does not simply involve residential mortgages. Securitization is a process whereby a financial firm purchases the assets of other firms, merges them into a single pool or portfolio, and sells the income flow from the underlying pool as a security to financial investors. The result of this process is an "asset-backed" security, which is a claim to payments from the pool. In most cases, the issuer of the security creates a pool by purchasing loans from commercial banks, which commonly include car loans, commercial mortgages, credit card accounts, personal loans, residential mortgages, or any other assets that generate income flows. The process of securitization creates a new financial structure that transforms lending and borrowing relationships. Prior to securitization, the borrower makes the contractual payments to the lender that originated the loan. The income flow from the repayment of the loan is simply from the borrower to the lender. With securitization, however, the original lender sells the loan to the issuer of the security, which now holds the right to be repaid in its portfolio. The borrower therefore makes the contractual payments to the issuer of the security, which the issuer then transfers to securities investors. Securities investors effectively function as lenders, since they are the ultimate recipients of the principal and interest payments from the borrower.

Proponents regard securitization as financial innovation and cite several benefits for all parties involved in the process. Securitization creates new profit opportunities for securities investors, which earn a rate of return from a diversified portfolio. The issuer of the security earns profit on the difference between the sales of asset-backed securities and the costs of acquiring the collateral that backs the portfolio. Lenders convert illiquid assets into cash, which they can use to create more loans. Borrowers in turn access more credit, which they can use to finance consumption and investment.

While the intent of securitization is to mitigate credit risk, it can also exacerbate it. The riskiness of an asset-backed security fundamentally depends upon the riskiness of the underlying assets in the pool. Volatility in the market value of the collateral in the pool will therefore contribute to volatility in the market value of asset-backed securities. Assuming that investors are risk averse, conventional economic theory states that a security backed by a pool of riskier assets should carry a higher rate of return, while a security backed by a pool of safer assets should carry a lower rate of return. However, investors must have full information about the risk profile of the portfolio in order for rates of return to properly align with the degree of risk. For whatever reason, if there is a lack of information or a lack of transparency about the quality of the collateral in the portfolio, the price of the asset-backed security will not properly reflect its risk. Furthermore, securitization exposes more parties to default risk in the event that the borrower stops making payments on the underlying loan. Prior to securitization, the negative effects of default do not extend beyond the lender. With securitization, default negatively affects not only the operations of the security issuer, which now holds the loan in its portfolio, but also the net worth of securities investors.

Mortgage securitization is simply a more specific form of this practice. In this case, a financial firm purchases residential mortgages from lending institutions, groups them into a larger portfolio, and sells claims to the monthly mortgage payments from the underlying pool. The result of this process is a new financial instrument known as a "mortgage-backed" security. As was the case with asset-backed securities, mortgage securitization transforms mortgage lending and borrowing relationships, as well as the property rights related to home ownership.

Mortgage-backed security investors effectively function as mortgagees, who now receive the principal and interest payments from the homeowner, whereas previously the homeowner made mortgage payments to a lending institution. The general benefits and risks of asset securitization discussed earlier apply to mortgage securitization, although a few caveats are important to note. Mortgage securitization creates a financial structure in which fluctuations in home values will contribute to fluctuations in the value of mortgage-backed securities. Should homeowners default on their mortgage payments, the decline in home values in local real estate markets will contribute to a decline in the value of mortgage-backed securities. Although the legal process of foreclosure facilitates opportunities for securities investors to receive compensation in part for their losses, mortgage-backed securities carry an additional risk of a differing nature. If homeowners pay off their mortgages early, the expected returns from mortgage-backed securities will be lower.

In order to establish a baseline for understanding the practice of mortgage securitization by different types of financial corporations, and the complexity of financial structure prior to the crisis, Figure 4.1 illustrates mortgage lending and borrowing relationships in the absence of securitization—a process known as portfolio lending. In this case, lenders raise financial capital primarily from their depositors in exchange for interest. Borrowers receive a sum of principal from lenders in order to purchase a home in the housing market. In exchange for accessing the benefits of home ownership, borrowers repay principal plus interest to their lenders.

In the United States, several institutions in both the private sector and the public sector engage in mortgage securitization. This chapter examines this process from a historical perspective by placing it within the evolutionary context of US capitalism. The remainder of this section focuses on the history and practice

FIGURE 4.1 Mortgage Lending and Borrowing Relationships: Portfolio Lending

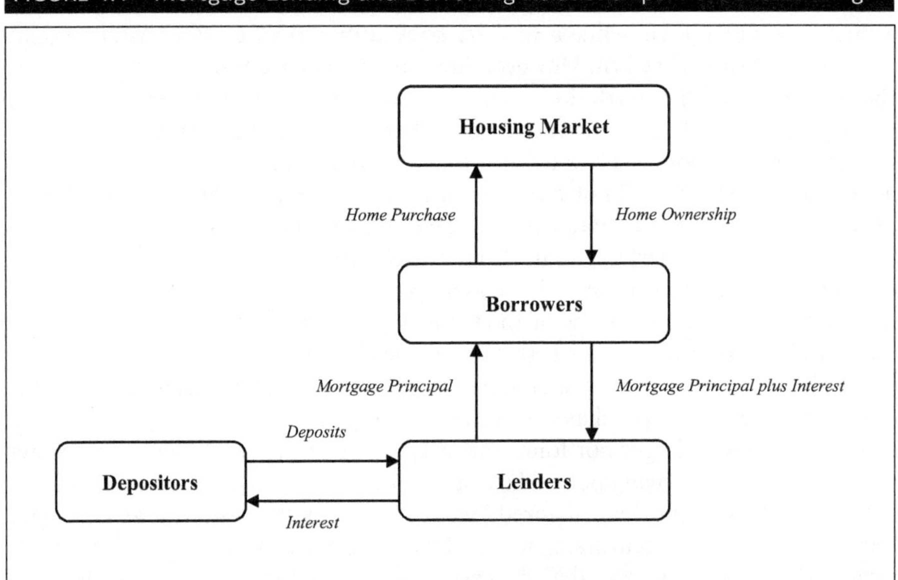

of mortgage securitization by government-sponsored enterprises, which arose during the 1970s. The next section focuses on the activities of Wall Street investment banks, and the creation of "private-label" mortgage-backed securities, during the 1980s.

Fannie Mae, Freddie Mac, and Agency Mortgage-Backed Securities

Government-sponsored enterprises are quasi-public organizations that feature characteristics of both private firms and government agencies. Government-sponsored enterprises are similar to private corporations in that their goal is to maximize profit. They sell stocks as well as bonds, meaning they are accountable to shareholders and external creditors. Unlike private corporations, however, government-sponsored enterprises receive their charters from Congress in order to mitigate credit risk in certain sectors. These charters also limit their operations to their respective sectors. For example, government-sponsored enterprises increase access to credit and lower borrowing costs for college students, farmers, and in this case, homeowners.

Two prominent corporations perform such functions in the area of home financing: the Federal National Mortgage Association (also known as Fannie Mae, or simply "Fannie") and the Federal Home Loan Mortgage Corporation (also known as Freddie Mac, or "Freddie"). Congress originally established Fannie Mae in 1938 as a federally funded government agency, another component of its strategy to revive mortgage lending and home ownership during the Great Depression. Taxpayer funding ceased in 1968 with the privatization of Fannie by the federal government, at which point it began selling stocks and bonds to investors. In 1970, Congress chartered Freddie Mac as a government-sponsored enterprise and competitor to Fannie Mae. As government-sponsored enterprises, their goals are to maximize profit in order to satisfy their investors, while also fulfilling their social purpose of expanding access to home ownership. In terms of their operations, however, neither corporation functions as a commercial bank. Neither corporation raises financial capital from depositors and issues mortgages directly to homeowners in the primary mortgage market. Instead, Fannie and Freddie expand the availability of credit for home financing through the secondary mortgage market. They engage in two primary activities in order to achieve their dual objectives.

First, both corporations purchase, and guarantee, residential mortgages between private lenders and homeowners. The only major difference between Fannie and Freddie concerns the type and size of lenders that each corporation works with. Fannie Mae purchases home loans from large commercial banks while Freddie Mac purchases loans from smaller lending institutions. These wholesale mortgage purchases provide fresh liquidity to lenders, which they prefer to the otherwise illiquid character of residential mortgages. This process benefits both homeowners and the economic system in multiple ways. When lenders sell mortgages to Fannie or Freddie for cash, they can utilize the new supply of loanable funds to create new mortgages for homeowners. According to conventional economic theory, an increase in the availability of credit creates a market surplus, which puts downward pressure on market interest rates. Competitive forces will pressure self-interested, profit-motivated lenders to convert their cash reserves into interest-bearing home loans, since reserves earn much less interest than loans. In order to entice homeowners to new lines of credit, they will lower mortgage rates. The expansion of net worth through home ownership creates a wealth effect that expands consumption and economic output. This process was therefore another key institution that supported aggregate demand during the regulated stage of US capitalism.

Second, both corporations sell mortgage-backed securities to investors. The term "agency mortgage-backed security" specifically refers to a security issued by a government-sponsored enterprise. The first activity fulfills their social motive to increase access to home ownership and middle-class wealth, while the second activity fulfills their private motive to earn profit. Fannie Mae and Freddie Mac finance these operations by selling short-term bonds. These short-term borrowings finance the purchasing of long-term mortgages from lenders in order to create mortgage pools. Fannie and Freddie therefore earn profit on the difference between the sales of agency mortgage-backed securities and the costs of borrowing. The sale of agency mortgage-backed securities first began during the early 1970s following the privatization of Fannie Mae and the chartering of Freddie Mac by the federal government. This is yet another common misconception about the crisis: the general provision of mortgage-backed securities well preceded the pre-Great Recession housing market bubble, and did not originate during the 1990s or 2000s. Furthermore, at this point, Wall Street investment banks did not yet engage in mortgage securitization.

Fannie Mae and Freddie Mac guarantee payments of principal and interest on agency mortgage-backed securities. Officially, this does not represent a guarantee by the US government, since both corporations operate as independent enterprises and receive no federal funding. According to a Fannie Mae Single-Family Mortgage-Backed Security Prospectus:

> We guarantee to each trust that we will supplement amounts received by the trust as required to permit timely payments of principal and interest on the certificates. We alone are responsible for making payments under our guaranty. The certificates and payments of principal and interest on the certificates are not guaranteed by the United States and do not constitute a debt or obligation of the United States or any of its agencies or instrumentalities other than Fannie Mae.

However, given that they received their charters from Congress, investors *perceived* that the federal government would intervene if either firm was unable to compensate securities investors. This question was the subject of debate within the financial sector and the federal government for many decades. For example, US Representative Barney Frank stated the following in 2003:

> The two government sponsored enterprises we are talking about here, Fannie Mae and Freddie Mac, are not in a crisis ... The more people, in my judgment, exaggerate a threat of safety and soundness, the more people conjure up the possibility of serious financial losses to the Treasury, which I do not see. I think we see entities that are

> fundamentally sound financially and withstand some of the disastrous scenarios. And even if there were a problem, the Federal Government doesn't bail them out. But the more pressure there is there, then the less I think we see in terms of affordable housing.

That question has technically been answered now, since the federal government placed both firms in conservatorship during the 2008 financial crisis. But regardless of their true or perceived backing, public or private, the activities of Fannie Mae and Freddie Mac constitute a major intervention in the mortgage lending system, the housing market, and the performance of US capitalism. Given that they are two of the largest corporations in the world, access to home financing, mortgage rates, home-ownership rates, and household consumption would be substantially different if they did not engage in these activities.

The analysis thus far has primarily focused on the supply side of the market for agency mortgage-backed securities; but what about the demand side? Until the 2008 financial crisis, securities investors deemed agency mortgage-backed securities to be attractive financial instruments in large part for their relative safety, meaning their perceived default risk was very low. The reason for this sentiment is that Fannie Mae and Freddie Mac maintained lending standards that limited securitization to primarily traditional mortgages—that is, 30-year, fixed-rate home loans. As noted earlier, the riskiness of the underlying mortgages in Fannie and Freddie's pools ultimately determines the riskiness of agency mortgage-backed securities. Since traditional mortgages feature high lending standards by loan originators in order to reduce their exposure to default risk, investors considered agency mortgage-backed securities to be relatively safe assets. If the underlying mortgages that backed Fannie and Freddie's portfolios were low-risk assets, then so too were any securities derived from them. Furthermore, the long-term stability of real home values following World War II ensured stability in the market value of agency mortgage-backed securities. For these reasons, large institutional investors throughout the global financial sector—including central banks, commercial banks, endowments, hedge funds, insurance companies, mutual funds, and pension funds—actively purchased mortgage-backed securities from government-sponsored enterprises as a strategy of risk diversification. In fact, to this day, traditional mortgage loans continue to serve as the collateral for agency mortgage-backed securities. At no point—including in the lead-up to the financial crisis—did either corporation securitize riskier, subprime mortgage loans.

Figure 4.2 illustrates the creation of agency mortgage-backed securities, and the transformation of mortgage lending and borrowing relationships brought about by government-sponsored securitization. The graphic builds upon the baseline understanding of these relationships presented in Figure 4.1, in the absence of securitization. In this case, a government-sponsored enterprise borrows money from the bond market in order to purchase traditional mortgages from lenders, which it places in a pool. The government-sponsored enterprise then sells agency mortgage-backed securities to investors. The goal is to encourage the process illustrated by Figure 4.1: lenders will have new cash reserves with which to create new mortgages; borrowers will use those funds to purchase new homes; and the increase in home ownership will accompany new repayments of principal and interest.

FIGURE 4.2 Creation of Agency Mortgage-Backed Securities

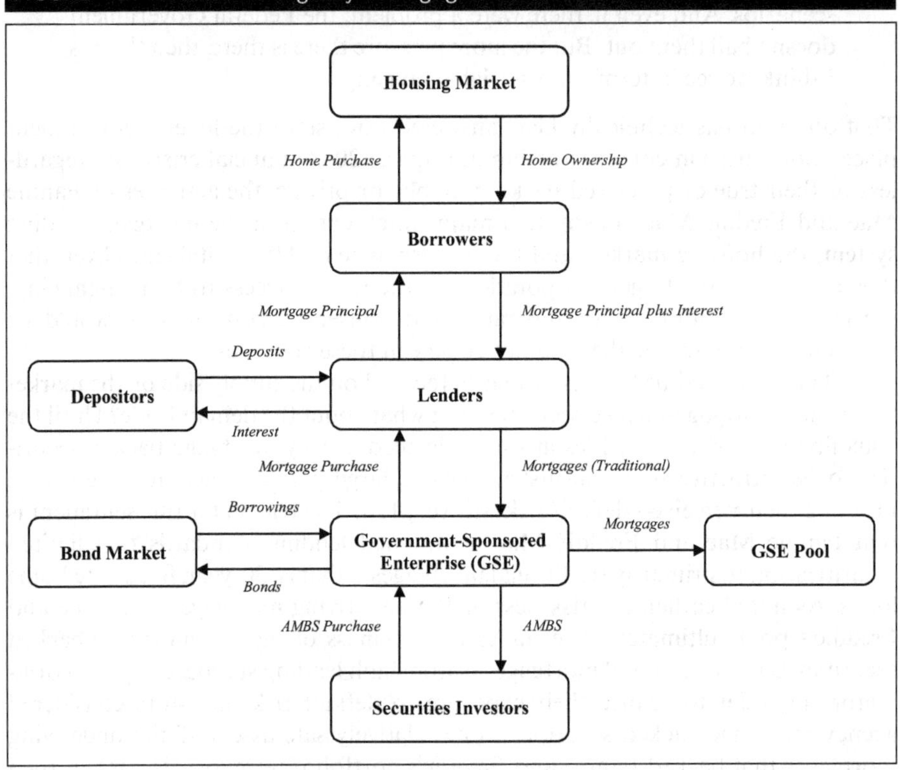

However, owners of mortgage-backed securities—not the loan originators—now receive the principal and interest payments from borrowers. Moreover, the availability of deposits no longer limits the creation of credit since lenders may now raise financial capital through the sale of their mortgages.

However, the evolution of capitalist institutions in profit making and investment, away from regulated capitalism and toward neoliberal capitalism, also led to the evolution of mortgage securitization. By the 1980s, the financialization of global capitalism—the rising influence of the financial sector in the economic system, politics, and society—led to greater demand for mortgage-backed securities from financial investors. The shift toward a deregulatory mindset that celebrated market competition and financial innovation, in lieu of government regulation, expanded the provision of mortgage-backed securities by the private sector, and eventually led to the securitization of subprime mortgages.

UNDERSTANDING FINANCIAL STRUCTURE PART II: MORTGAGE SECURITIZATION BY WALL STREET INVESTMENT BANKS

The origin of mortgage securitization by private investment banks lies in the crisis of the 1970s. During the crisis, high rates of inflation led to significant commercial bank losses due to lower real interest rates. By the early 1980s, these losses pressured commercial banks to engage in new forms of asset management, which included the provision of adjustable-rate mortgages as well as mortgage securitization.

Understanding Real Interest Rates: The Fisher Equation

In order to understand the effects of inflation on real interest rates, economists and financial professionals turn to the Fisher Equation. The Fisher Equation, developed by economist Irving Fisher, expresses the relationship between the nominal interest rate (i), the real interest rate (r), and the rate of inflation (π). The nominal interest rate is simply the interest rate specified in a loan contract, at the time of origination. For example, if the current 30-year mortgage rate is 5%, the nominal interest rate on a new loan equals 5%. The real interest rate, however, is the interest rate adjusted for inflation, at the end of the loan period. According to Fisher:

$$r = i - \pi$$

The real interest rate matters for the decision-making of both lenders and borrowers. For lenders, it represents the real rate of return, or purchasing power of interest income. For borrowers, it represents the real cost of borrowing, or burden of debt. The problem for commercial banks is that although they can specify the nominal interest rate at the time of origination, they cannot specify in advance the rate of inflation over the term of the loan. Commercial banks can only formulate an expectation of the inflation rate, and by consequence, their real rate of return.

This is a particularly important concern for long-term lending contracts such as residential mortgages. Following the Great Depression and World War II, the traditional mortgage product carried a fixed interest rate—that is, a fixed nominal interest rate. Even though future inflation rates were unknown variables, commercial banks secured stable real interest rates since inflation was largely stable during the regulated stage of capitalism. This practice changed, however, during the 1970s. Unexpectedly high inflation under fixed nominal interest rates led to lower real interest rates, and in many cases, negative real interest rates.

In order to understand this phenomenon, let's walk through an example using the Fisher Equation. Suppose Chase Bank issues a new home loan at a fixed nominal interest rate of 5%. If Chase expects an inflation rate (π^e) of 3%, the expected real interest rate (r^e) equals 2%. Using the Fisher Equation, at the time of origination:

$$r^e = i - \pi^e = 5\% - 3\% = 2\%$$

Suppose, however, that the actual inflation rate equals 8%, which is much higher than the expected inflation rate. Under the same nominal interest rate, the actual real interest rate at the end of the loan period equals -3%:

$$r = i - \pi = 5\% - 8\% = -3\%$$

This was a very real issue during the late 1970s and early 1980s, given the double-digit rates of inflation that plagued US capitalism at the time. By suppressing real interest rates, unexpected inflation redistributes income from lenders to borrowers. On the one hand, lenders lose purchasing power. In this example, instead of earning a 2% rate of return in real terms, Chase would take a loss of 3% on the loan. On the other hand, borrowers face a lower debt burden since the real cost of borrowing is now lower. Borrowers have an advantage because they can pay down their debt with money that is worth less.

Protecting Real Interest Rates: Adjustable Interest Rates and Private-Label Mortgage-Backed Securities

Commercial banks therefore developed two solutions. First, they expanded the provision of mortgages with adjustable interest rates, which keep nominal interest rates in line with market rates. An adjustable-rate mortgage gives the lender the right to increase the nominal interest rate in order to ensure the expected purchasing power of interest income. Using the scenario from this example, Chase could still ensure its 2% real interest rate by raising the nominal interest rate to 10%:

$$r = i - \pi = 10\% - 8\% = 2\%$$

This action prevents the redistributive effects of inflation under fixed nominal interest rates. Lenders secure a positive real of return, but borrowers do not see a reduction in the real cost of borrowing.

Second, commercial banks began selling mortgages in the secondary market to Wall Street investment banks. Salomon Brothers was one of the first private financial corporations to purchase residential mortgages as collateral for securitization. In contrast to the "agency" mortgage-backed securities sold by Fannie Mae and Freddie Mac, the term "private-label" mortgage-backed security refers to a financial instrument issued by an investment bank. The attributes of private-label securities differed from agency securities in several ways. Although they carried a higher degree of risk, they also carried a higher potential rate of return. Unlike Fannie and Freddie, investment banks did not guarantee payments of principal and interest on their securities. They were also not subject to the strict lending standards of Fannie and Freddie, meaning investment banks could purchase and securitize any type of mortgage, traditional or otherwise. The biggest difference, however, lay in the motivation for securitization. The singular motive for Wall Street was profit maximization. The creation of private-label mortgage-backed securities was not part of a larger social project to increase home ownership and middle-class wealth.

One way that investment banks raised funds in order to purchase mortgages from lenders was through repurchase agreements, or the "repo market." Repurchase agreements are in effect short-term loans. In a repurchase agreement, an investment bank borrows money by first selling assets in exchange for cash. The investment bank then repurchases the assets at some point in the near future, often the next day, for a higher price. The purchaser therefore functions as a lender and the assets serve as collateral on the loan. The difference between the repurchase price and the initial price represents the interest rate earned by the lender, and the cost of borrowing for the investment bank. As long as creditors were confident in the ability of the investment bank to repay its debt, these agreements rolled over on a daily basis in many cases.

Mortgage securitization by the private sector emerged at a time when corporations, especially financial corporations, began to consolidate their interests through lobbying. It occurred when the influence of the capitalist class overtook the influence of the working class in policymaking, away from fostering institutions that increased real wages, consumption, and spending, and toward institutions that increased profits, saving, and production. It also occurs when the merits of free market competition overtake the intent of government regulation, which in this case took the form of resistance to the lending standards set by Fannie Mae and Freddie Mac. During the late 1970s and early 1980s, the primary home loan product was still the traditional mortgage. Even though commercial banks expanded the provision of adjustable-rate mortgages, traditional mortgages served as the primary source of collateral for both government-sponsored and private-sector securitization. Eventually, however, securities investors pressured commercial banks to expand the availability of non-traditional mortgage products. As neoliberalism consolidated throughout the 1980s and 1990s, mortgage-backed securities investors faced the same dilemma as mortgage originators: the high lending standards associated with traditional mortgages limited the market from which mortgage lenders, and now securities investors, earned profit. The stagnant real wages and rising debt burdens of the working and middle classes amplified the risk of mortgage applicants. Restricting access to traditional mortgage loans would have restricted access to not only home ownership but also mortgage-backed securities. The expanded provision of riskier, subprime mortgages therefore flushed the secondary market with new assets for Wall Street to securitize in order to access the significant profits therein. For example, there was a reason that subprime mortgages carried pre-payment penalties: they reduced the value of mortgage-backed securities. Yet despite their riskier attributes, large institutional investors still regarded private-label mortgage-backed securities, just like agency mortgage-backed securities, as attractive financial instruments. This sentiment extended to Fannie Mae and Freddie Mac. Although Fannie and Freddie did not securitize subprime mortgages, they purchased private-label securities from investment banks for the same reason that other securities investors did: they considered them to be relatively safe assets.

Figure 4.3 summarizes the creation of private-label mortgage-backed securities. As compared to Figure 4.2, the practice of securitization by investment banks appears similar to the practice followed by government-sponsored enterprises. A few details and differences are important to note. First, investment banks financed their operations through overnight repurchase agreements. Second, government regulation did not limit mortgage purchases by investment banks to traditional mortgages. Third, private-label mortgage-backed securities carried no guarantee. Fourth, although the effects of private-sector securitization on mortgage lenders, borrowers, and home ownership rates were similar to government-sponsored securitization, the intent was solely profit maximization. Lastly, although government-sponsored enterprises did not securitize subprime mortgage loans, they purchased private-label securities as other institutional investors did.

FIGURE 4.3 Creation of Private-Label Mortgage-Backed Securities

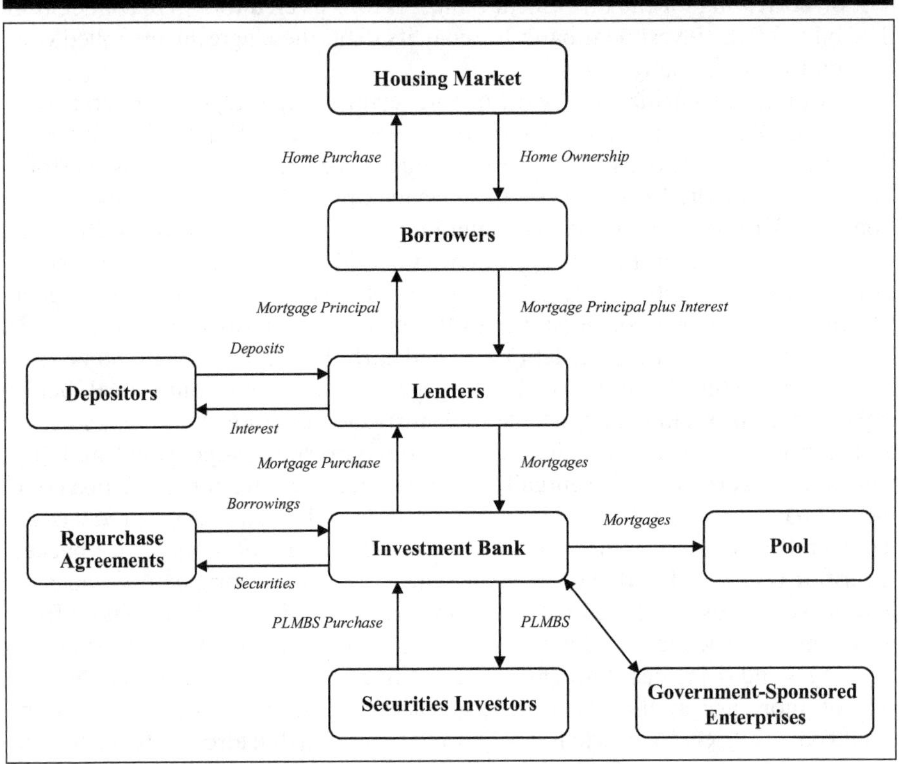

Collateralized Debt Obligations

The deeper question now is: why did institutional investors regard private-label mortgage-backed securities as relatively safe instruments, even without the guarantees and traditional lending standards that underlie agency mortgage-backed securities? Both investment banks and securities investors took actions that mitigated the default risk of private-label mortgage-backed securities. This chapter presents three major strategies—in this and the following two sections respectively—which involved further securitization by investment banks, the credit ratings process of the rating agencies, and the provision of insurance products by insurance companies.

The first action pursued by investment banks themselves involved the creation of yet another class of debt instrument: the collateralized debt obligation. The creation of collateralized debt obligations parallels the creation of private-label mortgage-backed securities. It essentially involves the re-securitization of securities. In this case, using funds acquired through short-term repurchase agreements, an investment bank purchases mortgage-backed and other asset-backed securities, pools them, and sells claims to the income flows from the underlying portfolio. Once again, global securities investors championed this practice as an exemplar of financial innovation and the advantages of unregulated financial markets. Collateralized debt obligations created new opportunities to invest in, and profit from, a diversified portfolio. Since these pools spread the risk of

FIGURE 4.4 Creation of Collateralized Debt Obligations

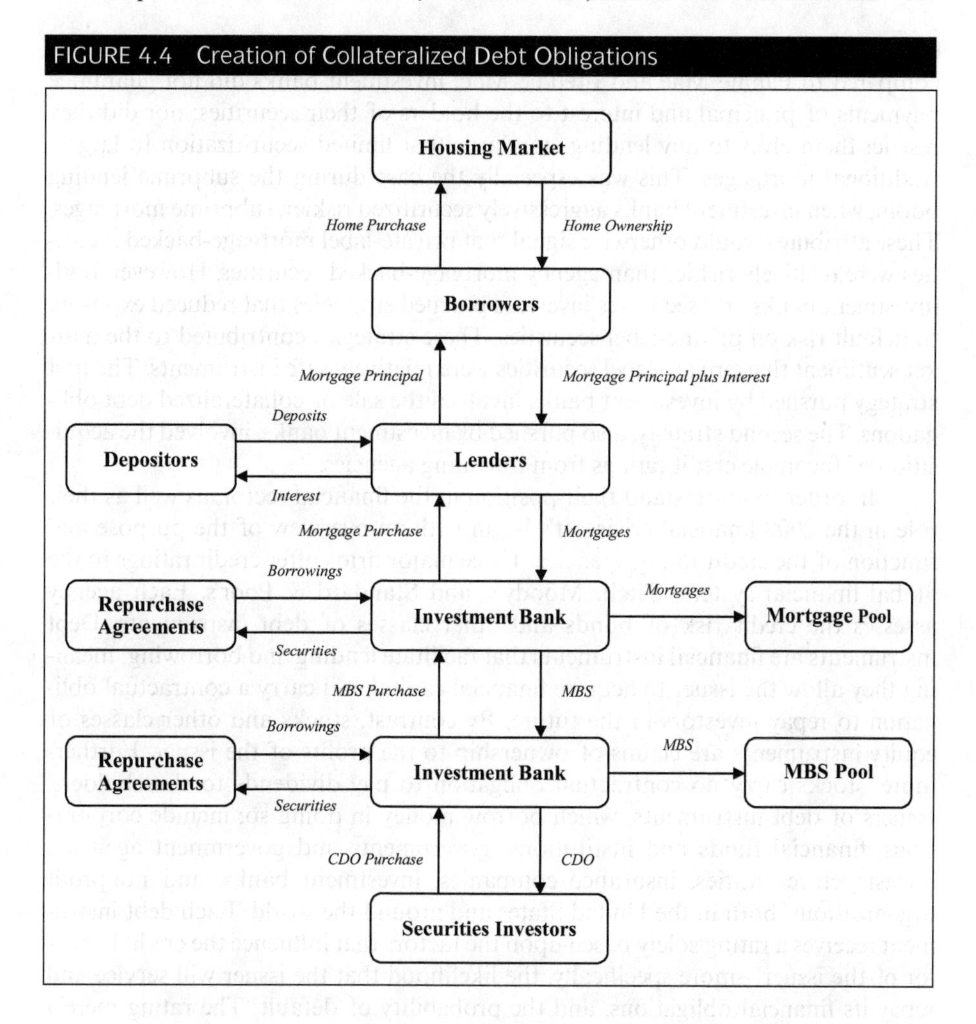

mortgage-backed securities, investors regarded collateralized debt obligations as high-quality financial instruments. The provision of collateralized debt obligations also enhanced liquidity. Wholesale purchases of mortgage-backed securities were a new source of financial capital for other investment banks to purchase more mortgages, lenders to issue more mortgages, and borrowers to purchase more homes. By consequence, they distributed the income flows from mortgage repayments in even more complex ways. Collateralized debt obligations exposed more parties to default risk and housing market volatility in the event that homeowners defaulted on their mortgages, but also in the event that investment banks defaulted on their mortgage-backed securities. Figure 4.4 illustrates this process by building upon the relationships presented in Figure 4.3.

UNDERSTANDING FINANCIAL STRUCTURE PART III: THE CREDIT RATING AGENCIES

The previous section presented some of the key differences in risk attributes between the agency mortgage-backed securities sold by government-sponsored enterprises and the private-label mortgage-backed securities sold by Wall Street. As compared to Fannie Mae and Freddie Mac, investment banks did not guarantee payments of principal and interest to the holders of their securities; nor did they restrict themselves to any lending standards that limited securitization to largely traditional mortgages. This was especially the case during the subprime lending boom, when investment banks aggressively securitized riskier, subprime mortgages. These attributes would otherwise signal that private-label mortgage-backed securities were relatively riskier than agency mortgage-backed securities. However, both investment banks and securities investors pursued strategies that reduced exposure to default risk on private-label securities. These strategies contributed to the market sentiment that private-label securities were relatively safe instruments. The first strategy pursued by investment banks involved the sale of collateralized debt obligations. The second strategy, also pursued by investment banks, involved the acquisition of favorable credit ratings from the rating agencies.

In order to understand their position in the financial sector, as well as their role in the 2008 financial crisis, let's begin with an overview of the purpose and function of the credit rating agencies. Three major firms offer credit ratings to the global financial system: Fitch, Moody's, and Standard & Poor's. Each agency assesses the credit risk of bonds and other classes of debt instruments. Debt instruments are financial instruments that facilitate lending and borrowing, meaning they allow the issuer to acquire financial capital and carry a contractual obligation to repay investors in the future. By contrast, stocks and other classes of equity instruments are claims of ownership to the profits of the issuer. Furthermore, stocks carry no contractual obligation to pay dividends to shareholders. Issuers of debt instruments, which borrow money in doing so, include corporations, financial funds and institutions, governments and government agencies, infrastructure entities, insurance companies, investment banks, and nonprofit organizations, both in the United States and around the world. Each debt instrument receives a rating solely based upon the factors that influence the credit behavior of the issuer—more specifically, the likelihood that the issuer will service and repay its financial obligations, and the probability of default. The rating merely represents the opinion of the agency. It does not represent a recommendation to investors. The purpose is to provide objective, independent information to investors about credit risk and changes in credit risk over time. Credit ratings therefore play a pivotal role in the determination of market interest rates and the allocation of global financial capital.

The agencies assign ratings using scales ranked according to credit risk. Rating scales vary according to the category of debt instrument as well as the term of the investment (e.g., short term, long term). With slight variations, the other rating agencies use similar scales in order to maintain consistency. Ratings at the top of the scale indicate a high likelihood of repayment and low probability of default. "Investment-grade" debt instruments receive these types of ratings, and carry low interest rates for their relative safety. Lower ratings indicate a lower likelihood of repayment and higher probability of default. "Speculative-grade" debt instruments receive these types of ratings, and carry higher interest rates for their higher degree of risk.

The ratings process is not a public service, however. The rating agencies, like their clients, are private firms in that they sell the information service of credit ratings in exchange for fees. Furthermore, the market structure of the credit rating industry features a high degree of concentration with very little competition. The operations of Fitch, Moody's, and Standard and Poor's combined cover the vast majority of the global ratings process. Economists classify this type of market structure, in which a small number of large firms holds significant market power, as an oligopoly. One of the defining characteristics of an oligopoly is mutual interdependence, in which the decisions of one firm influence the decisions of its rivals. According to financial industry advocates, this market environment is necessary in order to maintain a consistent and transparent ratings process that provides objective information to investors—a process that contributes to financial market efficiency and stability. Critics, however, argue that the organization of the industry grants excessive market power to individual agencies. Moreover, that power has intensified over the last few decades with the financialization of global capitalism, the wave of financial consolidation, and the growing reliance on financial markets for financial intermediation.

With regard to their role in the 2008 financial crisis, the credit rating agencies did not directly finance the operations and practices that facilitated the transmission of the crisis. The agencies themselves did not channel funds to investors in residential real estate, mortgages, mortgage-backed securities, or collateralized debt obligations. Rather, critics contend that the business practice and market structure of the credit rating industry created an inherent conflict of interest. The conflict of interest in this case centers on the fact that the issuers of the debt instruments pay fees to the credit rating agencies, in what is essentially a client relationship. Given the very limited number of agencies, and the relatively standardized product of credit risk analytics, an issuer can easily go to another agency in order to obtain a more favorable rating. The mutual interdependence of the industry implies that the potential loss of a client, which itself is typically an enormous firm, would directly benefit a rival agency. The argument is that the nature of the client relationship within this market environment pressured the agencies to assign premium, investment-grade ratings to private-label mortgage-backed securities and collateralized debt obligations, despite their underlying high-risk attributes. That pressure would not otherwise exist in a more competitive industry with a large number of small firms. Individual market shares would be much smaller, and the agencies would have limited market power. The decision by one agency to assign a rating would not directly affect the decision and market share of another agency in a much more dispersed market. At best, this process created a lack of transparency and disseminated misleading information to investors, which contributed to the over-investment in mortgage-related securities—the very outcomes the credit ratings process should have prevented. Figure 4.5 incorporates the position of the rating agencies into the broader pre-crisis financial structure analyzed in this chapter. For simplicity, Figure 4.5 builds on Figure 4.3 by illustrating the effects of the credit ratings process on the sale of mortgage-backed securities, although it certainly applies to the sale of collateralized debt obligations.

FIGURE 4.5 The Credit Ratings Process

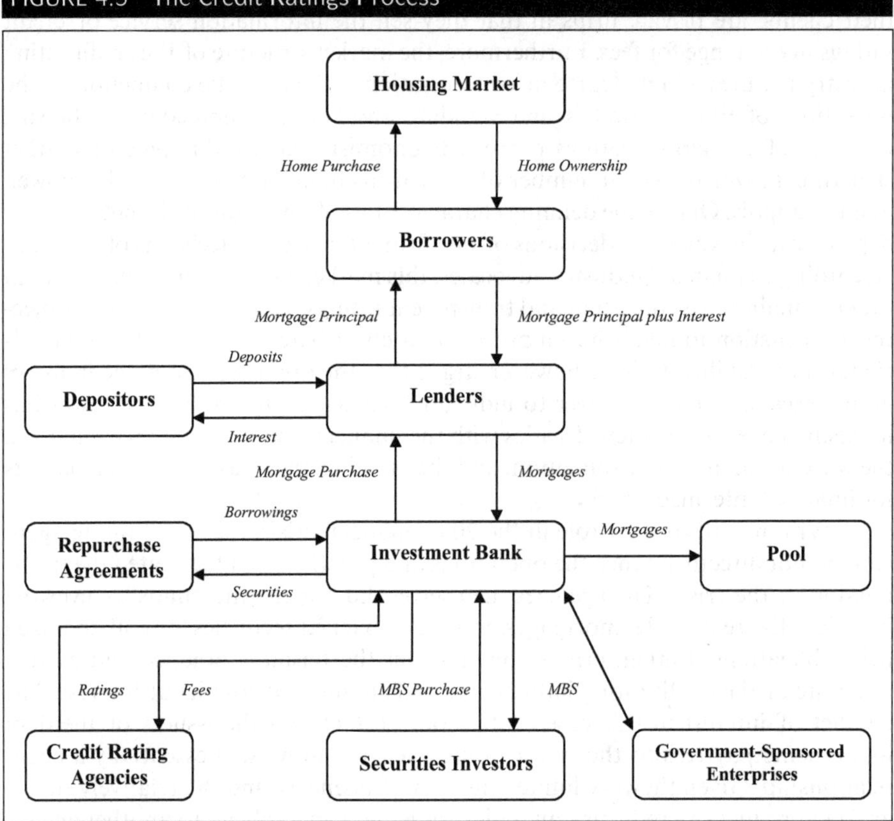

UNDERSTANDING FINANCIAL STRUCTURE PART IV: INSURANCE COMPANIES AND CREDIT DEFAULT SWAPS

The last two sections examined strategies pursued by investment banks in order to reduce exposure to default risk on private-label mortgage-backed securities. The first strategy involved the re-securitization of mortgage-backed securities into collateralized debt obligations. The second strategy involved the procurement of favorable credit ratings from the major rating agencies. This section focuses on a third action taken by securities investors with a similar motive: investment in insurance products known as credit default swaps. These strategies combined transformed private-label mortgage securities from high-risk debt instruments into low-risk debt instruments on par with agency mortgage-backed securities. This section completes the complex model of financial structure prior to the Great Recession, and the mechanisms and relationships that facilitated the transmission of the 2008 financial crisis.

In order to understand the contribution of credit default swaps to the 2008 financial crisis, let's begin with a primer on the general function of insurance contracts within the structure of the financial system, and the evolution of the regulatory environment in insurance. In an insurance contract, an individual or entity pays a premium to an insurer in exchange for financial protection against a loss.

The premium functions as the price of the contract, and reflects the risks of underwriting the policy. The premium accounts for the factors that influence the behavior of the insured and the likelihood of a loss—namely, the probability that the insured will file a claim, and the insurer will have to pay on the policy. Insurers impose higher premiums in cases with a higher degree of risk—that is, a higher probability that the insured will file a claim. Likewise, they impose lower premiums in cases with a lower degree or risk—that is, a lower probability that the insurer will have to pay on the policy.

The regulatory environment in insurance has evolved with the social structure of capital accumulation. In 1956, President Eisenhower signed the Bank Holding Company Act, which separated insurance underwriting from commercial banking activities, among other provisions that dissolved ownership stakes between banks and non-bank firms. Similar to the motives behind the Glass-Steagall Act, the purpose of the Bank Holding Company Act was to separate the risks and activities of commercial banks from insurance companies. For example, the Act prevented the use of the public's deposits to underwrite insurance products. As a result, it prevented the distribution of insurance claims from disrupting access to deposits and the availability of credit. Consistent with the social structure of regulated capitalism, the Act also featured a consumer protection motive. A large conglomerate offering multiple financial services could exercise significant market power by persuading consumers of one service into purchasing others—for example, such a conglomerate could market its insurance products to its banking customers, or vice versa. The argument was that this practice was anti-competitive since it reduced competitive pressures between conglomerates. The Act therefore limited market power and enhanced competition by limiting cross-marketing strategies that incentivized the creation of larger, and more complex, financial firms. In 1999, President Clinton signed the Gramm-Leach-Bliley Act, which eliminated regulatory barriers between commercial banks, investment banks, and insurance underwriters, and permitted the creation of financial holding companies. The social structure of neoliberal capitalism, which celebrated deregulation, facilitated new financial relationships and contracts between not only commercial banking and insurance, but also insurance and investment banking. The credit default swap is a prime example of the latter.

A credit default swap is a contract that provides insurance against the credit risk of debt instruments like mortgage-backed securities and collateralized debt obligations. In a credit default swap, a securities investor—the holder or owner of mortgage-related debt instruments—pays an insurer for protection against default by the issuer of the instruments. In simple terms, the securities investor "swaps" the risk of default with the insurer. Similar to other insurance contracts, the price of a credit default swap therefore operates as the premium and should reflect the risks to the insurer of underwriting the contract. The price should account for the factors that contribute to the probability of default by the securities issuer, would trigger a claim by the securities investor, and would therefore require payment by the insurer. Those factors include any circumstances that would diminish, or create volatility in, the value of the many layers of underlying assets that back mortgage-related securities. One of the important characteristics of credit default swaps is that they are traded in over-the-counter (OTC) markets. In an OTC market, participants trade directly with each other—that is, without the structure and

FIGURE 4.6 The Provision of Credit Default Swaps

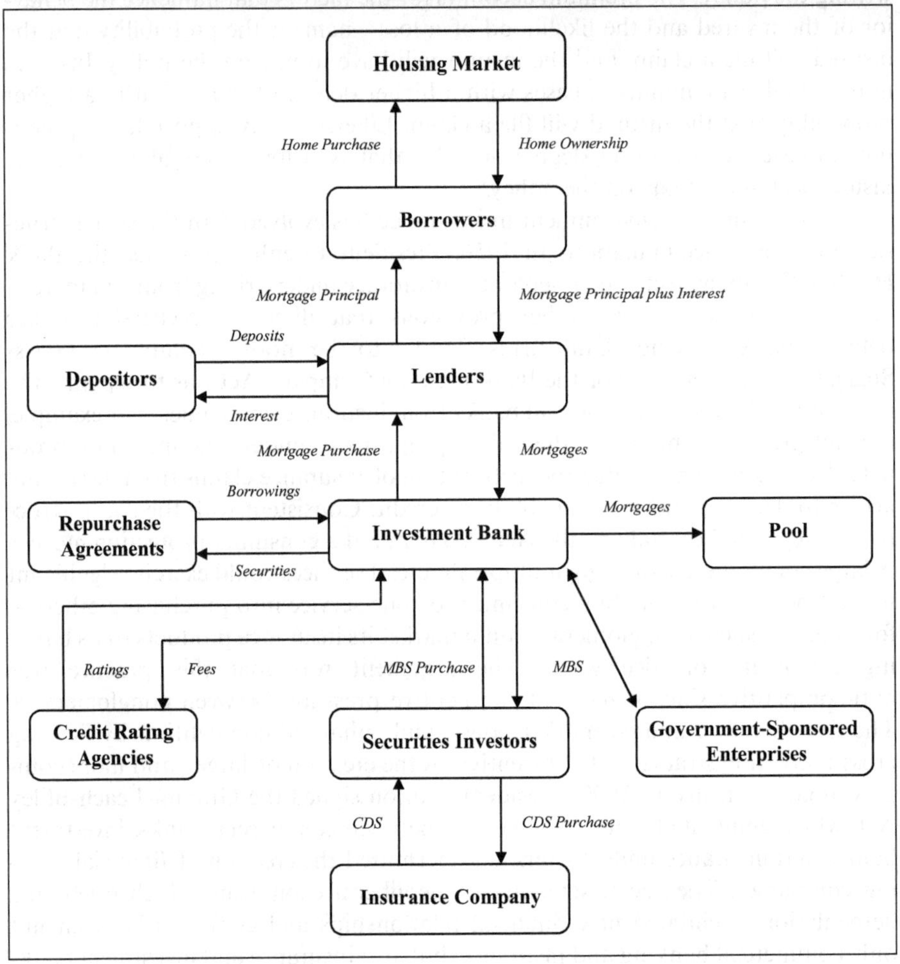

Housing Market
Home Purchase
Home Ownership
Borrowers
Mortgage Principal
Mortgage Principal plus Interest
Deposits
Depositors
Lenders
Interest
Mortgage Purchase
Mortgages
Borrowings
Repurchase Agreements
Investment Bank
Mortgages
Pool
Securities
Ratings
Fees
MBS Purchase
MBS
Credit Rating Agencies
Securities Investors
Government-Sponsored Enterprises
CDS
CDS Purchase
Insurance Company

organization of a formal exchange. Prior to the 2008 financial crisis, there was little to no regulatory oversight of these markets. However, there was also a lack of transparency within the financial sector, since other market participants could not readily observe the terms of these exchanges, such as the price and volume of trading. Figure 4.6 incorporates credit default swaps into the schematic of pre-crisis financial structure. Once again, for simplicity, Figure 4.6 builds on Figure 4.3 by illustrating the relationship between credit default swaps and mortgage-backed securities, although it certainly applies to collateralized debt obligations.

Like all financial contracts, credit default swaps carry a degree of risk, as there is some probability of default by the issuers of mortgage-related securities. Furthermore, like all of the financial contracts examined in this chapter, insurers regarded credit default swaps as high-quality, low-risk contracts on account of the high-quality, low-risk assets that backed the securities. Insurers perceived the probability of a claim by a securities investor—and indeed the probability of a systemic crisis that would require a massive payout by insurers—as low. Several longstanding conventions about the housing market, the mortgage market, the securitization process, and the credit ratings process informed this sentiment. Prior to the 2008 financial crisis, insurers assumed that:

- mortgage lenders maintained prudent lending standards;
- real home values were stable;
- homeowners always paid their mortgages;
- lenders could easily offload mortgages in the secondary market;
- government-sponsored enterprises had ample access to liquidity through the bond market;
- investment banks mitigated the default risk of mortgages by securitizing them, and selling mortgage-backed securities;
- investment banks mitigated the default risk of mortgage-backed securities by securitizing them, and selling collateralized debt obligations;
- investment banks had ample access to liquidity through repurchase agreements; and
- credit rating agencies disseminated objective assessments that private-label securities were low-risk financial instruments, meaning that investment banks would therefore make payments on mortgage-backed securities and collateralized debt obligations.

All of these conventions informed the sentiment that credit default swaps were low-risk contracts, but none were as important as the first two assumptions. For much of the postwar era, these were essentially stylized facts: the most common home financing product was a traditional mortgage, and real housing prices were indeed stable. During the 1990s and 2000s, however, the share of high-risk, subprime mortgage originations increased, and the housing market experienced an unprecedented speculative bubble. The heightened risk of mortgage lending and residential real estate consequently intensified the risk of all financial contracts, relationships, and securities derived from them—including credit default swaps. The problem is that these circumstances created yet another disconnect in the financial system between the price of a financial contract and its risk. Credit default swaps did not fully specify the probability that securities investors would have to file a massive scale of claims. Insurers priced credit default swaps as if mortgage-related securities carried a low risk of default, when in fact they carried a very high risk of default.

Yet another attribute elevated the risk of credit default swaps. Although insurers marketed credit default swaps as insurance contracts, they were actually financial instruments—just like the securities they insured—in order to avoid capital requirements, reserve requirements, and other government regulations. This means that they could be bought and sold in opaque, unregulated over-the-counter markets—in many cases, to investors that did not actually hold mortgage-related securities. It also means that credit default swaps were subject to speculative bubbles, just like the securities that they insured.

THE TRANSMISSION OF THE 2008 FINANCIAL CRISIS

Put simply: how, and why, did all of this go wrong? The model presented in this chapter incorporates five elements of financial structure related to residential real estate and home financing: the origination and repayment of residential mortgages; the underwriting and sale of agency mortgage-backed securities by government-sponsored enterprises; the underwriting and sale of private-label mortgage securities by Wall Street investment banks; the distribution of credit ratings by the rating agencies; and the provision of credit default swaps by insurance companies. What is more, this chapter has explored the evolution of the financial contracts, relationships, and securities related to home ownership and mortgage lending over time. This section carefully investigates the rapid deterioration of financial relationships in this context, and the transformation of mortgage-related securities and insurance contracts into "toxic assets." This analysis sets the stage for understanding the spillover of the 2008 financial crisis into an economic crisis, and the conduct of the Wall Street bailouts.

The financial structure that facilitated the transmission of the 2008 financial crisis evolved with the restructuring of capitalist production during the 1970s and 1980s. The transition to neoliberalism and the increasing financialization of capitalism led to a transformation in financial relationships, and especially financial behavior, that culminated in a subprime mortgage lending boom and speculative housing market bubble during the late 1990s and early 2000s. The collapse of the housing bubble in 2006 exposed the extent of systemic risk and the complex interdependent relationships that brought about a financial meltdown. This presentation differs greatly from neoclassical explanations, which apply the same model of economic structure and behavior to all economic interactions and financial transactions.

Let's first review the institutional context of home ownership and mortgage lending during the regulated stage of capitalism. In the aftermath of the Great Depression, federal interventions expanded the availability of the traditional mortgage loan in order to stabilize and expand wealth. The 30-year, fixed-rate mortgage allowed former owners to recover homes lost during a devastating foreclosure crisis, and borrowers to actually pay off their debt. The postwar expansion of wealth through home ownership was part of a larger strategy to stabilize household consumption and aggregate demand in order to reach full employment.

Mortgage lenders, on the other hand, faced significant restructuring, regulation, and oversight. Federal interventions separated and actively regulated commercial banking, investment banking, and insurance. These regulatory barriers insulated mortgage lending and home ownership from both financial market volatility and insurance underwriting. Risk-averse residential mortgage lenders maintained stringent lending standards during this period, which systematically excluded low-income and minority borrowers, for several reasons. First, the long-term nature of traditional mortgages exposed lenders to default risk. Second, traditional mortgages were relatively illiquid. Aside from Fannie Mae, there was a limited secondary market in which to sell issued mortgages. Deposits were therefore the primary source of funds with which commercial banks and savings and loan institutions created mortgages. Third, lenders incurred significant information expenses in determining the creditworthiness of mortgage borrowers. All of these policies and lending practices operated in an institutional environment of stable home-ownership rates, as well as stable real housing prices, following World War II.

The neoliberal stage of US capitalism, however, featured a larger strategy that prioritized corporate wealth and deregulation. For mortgage lenders, the crisis of the 1970s heightened default risk and plummeted real interest rates on traditional home loans. Securitization of traditional mortgages by government-sponsored enterprises, and later private investment banks, arose as a strategy to mitigate default risk and enhance liquidity in mortgage lending. Securitization elevated the importance of financial markets as sources of capital over financial institutions, and transmitted the income flows from housing markets and mortgage markets to multiple entities throughout the financial sector. Although homeowners theoretically benefited from mortgage securitization, it was of secondary importance (at best) to securing maximum financial profits. Greater competition between different sources of financial capital in a deregulated environment led to more risk-taking, and more debt.

For mortgage borrowers, however, the restructuring of capitalism led to lower real wages and higher debt burdens, which heightened their credit risk. Restricting access to traditional mortgages would have restricted the availability of mortgage-backed securities to investors. The immense demand for mortgage-backed securities from a much more complex financial system—which now integrated commercial banking, investment banking, and insurance—therefore led to an increase in riskier, subprime mortgage originations. As Fannie Mae and Freddie Mac continued to securitize traditional mortgages, Wall Street investment banks increasingly securitized subprime mortgage loans. However, broker incentives for subprime loans contributed to predatory lending practices that disproportionately affected minority homeowners, many of whom qualified for traditional mortgages. The re-securitization of mortgage-backed securities into collateralized debt obligations by investment banks, problematic ratings from the credit rating agencies, and the sale of credit default swaps by insurance companies transformed private-label mortgage securities into high-quality, low-risk investments. Beginning in the late 1990s, a tidal wave of new lines of credit resulted in a spike in home ownership rates and a speculative bubble that pushed real housing prices to unprecedented highs across the United States.

By the time of the US housing market bubble, the financial structure presented in Figure 4.6 was firmly in place. The housing market exhibited all of the classic behavioral characteristics of a speculative bubble. It instilled a belief in buyers and sellers that home values would rise without correction. Housing market participants exhibited herd behavior by basing their real estate decisions on the choices of others, and not on the potential risks to their individual wellbeing. The rapid home price appreciation created a bandwagon mentality, market euphoria, and a sense of optimism that superseded the underlying determinants of supply and demand. Both home buyers and home sellers displayed confirmation bias by disregarding information that suggested an extreme overvaluation of residential real estate was present. Home ownership was no longer a long-run productive investment that expanded wealth; instead, owners pursued short-run gains financed by a growing amount of riskier debt.

Throughout the financial structure developed in this chapter, the housing market bubble led private financial actors—ranging from homeowners to mortgage lenders, investment banks, insurance companies, and securities investors—to understate the degree of risk in subprime mortgage lending and securitization. Homeowners, especially those with subprime loans, believed that the home price appreciation protected them against default. Wall Street believed that the complex interconnectedness of the financial sector itself limited systemic risk—the risk that the failure of one entity to repay its financial obligations would destabilize the financial sector and the performance of the economic system. The logic was as follows:

- Homeowners could simply refinance or sell their homes if they were unable to pay their mortgages.
- Mortgage lenders could easily offload and sell issued mortgages in the secondary market, even if there was an increase in default risk.
- Investment banks could then securitize mortgages, and even re-securitize mortgage-backed securities, in order to reduce exposure to any heightened default risk.
- Insurance companies could sell credit default swaps as additional protection against potential losses.
- Given the vast global market for mortgage-related securities, securities investors could simply sell their holdings if negative expectations took hold. For similar reasons, they could even sell credit default swaps to other investors.

The problem was that all of these private actors were unaware of, lacked the capacity to understand, or simply disregarded the scale of subprime mortgage originations and securitization, and the overvaluation of housing. If residential real estate and subprime mortgages were riskier, then so too were all financial contracts derived from them. It is hard to understate this point based upon public remarks by policymakers and stakeholders on Wall Street. For example, in 2006, Moody's maintained that: "AIG will remain a leader in worldwide insurance and financial services." As the subprime meltdown unfolded in 2007, then-Chairman Ben Bernanke stated:

> We believe the effect of the troubles in the subprime sector on the broader housing market will likely be limited, and we do not expect significant spillovers from the subprime market to the rest of the economy or to the financial system.

Less than one year later, as financial institutions began to fail, US Treasury Secretary Hank Paulson stated: "Our financial institutions, our banks and investments banks are very strong, and I'm convinced that they're going to come out of this situation very strong."

Even in March 2008, Lehman Brothers received a vote of confidence from Moody's:

> Lehman has navigated quite well to date through persistently volatile and challenging financial markets, the sharp market-wide decline in valuations across numerous asset classes, tight global liquidity conditions, and the strong head winds facing Lehman's (and other securities firms') core-earnings drivers.

The precipitous collapse of home prices beginning in the summer of 2006 laid bare the extent of systemic risk, and initiated a wave of default and financial contagion across the system:

- Homeowners were unable to refinance or sell, since the outstanding balances on their loans far exceeded current market values. Homeowners with adjustable-rate mortgages faced significantly higher monthly payments after the initial term due to higher benchmark interest rates.
- A groundswell of mortgage defaults and foreclosures followed, many of which were voluntary, disrupting the widely held convention that mortgage borrowers always paid their mortgages.
- Consequently, lenders lost money on mortgages held in their portfolios, and could no longer offload mortgages in the secondary market.
- Given the widespread practice of mortgage securitization, private investment banks held subprime mortgages as collateral for their securities. The mortgage default crisis meant that they lost money on mortgages held in their pools, and defaulted on payments of principal and interest owed to private-label securities investors.
- Creditors quickly lost faith in their ability to mitigate mortgage default risk through securitization, regardless of the degree of their exposure to subprime mortgages. Insolvency ensued when investment banks could no longer borrow money through overnight repurchase agreements.
- Default by investment banks on mortgage-backed securities and collateralized debt obligations led to a sharp loss of net worth for securities investors around the world. Central banks, commercial banks, endowments, hedge funds, insurance companies, mutual funds, and pension funds all saw the value of their investment portfolios collapse.
- Fannie Mae and Freddie Mac lost money on mortgages held or guaranteed, and defaulted on payments to investors in agency mortgage-backed securities. Although they did not guarantee or securitize subprime mortgages, defaults on traditional mortgages rose with higher unemployment during the crisis. The principal issue that led to the collapse of Fannie and Freddie was, like other large institutional investors, their extensive investments in private-label mortgage securities, which were now in default.
- Creditors lost faith in their ability to fulfill either of their charges—that is, mortgage purchases and sales of agency mortgage-backed securities—due to rising uncertainty. Insolvency followed when Fannie Mae and Freddie Mac could no longer borrow money through the short-term bond market.
- Contagion, widespread uncertainty, and a crisis of confidence led to a credit freeze within the commercial banking system as well as runs on money market mutual funds. The credit freeze halted not only inter-bank lending, but also lending to the private sector. Borrowers, even those who were creditworthy, were unable to secure financing for consumption and investment.
- One of the most alarming consequences of the credit freeze was the seizure of commercial paper trading. Commercial paper is a short-term debt instrument used by corporations to make payroll and finance other short-term liabilities. A complete shutdown of the commercial paper market would have prevented

many non-financial corporations from making payroll and brought untold devastation to the broader economic system.

- Finally, insurance companies were unable to pay a massive scale of claims to holders of credit default swaps due to widespread defaults on mortgages and mortgage-related securities. Additionally, insurance companies were unable to acquire new loans due to the credit freeze. As traded securities themselves, the market value of credit default swaps collapsed across global financial markets.

THE TRANSMISSION OF THE ECONOMIC CRISIS

The transmission of the 2008 financial crisis extended well beyond Wall Street and the global financial system. Just as the pre-crisis financial structure evolved from changes in the structure of economic production, so too did financial instability develop into widespread economic instability. The interconnectedness of the financial sector and the real sector meant that the financial meltdown precipitated an economic crisis unseen in generations. The prime example of this relationship, of course, was the bankruptcy of the US auto industry. The "real sector" refers to the activities and processes pertaining to the production of goods and services. Those activities include investment in capital goods, infrastructure, and raw materials; employment of human labor; production of economic output; distribution of incomes; consumption of output; and the determination of prices. This section therefore investigates two critical questions: what were the transmission mechanisms that spread the financial crisis to the real sector? And how did the transmission of the economic crisis culminate in severe macroeconomic imbalances, such as a deep recession, high unemployment and deflation? In order to answer these questions, this section examines some of the principal measures of US economic activity maintained by the Bureau of Economic Analysis, the Bureau of Labor Statistics and the Census Bureau.

With regard to the first question, the 2008 financial crisis caused a massive reduction in both consumption and investment. As presented in Chapter 2, the US private sector has claimed an increasing share of US output during the neoliberal era, largely financed by an increasing amount of debt. A particularly large increase occurred during the 2001–07 recovery. During the 1982–90, 1991–2001 and 2001–07 recoveries respectively, consumption and investment combined grew from 81.3%, to 82.6%, and finally 85.8% of gross domestic product (GDP). Let's examine the contraction in each sector, and its respective linkage to the financial meltdown.

Figure 4.7 presents the growth rate of real personal consumption expenditures between the first quarter of 2002 (the beginning of the 2001–07 expansion) and the fourth quarter of 2010. Real personal consumption expenditures refer to inflation-adjusted spending on goods and services by individuals. The vertical reference line at the fourth quarter of 2007 marks the official peak of the 2001–07 expansion; while the reference line at the second quarter of 2009 marks the official trough of the Great Recession. The figure reports the compounded annual rate of change—that is, what the annual growth rate would be if the quarterly growth rate continued for a full year. As is the case during most economic expansions, consumption was stable prior to the Great Recession. Quarterly growth rates during

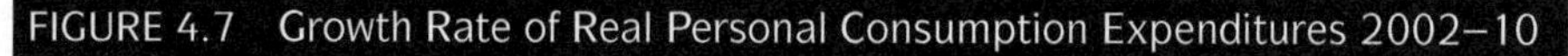

FIGURE 4.7 Growth Rate of Real Personal Consumption Expenditures 2002–10

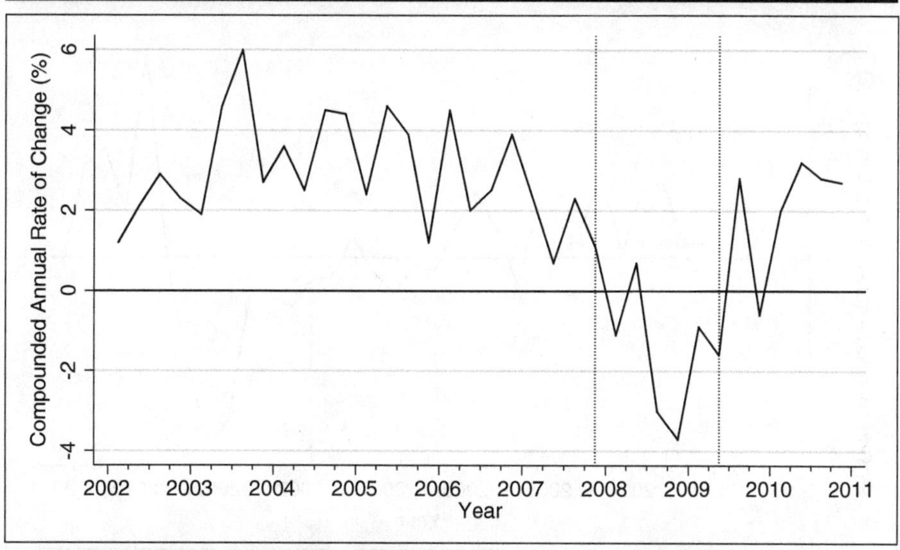

Units—compounded annual rate of change | Seasonally adjusted annual rate | Quarterly.
Source: Federal Reserve Bank of St. Louis FRED economic data (https://fred.stlouisfed.org).

the 2001–07 expansion ranged between 2% and 4%. However, the data show multiple contractions of consumption throughout 2008 and 2009, the largest of which occurred during the fourth quarter of 2008, at 3.7%. Considering that consumption itself constitutes two-thirds of US output, the reversal in consumer spending represented an enormous shock to the real sector.

Several factors contributed to the cutback in consumption. First, the bursting of the housing market bubble led to a collapse in wealth. The collapse in home values had both material and psychological effects on consumption. Millions of homeowners—a substantial proportion of whom had either bought or refinanced homes during the bubble—lost properties to foreclosure. Even for those who did not, US homeowners could no longer borrow against home equity, which they had used to finance other consumer expenditures (e.g., on cars, education, and travel), but especially to manage other debts (e.g., credit cards, student loans and home equity lines of credit). A period of deleveraging followed, whereby homeowners began paying down debt and reducing spending on new goods and services. Just as important, however, was the psychological effect of the housing market bust. Given that housing is the primary financial asset that most working-class and middle-class households own, the loss of net worth hindered consumer spending simply by damaging confidence. A second wealth effect resulted from the collapse in the value of mortgage-backed securities. Like other investors, workers had significant holdings of mortgage-backed securities in investment portfolios, especially 401(k) retirement plans. Since the early 1990s, private-sector retirement benefits had shifted away from employer-funded pensions and toward employee-funded, defined contribution plans. Workers increasingly relied upon the performance of riskier investment portfolios—not guaranteed retirement benefits—to supplement Social Security, which itself continued to face calls for reform and privatization.

FIGURE 4.8 Growth Rate of Real Gross Private Domestic Investment 2002–10

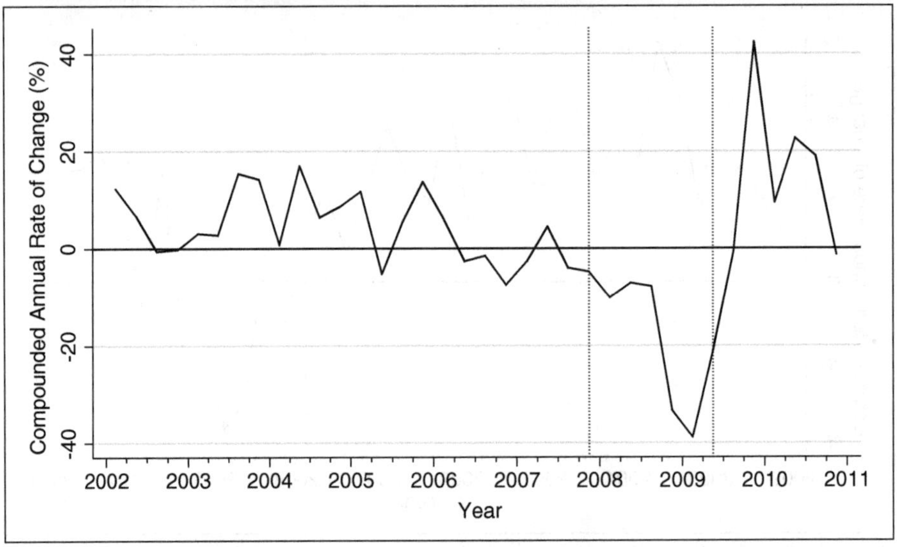

Units—compounded annual rate of change | Seasonally adjusted annual rate | Quarterly.
Source: Federal Reserve Bank of St. Louis FRED economic data (https://fred.stlouisfed.org).

Losses in mortgage-backed securities not only devastated retirement security but also confidence as workers saw years' worth of savings disappear during the 2008 financial crisis.

Figure 4.8 presents the growth rate of real gross private domestic investment, the second component of private-sector spending on US output. Real gross private domestic investment includes inflation-adjusted expenditures on computer software, equipment, and structures, as well as changes in inventories, primarily by private enterprises. Although investment constitutes a smaller share of GDP as compared to consumption—less than 20% on average—it is much more volatile. Unlike consumption, investment experiences wider swings even during economic expansions. Note the difference in the scales of the y-axes between Figures 4.7 and 4.8. Whereas the growth rate of consumption oscillated between 2% and 4% throughout the 2001–07 expansion, the growth rate of investment ranged between -5% and 15%. After the second quarter of 2007, investment contracted until the fourth quarter of 2009. At the height of the Great Recession, investment dropped by an astounding 38% during the first quarter of 2009.

Two mechanisms led to the falloff in investment. The first was a significant increase in uncertainty. Uncertainty surrounding the extent of the financial meltdown, as well as the reversal in consumer sentiment, fueled negative expectations of the future direction of the economic system and the ability to earn profit. Capitalists therefore canceled or postponed plans for new investments in capital goods and technology for their production processes. The second factor was an enormous drop in real residential investment during the housing market bust, as detailed in Figure 4.9. Private residential fixed investment includes new construction of, as well as improvements to, single-family and multi-family residential structures. The data shows multiple expansions of the residential capital stock

FIGURE 4.9 Growth Rate of Real Private Residential Fixed Investment 2002–10

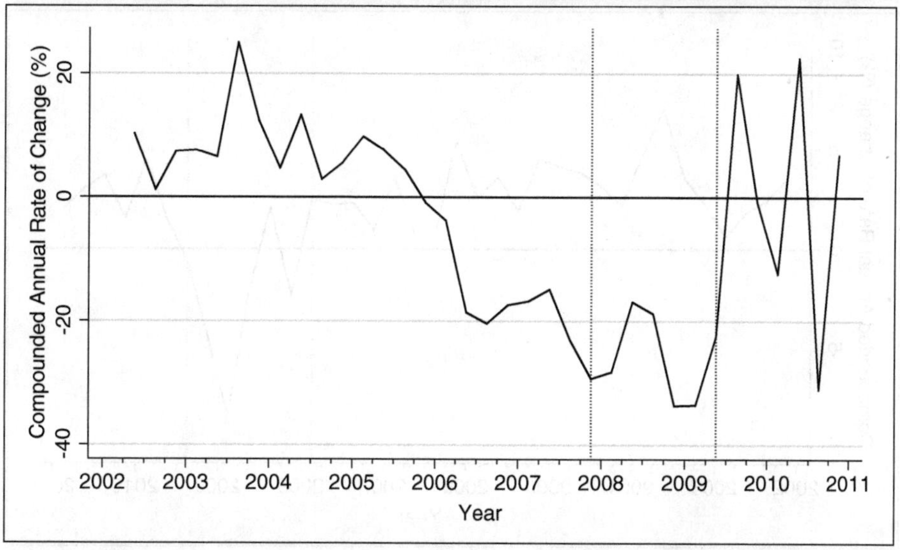

Units—compounded annual rate of change | Seasonally adjusted annual rate | Quarterly.
Source: Federal Reserve Bank of St. Louis FRED economic data (https://fred.stlouisfed.org).

between 2002 and 2005. Note that the largest quarterly growth rate occurred during the third quarter of 2003, which coincides with the largest quarterly increase in consumption during the 2001–07 expansion. However, residential investment began to decrease during the fourth quarter of 2005. Sharp reductions then followed in 2006, 2007, and 2008.

Let's now examine the macroeconomic imbalances that occurred during the Great Recession using the standard performance measures of the US business cycle. First, the extreme shortfall in private-sector expenditures on goods and services, which together constituted over 85% of US economic activity, resulted in severe cutbacks in production as measured by real GDP. According to Figure 4.10, quarterly growth rates of real GDP ranged between 2% and 5% between 2002 and 2005. Note again that the largest quarterly growth rate in output occurred during the third quarter of 2003, coinciding with peaks in both consumption and residential investment. The data then show weaker growth beginning in 2006, followed by negative growth during 2008 and 2009. At the height of the Great Recession, US output contracted by 8.4% during the fourth quarter of 2008.

Second, cutbacks in production led to a massive increase in layoffs. Figure 4.11 presents the rate of unemployment—the number of unemployed individuals relative to the labor force. After reaching a low of 4.4% during the fourth quarter of 2006, the national unemployment rate more than doubled to 9.3% by the second quarter of 2009. However, the unemployment rate does not fully capture the dire labor market situation faced by US workers, both before and during the crisis. For example, Figure 4.12 presents the growth rate of total employment. The sharp reduction in the number of employed workers during the Great Recession is quite clear. The problem is that the jobless recovery limited the degree of substantive employment growth during the 2001–07 expansion. Employment only began

FIGURE 4.10 Growth Rate of Real Gross Domestic Product 2002–10

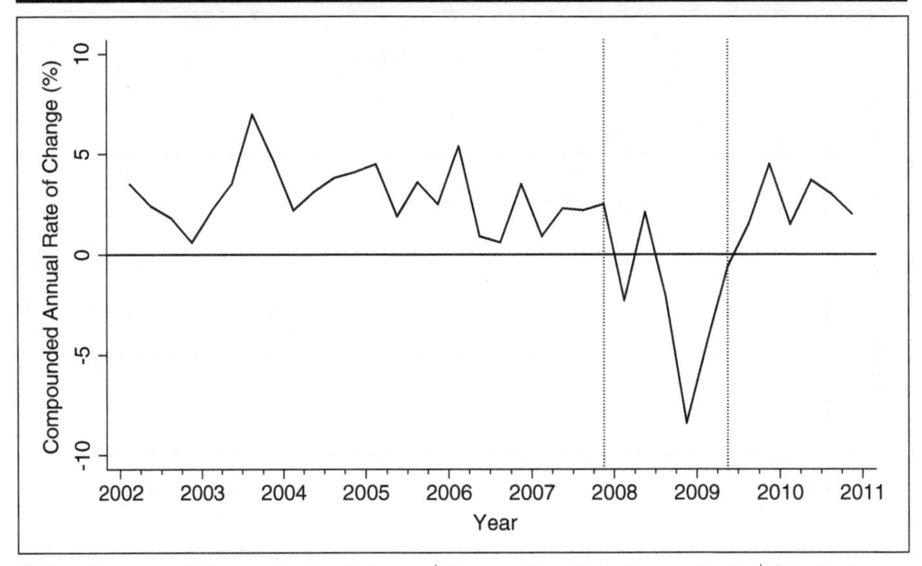

Units—Compounded annual rate of change | Seasonally adjusted annual rate | Quarterly.
Source: Federal Reserve Bank of St. Louis FRED economic data (https://fred.stlouisfed.org).

FIGURE 4.11 Rate of Unemployment 2002–10

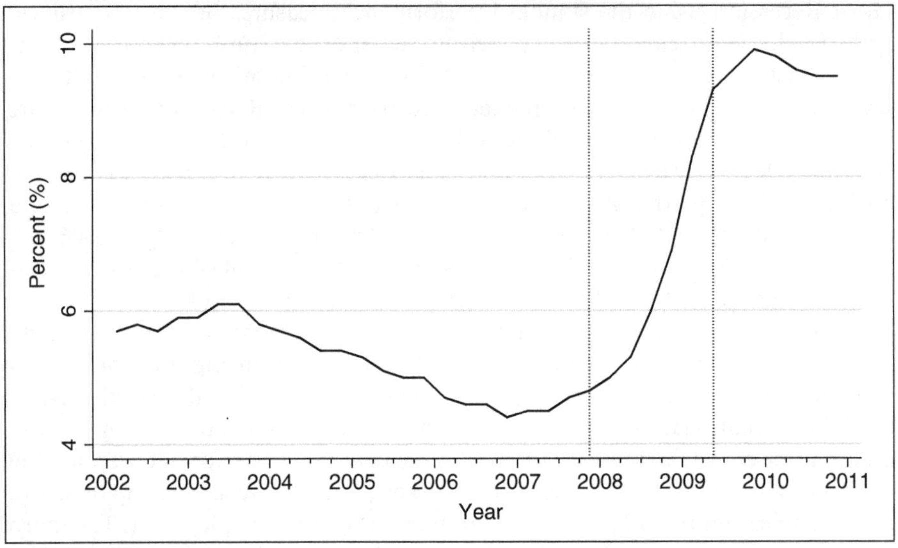

Units—Percent | Seasonally adjusted | Quarterly average.
Source: Federal Reserve Bank of St. Louis FRED economic data (https://fred.stlouisfed.org).

FIGURE 4.12 Growth Rate of Total Non-Farm Payroll Employment 2002–10

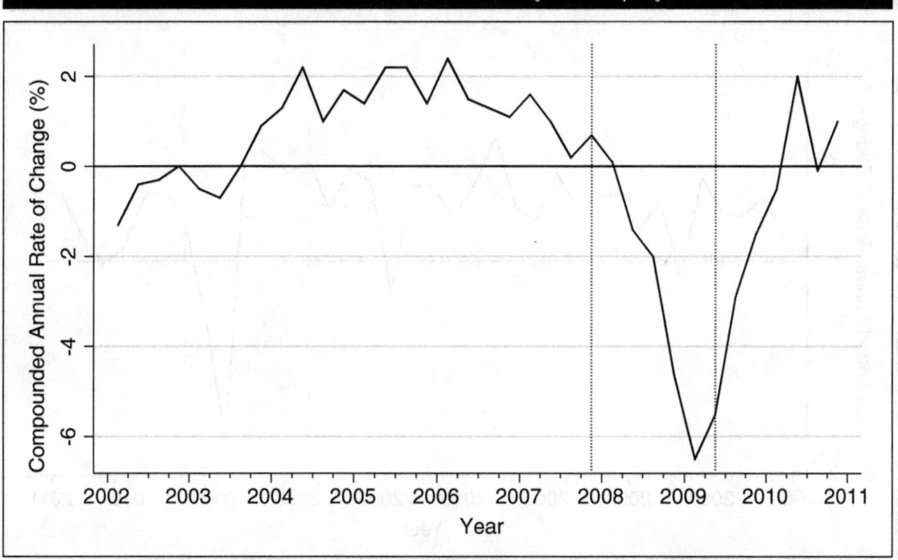

Units—Compounded annual rate of change | Seasonally adjusted annual rate | Quarterly average.

Source: Federal Reserve Bank of St. Louis FRED economic data (https://fred.stlouisfed.org).

FIGURE 4.13 Growth Rate of Real Median Household Income 2002–10

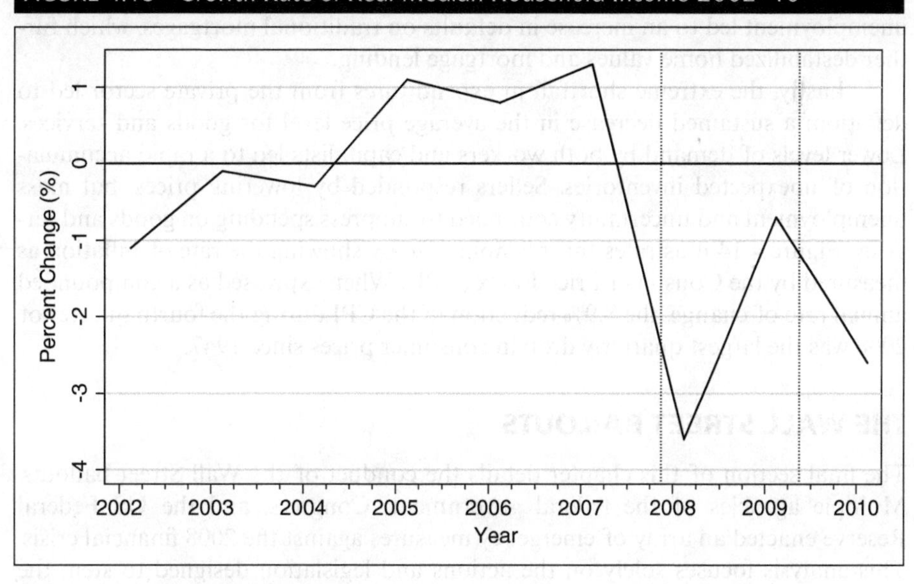

increasing during the fourth quarter of 2003 and peaked during the first quarter of 2006. Figure 4.13 shows a similar trend for the growth rate of real median household income. After shrinking between 2002 and 2004, the annual percent change in real median household income averaged a meager 1% between 2005 and 2007. These reductions in employment and income further suppressed

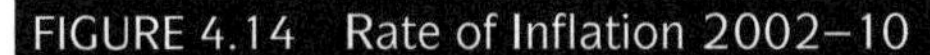

FIGURE 4.14 Rate of Inflation 2002–10

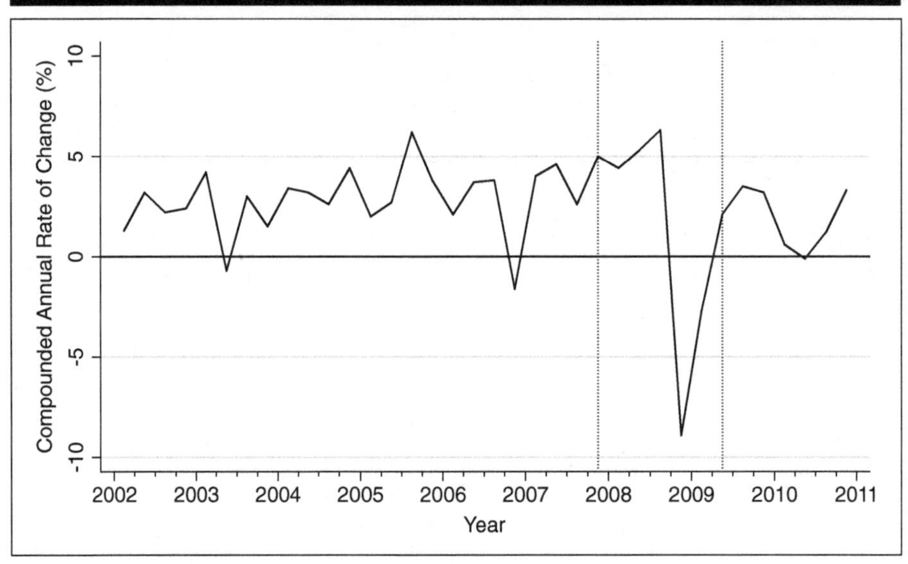

Units—compounded annual rate of change | Seasonally adjusted annual rate | Quarterly average.

Source: Federal Reserve Bank of St. Louis FRED economic data (https://fred.stlouisfed.org).

consumption, and thereby production of goods and services. In addition, higher unemployment led to an increase in defaults on traditional mortgages, which further destabilized home values and mortgage lending.

Lastly, the extreme shortfall in expenditures from the private sector led to deflation: a sustained decrease in the average price level for goods and services. Lower levels of demand by both workers and capitalists led to a rapid accumulation of unexpected inventories. Sellers responded by lowering prices, but mass unemployment and uncertainty continued to suppress spending on goods and services. Figure 4.14 illustrates this phenomenon by showing the rate of inflation as measured by the Consumer Price Index (CPI). When expressed as a compounded annual rate of change, the 8.9% reduction in the CPI during the fourth quarter of 2008 was the largest quarterly drop in consumer prices since 1947.

THE WALL STREET BAILOUTS

The final section of this chapter details the conduct of the Wall Street bailouts. Multiple agencies of the federal government, Congress, and the US Federal Reserve enacted an array of emergency measures against the 2008 financial crisis. This analysis focuses solely on the actions and legislation designed to stem the contagion and crisis of confidence within the financial sector. Part III of this textbook will then focus on measures largely taken after the financial crisis, such as financial reform, the traditional and non-traditional tools of monetary policy deployed against both the financial crisis and the economic crisis, and the fiscal policies enacted to combat the economic crisis.

TABLE 4.1 Summary of the Wall Street Bailouts

March 2008	Bear Stearns - Arranged merger with JPMorgan Chase
September 2008	Fannie Mae and Freddie Mac - Nationalization by the US Treasury Department
	Lehman Brothers - Bankruptcy due to failed arranged merger
	American International Group - Nationalization by the US Federal Reserve
October 2008	Congress passes the Emergency Economic Stabilization Act:
	Troubled Asset Relief Program (TARP) - Federal government purchases mortgage-related securities
	Capital injections - Federal government becomes a major shareholder in largest banks
	Federal Deposit Insurance Corporation (FDIC) raises limit on deposit insurance coverage
	FDIC guarantees bank debt
November 2008	Supplemental rescue package for Citigroup
January 2009	Supplemental rescue package for Bank of America

The conduct of the Wall Street bailouts essentially mirrors the financial structure and transmission of the 2008 financial crisis presented in this chapter. An unyielding collapse of confidence spread across the financial system—from housing markets to mortgage markets, investment banks, financial markets, government-sponsored enterprises, commercial banks, and insurance companies—revealing a high degree of systemic risk and, most importantly, cutting off liquidity. The inability of the government to resolve the unfolding financial crisis through individual rescue packages—due in large part to a lack of understanding about the interdependent financial relationships throughout Wall Street—eventually led to the enactment of an industry-wide bailout. The federal government's response in this case differed greatly from its response to homeowners and the foreclosure crisis. In the years that followed, both Democrats and Republicans seized upon popular animosity toward the conduct of the bailouts, resulting in an ideological realignment within both major political parties on the role of government. The remainder of this section discusses each action in roughly chronological order. Table 4.1 presents a brief summary of these actions taken during 2008 and 2009.

Bear Stearns

Bear Stearns was a private investment bank that engaged heavily in mortgage securitization, especially securitization of subprime loans. By March 2008, higher default rates on subprime mortgages, falling housing prices, and weaker economic growth fueled speculation that Bear was losing money on the assets held in its portfolios and would soon default on its securities. Fearful that it would be unable to service its extensive financial obligations, creditors ceased lending to Bear through short-term repurchase agreements. The result was what investors feared: Bear's insolvency. In response, the New York Federal Reserve Bank arranged a merger with JPMorgan Chase in what constituted an indirect bailout.

The problem was not necessarily the size of Bear's financial dealings; in fact, it was relatively smaller than the institutions that subsequently collapsed during the crisis. Regulators feared that the rapid drop in confidence and disintegration of liquidity, which brought down one of Wall Street's oldest firms, would spread to larger institutions. As an investment bank, Bear Stearns was not a member of the Federal Reserve system, which meant the Federal Reserve could not lend directly to Bear. The New York Federal Reserve Bank therefore lent money to JPMorgan Chase, with loan guarantees from the US Treasury Department, in order to purchase Bear Stearns.

Fannie Mae and Freddie Mac

Nevertheless, the Bear Stearns bailout did not stem the tide of uncertainty moving through the financial system. Congress passed the Housing and Economic Recovery Act during the summer of 2008, which authorized capital injections—direct infusions of cash—into Fannie Mae and Freddie Mac. By September, however, questions surrounding their solvency centered on two issues. First, the accelerating economic crisis and rise in unemployment led to higher default rates on traditional mortgages, which destabilized the value of agency mortgage-backed securities. Second, Fannie and Freddie lost money on their investments in private-label mortgage securities. Once again, fearful that they would be unable to service their financial obligations, creditors ceased lending to Fannie and Freddie through the short-term bond market. Given their extensive involvement in mortgage markets and housing markets, the government believed that the failure of Fannie and Freddie would have heightened systemic risk to a far greater degree than Bear Stearns. In response, the Treasury Department placed both firms in conservatorship under the direction of the Federal Housing Finance Agency.

Lehman Brothers

The rapid erosion of investor confidence spread to more financial firms in September 2008. Lehman Brothers—one of the largest private investment banks on Wall Street—had also engaged heavily in subprime mortgage securitization and faced the same questions of solvency that led to a run on Bear Stearns. Analysts initially expected a government rescue package similar to that received by Bear—in this case, an arranged merger with either Bank of America or Barclays. However, the federal government was unwilling to provide the same loan guarantees that secured the Bear Stearns deal. Negotiations fell through without government guarantees from the Treasury Department and Lehman filed for bankruptcy. The collapse of one of the largest corporations in the world eroded confidence even further. Uncertainty about the degree of exposure to the subprime mortgage meltdown led to a credit crisis in the commercial banking system. Not only did banks stop lending to each other, they also stopped lending to the private sector. While Lehman Brothers was inarguably the most consequential firm to collapse during the financial crisis, Wachovia and Washington Mutual were also brought down during the fall of 2008.

American International Group

During the housing market bubble and subprime mortgage boom, American International Group (AIG) —a multinational insurance corporation—insured private-label mortgage securities against default. As the subprime mortgage meltdown unfolded, AIG lacked the collateral and reserves to pay claims on credit default swaps due to their status as unregulated securities. Furthermore, AIG was unable to borrow money from commercial banks due to the credit crisis. If AIG was unable to meet its obligations, it would assuredly destabilize its business partners, which were the largest financial firms on Wall Street. The Federal Reserve therefore expanded its emergency powers even further by nationalizing AIG.

The Emergency Economic Stabilization Act

By October, it was clear that individual rescue packages were not slowing financial contagion. In fact, the differing structure of the rescue packages to that point—an arranged merger, a public takeover by the Treasury, a failed arranged merger, a public takeover by the Federal Reserve—exacerbated uncertainty, but especially the credit freeze. Regulators decided that a direct, industry-wide rescue package was necessary to prevent a complete collapse of the financial system, and likely another depression. Such an action, which required legislation by Congress, was not uncontroversial. Conservative House Republicans railed against the expansion of government intervention proposed by members of their own party, sinking the initial bill and damaging investor confidence even further.

Upon its eventual passage, the Emergency Economic Stabilization Act established the infamous Troubled Asset Relief Program (TARP), which originally authorized the federal government to purchase up to $700 billion in toxic mortgage-related securities from the financial system. The principal goal of TARP was to stem widespread volatility in financial markets. Mass selloffs of mortgage-related securities continued to flood global markets with excess supply, leading to precipitous collapses in asset prices. But the government soon revised the program by using TARP funding for capital injections to unfreeze the credit system. TARP further supported anti-foreclosure initiatives, lending to small businesses, and the restructuring of the US auto industry. In addition, the Federal Deposit Insurance Corporation temporarily increased the limit on federal deposit insurance coverage, and guaranteed bank debt. The government later organized supplemental rescue packages for Citigroup in November 2008, and Bank of America in January 2009.

Let's look more closely at the actual provision of TARP funds. Economists Alan Blinder and Mark Zandi published two landmark analyses of the policy responses to the 2008 financial crisis and Great Recession—the first in 2010 for Moody's, and the second in 2015 for the Center on Budget and Policy Priorities. The studies include a full accounting of the emergency measures enacted by the government and estimate the effects of those measures on macroeconomic performance under alternative scenarios. According to Blinder and Zandi, the original aim of TARP—to purchase toxic assets from the financial sector—ended up comprising a relatively small share of its costs. During the financial crisis, both the

Federal Reserve and the Treasury Department established programs that financed asset purchases. In practice, TARP funding supported potential losses to investors through such programs. TARP also financed purchases of toxic assets held by AIG, Bank of America, and Citigroup. By far the largest component of TARP was the Capital Purchase Program, which financed capital injections into financial institutions. In order to boost investor confidence, the government became a major shareholder in the largest banks on Wall Street. Third, TARP supported two of the government's major initiatives to address the foreclosure crisis: the Home Affordability Mortgage Plan (HAMP) and the Home Affordability Refinance Program, both of which were analyzed in Chapter 3. Lastly, the most important use of TARP funds for the stability of the real sector was the auto industry bailout. As the transmission of the financial crisis into the real sector accelerated through the end of 2008, the collapse of General Motors (GM) and Chrysler would have almost certainly multiplied through auto supply chains, and inevitably led to the collapse of Ford. Given the state of the credit freeze at the time, a solution from the private sector was highly unlikely. TARP therefore facilitated the restructuring of GM and Chrysler through a more orderly bankruptcy process.

The Legacy—and Cost—of the Wall Street Bailouts

Taken together, the federal government's response toward Wall Street and the 2008 financial crisis differed greatly from its response toward homeowners and the foreclosure crisis. The guiding principle behind the government's response to homeowners, by both the W. Bush and Obama administrations, was that the foreclosure crisis resulted from a deficit of personal responsibility. Homeowners received mortgage workouts on a case-by-case basis. Government intervention was indirect through the use of incentives, which left the decision to initiate workouts to lenders. As a result, the vast majority of workouts were modified repayment plans, not loan modifications. Wall Street, on the other hand, received a comprehensive, industry-wide bailout. The guiding principle behind the government's response to Wall Street was "too big to fail"—the principle that the government would prevent the failure of large institutions that would threaten the stability of the financial sector and the economic system. Intervention was direct, through purchases of toxic mortgage-related securities and capital injections. Moreover, the government provided debt guarantees to bondholders throughout the bailouts.

According to the Blinder and Zandi studies, the Wall Street bailouts were successful in the sense that they contributed significantly to halting the crisis of confidence, resetting the financial system, and averting another depression. More specifically, the implementation of stress tests ultimately restored investor confidence in the financial system. In early 2009, federal regulators directed large commercial banks to assess whether they held enough capital to endure another financial crisis. Banks that failed their stress tests were required to recapitalize through either private sources or more TARP funds. Financial market volatility subsided once the government publicly confirmed the recapitalization of the banking sector.

In 2015, Blinder and Zandi calculated the ultimate cost of TARP for US taxpayers. While the government certainly incurred losses on individual initiatives, it either recovered the original funds committed or earned a profit on several programs. There are two reasons for this outcome. First, most financial institutions repaid the government with interest, in many cases quite quickly, in order to avoid further restrictions and stipulations from the government. Second, the government initially acquired toxic assets during a market crash when prices were at rock bottom. Since it later resold its holdings during a more stable market environment, in which asset prices had recovered, it sometimes made capital gains. Table 4.2 presents their results for each of the major components of TARP. The first column itemizes each component and program; the second column reports the original commitment by the government; while the third column reports the ultimate cost to taxpayers. The third column is the most important. A negative figure indicates that the government made a profit, meaning it earned more than it originally committed. A positive figure indicates that the government took a loss, meaning it was unable to recover all of the funds committed. Zero indicates that the government recovered all funds committed, with no net earnings or losses to taxpayers. In total, the government committed $600 billion of the $700 billion authorized by the Emergency Economic Stabilization Act. The ultimate cost of TARP to US taxpayers, however, was *$40 billion*—not insignificant, but a relatively small share of the original funds committed by the government. The Capital Purchase Program, which financed capital injections, was the largest and most successful TARP initiative, as the government ultimately earned $16 billion. Toxic asset purchases were less successful and cost taxpayers $11 billion. However, both the Federal Reserve and the Treasury Department earned a profit on their

TABLE 4.2 Total Cost of the Troubled Asset Relief Program ($ billions)

	Original Commitment	*Ultimate Cost*
Total	**600**	**40**
Wall Street Bailouts	450	−5
Capital Injections	*250*	*−16*
Capital Purchase Program	250	−16
Toxic Asset Purchases	*200*	*11*
Systemically Important Institutions (AIG, BoA, Citi)	115	15
Federal Reserve (TALF)	55	−1
Treasury (PPIP)	30	−3
Auto Industry Bailouts	84	17
GM	64	14
Chrysler	15	3
Auto suppliers	5	0
Anti-Foreclosure Initiatives	52	28
Homeowner Affordability and Stability Plan	52	28
FHA Short Refinance program	N/A	0
Aid to Small Businesses	15	0
SBA loan purchase	15	0
Community Development Capital Initiative	N/A	0

Source: Blinder and Zandi (2015).

This material was created by the Center on Budget and Policy Priorities (www.cbpp.org).

respective programs. The individual rescue packages for AIG, Bank of America, and Citigroup proved to be costly, but the government's loss was almost entirely from the AIG bailout. Taken together, the government earned $5 billion from the Wall Street bailouts. Although the government recovered most of the funds committed to the auto industry bailouts, taxpayers incurred a loss of $17 billion, most of which was from GM. The government's anti-foreclosure initiatives were the least successful in this accounting, largely due to the problematic incentive structures for both lenders and homeowners. Taxpayers ultimately took a loss of $28 billion, which was over half of the original funds committed. Finally, the government recovered all funds committed toward its small business lending initiatives during the crisis.

In the years after the 2008 financial crisis, however, both the Democratic and Republican Party establishments paid a political price for the conduct of the bailouts, albeit for different reasons. Fiscal conservatives pushed the Republican Party to the right by denouncing government intervention and the enormous increase in the federal deficit. Progressives pushed the Democratic Party to the left by maligning the formation of even larger banks and the increase in income inequality that followed the crisis. Unlike its response to the Great Depression, the government's response to the Great Recession fueled polarization, not consensus, on the role of government in the financial sector.

FINAL THOUGHTS

This chapter has brought us to a pivotal point in this comprehensive investigation of the lead-up to the crisis, and its transmission across the financial sector and the economic system. The next chapter completes this part with an overview of the major explanations of the crisis offered by both mainstream and heterodox economists. Part III then investigates the different policy responses to the Great Recession. While the Wall Street bailouts ended the 2008 financial crisis, policymakers continued to face daunting and divisive questions about how to resolve the unfolding economic crisis and regulate the financial sector during the ensuing recovery.

Sources

Bernanke, B.S. (2007, May 17). The subprime mortgage market [Transcript]. Remarks by Chairman Ben S. Bernanke before the Federal Reserve Bank of Chicago's 43rd Annual Conference on Bank Structure and Competition. Retrieved from https://www.federalreserve.gov.

Blinder, A.S. & Zandi, M. (2010, July 27). *How the Great Recession was brought to an end*. Moody's Analytics.

Blinder, A.S. & Zandi, M. (2015, October 15). *The financial crisis: Lessons for the next one*. Center on Budget and Policy Priorities.

Fannie Mae. (2019a, June 1). *Single-family MBS prospectus*. Retrieved from http://www.fanniemae.com.

Fannie Mae. (2019b, October). *Basics of Fannie Mae single-family MBS*. Retrieved from http://www.fanniemae.com.

Federal Reserve Bank of St. Louis. (n.d.). *FRED economic data* [Data file and codebook]. Retrieved from https://fred.stlouisfed.org.

Kelly, K., Ip, G., & Sidel, R. (2008, March 16). Fed races to rescue Bear Stearns in bid to steady financial system. *The Wall Street Journal*. Retrieved from https://www.wsj.com.

Moody's. (2020, January 16). *Rating symbols and definitions*. Retrieved from http://www.moodys.com.

Moody's Investor Service. (2006, June 19). *Moody's rates AIG's senior notes Aa2; stable outlook*. Retrieved from https://www.moodys.com.

Moody's Investor Service. (2008, March 17). *Moody's affirms Lehman's A1 rating; outlook stable*. Retrieved from https://www.moodys.com.

Shiller, R.J. (n.d.). *Online data – Robert Shiller* [Data file and codebook]. Retrieved from http://www.econ.yale.edu/~shiller/data.htm.

The Treasury Department's views on the regulation of government sponsored enterprises: Hearings before the U.S. House of Representatives Committee on Financial Services, 108th Congress. (2003).

US Bureau of Economic Analysis. (n.d.). *A guide to the National Income and Product Accounts of the United States*. Author.

Further Reading

Aalbers, M.B. (ed.). (2012). *Subprime cities: The political economy of mortgage markets*. Malden, MA: Wiley-Blackwell.

Aliber, R.Z. & Kindelberger, C.P. (2015). *Manias, panics, and crashes: A history of financial crises*. New York, NY: Palgrave Macmillan.

Crotty, J. (2017). *Capitalism, macroeconomics and reality: Understanding globalization, financialization, competition and crisis*. Cheltenham, UK: Edward Elgar Publishing.

Fisher, I. (1930). *The theory of interest as determined by impatience to spend income and opportunity to invest it*. New York, NY: Macmillan.

Foster, J.B. & Magdoff, F. (2009). *The Great Financial Crisis: Causes and consequences*. New York, NY: Monthly Review Press.

Harvey, D. (2010). *The enigma of capital and the crises of capitalism*. New York, NY: Oxford University Press.

Sherman, H. (2016). *The roller coaster economy: Financial crisis, Great Recession, and the public option*. Abingdon, UK: Routledge.

Wolfson, M.H. & Epstein, G.A. (eds.). (2015). *The handbook of the political economy of financial crises*. New York, NY: Oxford University Press.

CHAPTER 5

Competing Explanations of the Crisis

This chapter completes this focused investigation of the lead-up to and transmission of the Great Recession. Chapter 2 opened Part II of the book with an analysis of the long-term restructuring of US capitalism prior to 2008. Chapter 3 delved further into the origins of the housing market bubble, the subprime mortgage lending boom, and the foreclosure crisis. Chapter 4 then examined the evolution of financial structure prior to the subprime mortgage meltdown, the transmission of the financial and economic crises, and the conduct of the Wall Street bailouts. Drawing upon the perspectives introduced in Chapter 1, and in keeping with the pluralist approach of this textbook, Part II concludes with a reflective chapter on competing theoretical explanations of the crisis. This chapter examines not only the critical differences between heterodox and mainstream explanations, but also the important variations within heterodox economics itself. The purpose of this exercise is to apply the principles, logic, and arguments of competing schools of economic thought, and their differing interpretations of economic phenomenon, to the Great Recession—a situation in which the capitalist economic system failed. To be clear, this is by no means an exhaustive investigation. There are certainly more schools of thought within the field of economics, just as there are divergences within the frameworks presented here. However, after completing this chapter, readers will have the understanding and resources to explore other theories or variations of these theories for further study.

This chapter presents seven distinct frameworks for understanding the 2008 financial crisis and the Great Recession. The organization of the content differs slightly from the other chapters of this textbook. Each section can be read individually, but all refer in some way to the conventional adjustment process advanced by neoclassical economics. Since they are largely independent, sources and recommendations for further reading are listed after each section. Each section also includes an accompanying table that briefly summarizes the major points from the framework.

The first section begins with a presentation of mainstream explanations of the crisis. Mainstream economists argue that capitalism features self-adjusting

DOI: 10.4324/9780429461316-7

mechanisms that maintain full employment. Although exogenous shocks may create recessionary gaps, deflationary forces in free markets will automatically return the economic system to full employment. As a result, government intervention and management of the macro economy are unnecessary and counterproductive. This section concludes with an explanation of the crisis advanced by Nobel Laureate Robert E. Lucas, Jr., who draws parallels between the Great Depression of the 1930s and the Great Recession using the conventional framework.

The second section analyzes the perspectives of Alan Greenspan, the former chair of the US Federal Reserve Board of Governors, who famously testified before the House Committee on Oversight and Government Reform during the 2008 financial crisis. Although Greenspan admits flaws in the mainstream understanding of the behavior of lending institutions, and supports new regulations on securities firms, he largely defends the financial structure and regulatory environment that preceded the crisis.

The third and fourth sections emphasize the origins of the speculative bubble and the historical severity of the crash. Although both were developed well before the Great Recession itself, they are widely regarded as compelling explanations of the crisis. For example, the third section applies Irving Fisher's theory of debt-deflation to the Great Recession. Fisher, whose work has influenced both mainstream and heterodox schools of thought, argued that the combination of debt accumulation and deflation triggers severe economic crises. Far from being the solution to recessionary gaps, as posited by conventional economists, deflation accelerates the severity of downturns by significantly increasing real debt burdens.

The fourth section presents Hyman Minsky's financial instability hypothesis—a post-Keynesian framework that explains the origins of financial instability. In contrast to the conventional adjustment process, which emphasizes exogenous shocks and self-interested behavior, Minsky emphasizes the endogenous forces and complex shifts in market psychology that generate market bubbles. Intervention and management of the macro economy therefore remain legitimate interests of the government.

The fifth section highlights two explanations of the crisis from the field of institutionalist economics. First, radical institutionalists critique the policy responses to the crisis by arguing that they failed to address institutional barriers to society's joint stock of knowledge. Radical institutionalists promote institutional changes that reduce inequality and exclusion, such as universal employment programs, in order to promote the full utilization of knowledge. Second, feminist institutionalists critique the so-called "Great Mancession," a popular narrative that circulated within conservative media following the crisis. According to the Great Mancession, men allegedly experienced an unprecedented increase in unemployment relative to women. Feminist institutionalists critique not only the empirical basis of the Mancession, but also the gendered construct of the narrative and the neoclassical principles that support it.

The final section presents a Marxist account of the crisis by drawing upon the work of David Harvey. According to Harvey, capitalism has never resolved its historical tendency toward crisis; it simply relocates it to different sectors in order to maintain compound growth. The Great Recession is no different in this regard, as its origins lie in the resolution of the crisis of the 1970s. However, he argues that capitalism has reached new limits on the ability to relocate its crisis tendency. The resolution of this crisis requires the consolidation of political power by the working class, and the reorganization of economic production away from capitalism.

MAINSTREAM EXPLANATIONS

To begin this chapter, let's scrutinize the arguments behind mainstream explanations of the Great Recession—and recessions in general. Although a certain degree of variation exists, several foundational assumptions underlie mainstream accounts of the crisis and the subsequent recovery—the most important of which is the principle that capitalism features self-adjusting mechanisms that maintain full employment. Mainstream or conventional economists do not disregard the occurrence of recessions. They acknowledge that circumstances may arise when aggregate demand is unable to maintain current production and employment levels. Rather, they believe that free markets automatically correct excessive fluctuations in economic activity through adjustments in factor prices, wages, and interest rates. The belief that aggregate demand is inherently stable implies that government intervention to correct the business cycle is unnecessary.

The Conventional Adjustment Process

According to conventional economic analysis, recessions occur when the overall level of household saving exceeds business investment. Whereas "saving" refers to the share of household income not spent on current output, "investment" refers to business spending on capital goods, raw materials, and inventories in order to produce output. A combination of weak investment plus weak consumption (due to excessive saving) produces an insufficient level of aggregate demand that could initiate a recessionary spiral. These imbalances occur from time to time simply because they reflect decision making by different sectors of the economic system. Conventional analysis attributes the causes of recessionary imbalances to exogenous shocks, or forces external to the operation of capitalism—for example, natural disasters, wars, public health emergencies, disruptions in supply chains of technology and resources, or bad government policies.

How does capitalism self-stabilize when an insufficient level of aggregate demand arises? A higher savings rate constrains consumer spending, which causes excess capacity and unexpected inventories in industries that produce goods and services—notably cars, housing, manufacturing, retail, and travel. Firms will reduce planned investment in response, which likewise causes gluts in industries that produce capital goods (e.g., tools, equipment, and machinery), as well as raw materials (e.g., fuels, lumber, plastics, and metals). In order to clear factor markets of surpluses, prices will fall until those markets reach equilibrium. A similar process takes place in the labor market. Weak investment reduces labor demand and creates excess supply, or unemployment, which puts downward pressure on wages. The key point is that lower factor prices—as long as they can freely adjust—will entice capitalists to reinvest and rehire. These market adjustments avert a more protracted downturn.

In particular, mainstream explanations emphasize that self-adjustment takes place in a free and flexible credit market. An excess of saving over investment has two effects. First, an increase in saving leads to an increase in the supply of credit. Financial institutions will see an influx of cash as people save more money in banks, increase investments in financial markets, or pay down debts. Second, a decrease in investment leads to a decrease in the demand for credit. For large corporations that engage in mass production, investments in capital goods and infrastructure are typically long-term expenditures, which they finance through borrowings. A reduction in planned investment, for the reasons stated above, reduces the ability and willingness to borrow. A surplus of credit will emerge at current interest rates due to a combination of lower demand and greater supply. In order to reach equilibrium in the credit market, interest rates will fall. This adjustment in market interest rates stabilizes aggregate demand by decreasing saving and increasing investment until the economic system reaches full employment again. Lower interest rates reduce the incentive to save, due to lower rates of return, and thereby increase the incentive to consume. Lower interest rates also increase the incentive to invest due to lower costs of borrowing. In practice, this adjustment process informed the views of policymakers like Ben Bernanke, who believed that the financial sector was a protective factor against economic instability.

In sum, mainstream economists argue that the solution to a recession is essentially deflation. Excessive saving relative to investment suppresses demand and generates surpluses across multiple sectors of the economic system. However, market forces will eventually drive down prices for key inputs, such as capital goods, raw materials, labor, and credit. Left to themselves, markets will recalibrate spending and employment until the economic system reaches full employment. This inherent stability of aggregate demand implies that government intervention to alleviate economic instability serves no purpose, and only disrupts the natural adjustment process of the market mechanism.

Robert Lucas's Explanation

Let's now examine a specific analysis of the Great Recession conveyed by Nobel Laureate Robert E. Lucas, Jr, who draws upon the general principles of the conventional adjustment process. Throughout his career, Lucas contributed to the development of new classical economics, a school of thought that emerged during the 1970s. Along with Milton Friedman and Friedrich Hayek, Lucas was instrumental in the paradigm shift away from Keynesianism, and toward theories of macroeconomic activity and behavior based upon microeconomic models. The new classical school departed from postwar Keynesian orthodoxy by reviving market-clearing assumptions and *laissez-faire* policy prescriptions, repositioning full employment as the general case in its theoretical models, and replacing the theory of animal spirits with a theory of rational expectations. In his 2003 presidential address to the American Economic Association, Lucas offers a clear summary of his views:

> Macroeconomics was born as a distinct field in the 1940's, as a part of the intellectual response to the Great Depression. The term then referred to the body of knowledge and expertise that we hoped would prevent the recurrence of that economic disaster. My thesis ... is that macroeconomics in this original sense has succeeded: Its central

> problem of depression prevention has been solved, for all practical purposes, and has in fact been solved for many decades. There remain important gains in welfare from better fiscal policies, but I argue that these are gains from providing people with better incentives to work and to save, not from better fine-tuning of spending flows. Taking U.S. performance over the past 50 years as a benchmark, the potential for welfare gains from better long-run, supply-side policies exceeds *by far* the potential from further improvements in short-run demand management.

In 2011, Lucas delivered the Milliman Endowed Lecture in Economics at the University of Washington, entitled "The U.S. Recession of 2007–201?" Lucas begins by acknowledging the severity of the crisis and the need to consider policies that promote recovery, while also stressing the importance of long-run productive capacity and the efficient use of resources when evaluating economic performance. To set the stage, he first compares the United States to other advanced economic systems in North America, Europe, and Asia in terms of their historical growth rates. Despite sporadic deviations from its long-run trend, like wars and depressions, US capitalism has sustained an annual growth rate of approximately 3% since the late nineteenth century. In fact, Lucas minimizes the significance of most postwar recessions: "Who remembers them?" he asks. While not discounting the government's contribution of providing education and a stable context of individual rights, Lucas attributes the rapid expansion of US living standards, and the tendency of growth to return to its long-run trend, to free-market capitalism. Furthermore, despite similar growth rates since the 1970s, US real incomes have been 20% to 40% higher than those in other advanced economic systems. Lucas attributes this income gap to the more substantial taxes, regulations, and social welfare programs in those countries, which he contends diminish work effort and saving.

The principal focus of his analysis is a comparison of the Great Recession to the Great Depression of the 1930s. Lucas argues that, prior to the Great Recession, the increasing reliance on investment banks for financial intermediation was due to government regulations that forbade interest payments on commercial bank deposits. In response, institutional investors turned to short-term debt instruments sold by investment banks that offered higher returns, greater liquidity, and relative safety. The collapse of Lehman Brothers in particular set in motion a credit freeze that paralleled the commercial bank runs of the 1930s. Unlike in the 1930s, however, the US Federal Reserve appropriately intervened and expanded liquidity. What, then, explains the prolonged lack of recovery from the Great Recession during the early 2010s? Despite the reset in liquidity, consumption and investment remained suppressed during the initial years of the recovery, while unemployment was persistently high. Here again, Lucas draws parallels to the Great Depression by concluding that government intervention and spending were too significant—not inadequate. He argues that the anemic recovery following the Depression-era bank runs was due to high tariffs, the creation of industrial unions, and the "demonization of business." The sluggish recovery following the 2008 financial crisis was likewise due to the prospect of higher taxes on the wealthy by the Obama administration, the expected increase in medical costs through the Affordable Care Act, and the expansion of central bank oversight through the Dodd-Frank Act. Lucas's presentation of the intercountry income gap therefore

TABLE 5.1 Mainstream Explanations

Conventional Adjustment Process	- Capitalism features self-adjusting mechanisms that maintain full employment - Exogenous shocks cause recessions - Free markets correct instability in aggregate demand through price adjustments - Deflation is the solution to recessions - Government intervention is unnecessary and counter-productive
Robert Lucas (New Classical)	- Commercial bank regulations led to an increase in demand for short-term debt securities - The bankruptcy of Lehman Brothers led to the credit freeze - Expansionary monetary policy was necessary and appropriate - Expansionary fiscal and financial policies were too significant - The sluggish recovery was due to higher taxes, medical costs, and financial regulations

serves as a warning: should the United States adopt the tax-and-spend policies of other advanced economic systems, it faces the prospect of a weaker long-run trend in economic growth.

Sources

Lucas, R.E. (2003). Macroeconomic priorities. *American Economic Review, 93*(1), 1–14. doi: 10.1257/000282803321455188

Lucas, R.E. (2011, May 19). The U.S. recession of 2007–201? Remarks at the Milliman Endowed Lecture in Economics, University of Washington.

Further Reading

Lucas, R.E. (1972). Expectations and the neutrality of money. *Journal of Economic Theory, 4*(2), 103–24. doi: 10.1016/0022-0531(72)90142-1

Lucas, R.E. (1976). Econometric policy evaluation: A critique. *Carnegie-Rochester Conference Series on Public Policy, 1*, 19–46. doi: 10.1016/0167-2231(76)90007-7

Snowdon, B., Vane, H., & Wynarczyk, P. (1994). *A modern guide to macroeconomics*. Aldershot, UK: Edward Elgar Publishing.

ALAN GREENSPAN'S EXPLANATION

Alan Greenspan was chair of the US Federal Reserve Board of Governors from 1987 until 2006. In his role he oversaw monetary policy during the Great Moderation—the so-called period of reduced macroeconomic volatility prior to the crisis. During this time, the central bank largely pursued monetary policies that expanded liquidity and lowered interest rates. Critics and defenders alike recognize Greenspan as one of the most consequential stewards of monetary policy since the founding of the Federal Reserve. In addition to his service to the Federal Reserve, Greenspan had a distinguished career as a private consultant and advisor in other areas of policymaking, such as commodity markets, financial regulation, fiscal policy, foreign affairs, and international economic policy.

Greenspan's views were consistent with the philosophical and ideological mindset of policymakers during the neoliberal stage of US capitalism. He was a proponent of deregulation and free market competition. He believed that low inflation, not full employment, should be the principal goal of monetary policy. In the realm of fiscal policy, he supported lower taxes, lower deficits, and the privatization of Social Security. In the realm of foreign affairs, he supported the invasion of Iraq in 2003. In fact, libertarianism informed many of Greenspan's views, as he was a longtime confidant of the philosopher Ayn Rand.

In a now-famous Congressional hearing at the height of the 2008 financial meltdown, Greenspan offered his own explanation of the crisis. On October 23, Greenspan testified before the House Committee on Oversight and Government Reform on "The Financial Crisis and the Role of Federal Regulators." In prepared testimony, he outlines his perspectives on the sources of the crisis, appropriate policy responses, the performance of the US and global economic systems, and the evolution of his beliefs on such matters. Although his opening statement is short—only 1,133 words—Greenspan delivers a succinct explanation of the crisis that still resonates and is the subject of debate, like so many of the views and decisions throughout his career.

Greenspan first discusses the effects of the 2008 financial crisis on unemployment. He attributes the economic crisis to a massive reduction in consumption due to restricted access to credit, widespread losses in retirement savings, and a rapidly weakening labor market. In order to recover financial losses incurred from the stock market crash and housing market bust, individuals allocated a larger share of their disposable income toward saving. He argues that ending the crisis would require the stabilization of home values—the collateral that supported mortgage securitization—in order to stabilize the value of mortgage-related securities. The appropriate pricing of risk would subsequently resume, stable relationships within the financial system would return, and the economic system would recover.

The most notable line from the hearing is this *mea culpa* from Greenspan: "... those of us who have looked to the self-interest of lending institutions to protect shareholder's equity (myself especially) are in a state of shocked disbelief."

Greenspan finds that the international economic policy framework following the 1970s worked well; but a surge in global demand for mortgage-backed securities, combined with questionable credit ratings, created the impetus for the subprime mortgage lending boom. He frames the financial crisis as a failure to properly price risk. Again, Greenspan lauds the risk management models and financial structure that evolved during his tenure at the Federal Reserve. The problem was that the models only accounted for the previous two decades of financial activity, which was a period of market exuberance. When investors realized the disconnect between asset prices and asset ratings, volatility and uncertainty emerged in financial markets with any connection to subprime mortgage lending. Greenspan therefore supports new regulations that would require security issuers to hold a certain percentage of their securities.

On the one hand, several aspects of Greenspan's analysis are consistent with the multitude of explanations offered by economists, policymakers, and media analysts. These features are largely uncontroversial and agreed upon in the literature. He attributes the 2008 financial crisis to an underpricing of risk, due in part to unrealistic credit ratings. He argues that excess demand for mortgage-related securities fueled the wave of subprime mortgage originations. He identifies a severe reversal of consumption as the primary mechanism that transmitted the financial crisis to the real sector. On the other hand, certain aspects of Greenspan's analysis cut against conventional explanations of the crisis and the federal government's response to it. His admission that the self-interest of lending institutions failed to safeguard shareholder equity is notable, especially for someone who was so heavily involved in the processes that generated the crisis. His advice to stabilize home prices is a subtle commentary on the government's response to the financial crisis. The federal government put much more emphasis on the stabilization of mortgage-related securities and the solvency of financial institutions, as compared to the foreclosure crisis and the stabilization of household net worth.

There are many instances, however—both in his prepared statement and under questioning—in which Greenspan defends the business practices, economic processes, and regulatory environment prior to the crisis. Although he recognizes the *effects* of the 2008 financial crisis on the real sector, he does not acknowledge the *origins* of the financial crisis in the real sector and the restructuring of capitalist production. Throughout the hearing, he does not question the complex, interconnected structure of the financial system. With the exception of credit default swaps, he finds nothing wrong with securitization. Greenspan merely assumes that the global economic policy framework worked well by not acknowledging the growing degree of financial instability during the Great Moderation; nor does he examine why the rating agencies granted unrealistic credit ratings. While most analysts agree that financial markets failed to properly price risk, Greenspan views that failure as a forecasting problem, not a historical problem. The risk management models—which reflected the best innovations in finance, the sciences, and technology—were simply not calibrated appropriately to the financial market behavior of the time. However, he does not fully explain why market behavior shifted decisively toward euphoria. Lastly, although he supports new regulations on securitization, Greenspan does not cite the lack of regulation as a contributing factor in the crisis, arguing that market forces alone have eliminated the prevalence of toxic assets. A new regulatory structure that would prevent a similar crisis, which he views as a "once-in-a-century phenomenon," would suppress long-run economic growth. In fact, at the end of his prepared statement, Greenspan recommends the reestablishment of "sustainable" subprime lending practices.

Sources

The financial crisis and the role of federal regulators: Hearings before the U.S. House of Representatives Committee on Oversight and Government Reform, 110th Congress. (2008).

TABLE 5.2 Alan Greenspan's Explanation

- Credit restrictions, financial losses, and high unemployment led to a massive contraction in household consumption
- Stabilization of securities markets requires stabilization of home values
- The self-interest of lending institutions failed to protect shareholder equity
- Global demand for mortgage-backed securities and questionable credit ratings led to the subprime lending boom
- The 2008 financial crisis was a failure to properly price risk

IRVING FISHER'S DEBT-DEFLATION THEORY

Irving Fisher was a prominent American economist during the early half of the twentieth century. Fisher holds an intriguing place in the history of economic thought. For much of his career, he was an adherent of neoclassical economics. For example, Chapter 4 applied his theory of interest using the Fisher Equation. Fisher was also a popular figure in the press, in addition to his scholarly work in books and academic journals. Shortly before the stock market crash of 1929, he famously told the *New York Times* that stock values had reached "what looks like a permanently high plateau." In large part for this reason, economists discounted his contributions to the discipline for many years, as the work of John Maynard Keynes became the principal framework for explaining the Great Depression of the 1930s.

Nonetheless, by the early 1930s, Fisher realized that capitalism lacked the self-adjusting mechanisms promoted by mainstream economics. In an article published in *Econometrica*, Fisher advances a theory of debt-deflation. His goal is not to explain the business cycle *per se*—that is, the regular oscillations in economic activity that generate recessions—but rather the types of disruptions that cause severe depressions. Fisher identifies two such forces: the rapid accumulation of debt during an economic expansion, followed by a period of deflation during a contraction. The term "debt deflation" refers to a process whereby deflation leads to significantly higher real debt burdens. The increase in real debt burdens not only redistributes income from borrowers to lenders, but also initiates a vicious cycle of suppressed economic activity. Far from being the solution to recessions, as predicted by the conventional adjustment process, deflation following a period of rapid debt accumulation exacerbates the severity of downturns. As there are many parallels between the forces that contributed to the Great Depression and the Great Recession, since 2008, Fisher's debt-deflation theory has re-emerged among both mainstream and heterodox economists as a forceful explanation of the historical severity of the crisis.

Fisher explains the process of debt deflation in nine steps. During the 1920s, individuals, homeowners, and firms accumulated more debt. Fisher argues that the proclivity for debt accumulation eventually ceased, which initiated a period of debt liquidation:

- Debt liquidation first results in mass selloffs of assets.
- A period of deleveraging follows as borrowers pay down or pay off their debts. Lending and deposit creation in the banking system slow.
- Mass selloffs and deleveraging lead to lower asset prices. The value of money rises.

- Lower asset prices erode the net worth of firms, resulting in bankruptcies.
- Firms incur profit squeeze or losses.
- Losses lead to cutbacks in production and employment.
- Economic instability generates negative expectations about the future direction of the economic system.
- Cash hoarding begins as negative expectations take hold.
- Although *nominal* interest rates fall, *real* interest rates rise.

Two questions are worth clarifying. First, why does this process create deflation? The reason is that when individuals and firms try to liquidate their debts, they sell their assets. This response significantly increases supply in asset markets, which puts downward pressure on prices. For firms, this process lowers market prices for capital goods, raw materials, and inventories. For individuals, it lowers prices for consumer durables, such as housing and cars. Second, why does this process increase real interest rates? Fisher argues that, unlike asset prices, debt does not deflate when the economic system contracts. By increasing the value of money, deflation results in higher real interest rates, or higher real debt burdens for borrowers. Therein lies Fisher's most important point: "... the very effort of individuals to lessen their burden of debts increases it, because of the mass effect of the stampede to liquidate in swelling each dollar owed."

In order to understand this critical aspect of his analysis, let's take an example.

Both lenders and borrowers base their decisions upon real interest rates. Although lenders can specify the nominal interest rate (i) on a loan, they can only formulate an expectation of the real interest rate (r) at the time of origination, since the actual inflation rate (π) is unknown. Given that expected inflation (π^e) erodes the purchasing power of the expected return to lending (r^e):

$$r^e = i - \pi^e$$

Lenders therefore specify a nominal interest rate according to the expected real rate of return and expected rate of inflation. Rearranging the above equation yields the following relationship:

$$i = r^e + \pi^e$$

Returning to Fisher's scenario, during a period of economic expansion, individuals and firms take on more debt. Profits, wages, asset prices, consumer prices—and especially confidence—are all higher when borrowers initially acquire these loans. For example, if a lender expects an inflation rate of 2%, and a real interest rate of 3%, it will charge a nominal interest rate of 5%:

$$i = r^e + \pi^e = 2\% + 3\% = 5\%$$

However, when the incentives for debt accumulation inevitably erode, and borrowers attempt to liquidate their debts, the economic system enters a period of deflation. Profits, wages, asset prices, consumer prices, and confidence are now

TABLE 5.3 Irving Fisher's Debt-Deflation Theory
- Capitalism lacks self-adjusting mechanisms
- Rapid debt accumulation followed by deflation leads to severe economic crises
- Deflation leads to higher real debt burdens
- Higher real debt burdens redistribute income from borrowers to lenders, and further restrain economic activity
- Deflation does not correct, but exacerbates, the severity of recessions

lower. In this example, if the economic system actually experiences a 1% rate of deflation, instead of the expected 2% rate of inflation, the real interest rate on the loan equals 6%:

$$r = i - \pi = 5\% - (-1\%) = 6\%$$

Although lenders secure a higher real interest rate, borrowers face a higher real cost of borrowing. The crucial point is that when borrowers attempt to reduce their debt burdens, they unleash deflationary forces that end up increasing their debt burdens—the very outcome they sought to avoid. Individuals and firms will make more debt payments to lenders, resulting in less consumption and investment. The danger is that less demand for goods and services from the private sector will put further downward pressure on prices, and consequently more upward pressure on real interest rates, in a potentially vicious cycle.

Fisher's debt-deflation theory is a useful framework for understanding the severity of the Great Recession, as it incorporates many features of the period before and during the crisis. Fisher stresses that the combination of rapid debt accumulation followed by deflation is what triggers prolonged economic contractions like the Great Depression and, in this case, the Great Recession. Excessive investment, excessive speculation, or excessive confidence alone is not sufficient to trigger such crises; but when financed with borrowed funds, they are lethal to the operation of the economic system. If a prolonged period of leveraging is followed by inflation, it is less likely to trigger a severe downturn. Similarly, if deflation is not the result of deleveraging, the consequences are less harmful. It is the synthesis of debt and deflation that distinguishes the regular occurrence of recessions from the irregular occurrence of depressions.

Sources

Fisher, I. (1933). The debt-deflation theory of great depressions. *Econometrica*, *1*(4), 337–57. doi: 10.2307/1907327

Fisher sees stocks permanently high. (1929, October 16). *The New York Times*. Retrieved from http://www.proquest.com.

Further Reading

Fisher, I. (1930). *The theory of interest as determined by impatience to spend income and opportunity to invest it*. New York, NY: Macmillan.

HYMAN MINSKY'S FINANCIAL INSTABILITY HYPOTHESIS

Although Fisher's debt-deflation theory offers a compelling explanation of the *severity* of the Great Recession, it does not fully explain the *formation* of the speculative bubble itself. Why do certain economic expansions feature a substantial increase in debt in the first place? In order to examine this question, this section presents the financial instability hypothesis of Hyman P. Minsky. Minsky advanced the understanding of financial crises, macroeconomics, and monetary policy throughout the postwar period. While Minsky's work has influenced multiple heterodox schools of thought, he identified himself as a post-Keynesian economist.

Post-Keynesians expand upon the contributions of John Maynard Keynes following the publication of *The General Theory of Employment, Interest, and Money* in 1936, as well as the great Polish economist Michał Kalecki. The prefix "post-" is not simply a chronological distinction, however. Post-Keynesians actively reject the assumptions, methods, and policy prescriptions of mainstream macroeconomics. For example, mainstream schools, such as monetarism and new classical economics, dilute or disregard the radical insights of Keynes and realign them with neoclassical theory. Given its broad purpose and scope, post-Keynesianism is a diverse project within heterodox approaches to economic analysis. Still, it features a number of recurring principles and themes. Post-Keynesians emphasize the role of uncertainty in human behavior in opposition to the neoclassical vision of Economic Man. They reject the neoclassical preoccupation with scarcity and the efficient use of resources by incorporating the general circumstances of excess capacity and unemployment into their theoretical models. The endogeneity of money and credit is also a key principle, in which the operation of capitalism itself generates financial and economic instability. Post-Keynesians integrate the complex influences of time and access to credit into theories of production. They integrate the interconnectedness of the real and financial sectors into theories of the business cycle. Given these inherent conditions of capitalist economic systems—fundamental uncertainty, excess capacity, unemployment, and money endogeneity—post-Keynesians promote financial regulations and policies that manage aggregate demand in order to achieve full employment. In stark contrast to Robert Lucas, post-Keynesians do not view the problem of depression economics as solved. Although Minsky contributed an array of insights on these subjects, this section examines his renowned financial instability hypothesis. Similar to Fisher's debt-deflation theory, the 2008 financial crisis and Great Recession gave new prominence to Minsky's work on the origins of financial instability.

Minsky builds a framework for understanding financial instability based upon the historical reality of capitalism itself—a common characteristic of post-Keynesian method. Despite the efforts of government intervention in many instances, there are periods when capitalist economic systems experience uncontrollable, self-perpetuating debt deflation (or inflation). In contrast to mainstream assumptions, Minsky views the business cycle as a dynamic process. Instead of self-adjustment toward stable points of equilibrium in flexible markets, capitalism may deviate away from market-clearing conditions in accelerating fashion: "… the economic system's reactions to a movement of the economy amplify the movement …"

The following dimensions inform the theoretical basis of the financial instability hypothesis:

- Capitalist production by industrial firms requires investment in costly capital goods, infrastructure, and other physical assets.
- An important aspect of that system is a multi-faceted financial sector.
- The core dilemma facing capitalist economic systems is capital accumulation, not the efficient use of resources.
- Capital accumulation is a process that takes place over time.

Although Minsky focuses on the behavior of capitalist firms, as he notes, the financial instability hypothesis certainly applies to governments, international financial relations, and—with particular relevance to the Great Recession—households. Let's examine his logic more closely.

Minsky argues that capital accumulation by industrial firms involves an exchange of present money for future money. In the present, firms organize a production process by paying for inputs (labor, capital goods, and raw materials) using an initial sum of money. In the future, they receive another sum of money upon the sale of the resultant output. The schematic below summarizes the sequence of this circuit, where M equals the initial sum of money, C represents the firm's inputs, P denotes the production process, C' represents the firm's output, and M' equals the sale price of output:

$$M - C - P - C' - M'$$

The difference between $M'$and M is capitalist profit. However, firms must typically borrow some portion of the initial sum of money (M) from banks or other financial intermediaries. In this sense, a key qualification of the defining characteristics of capitalism—that is, private ownership of the means of production contained in C, and the ability to organize the production process (P)—involves the undertaking of financial liabilities. The business of banking and the circulation of money therefore interact with capitalist property rights and production. Banks collect cash savings from depositors and convert them into interest-bearing assets, which include loans to firms for investment. Firms realize profit when the product of the investment is sold and must then repay banks. Since these two interrelated activities of the industrial firm—investment and profit making—take place at different points in time, the *expectation* of future profits conditions the level and cost of borrowing, just as the realization of profits conditions the likelihood of repayment to lenders.

In another circuit, banks earn financial profit on the difference between the interest earned on loans (and other assets) relative to the interest owed to their depositors. Similarly, the two primary functions of banks—deposit servicing and lending—take place at different points in time. Banks must formulate an expectation of future profits, according to the risk and creditworthiness of industrial firms, when determining interest rates and the volume of lending. Repayment of principal and interest over time determines the ability to compensate depositors and service other bank liabilities.

The value added of the financial instability hypothesis is its articulation of the impact of debt and debt repayment on the stability of capitalist economic systems. Just as industrial production is a profit-driven process, so too is the business of banking and financial intermediation. By consequence, the creation of money is not exogenous, but endogenous to the process of capital accumulation.

Minsky posits three forms of financial relations or positions. Under "hedge" finance, industrial firms have sufficient income to repay both principal and interest to lenders. Under "speculative" finance, firms have sufficient income to repay interest, but not principal. Under "Ponzi" finance, firms are unable to repay principal and interest. Minsky's first theorem of the financial instability hypothesis is that capitalism features financial relations that are both stable and unstable. If hedge finance prevails, the economic system tends toward stability. But if the riskier speculative or Ponzi forms prevail, the system tends toward instability. Minsky's second theorem is that during long periods of expansion, the economic system evolves from stable to unstable financial relations—that is, from hedge finance to speculative finance, and then to Ponzi finance. Shifts in market psychology over the course of the business cycle play a pivotal role in this process.

Coming out of a downturn, industrial firms typically hold negative expectations. A high degree of risk aversion implies that firms will likely hold more cash reserves and only take on safer lines of credit for investment, such as hedge finance. As the economic system expands, however, the combination of frugal investment plus economic growth leads to higher profits, and subsequently positive expectations. Firms will reinvest their profits, but they shift their behavior toward more risk taking and more speculation. As a result, they will hold less cash reserves and take on more debt through riskier lines of credit. Moreover, banks exhibit a similar shift in market sentiment, from pessimism to optimism. Coming out of a downturn, they will likely maintain high lending standards and adhere to hedge finance. As profitability and economic growth rebound, however, and frugal investors pay down their debts, banks revise their lending standards toward a willingness to engage in speculative, and eventually Ponzi, finance. A financial crisis occurs when a high propensity of Ponzi investors must sell assets in order to repay their debts. As asset prices collapse in response to a surge in selloffs, market panic and pessimism overtake speculative euphoria, leading to sharp reductions in investment and job creation in the real sector. Crises are not the result of exogenous shocks to the economic system. Rather, they originate from the operation of capitalism and its complex interconnections with the financial sector.

TABLE 5.4 Hyman Minsky's Financial Instability Hypothesis

- Capitalism features financial relations that are both stable and unstable
- Capitalism evolves from stable to unstable financial relations over long periods of expansion
- During expansions, investors shift their behavior towards speculation, and accumulate more debt
- Financial crises occur when over-leveraged investors must sell assets to repay debts
- Crises are the result of endogenous changes to the economic and financial systems - not exogenous shocks

Sources

Minsky, H.P. (1994). The financial instability hypothesis. In P. Arestis & M. Sawyer (eds.), *The Elgar companion to radical political economy* (pp. 153 – 158). Aldershot, UK: Edward Elgar Publishing.

Further Reading

Kalecki, M. (2003). *Essays in the theory of economic fluctuations*. Abingdon, UK: Routledge.

Keynes, J.M. (1964). *The general theory of employment, interest, and money*. San Diego, CA: Harcourt.

Minsky, H.P. (1975). *John Maynard Keynes*. New York, NY: Columbia University Press.

Minsky, H.P. (1982). *Can "it" happen again?* Armonk, NY: M.E. Sharpe.

Minsky, H.P. (1986). *Stabilizing an unstable economy*. New Haven, CT: Yale University Press.

INSTITUTIONALIST EXPLANATIONS

Institutionalists principally reject the ahistorical character of neoclassical economics. Instead, they examine the evolutionary character of economic and social institutions, and the process of long-run historical change. The term "institution" refers to the complex influences on human agency—such as conventions, customs, habits, or routines—that govern the major sectors, organizations, and activities of economic systems. Institutionalist analysis is holistic in that it examines the interactions between the economic and non-economic spheres of societies. Culture plays a particularly significant role in this regard; as do the interactions of politics, social forces, and ecology with the operation of economic systems. Institutionalists emphasize pragmatism and realism in economic analysis. In this sense, they underscore the evolutionary nature of knowledge itself. Policy relevance and the ability of government to improve wellbeing are also essential characteristics of institutionalist analysis. This approach differs, of course, from neoclassical economics and its single-minded focus on Economic Man and methodological individualism; its limited understanding of capitalism as a system of competitive markets under scarcity; its reverence for mathematical and statistical modelling; and its advocacy for *laissez-faire* policies.

Institutionalism is a diverse tradition that intersects not only with other schools within heterodox economics, but also with some traditions within mainstream economics. The central figure in the historical development of institutionalism during the early twentieth century was, without question, Thorstein Veblen. Similar to what transpired in the field of macroeconomics, subsequent developments have either extended or diminished Veblen's distinctive critique of neoclassical economics. In the latter case, a movement within mainstream economics has rebuffed Veblen's analysis of capitalism and reframed the principles of institutionalism to align with neoclassical theory. In the former case, heterodox economists have synthesized the tenets of institutionalism with other schools of radical thought. For example, institutionalists and post-Keynesians have a mutual affinity for Minsky's financial instability hypothesis, which incorporates the interactions of the real and financial sectors, and the evolution of investor behavior over the course of the business cycle. Institutionalists find common ground with feminist and stratification economists for their shared focus on intergroup inequality by gender and race. Radical institutionalists advance an understanding of class that integrates the original insights of Veblen with Marx's critique of capitalism. Radical institutionalists investigate the exploitative and evolutionary character of power relations, and how they condition income and wealth inequality. To this end, they advocate for radical policies that redress capitalist hegemony, and expand popular participation in economic planning and decision making.

Given the diversity of thought and analysis within this tradition, this chapter presents two exemplars of institutionalist explanations of the Great Recession. Each study was published in the *Journal of Economic Issues,* an academic journal that promotes research in the field of institutionalism. Each study also represents an example of the aforementioned intersections between institutionalism and other heterodox schools of economics. In the first piece— "Abundance Denied: Consequences of the Great Recession"—William M. Dugger and James T. Peach present a radical institutionalist analysis of the crisis and the policy responses to it. In the second piece—"The Great Crisis and the Significance of Gender in the U.S. Economy"—Janice Peterson offers a feminist-institutionalist critique of the "Great Mancession" narrative that emerged during the crisis.

A Radical Institutionalist Explanation

The Dugger and Peach study extends their work on "economic abundance." Abundance is a different entry point to understanding the structure and operation of economic systems. According to neoclassical economics, the core dilemma facing all economic systems is scarcity: in a given time period, the stock of resources is limited and unable to achieve all goals. Moreover, scarcity implies the presence of opportunity costs: the investment of resources in one economic activity requires, by definition, the reallocation of resources from an alternative activity. Dugger and Peach concur that economic systems face such dilemmas—at least in the short run. Abundance, on the other hand, involves the full utilization of society's joint stock of knowledge. Knowledge is a unique resource in that it is *not* limited. The application of knowledge toward an economic activity does *not* require the reallocation of knowledge from another activity. Since multiple economic activities can utilize knowledge, it carries no opportunity cost. Further, knowledge changes and evolves over time. However, there are institutional barriers to accessing the joint stock of knowledge, meaning there are institutional barriers to achieving abundance. The core dilemma facing all economic systems is not scarcity, but a lack of abundance. Inequality and exclusion based upon class, nationality, race, and sex prevent full and genuine participation in capitalist economic systems. Universal access to the joint stock of knowledge requires radical changes in institutions, from those that create scarcity to those that promote abundance.

Dugger and Peach apply the concept of abundance to the Great Recession by examining the substantial output gap that emerged during the crisis. The output gap is simply the difference between actual output, measured as real gross domestic product, and potential output. Institutionalists and post-Keynesians acknowledge that such gaps are a regular feature of capitalist societies. Conventional economists do not. They calculate potential output by applying the long-run compounded annual growth rate of 3.3% to actual US output between 2008 and 2012. Over this period, they estimate a cumulative output gap of $6.6 trillion. However, nothing about the Great Recession suggests that the joint stock of knowledge shrunk during this time. In fact, labor productivity increased as US capitalism emerged from the crisis.

Dugger and Peach argue that the output gap resulted from policy responses that did not foster abundance. None of the fiscal policies, monetary policies, or bailouts during the Great Recession sought to expand access to the joint stock of knowledge. They merely reset short-run economic and financial activity. In contrast to post-Keynesian economists, Dugger and Peach argue that full employment is also not enough to achieve abundance. Although full employment eliminates cyclical unemployment—that is, unemployment caused by the business cycle—it allows for frictional, seasonal, and structural unemployment. From an institutionalist perspective, full employment does not alter the barriers that limit access to the joint stock of knowledge. Dugger and Peach call for abundance policies that guarantee access to the joint stock of knowledge for all. In this study, they discuss the prospect of universal employment programs. Universal employment goes beyond full employment by eliminating all forms of unemployment and employing all workers. Unlike full employment, universal employment involves radical institutional change through the creation of an "employer of last resort" in the labor market. An employer of last resort would assist workers with job searches and retraining. If necessary, it would provide direct employment. Unlike full employment policies, universal employment policies would address the frictional, seasonal, and structural forms of unemployment that perpetually exist in capitalist societies. They could also reduce inequality by setting living wage standards and expanding the bargaining power of workers and historically under-represented groups in the workplace. While the establishment of an employer of last resort is indeed a challenging endeavor, Dugger and Peach note that the opportunity cost of not pursuing abundance during the Great Recession is both clear and significant: $6.6 trillion in lost output.

A Feminist-Institutionalist Explanation

In her presidential address to the Association for Evolutionary Economics, Janice Peterson draws parallels between the fields of feminism and institutionalism in order to debunk the "Great Mancession" narrative—a popular account of the crisis spread by blogs, conservative thinktanks, and the press. Proponents of the Mancession narrative argued that the crisis would lead to structural changes in both the labor market and the household for men. This characterization essentially centers on a singular labor market outcome during the Great Recession: namely, that men experienced a purportedly unprecedented increase in the rate of unemployment relative to women. This gap reflects the high concentration of men in industries hit hardest by the recession, such as construction and manufacturing, versus the high concentration of women in industries that supposedly weathered the recession, such as education, government, and healthcare. Furthermore, the fiscal stimulus policies of the Obama administration exacerbated the gender unemployment gap by directing stimulus toward sectors with a high concentration of women. Given the growing labor force participation of women, which began prior to the Great Recession, proponents argue that women will eventually constitute a majority of the US labor force. The realignment of the labor market could subsequently relegate men to greater responsibilities within the household.

From an empirical perspective, there are several flaws with the Mancession narrative noted in the literature. First, the larger increase in unemployment experienced by men is actually not at all unprecedented. The narrative focuses on differences in unemployment rates and employment by sector, but to the exclusion of other gender disparities in labor market outcomes, such as earnings and benefits. It does not consider the complexity of gender inequality, and the differing experiences of women (and men) by age, educational attainment, marital status, and race, among other demographic characteristics. For example, further research shows that female heads of households suffered disproportionately during the Great Recession. Lastly, the shift toward austerity brought about by the conservative Tea Party wave led to significant cutbacks in education and healthcare during the recovery—the very sectors that supposedly favored women during the recession. In addition to its shaky empirical grounds, however, the Great Mancession narrative reflects underlying cultural anxieties about the reversal of gender roles in the household, as well as the diminished relevance and power of men in the workforce. Peterson draws insights from feminist and institutionalist thought in order to develop a theoretical understanding of this problematic aspect—and the inherent inability of neoclassical economics to address it.

Peterson applies a feminist-institutionalist framework to three facets of the Great Mancession narrative. First, the narrative presumes a neoclassical separation between the economic and non-economic spheres of capitalist societies—a separation that both schools of thought reject. More specifically, it privileges the market over both the household and the government as credible economic processes, which systematically undervalues the economic contributions of women in several ways. The narrative overemphasizes the cyclical unemployment of men during the crisis while discounting the persistent structural barriers that women face in the labor market. It laments the loss of status of men as primary income earners, and the shift in the household division of labor, while overlooking the increasing role of women as income earners. It regards the stratification of the labor market by gender—that is, the disproportionate employment of men in the private sector versus the disproportionate employment of women in the public sector—as an advantage for women. It also celebrates the post-crisis austerity measures that reduced government intervention at the state and federal levels, which resulted in greater job losses for women.

Second, the Mancession narrative engages the neoclassical principle of scarcity. It envisions a zero-sum game whereby women benefit at the expense of men in a competitive pursuit for limited resources. It thereby disregards the growing dependence of US households on multiple income earners due to the long-term suppression of real labor income, rising household debt loads, and increasing financial instability. By contrast, feminists and institutionalists argue that gender inequality, and the economic dislocations caused by the Great Recession, are harmful to both women and men.

Finally, enabling myths inform the logic behind the so-called Great Mancession. Enabling myths are conventions that reinforce existing power structures,

TABLE 5.5 Institutionalist Explanations

Radical Institutionalists	- Abundance refers to the full utilization of society's joint stock of knowledge - Policy responses did not address institutional barriers to abundance, such as inequality and exclusion - Policy responses to the crisis only reset short-run economic and financial activity - Full employment is not enough to achieve abundance - Universal employment would guarantee access to the joint stock of knowledge for all
Feminist Institutionalists	- The larger increase in male unemployment relative to female unemployment is not unprecedented - The Mancession narrative ignores other gender disparities in the labor market and their complexity - The narrative privileges the market, and delegitimizes both the household and the government - The narrative presumes that women compete against men in the pursuit of scarce resources - The narrative reflects enabling myths about gender norms and power dynamics

such as racism, classism, and sexism. In this case, underlying the Mancession narrative is a resistance to change in gender norms and power dynamics between women and men. Enabling myths are institutions that maintain inequality, create barriers to abundance, and distort the appropriate policy responses to the crisis. Institutional change will therefore facilitate a deeper understanding of gender inequality and the complex distributional consequences of the Great Recession.

Sources

Dugger, W.M. & Peach, J.T. (2013). Abundance denied: Consequences of the Great Recession. *Journal of Economic Issues*, *47*(2), 351–58. doi: 10.2753/JEI0021-3624470210

Peterson, J. (2012). The great crisis and the significance of gender in the U.S. economy. *Journal of Economic Issues*, *46*(2), 277–90. doi: 10.2753/JEI0021-3624460203

Further Reading

Veblen, T. (1975). *The theory of the leisure class*. New York, NY: A.M. Kelley.

Veblen, T. (1978). *The theory of the business enterprise*. New Brunswick, NJ: Transaction.

A MARXIST EXPLANATION

To conclude this chapter, let's investigate a Marxist analysis of the Great Recession. Like all of the schools of thought surveyed in this chapter—and to an even greater extent—Marxism is a diverse tradition. In keeping with the presentation of previous sections, this section focuses on a particular body of work that has received widespread attention since the crisis in both academic and popular circles. This framework also relates to and builds upon topics explored in previous chapters of this book, such as the emergence of neoliberal capitalism, racial stratification in housing markets, and the evolution of financial structure.

Although David Harvey is a geographer by trade, his work has influenced multiple disciplines during the late twentieth and early twenty-first centuries, including anthropology, history, philosophy, and of course, heterodox economics. Throughout his career, Harvey has developed and applied radical theories in the field of urban geography. Harvey's early work examined the nexus between social justice, racism, and the urban setting of capitalism. During the early 1970s, he famously applied a revolutionary theory of social justice and urban space to the racially segregated neighborhoods of Baltimore, Maryland. His more recent work investigates the historical development of neoliberalism, the geography of capitalist development, and the internal contradictions of capitalism that generate crises. Prior to the Great Recession, Harvey advanced Marxist theories of money and credit, and examined the origin of financial crises in the urban built environment. Geographic expansion, including the 2003 US invasion of Iraq, has been a recurring solution to the crisis-prone period of neoliberal capitalism, which relies in part upon processes of dispossession.

Following the 2008 financial crisis and the Great Recession, Harvey comprehensively investigated these themes in *The Enigma of Capital*. His goal is explain not only the particular causes of the crisis, but also the general function of crises in the history of global capitalism. According to Harvey, capitalism never resolves its tendencies toward crises; it simply relocates them to different sectors, and especially different spaces, in order to maintain compound growth. The history of capitalism is therefore one of both instability and persistence. It persisted following the Great Depression of the 1930s with the emergence of regulated capitalism. It persisted following the crisis of the 1970s with the emergence of neoliberal capitalism. And it certainly persisted following the Great Recession of 2007–09. Harvey does not anticipate an inevitable end to neoliberalism; nor does he foresee another restructuring of capitalist production. Whereas the 1930s and 1970s led to reconfigurations of class power (albeit in opposing ways), the Great Recession did not. The recovery that followed the Great Recession only exacerbated wealth inequality and consolidated the power of financial capitalists, in large part due to their sizable contributions to Obama's 2008 presidential campaign. Nonetheless, Harvey argues that capitalism is reaching new limits on the ability to relocate its crisis problematic. Let's examine the theoretical and historical aspects of his analysis in *The Enigma of Capital* more closely.

Marxists regard capital as a *process* involving the purposeful advancement of money in order to realize a greater sum of money. This process occurs in the realm of industrial production. Harvey applies the model of capital accumulation presented earlier in the Minsky section:

$$M - C - P - C' - M'$$

At the beginning of the cycle, the capitalist advances an initial sum of money (M) in order to purchase commodities (C) that serve as inputs: means of production and labor power. Means of production include non-labor inputs, such as capital goods and raw materials. Labor power refers to the *capacity* for work, meaning the mental and physical abilities of labor. Marx assumes in Volume I of *Capital* that wages fully compensate labor for the consumer goods needed to replenish work effort. The capitalist then organizes a production process (*P*) with a technological dimension (relations between inputs and output) as well as an organizational dimension (social relations between people). The result is a new commodity with a higher value (*C*′). *C*′ has a higher value than *C* because labor not only transfers the value of the means of production to the new commodity, but also adds new value. Otherwise, there would be no incentive for the capitalist to employ labor. Finally, the capitalist must sell *C*′ in a market for a new sum of money (*M*′). Marxists define the difference between *M*′and *M*—the change in money—as surplus value (ΔM). Surplus value arises because wages do not compensate workers for the value produced beyond the value of labor power. This new sum of money includes the original money advanced plus a surplus value:

$$M' = M + \Delta M$$

Money has now been transformed into capital.

The capitalist must then allocate a portion of surplus value toward reinvestment, which initiates another cycle of capital accumulation, for two reasons. First, the capitalist faces competition from other capitalists. Without reinvestment, he or she will no longer remain a capitalist. Second, the social power of money has no inherent limit, so there is every incentive to advance money again. However, there are real limits within the process of capital accumulation that can prevent the realization of surplus value. These limits exist at every stage of the model discussed above:

- At the beginning of the cycle, the capitalist could face difficulties accessing the initial sum of money—for example, if there are disruptions in credit markets due to market forces or central bank interventions that restrict the availability of money.
- The capitalist could face difficulties in the labor market. Indeed, Harvey cites the labor market as a center of crisis formation during the 1970s. Prior to neoliberal capitalism, full employment policies and reliance upon national labor markets granted substantial power to labor relative to capital, which eventually thwarted capitalist investment. The solution was therefore greater labor market competition through globalization.
- Natural limits could disrupt access to raw materials and the ability to manufacture capital goods.
- Crises can emerge if rapid technological advancements disrupt the production process necessary to create new value.
- Similarly, certain organizational forms and configurations of the capitalist labor process can limit capital accumulation. Harvey again cites the excessive power of labor unions within the workplace as a center of crisis formation during the 1970s. Neoliberal capitalism resolved this limit through de-unionization and labor discipline, which further shifted the balance of class power toward capital.
- At the end of the cycle, the capitalist could face difficulties in the market. In order to realize surplus value, the capitalist must exchange the new commodity for money, which requires new effective demand.

Harvey notes the importance of time, space, and finance throughout the entire cycle. If accumulation is too slow, the capitalist will incur losses and be unable to realize surplus value. Geographic barriers can limit access not only to labor and raw materials, but also to money. For example, Harvey argues that the emergence of offshoring and globalization necessitated the development of a new global financial architecture. Financial innovation is indeed critical at every point, which grants a significant amount of power to financial capitalists. There is therefore an incentive to accelerate the process and reduce barriers therein. Capitalists must convert the real limits within the process of capital accumulation into barriers that they can surpass, which could involve both legal strategies and illegal strategies of dispossession.

The fundamental question is: once the capitalist realizes surplus value, where exactly does it go? As noted earlier, at the last stage in the cycle of capital accumulation, the realization of surplus value requires new effective demand. The result of the accumulation process is a new commodity with a higher value, which the capitalist must sell in a competitive market. But in an equal exchange, that requires new effective demand. The source of new effective demand could originate from multiple sources. One possibility is through greater worker consumption. While that was a solution during regulated capitalism, it is limited by the fact that the wage bill is always less than the value of capital in circulation. Wages alone could not claim all output, since profits would be zero. Another possibility is through greater capitalist consumption. Given the degree of inequality, however, personal consumption by the capitalist class itself will be insufficient to absorb surplus value. Lacking any external sources of surplus absorption, the solution is new effective demand generated by expansion of the system. Capitalism internalizes its effective demand problem by claiming output produced in the *current* period through expansion of the system in the *next* period. The solution involves reinvestment by capitalists, but continuous accumulation necessitates new profitable investment opportunities at a compound rate. The system can stagnate, or fall into crisis, if substantial barriers limit opportunities for reinvestment. Excessive accumulation without sufficient investment opportunities will then devalue capital.

Harvey's argument is that the origins of this crisis lie in the resolution of the crisis of the 1970s. Capitalism relocated its crisis problematic away from the barriers in the labor market and the workplace, and recalibrated power relations to favor capital—in particular, financial capital. In the lead-up to the crisis, financialization generated continuous investment opportunities in financial markets and real estate, and devalued opportunities in the real sector. Expanded access to credit in the housing market sustained worker consumption under stagnant real wages; otherwise, neoliberal capitalism would have faced a serious crisis of underconsumption much earlier. Capitalist reinvestment favored speculative investment in assets over productive investment in capital goods with the formation of fictitious financial securities. This created an unstable environment in which capitalism required not simply accumulation at a compound rate, but *credit-fueled* accumulation at a compound rate. Credit bridged the gap between the absorption of today's surplus and tomorrow's expansion of the system.

But in doing so, capitalism created a new problematic. Whereas property markets resolved the previous crisis in the labor market and the capitalist workplace, they became the center of crisis formation with the collapse of the housing

TABLE 5.6 A Marxist Explanation

- Capitalism must continuously relocate its crisis problematic in order to maintain compound growth
- The origins of the crisis lie in the resolution of the Crisis of the 1970's
- The crisis exacerbated inequality and consolidated the power of financial capitalists
- Capitalism now faces new limits on the ability to relocate its crisis problematic
- Resolution of the crisis requires consolidating the power of the working class, and transitioning away from capitalism

market bubble. In general, such crises tend to be longer and more severe, given that they involve more debt, carry higher risk, and take more time to reveal themselves. Harvey's principal argument is that it is no longer possible to maintain compound growth. Capitalism simply cannot generate the value of profitable investment opportunities necessary to maintain its long-run compound growth rate. In fact, this problem emerged well before the 2008 financial crisis and the Great Recession, given the increasing frequency of financial crises and financial volatility since the transition to neoliberal capitalism. However, he does not anticipate an inevitable end to neoliberalism. For Harvey, the resolutions of previous crises have never been inevitable. The resolution of this crisis requires the organization of political power on the part of the working class, and social control of the surplus. He advocates for greater social control of money and wealth, and the reorganization of economic production away from capitalist class relations and property rights.

Sources

Harvey, D. (2011). *The enigma of capital: and the crises of capitalism*. New York, NY: Oxford University Press.

Further Reading

Harvey, D. (2003). *The new imperialism*. New York, NY: Oxford University Press.

Harvey, D. (2005). *A brief history of neoliberalism*. New York, NY: Oxford University Press.

Harvey, D. (2007). *The limits to capital*. Brooklyn, NY: Verso.

Harvey, D. (2009). *Social justice in the city*. Athens, GA: University of Georgia Press.

Harvey, D. (2014). *Seventeen contradictions and the end of capitalism*. New York, NY: Oxford University Press.

PART III

Policy Responses to the Great Recession

CHAPTER 6

Financial Reform

On June 17, 2009, newly inaugurated US President Barack Obama took the first step in transforming a major campaign promise into concrete legislative action: "A sweeping overhaul of the financial regulatory system." By that point, the emergency policy responses of the W. Bush administration, the nascent Obama administration, and the US Federal Reserve had halted the worst volatility of the crisis and reset economic and financial activity. In fact, although it was not known at the time, US capitalism had already reached the official "trough" of the Great Recession. The next phase in the government's response—arguably more complex and challenging than the foregoing emergency measures—was the development of policies that would foster economic recovery and financial stability. In his remarks, Obama set three priorities for financial reform. First, the new regulatory structure should include mechanisms that monitor systemic risk, and not simply the solvency of individual financial firms. Second, the post-crisis regulatory structure should include a new federal agency devoted to consumer financial protection. Third, financial reform should close regulatory gaps and inefficiencies throughout the US and international financial systems.

The final outcome—which would take over a year to pass, but would largely cover the vast majority of Obama's original proposal—was the Dodd-Frank Wall Street Reform and Consumer Protection Act, or simply "Dodd-Frank." Critics and defenders alike recognize Dodd-Frank as a significant and meaningful piece of legislation. The Act itself is enormous, encompassing 849 pages and 16 titles. More substantively, there is now a clear distinction between pre- and post-Dodd-Frank financial regulation. Yet Obama himself described his vision as a "careful balance." He maintained that free and competitive markets are the essential source of economic prosperity and innovation; that job creation is the purview of risk-taking capitalists; and that government should facilitate wealth building. In short, a restructuring of the financial *system* was never the goal. Rather, he charged Congress with addressing structural weaknesses in the financial system; limiting financial practices that fueled reckless and abusive behavior; improving transparency; and preventing normal fluctuations in the business cycle from triggering financial crises.

DOI: 10.4324/9780429461316-9

This chapter begins an investigation of the policy responses to the Great Recession. Whereas Part II examined the origins of the Great Recession, Part III investigates how the Great Recession was ultimately ended. Each of the three chapters in this part focuses on the purpose and conduct of a major policy response to the crisis. Chapter 6 opens with an analysis of financial reform. Chapter 7 then examines monetary policy responses to both the 2008 financial crisis and the economic crisis; while Chapter 8 discusses fiscal policy responses to the economic crisis.

This chapter is divided into two major sections. The first and largest section outlines the key provisions of Dodd-Frank—but not in sequential order as defined in the law. Instead, it uses the model of financial structure presented in Chapter 4 as an outline, and relates the interconnected components of financial structure, the transmission of the 2008 financial crisis, and the conduct of the Wall Street bailouts to the provisions of Dodd-Frank. The final section considers the merits and limits of Dodd-Frank, particularly from the perspectives of heterodox economists and consumer advocates for financial reform.

THE DODD-FRANK WALL STREET REFORM AND CONSUMER PROTECTION ACT

The long title of Dodd-Frank summarizes how the law seeks to achieve financial stability in the aftermath of the 2008 financial crisis:

> An Act to promote the financial stability of the United States by improving accountability and transparency in the financial system, to end "too big to fail", to protect the American taxpayer by ending bailouts, to protect consumers from abusive financial services practices, and for other purposes.

But how do the provisions of Dodd-Frank accomplish these goals specifically? For reference, Table 6.1 outlines the major titles of Dodd-Frank in sequential

TABLE 6.1 Titles of the Dodd-Frank Wall Street Reform and Consumer Protection Act

I.	Financial Stability
II.	Orderly Liquidation Authority
III.	Transfer of Powers to the Comptroller of the Currency, the Corporation, and the Board of Governors
IV.	Regulation of Advisers to Hedge Funds and Others
V.	Insurance
VI.	Improvements to Regulation of Bank and Savings Association Holding Companies and Depository Institutions
VII.	Wall Street Transparency and Accountability
VIII.	Payment, Clearing, and Settlement Provision
IX.	Investor Protections and Improvements to the Regulation of Securities
X.	Bureau of Consumer Financial Protection
XI.	Federal Reserve System Provisions
XII.	Improving Access to Mainstream Financial Institutions
XIII.	Pay It Back Act
XIV.	Mortgage Reform and Anti-Predatory Lending Act
XV.	Miscellaneous Provisions
XVI.	Section 1256 Contracts

TABLE 6.2 Provisions of Dodd-Frank in Relation to Financial Structure

Area	*Title or Subtitle*
Mortgage Lending and Homeownership	XIV. Mortgage Reform and Anti-Predatory Lending Act
Commercial Banking	VI. Improvements to Regulation of Bank and Savings Association Holding Companies and Depository Institutions
	III. Transfer of Powers to the Comptroller of the Currency, the Corporation, and the Board of Governors
	XII. Improving Access to Mainstream Financial Institutions
Mortgage Securitization	IX.D. Improvements to the Asset-Backed Securitization Process
	IX.E. Accountability and Executive Compensation
	IX.G. Strengthening Corporate Governance
Financial Stability Oversight Council	I. Financial Stability
Securities Markets	IX.A. Increasing Investor Protection
	IX.B. Increasing Regulatory Enforcement and Remedies
	IV. Regulation of Advisors to Hedge Funds and Others
	IX.F. Improvements to the Management of the Securities and Exchange Commission
	IX.J. Securities and Exchange Commission Match Funding
Credit Ratings	IX.C. Improvements to the Regulation of Credit Rating Agencies
Insurance	V.A. Office of National Insurance
	VII. Wall Street Transparency and Accountability
Bailout Reform	II. Orderly Liquidation Authority
	XI. Federal Reserve System Provisions
	XIII. Pay It Back Act
Consumer Financial Protection Bureau	X. Bureau of Consumer Financial Protection

order. Table 6.2 summarizes the analysis presented throughout this section, which relates the components of financial structure to the titles and subtitles of the law.

Mortgage Lending and Homeownership

This analysis begins with surely the most important catalysts of the Great Recession: the subprime mortgage boom and the subsequent foreclosure crisis. Title XIV of Dodd-Frank ("Mortgage Reform and Anti-Predatory Lending Act") contains multiple provisions related to mortgage lending and homeownership. Regarding mortgage reform, the law sets both general and specific standards. In general, the objective of Title XIV is to contribute to economic stability by regulating mortgage lending without constraining the availability of credit. The law also provides a new standard for residential mortgage origination: the contractual terms should "reasonably reflect" the ability of the borrower to pay back the loan, and must be "understandable and not unfair, deceptive or abusive." More specifically, Title XIV requires mortgage originators to be qualified, registered, and licensed. It prohibits all steering incentives based upon the contractual terms of a mortgage product, which had led to predatory marketing strategies in the subprime market. It empowers the Federal Reserve Board of Governors with the discretionary authority to write rules that prohibit many of the lending practices that preceded the crisis: steering borrowers toward loans they are unlikely to repay; steering borrowers toward predatory loans; steering borrowers who otherwise qualify for traditional loans toward subprime loans; discriminating against borrowers with equal credit characteristics on the basis of race, ethnicity, gender, or age; and misrepresenting a borrower's credit history, the availability of certain loan products to a borrower, or the appraised value of collateral property. Mortgage originators that violate these standards are now subject to legal liability.

Title XIV sets minimum standards on the range of mortgage products available in the market. In order to determine a borrower's ability to repay, creditors must utilize payment schedules that include the full amortization of the loan over the entire term, and account for taxes, insurance, and assessments. In addition, creditors must include second mortgages in their determinations, and verify borrower income. This standard applies not only to traditional loans but also adjustable-rate, interest-only, and negative amortization loans. For example, in the case of an interest-only loan, the creditor must disclose the monthly payment that will pay off the remaining loan balance after the initial period. Likewise, in the case of a negative amortization loan, the creditor must account for any increase in the principal, and disclose the monthly payment that will pay off the entire loan balance. However, the law does not impose similar restrictions on shared appreciation loans. In fact, Title XIV first calls for a study in order to determine rules that promote the sustainable provision of shared appreciation mortgages.

Creditors that violate these standards cannot foreclose on borrowers. Moreover, the law establishes new requirements for the contractual terms of specific mortgage products. For example, it prohibits pre-payment penalties on non-traditional loans, requires consumer disclosure statements for negative amortization loans, and significantly limits the size of balloon payments. Several sections impose further disclosure requirements on creditors. Creditors must notify borrowers of interest resets six months in advance. For adjustable-rate mortgages, they must disclose not only the initial monthly payment but also the fully indexed payment, and the total amount of settlement charges, fees, and interest to be paid over the entire term. For any subprime mortgage, a borrower must receive pre-loan counseling before a creditor issues the loan.

Regarding the foreclosure crisis, Title XIV establishes an Office of Housing Counseling within the Department of Housing and Urban Development (HUD) for both homeowners and renters. It establishes a program within HUD to protect tenants of multi-family properties that are at risk of foreclosure. Title XIV also provides direct funding for homeowners, renters, and communities afflicted by the foreclosure crisis. The Emergency Homeowners' Relief Fund assists borrowers who are likely to make their payments again; while the Neighborhood Stabilization Program aids state and local governments with the rehabilitation of abandoned properties lost to foreclosure. Another grant program within HUD provided legal assistance to low-income homeowners facing foreclosure, as well as renters facing eviction due to foreclosure, with priority given to the metropolitan areas with the highest foreclosure rates. Funding for this program ceased in 2012, however.

Commercial Banking

In addition to mortgage reform and limits on predatory lending, Dodd-Frank includes multiple titles that regulate the operations of bank holding companies, commercial banks, and other depository institutions, the largest of which is Title VI ("Improvements to Regulation of Bank and Savings Association Holding Companies and Depository Institutions"). First, Title VI strengthens reporting and examination requirements for bank holding companies. When requested by the Federal Reserve Board of Governors, a bank holding company must provide reports and information submitted to state and federal regulatory agencies, as well as externally audited financial statements. Title VI authorizes the Board of Governors to examine a bank holding company and its subsidiaries for the purpose of verifying compliance with federal law, and notifying the Federal Reserve as to its financial situation. When under examination, a bank holding company must report any risks that could threaten the stability of the firm, a depository institution subsidiary, or the financial system, as well as how the firm monitors and limits such risks. It notably subjects a non-depository institution subsidiary engaged in lending activities to the same examination requirements as a depository institution subsidiary, closing a previous inconsistency in regulatory oversight. Second, Title VI strengthens regulations related to mergers, acquisitions, and consolidations. For example, it imposes concentration limits on large financial firms. No financial firm may complete a merger if the new firm accounts for more than 10% of the total liabilities of all financial firms. It prohibits regulators from approving an interstate merger if the new insured depository institution accounts for more than 10% of the total deposits of all insured depository institutions. The law requires the Board of Governors to consider the degree to which any bank acquisition threatens financial stability. However, acquisitions of non-banks by a financial holding company do not require Board approval, unless the assets acquired in the deal exceed $10 billion. Title VI also prohibits a national bank from converting to a state bank (and vice versa) in order to evade a regulatory investigation. Third, Title VI sets new standards and limits on balance sheet activities. In general, a bank holding company must function as a "source of financial strength" for any depository institution subsidiary. A financial holding company must similarly remain "well capitalized and well managed." One of the more consequential provisions of Title VI is the inclusion of credit exposure from derivative transactions, repurchase agreements, and other securities transactions in bank lending limits. It restricts conflicts of interest by limiting lending to, and asset purchases from, industry insiders. Moreover, the law requires the Board of Governors to develop capital regulations such that capital levels will increase during expansions and decrease during recessions in order to mitigate financial instability. Lastly, Title VI is the home of the "Volcker Rule." Named after former Federal Reserve Chair Paul Volcker, the Volcker Rule encompasses a series of provisions that limit risky, proprietary trading by banks, as well as ownership stakes in hedge funds or private equity funds. Non-bank financial firms regulated by the Board of Governors also face stronger capital requirements, and similar restrictions on proprietary trading and relationships with funds. The law provides for several permitted activities in this area. However, it explicitly prohibits any trade that could cause a "material conflict of interest," expose the bank to high-risk assets, endanger the solvency of the bank, or endanger the stability of the financial sector. Banks are prohibited from owning more than 3% of a fund and investing more than 3% of Tier 1 capital in all funds.

Whereas Title VI implements new rules and requirements, Title III ("Transfer of Powers to the Comptroller of the Currency, the Corporation, and the Board of Governors") improves consistency and efficiency in banking regulation—one of Obama's chief goals. In addition to ensuring a stable banking system, Title III seeks to maintain the dual system of state and national banks in the United States, establish a "fair and appropriate" level of regulation irrespective of bank size or charter, and streamline the regulatory structure of banking. The most notable provision to that end is the elimination of the Office of Thrift Supervision, which transfers its powers to the Comptroller of the Currency, the Federal Deposit Insurance Corporation (FDIC), and the Federal Reserve Board of Governors. In addition, Title III permanently increases federal deposit insurance to $250,000, and establishes an Office of Minority and Women Inclusion at all financial regulatory agencies within the federal government.

Although one of the smaller titles of Dodd-Frank, Title XII ("Improving Access to Mainstream Financial Institutions") facilitates greater access to financial institutions for those outside the "financial mainstream," such as the unbanked and other underserved communities. Title XII creates grant programs in order to establish bank accounts for low-income individuals and provide low-cost, small-dollar loans to borrowers. It likewise provides funding for community development financial institutions in order to offset the costs of small-dollar consumer loans through loan-loss reserve funds.

Mortgage Securitization

Turning now to the secondary mortgage market and the process of mortgage securitization, Title IX Subtitle D ("Improvements to the Asset-Backed Securitization Process") prescribes new regulations for securities issuers. In particular, it contains one of the principal recommendations made by Alan Greenspan during the 2008 financial crisis: securities issuers must hold at least 5% of the credit risk for the securities that they sell. This rule applies to all asset-backed securities including mortgage-backed securities. Issuers may not hedge or transfer any retained credit risk as required by law. Subtitle D also implements new disclosure requirements for securities issuers. Issuers must now report detailed data and information related to the collateral that back their securities. In the case of mortgage-backed securities, this standard requires an investment bank to divulge mortgage-level data, such as the identity of the mortgage originator, the form and amount of compensation of the mortgage originator, and the credit risk retained by the mortgage originator and the issuer of the mortgage-backed security.

Title IX ("Investor Protections and Improvements to the Regulation of Securities") further addresses executive compensation and corporate governance at securities firms. Subtitle E ("Accountability and Executive Compensation") provides shareholders a non-binding vote on executive compensation and "golden parachute" agreements. It requires issuers to disclose information to shareholders regarding executive pay in relation to stock performance; median employee pay, excluding the chief executive officer (CEO); CEO pay; the ratio of median employee pay to CEO pay; and any hedging by employees or directors of the firm. Issuers that violate accounting standards by releasing erroneous financial statements must reclaim any incentive-based executive compensation. More broadly, federal regulators will develop rules that require financial institutions to report on incentive-based executive compensation systems, in order to determine whether such systems are excessive and "could lead to material financial loss." Regulators will accordingly develop prohibitions on certain incentive-based compensation systems that promote excessive risk-taking. Subtitle G ("Strengthening Corporate Governance") contains a small but important improvement to corporate governance at securities firms: an issuer must explain to shareholders the selection of one person as board chair and CEO, or the selection of different persons for each position.

Preventing Systemic Crises: The Financial Stability Oversight Council

Thus far, this chapter has focused on the sections of Dodd-Frank that address the operations of individual financial firms, such as mortgage lenders, depository institutions, and securities firms. However, Dodd-Frank includes key mechanisms that monitor the interconnectedness of financial firms and the stability of the financial system—another priority of the Obama administration. The most important title to that effect is Title I ("Financial Stability"), which establishes the Financial Stability Oversight Council. The purpose of the Council is threefold: to assess systemic risk in the financial system; to abolish moral hazard within the financial system, meaning the government will no longer protect the stock and bond holders of financial firms from losses; and to act against future occurrences of financial instability. The Council, chaired by the secretary of the Treasury, comprises federal and state regulators from across the financial services sector. Some of its general duties include collecting information from regulators, enabling knowledge sharing between regulators, systematizing cooperation between regulators, locating regulatory gaps within the financial sector, and advising and reporting to Congress. In its annual report to Congress, each voting member must sign a statement that the Council, the federal government, and the financial sector are "taking all reasonable steps" to prevent financial instability and limit systemic risk to the economic system. If a voting member disagrees, he or she must submit a statement that identifies the measures necessary to achieve such outcomes. In order to assist the Council with these duties, the law establishes an Office of Financial Research within the US Treasury Department, which is responsible for data collection, research, and analytics.

A number of sections of Title I represent an important pivot in the comprehensive monitoring of interconnected financial institutions. First, by a two-thirds majority vote, and with the consent of the Treasury, the Council may subject a non-bank financial firm to supervision and regulation by the Federal Reserve

Board of Governors, if the Council establishes that the financial activities or potential failure of the firm presents a systemic risk. Specific considerations include "the importance of the company as a source of credit for low-income, minority, or underserved communities, and the impact that the failure of such company would have on the availability of credit in such communities." Furthermore, this section includes an important anti-evasion measure: *any* firm, regardless of legal status or structure, is subject to this provision if its financial activities present a systemic risk. Second, the Council may recommend new or stronger regulations on bank holding companies and non-bank financial firms under the supervision of the Board of Governors, or the principal regulatory agency. The Board may also impose new or stronger regulations independently. These measures include mandatory annual stress tests and the submission of "resolution plans" for systemically important financial firms. Resolution plans must detail how a firm will cease operations should it fail. If a financial firm does not submit a convincing plan that would result in the orderly shutdown of the firm, the Board of Governors and the FDIC may impose stricter capital and liquidity requirements, limit the growth of the firm, or force the firm to divest assets. Firms cannot evade these heightened regulations by no longer operating as bank holding companies, especially if they received bailout funds from the Emergency Economic Stabilization Act. Third, the law authorizes the Board of Governors to intervene against large bank holding companies or non-bank financial firms that present a systemic risk. By a two-thirds majority vote of the Council, and with the consent of the Treasury, the Board can prohibit a merger, acquisition, or consolidation; limit the sale of a particular financial product; force the firm to cease a particular activity; or impose conditions on an activity. If those measures are insufficient, the Board can force the firm to liquidate its assets.

Securities Markets

The recognition that large, interconnected financial institutions pose a systemic risk to the financial sector and the economic system is an essential feature of Dodd-Frank. However, another essential feature is the recognition that financial markets account for an increasing share of financial intermediation. To that end, Dodd-Frank expands protections for securities investors, implements new regulations on securities markets, and reforms the management and funding of the Securities and Exchange Commission (SEC). Title IX of Dodd-Frank addresses most of these issues. For example, Subtitle A ("Increasing Investor Protection") expands the advice and influence of securities investors within the SEC. It establishes an Investor Advisory Committee, the purpose of which is to confer with the SEC on securities regulations, investor interests, investor confidence, and other issues related to securities market activities. The Committee will also submit policy recommendations to the SEC. As part of this new structure, a new Office of Investor Advocate will settle disputes between securities investors and the SEC, communicate investor concerns with a particular financial firm or security, and promote the policy interests of securities investors.

Subtitle A further establishes new regulations on securities markets. The law empowers the SEC to impose a fiduciary duty on brokers. Investment advice must be "in the best interest of the customer without regard to the financial or other interest of the broker, dealer, or investment adviser providing the advice." Investment advisers must also disclose conflicts of interest to their customers. The SEC may consider and develop additional regulations that limit or forbid specific sales techniques, conflicts of interest, or compensation systems for investment advisers. Subtitle B ("Increasing Regulatory Enforcement and Remedies") builds upon these rules by establishing financial incentives and protections for whistleblowers who report securities law violations. It bans convicted felons and "bad actors" from selling securities, and makes manipulative short selling illegal. Title IV of Dodd-Frank ("Regulation of Advisers to Hedge Funds and Others") specifically requires hedge fund advisers to register with the SEC, removing a previous exemption in federal law. When requested by the SEC, registered investment advisers must submit reports on their activities to the SEC in order to protect the interests of securities investors, or to the Financial Stability Oversight Council in order to identify systemic risk.

Finally, Title IX Subtitle F ("Improvements to the Management of the Securities and Exchange Commission") mandates a series of reports and studies on the organization and management of the SEC. Subtitle J ("Securities and Exchange Commission Match Funding") increases SEC funding through transaction fees and assessments, as well as expanded Congressional appropriations.

Credit Ratings

Favorable credit ratings contributed in part to the investor sentiment that mortgage-backed securities were relatively safe. Those ratings, of course, were fundamentally flawed. Moreover, the transmission of the 2008 financial crisis revealed the significance and complexity of the ratings process in financial intermediation, beyond the fact that the ratings themselves were inaccurate. Several factors therefore motivated Congress to increase federal oversight of the credit rating agencies, including the recognition that credit ratings are systemically important; that rating agencies perform services comparable to auditors and securities analysts; that the production of credit ratings is a commercial endeavor; and that the client relationship between the rating agencies and securities issuers involves conflicts of interest. Consistent with the overall premise of Dodd-Frank, Title IX Subtitle C ("Improvements to the Regulation of Credit Rating Agencies") increases the accountability and transparency of the credit rating agencies. It states:

> Because of the systemic importance of credit ratings and the reliance placed on credit ratings by individual and institutional investors and financial regulators, the activities and performances of credit rating agencies ... are matters of national public interest, as credit rating agencies are central to capital formation, investor confidence, and the efficient performance of the United States economy.

The law now requires each agency to maintain an internal control process related to the production of credit ratings, and report on this process annually to the SEC. If an agency has a record of producing inaccurate ratings, the SEC has the authority to deregister the agency from rating a particular security. The SEC has the authority to issue regulations that separate marketing interests from the ratings process. In order to address conflicts of interest, Dodd-Frank mandates that each rating agency have a board of directors, half of which are independent. Each agency must also submit a report to the SEC on employment transitions between the agency and securities issuers. In a further enhancement to accountability, the law establishes an Office of Credit Ratings within the SEC that carries out these provisions. One of the primary responsibilities of the Office is to perform annual examinations of each rating agency, which the SEC will make public. The law ultimately grants the SEC the authority to develop regulations in order to carry out these duties, and levy fines or penalties for violations.

For the purpose of improving transparency in the credit ratings process, Dodd-Frank requires a rating agency to release its initial credit rating for a security and any changes over time. Each agency must disclose both the qualitative and quantitative content behind its rating methodologies, as well as any changes to such procedures. More specifically, each agency must release a user-friendly form for each credit rating that explains the assumptions and data used in the rating process. Throughout this process, credit rating analysts must now meet qualification standards in training and testing. Furthermore, the law requires a rating agency to consider credible information about a securities issuer from other sources. If that information includes violations of the law by a securities issuer, the rating agency must report such allegations to the authorities.

Insurance

The 2008 financial crisis laid bare not only the systemic importance of insurance *institutions* in the operation of the financial system, but also the lack of regulatory oversight of insurance contracts in financial *markets*. The most striking example of both concerns, of course, was the collapse of American International Group (AIG). Prior to the crisis, AIG extensively wrote and sold credit default swaps—the opaque instruments that insured mortgage-backed securities against default—to securities investors. Two titles of Dodd-Frank therefore address matters of insurance in financial regulatory reform. Title V ("Insurance") enhances state, federal, and international oversight of insurance companies; while Title VII ("Wall Street Transparency and Accountability") resolves gaps in the regulation of credit default swaps. In response to the controversial bailout of AIG by the Federal Reserve, Title VII also prohibits federal bailouts of swap entities.

In order to increase supervision of insurance companies, Title V, Subtitle A ("Office of National Insurance") establishes a federal insurance agency within the Treasury Department. The responsibilities of this agency include, among other functions, monitoring the insurance sector; assessing regulatory gaps that could pose a systemic risk to the insurance sector or the financial system; advancing national insurance policy related to international concerns; and working with the states on national and international insurance issues. The Federal Insurance Office has the authority to recommend to the Financial Stability Oversight Council the supervision of an insurance company by the Federal Reserve Board of Governors. In addition, the Office will examine access and barriers to insurance for low-income and minority consumers. However, its authority excludes three forms of insurance: crop, long-term care, and health insurance. Similar in purpose to other provisions of Dodd-Frank, the Federal Insurance Office serves as a hub for the gathering, sharing, and analyzing of information from the insurance sector.

Title VII improves transparency in the provision and supervision of credit default swaps, and other securities regarded as "toxic assets" during the 2008 financial crisis. The law first delineates regulatory jurisdiction over "swap" markets: the Commodity Futures Trading Commission (CFTC) is responsible for the supervision of over-the-counter swaps (e.g., credit default swaps); while the SEC is responsible for the supervision of "security-based swaps" (e.g., mortgage-backed securities). The latter provision is particularly significant, as it repeals a previous ban on the regulation of security-based swaps contained in the Gramm-Leach-Bliley Act. However, in order to maintain consistency, each agency must coordinate with the other "to the extent possible" when it writes a new rule. For example, if the SEC proposes a regulation on mortgage-backed securities, it will consult the CFTC. Likewise, if the CFTC issues an order concerning credit default swaps, it will consult the SEC. The law requires both agencies to work jointly with the Federal Reserve Board of Governors to continue to define the securities and entities under their respective authorities. Each agency can obtain information and issue reports on any swap or security-based swap that contributes to financial market volatility. For similar reasons, after consulting with the Treasury Department, each agency can ban foreign entities from US swap markets.

In a further step toward transparency in swap markets, Title VII mandates the clearing of a swap through an exchange or a registered derivatives clearing organization, although not all swaps are required to do so. Swap dealers and major swap participants must now register with the CFTC. In order to mitigate systemic risk and financial market instability, they are subject to capital and margin requirements. The law makes it illegal for any individual to engage in a "manipulative or deceptive device of contrivance." Following a swap transaction, the CFTC has the authority to release price and quantity data to the public in real time.

The most consequential section of Title VII is the ban on federal bailouts of any swaps entity: "No Federal assistance may be provided to any swaps entity with respect to any swap, security-based swap, or other activity of the swaps entity." The law defines "federal assistance" as any use of funds from a Federal Reserve credit program that does not feature "broad-based" eligibility, such as lending to a swaps entity; purchasing the stock, equity, debt, or assets of a swaps entity; or guaranteeing the debt of a swaps entity. However, this provision does not apply to a swap or security-based swap activity by an insured depository institution. If a swap or security-based swap activity leads to the insolvency or receivership of a financial institution, the firm must cease the contributing activity. The law also prohibits the use of taxpayer funds to avoid receivership of a swap entity. In the execution of this authority, the government will recoup any costs incurred through the liquidation of the swap entity's assets—not from taxpayer dollars.

Bailout Reform

During the 2008 financial crisis, the US government took unprecedented actions to stabilize the operation of both financial institutions and financial markets. There were two main characteristics of the initial interventions by the W. Bush administration. First, they were largely arranged on an emergency basis. Absent a clear federal policy in this area, the government simply had no plan as to how to manage institutional failures and financial market volatility, and could only respond to circumstances as they arose. There was no mechanism to prevent or contain a systemic crisis. The only guiding principle, of course, was "too big to fail." Second, the initial interventions were arranged on a case-by-case basis, which resulted in disparate responses. The New York Federal Reserve Bank organized the merger of Bear Stearns with JPMorgan Chase; the Treasury Department nationalized Fannie Mae and Freddie Mac; Lehman Brothers was allowed to declare bankruptcy; and the Federal Reserve nationalized AIG. Both factors fueled a crisis of confidence, culminating in a credit freeze, which eventually led to more concerted actions through the Emergency Economic Stabilization Act.

Once the crisis subsided, the task left to the Obama administration was how to deal with future cases of financial instability in an orderly and uniform way. The premise for bailout reform was this: institutional failures themselves are not necessarily the problem; rather, *unexpected* institutional failures are the problem. Unexpected institutional failures lead to crises of confidence, market volatility, and instability in the real sector—all of which require government intervention, and thus taxpayer dollars, to cover losses and resuscitate economic growth. This was especially the case for the complex, interconnected financial firms that collapsed in 2008. For commercial banks, there is such a mechanism for handling institutional failures. The FDIC insures the depositors of a failed bank, liquidates its assets, and then settles its debts. Since the Great Depression of the 1930s, this process has successfully prevented bank failures from destabilizing the financial sector, destabilizing the economic system, and eroding investor confidence. However, prior to Dodd-Frank, no such mechanism existed for non-bank financial firms like investment banks and insurance companies. Three titles of Dodd-Frank therefore address bailout reform. Title II ("Orderly Liquidation Authority") establishes a comprehensive Orderly Liquidation Authority for containing institutional failures. Title XI ("Federal Reserve System Provisions") reforms the emergency authority, governance, and public oversight of the Federal Reserve. Title XIII ("Pay It Back Act") limits the availability of funds for the Troubled Asset Relief Program (TARP), and restricts the allocation of any unused funds.

Title II establishes a process for liquidating failing financial firms in order to limit systemic risk and moral hazard problems. The purpose is not to protect a financial firm from failure, as was the case under "too big to fail." The law clearly states that shareholders and creditors will incur losses; that the management and directors of the firm will be dismissed; and that the distribution of losses will be proportional to responsibility for the financial condition of the firm. The FDIC will serve as receiver in all determinations, but the process for initiating liquidation varies by the category of financial firm. A recommendation for placing a financial firm into receivership requires a two-thirds majority vote of both the FDIC and the Federal Reserve Board of Governors. For a broker or dealer, however, a recommendation requires a two-thirds majority vote of both the SEC and the Board of Governors. For an insurance company, it requires a two-thirds majority vote of the Board of Governors and the consent of the director of the Federal Insurance Office. Recommendations for receivership must consider and assess the following questions:

- Is the firm in, or at risk of, default?
- What are the repercussions of default on the stability of the financial sector?

- What are the repercussions of default on the financial and economic circumstances of low-income and minority groups?
- What interventions should the government pursue, and to what degree?
- What is the probability of a private sector solution?
- Why is resolution through bankruptcy inappropriate?
- What are the repercussions of default on financial market participants, such as creditors and shareholders?
- Is the failing firm a "financial firm" as defined in the law?

If the Treasury Department accepts the recommendation, after consulting the president of the United States, the secretary will appoint the FDIC as receiver of a failing financial firm for a period of three years. However, the FDIC may not acquire any ownership interests in the firm under receivership. The secretary will then issue reports to Congress and the public; while the Government Accountability Office (GAO) will issue its own report on the determination. Firms that do not consent to the receivership may pursue a judicial review and appeals process. Once placed under receivership, the law requires that the FDIC liquidate the firm, and that the costs incurred to the FDIC be financed through the sale of the firm's assets. The law explicitly prohibits the appropriation of any tax dollars to protect a firm from liquidation. In fact, taxpayers are legally protected from any losses related to this process.

Title XI contains several key provisions related to Federal Reserve reform. First, Title XI alters the scope and conduct of Federal Reserve emergency lending. All emergency lending programs now require the approval of the secretary of the Treasury. Eligibility for such programs must be "broad-based," meaning the Federal Reserve may no longer purchase the assets of an individual organization, or protect it from bankruptcy, as it did during the 2008 financial crisis. In fact, borrowers must certify that they are not insolvent. The law directs the Board of Governors to develop rules and practices, with the approval of the secretary of the Treasury, in order to:

> ensure that any emergency lending program or facility is for the purpose of providing liquidity to the financial system, and not to aid a failing financial company, and that the security for emergency loans is sufficient to protect taxpayers from losses and that any such program is terminated in a timely and orderly fashion.

When the Board of Governors engages in emergency lending, the law requires a report to Congress on the nature and scope of the assistance. Second, Title XI imposes limits on debt guarantees for solvent banks—another controversial action taken during the financial crisis. The law permits the government to make such guarantees, but there must be clear evidence that a threat to financial or economic stability exists. A debt guarantee requires a two-thirds majority vote of the Board of Governors and the FDIC, as well as the approval of the secretary of the Treasury. The secretary determines the amount of the guarantee, and the president of the United States may report to Congress and seek approval. Third, Title XI reforms the governance of the Federal Reserve system. Federal Reserve Bank presidents will now be elected by directors that represent the public, not member banks. The law also establishes a vice chairman for supervision on the Board of

Governors, who will develop proposals for financial regulatory policies, and supervise Board regulation of financial firms. Fourth, Title XI calls for a number of measures that increase public oversight of the Federal Reserve and the transparency of monetary policy. It subjects the Federal Reserve to GAO audits of its credit programs and open market operations. It mandates that the Board of Governors release all audits to the public, including detailed information about the participants and terms of such programs. Title XI calls for a one-time GAO audit and publication of all measures and actions taken by the Federal Reserve during the financial crisis. The GAO will also conduct a study of Federal Reserve governance in order to determine whether the appointment process for Federal Reserve Bank directors represents the public, in terms of both demographic and economic interests, or involves conflicts of interest.

Lastly, Title XIII cuts funding for TARP, and prohibits the use of TARP funds for any new initiatives following the final passage of Dodd-Frank. It further stipulates that any receipts from the sale of Fannie Mae and Freddie Mac securities must be used for deficit reduction, and cannot be used for spending increases or tax cuts.

The Consumer Financial Protection Bureau

Title X ("Bureau of Consumer Financial Protection") remains one of the more controversial provisions of Dodd-Frank since its passage. This new, independent agency within the Federal Reserve is responsible for overseeing and regulating the market for "consumer financial products or services," meaning those sold to individuals, families, or households. Dodd-Frank consolidates the formerly piecemeal consumer financial protection authorities of the federal government, which were spread across multiple agencies, into a single authority. Funded by the Federal Reserve, the Bureau operates autonomously within the Federal Reserve and the federal government. The law prevents the Board of Governors from intervening in the actions, personnel matters, organization, or duties of the Bureau. Moreover, the regulations issued by the Bureau are not subject to Board approval. Like other federal agencies, the Bureau is headed by an independent director appointed by the president of the United States, and confirmed by the Senate, for a term of five years. Several units and offices comprise the Bureau, including a research unit; a community affairs unit; a centralized database for managing consumer complaints; an Office of Fair Lending and Equal Opportunity; an Office of Financial Education; an Office of Service Member Affairs; and an Office of Financial Protection for Older Americans. A Consumer Advisory Board will meet with the Bureau to discuss developments in industry and other matters of consumer financial protection. In particular, membership of the Consumer Advisory Board will include "representatives of depository institutions that primarily serve underserved communities, and representatives of communities that have been significantly impacted by higher-priced mortgage loans," among other experts.

Like other provisions of Dodd-Frank, the purpose of the Bureau is not simply to strengthen consumer financial protections, but also to apply them consistently and improve market efficiency:

> The Bureau shall seek to implement and, where applicable, enforce Federal consumer financial law consistently for the purpose of

> ensuring that all consumers have access to markets for consumer financial products and services and that markets for consumer financial products and services are fair, transparent, and competitive.

The objective is to protect consumers from predatory and discriminatory practices, while ensuring sufficient access to information in order to "make responsible decisions about financial transactions." Although it will consult and coordinate with other regulatory agencies in the interest of consistency—such as the CFTC, the Federal Trade Commission and other regulators at the state level—the Bureau has the exclusive authority to issue regulations and enforce federal consumer financial law. For example, the Bureau can prohibit a consumer financial transaction that it deems "unfair, deceptive, or abusive." It can also issue an order requiring the full disclosure of the terms of a financial transaction to consumers. The Bureau has the authority to submit large banks and credit unions to examinations for compliance and risk, while the relevant regulatory agency will conduct similar examinations of smaller depository institutions. In order to avoid excessive regulatory oversight, the law excludes several categories of small businesses and independent producers from Bureau supervision.

DODD-FRANK IN PERSPECTIVE: SUCCESSES, CHALLENGES, AND QUESTIONS

Since its passage in 2010, heterodox economists and consumer advocates have cited a number of successes of Dodd-Frank. These successes are by no means final, as they continue to evolve, but constitute notable improvements in the financial sector and financial regulation. First, Dodd-Frank reorients the financial regulatory system from the solvency of individual financial firms, and the principle of "too big to fail," to systemic risk. Second, the law recognizes the structural shift away from an institution-based financial sector and toward a market-driven financial sector. Third, the law addresses the disproportionate impact of the 2008 financial crisis on low-income, minority, and other historically under-represented groups. In all three areas, Dodd-Frank indeed represents a clear demarcation in financial regulatory policy.

According to a 2015 study by Gerald Epstein and Juan Antonio Montecino of the Political Economy Research Institute, the capital and leverage rules of Dodd-Frank have enhanced the safety and resiliency of the financial sector. Jane D'Arista—a prominent heterodox economist in the fields of financial regulation, monetary policy, and international finance—cites the inclusion of credit exposure from derivatives, repurchase agreements, and securities lending and borrowing in bank lending limits as an important achievement. These provisions, which effectively broaden the legal definition of credit exposure, curb the interconnectedness of the financial sector by restraining the exposure of banks to other financial institutions. Financial institutions will have less of an incentive to accumulate debt and engage in speculative activities, which will strengthen the connection between the financial system and the real sector, particularly by restoring investment in the real sector as the primary source of bank profits. According to Americans for Financial Reform—a broad coalition of state and national organizations that advocates for financial reform—Dodd-Frank has delivered several victories. Among these are legitimate accountability for Wall Street, stronger regulations, and prohibitions against risky and predatory practices; the ability to actually enforce the stronger consumer financial protections embedded in the law; greater supervision and transparency of financial markets, especially for derivatives; greater safety in financial markets through capital requirements; limits on the business practices that resulted in government bailouts; new investor protections and improvements in corporate governance; and a strong, independent consumer financial protection bureau.

Yet many challenges remain. Although Dodd-Frank has improved accountability and transparency, it has not fundamentally altered financial structure. No one really disputes this point, since restructuring was not the aim of the Obama administration. The complex interconnected financial firms that precipitated the crisis remain largely intact; as does the significance of financial markets for financial intermediation. What the law principally does is improve access to information, both among regulators and between government and the financial sector, in order to act against systemic threats to the financial sector and the economic system. Dodd-Frank overhauls financial *regulation*, but it does not overhaul financial *structure*. There are certainly provisions of Dodd-Frank that provide for clear, heightened rules, as well as penalties for violations. However, many provisions are vague, or give regulators the discretionary authority to write new rules. Both factors favor the interests and influence of the financial sector. Many provisions require studies prior to the development of new rules, while others were slow to implement, or expired shortly after passage.

According to Epstein and Montecino, the business of banking itself has not changed since the 2008 financial crisis. In fact, the banking sector is once again extremely profitable, in part due to higher consumer financial fees. Access to credit is still a real barrier for small businesses, while households continue to face debt overhang from the subprime mortgage meltdown. Americans for Financial Reform, which lobbied for the passage of Dodd-Frank, has identified the following specific proposals that either did not make it into the final bill or led to compromises:

- stronger regulatory limits on bank size;
- the complete separation of proprietary trading and banking beyond the scope of the Volcker Rule, akin to the Glass-Steagall Act;
- the election of corporate boards of directors by majority voting of shareholders;
- annual, binding shareholder voting on executive compensation as opposed to the non-binding voting that occurs at least every three years;
- a compulsory leverage ratio of $1 in capital per $15 in debt for systemically important financial firms;
- a rule that would require the rating agencies to revise credit ratings with changes in market conditions;
- the establishment of a public credit rating agency;
- stricter limits on permitted swaps activities by banks;
- a new financial speculation tax;
- the creation of a fund in order to finance the liquidation of failed financial firms, to be paid for by assessments on financial funds and institutions;
- greater democratization of Federal Reserve governance;

- a full audit of the Federal Reserve System;
- the ability to subject small depository institutions to examinations for compliance and risk by the Bureau of Consumer of Financial Protection;
- the ability of the Bureau to compel the relevant regulatory agency to conduct thorough examinations of small depository institutions; and
- regulatory oversight of auto dealers and auto financing by the Bureau of Consumer Financial Protection

Financial reform advocates admit that Wall Street invested millions of dollars to limit the scope of Dodd-Frank and prevent a comprehensive restructuring of the financial system. In this regard, Dodd-Frank differs greatly from the actions taken by the US government in response to the Great Depression. Following the Great Depression, the government intervened and restructured the financial organizations and practices that precipitated that crisis. Although many of those regulations were eventually repealed, or simply not enforced by industry-friendly regulators, it was a gradual process that took many decades to complete. For example, the Glass-Steagall Act of 1933 was not repealed until 1999 with the passage of the Gramm-Leach-Bliley Act. But following the 2008 financial crisis and the Great Recession, industry advocates were involved in the reform process from the very beginning. As a result, the balance of power between Wall Street lobbyists and consumer advocates within the new financial regulatory system will ultimately determine the effectiveness of Dodd-Frank over the long term. Jane D'Arista offers a compelling perspective on the complexity of the merits—and limits—of the law:

> To many [Dodd-Frank] seemed to go through the motions of a major reform effort, giving nominal recognition to problem areas without, however, confronting many of the structural issues that had caused the collapse. But Dodd-Frank is worthy of careful analysis precisely because it helps lay out the structural issues in ways that could move the reform effort in a more constructive direction.

FINAL THOUGHTS

Dodd-Frank is widely regarded as a significant legislative achievement, if not the most significant legislative achievement, of the Obama presidency. Given the sizable Democratic majorities in both Houses of Congress at the time, there was a perception that Dodd-Frank was the first step toward a continuing process of financial reform. But Dodd-Frank is where those efforts would end. Following the 2010 midterm elections, the conservative Tea Party wing of the Republican Party would formulate an ideological opposition to government intervention, and stall further efforts at not only financial reform, but any priorities of Obama's domestic economic agenda. After several unsuccessful constitutional challenges, President Trump signed a partial repeal of Dodd-Frank in 2018, which the upcoming part on the recovery from the Great Recession will examine further. For now, the next chapter explores monetary policy responses to the 2008 financial crisis and the economic crisis, as well as contemporary heterodox research on these important issues.

Sources

Americans for Financial Reform. (n.d.). *What the law does: Wins and losses.* Retrieved from https://ourfinancialsecurity.org.

D'Arista, J. (2011). *Reregulating and restructuring the financial system: Some critical provisions of Dodd-Frank* (Working Paper #272). Amherst, MA: Political Economy Research Institute.

Dodd-Frank Wall Street Reform and Consumer Protection Act, 12 U.S.C. § 5301 (2010).

Epstein, G. & Montecino, J.A. (2015). *Banking from financial crisis to Dodd-Frank: Five years on, how much has changed?* Amherst, MA: Political Economy Research Institute.

Epstein, G. & Pollin, R. (2011). Regulating Wall Street: Exploring the political economy of the possible. In P. Arestis (ed.), *Microeconomics, macroeconomics and economic policy: Essays in honour of Malcom Sawyer* (pp. 268–85). New York, NY: Palgrave Macmillan.

Obama, B. (2009, June 17). Remarks on financial regulatory reform [Transcript]. Retrieved from https://www.presidency.ucsb.edu

Further Reading

D'Arista, J. (1994). *The evolution of U.S. finance, volume II: Restructuring institutions and markets*. New York, NY: Routledge.

D'Arista, J. (2009). *Rebuilding the framework for financial regulation*. Washington, DC: Economic Policy Institute.

Dymski, G. (2009). Financing community development in the US: A comparison of "War on Poverty" and 1990s-era policy approaches. *The Review of Black Political Economy*, *36*(3–4), 245–73. doi: 10.1007/s12114-009-9058-2

Jarsulic, M. (2010). *Anatomy of a financial crisis: A real estate bubble, runaway credit markets, and regulatory failure.* New York, NY: Palgrave Macmillan.

CHAPTER 7

Monetary Policy Responses to the Great Recession

This chapter continues our examination of the comprehensive policy responses to the Great Recession. Taken together, the actions and interventions by national policymakers in the United States addressed either the 2008 financial crisis (i.e., the crisis of confidence in financial markets and widespread failures of financial institutions), the economic crisis (i.e., the severe recession and high unemployment), or both. Chapter 6 presented the ways in which Dodd-Frank addressed financial structure, the transmission of the financial crisis, and the conduct of the Wall Street bailouts. Chapter 7 now investigates the ways in which the Federal Reserve—the central bank of the United States—addressed both the financial crisis and the economic crisis. In terms of both price tag and time, expansionary monetary policy was the most significant policy response to the financial crisis and the Great Recession. Between 2007 and 2014, the Federal Reserve injected trillions of dollars into the financial sector and the economic system in order to stabilize financial markets, support financial institutions, and resuscitate economic growth. Most importantly, these interventions led the Federal Reserve to alter the tools of monetary policy, and therefore how it has responded to crises since the Great Recession.

In keeping with the theme of this textbook, Chapter 7 uses this aspect of the crisis as a case study for understanding the conduct and effectiveness of monetary policy. It explains how the Great Recession itself led to changes in the policy instruments of monetary policy and the ways in which the Federal Reserve manages interest rates. It also presents arguments by both mainstream and heterodox economists that attribute the crisis to monetary policy failures. In keeping with a further aim of the book, this chapter uses this aspect of the crisis as a lens for understanding competing schools of thought in the area of monetary economics.

The first section is an extensive primer on the conventional tools of monetary policy, the structure of the Federal Reserve System, and the transmission mechanisms of monetary policy. In particular, the first section establishes an important baseline by explaining the context and conduct of monetary policy *prior* to the 2008 financial crisis. The second section examines the philosophy of

DOI: 10.4324/9780429461316-10

Ben Bernanke, who chaired the Federal Reserve Board of Governors from 2006 to 2014. A scholar of the Great Depression of the 1930s, Bernanke was a proponent of the monetarist school of economic thought, which guided his decision making throughout his tenure. The next section investigates the conduct of monetary policy *during* the crisis. Between 2007 and 2010, the Federal Reserve not only implemented traditional monetary stimulus but also invoked its emergency authority under the Federal Reserve Act, for the first time since the Great Depression, in order to conduct significant quantitative easing. But as a result of these responses, the central bank would need to develop new policy instruments, and reorient the use of its conventional tools, during Janet Yellen's tenure as chair of the Federal Reserve Board of Governors. The next section then presents the conduct of monetary *following* the crisis and the shift toward policy normalization in 2014. The final section of the chapter highlights the important work of heterodox economist Jane D'Arista. Instead of moderating financial markets and the business cycle, D'Arista argues that monetary policy now exacerbates economic and financial instability, and makes a compelling case for monetary reform.

PRIMER ON MONETARY POLICY AND THE US FEDERAL RESERVE SYSTEM: MONETARY POLICY BEFORE THE GREAT RECESSION

The Federal Reserve System—or simply "The Fed" —functions as the central bank of the United States. Congress originally established the Federal Reserve in 1913, in large part due to a series of banking crises that once again plagued US capitalism during the late nineteenth and early twentieth centuries. The long title of the law summarizes the original intent of Congress: "An Act To provide for the establishment of Federal reserve banks, to furnish an elastic currency, to afford means of rediscounting commercial paper, to establish a more effective supervision of banking in the United States, and for other purposes."

Although its functions have evolved considerably since the enactment of the Federal Reserve Act, its major duties today are as follows:

- First and foremost, the Federal Reserve conducts monetary policy. "Monetary policy" refers to changes in the money supply, the availability of credit, and interest rates by a central bank.
- The Federal Reserve is a "banker's bank," in that it accepts deposits from, and provides loans to, member commercial banks and other depository institutions. In particular, the Federal Reserve is a lender of last resort to the banking sector during periods of economic and financial uncertainty.
- The Federal Reserve manages the payments system. When needed, it provides currency to depository institutions. It also provides the financial service of check clearing.
- The Federal Reserve examines and regulates individual financial firms.
- The Federal Reserve monitors systemic risks to the financial sector and the economic system.
- The Federal Reserve advances consumer financial protection.
- The Federal Reserve monitors, and sometimes adjusts, the value of the US dollar relative to foreign currencies.

Instruments of Monetary Policy Prior to the Great Recession

The principal focus of this chapter, of course, is the evolution of the conduct of monetary policy since the Great Recession. *Prior* to the 2008 financial crisis, the Federal Reserve utilized three policy instruments over different time frames. Table 7.1 summarizes the conventional tools of monetary policy presented here and in most macroeconomics textbooks: open market operations, the discount rate, and the required reserve ratio. There are two critical features of the conduct of monetary policy in the decades leading up to the financial crisis:

- The Federal Reserve conducted monetary policy in a context of *relatively scarce* reserves. Since the Federal Reserve did not pay interest on reserve balances, banks only held enough reserves to meet their required reserve ratio and a minimal level of excess reserves to accommodate unexpected demand for currency from depositors. For perspective, total reserves of depository institutions stood at $38.7 billion (adjusted for inflation) in December 2007. By comparison, once the recovery from the Great Recession was underway, total reserves peaked at $2.8 trillion in August 2014.
- The regulatory and oversight authorities of the Federal Reserve, as well as the transmission mechanisms of monetary policy, were limited to banks and did not extend to non-bank financial intermediaries. As this chapter shows, both features would change following the Great Recession.

First, in order to initiate short-run changes in the US money supply and interest rates, the Federal Reserve conducted "open market operations." Open market operations involve the purchase or sale of securities by the central bank. Although the central bank could technically trade with any individual or organization in securities markets, it typically traded with banks and other depository institutions in order to influence the availability of credit. And although the central bank could technically buy or sell any class of security, prior to the 2008 financial crisis, it primarily traded in short-term government bonds in order to target short-term interest rates.

TABLE 7.1 Conventional Tools of Monetary Policy

Tool	Description
Open Market Operations	- Buying and selling of securities by the Federal Reserve - Used to target the effective federal funds rate - Conducted over the short run
Discount Rate	- Interest rate on bank borrowings from the Federal Reserve - Set above the effective federal funds rate - Conducted over the medium run
Required Reserve Ratio	- Percentage of transaction accounts that must be held as reserves - Held as vault cash or in a Federal Reserve bank account - Conducted over the long run

The immediate effects of open market operations take place in the federal funds market. The federal funds market is an overnight, inter-bank market for reserves. Banks with ample excess reserves can lend to other banks by supplying federal funds. Banks that are unable to meet their required reserve ratio, or that simply wish to hold more excess cash reserves, can borrow from other banks by demanding federal funds. The interest rate on inter-bank lending and borrowing—the federal funds rate—is therefore a key benchmark interest rate. In the pre-crisis context of *relatively scarce* reserves, the Federal Reserve could significantly influence the direction of the federal funds rate through small changes in the supply of reserves. However, it could only establish a target for the federal funds rate due to countervailing forces on the demand side of the federal funds market. This is why publicly available data sources refer to it as the "effective" federal funds rate.

In the case of an open market purchase, the Federal Reserve buys government bonds from banks (which implies that banks sell bonds to the Federal Reserve). When the central bank pays for bonds, it replaces bank assets with new cash reserves. An open market purchase expands the availability of credit, since banks have new funds with which to create loans to households and businesses. As the exclusive monetary authority, the central bank essentially finances the operation with new money, which banks in turn release into circulation through lending. In the federal funds market, an open market purchase expands the supply of reserves, which puts downward pressure on the federal funds rate target.

In the case of an open market sale, the Federal Reserve sells bonds to banks (which means that banks buy bonds from the Federal Reserve). When banks pay for bonds, they draw upon their reserves in order to acquire new assets. An open market sale ultimately constrains the availability of credit, since banks will have fewer funds to lend to households and businesses. This operation therefore indirectly withdraws money from circulation. Although the size of an open market sale is in theory limited by the central bank's asset holdings, the Federal Reserve has enormous holdings of government bonds and other securities on its balance sheet. In the federal funds market, an open market sale constrains the supply of bank reserves, which puts upward pressure on the federal funds rate target.

In either scenario, this tool of monetary policy holds several advantages. First, the Federal Reserve exclusively controls the change in bank reserves through the purchase or sale of securities. For example, if the central bank wishes to increase bank reserves by $800 million, it simply purchases $800 million in government bonds. Second, open market operations are flexible, in that the Federal Reserve can initiate transactions of any denomination, small or large. Third, open market operations are easily reversible. Using the previous example, if the Federal Reserve determines that an $800 million increase in bank reserves was too much, it can correct course by selling bonds.

The second conventional tool of monetary policy is the discount rate. The discount rate is the interest rate on a loan from the Federal Reserve to a bank or other depository institution. This special line of credit—also known as the "discount window"—fulfills the Federal Reserve's function as a lender of last resort. The discount window is at times a critical source of liquidity for banks, especially during periods of economic and financial instability. However, the Federal Reserve provides three different types of credit depending upon bank needs. The "primary" credit window is intended for stable banks. The discount rate on primary credit is typically set above the federal funds rate target in order to encourage banks to resolve their short-term liquidity issues in the federal funds market. The "secondary" credit window, on the other hand, is intended for banks experiencing persistent financial distress. The discount rate on secondary credit is typically set above the primary rate in order to discourage bank practices that create liquidity crises. The "seasonal" credit window is for banks that predominantly serve regions and sectors with pronounced seasonal variations in economic activity. In each case, the discount rate functions as an upward bound on the cost of borrowed reserves in the federal funds market.

Like open market operations, the Federal Reserve uses the discount rate to indirectly influence the availability of credit. Unlike open market operations, the Federal Reserve adjusts the discount rate over longer periods of time—usually when there are pronounced shifts in the US business cycle. The Federal Reserve lowers the discount rate during periods of sluggish economic growth in order to stimulate lending to households and businesses. During periods of rising inflation or accelerating economic growth, the Federal Reserve raises the discount rate in order to restrain access to credit.

One of its key advantages as a tool of monetary policy is that the Federal Reserve exclusively controls the discount rate. Unlike the federal funds rate, there are no market forces for these types of loans that could put upward or downward pressure on the interest rate administered by the Federal Reserve. However, the Federal Reserve does not control the volume of discount lending and, by implication, the change in bank reserves. For example, a lower discount rate during a recession reduces the cost of borrowing from the central bank. The expectation is that banks will then acquire new reserves (along with a new liability to repay the central bank), which they can use to expand the availability of credit to households and businesses. But the decision to accept a discount loan rests entirely with the banks. If banks hold negative expectations, they may not be willing to take on more debt, which limits the effectiveness of the intended policy. Furthermore, the size of the discount loan, and therefore the volume of new lines of credit to households and businesses, could be higher (or lower) than what the central bank intended. During a period of rising inflation, on the other hand, a higher discount rate raises the cost of borrowing from the central bank. The expectation is that banks are less likely to use the discount window to acquire reserves, which would then restrict access to credit. Once again, though, the decision to accept a discount loan rests entirely with the banks. If banks continue to utilize the discount window and expand lending, despite a higher discount rate, the intended policy is less effective. Similar to open market operations, the Federal Reserve finances the expansion of discount lending using new money while it withdraws money from circulation through restrictions on discount lending.

The third conventional tool of monetary policy is the required reserve ratio. The required reserve ratio is a regulation that obliges banks and other depository institutions to hold a specified percentage of their transaction accounts as reserves, either as vault cash or in an account with a Federal Reserve bank. Banks cannot use required reserves to acquire or create any other assets, such as government bonds or loans to bank customers. Like the discount rate, there are multiple required reserve ratios in practice, which vary according to bank size. Prior to the

Covid-19 pandemic recession, small banks faced a reserve requirement of between 0% and 3%, while large banks faced a 10% reserve requirement. If the central bank lowers the reserve requirement, banks will have access to more reserves, which increases their ability to create loans to households and businesses. This policy would likely ease the demand for reserves in the federal funds market, which would lead to a lower effective federal funds rate. If the central bank raises the reserve requirement, banks must hold more reserves, which limits their ability to create loans to households and businesses. Such a change would likely increase the demand for bank reserves and lead to a higher effective federal funds rate. Although the Federal Reserve can utilize this mechanism as an instrument of monetary policy, it rarely does so due to its uncertain and sometimes volatile effects on the money supply. Before the Covid-19 pandemic recession, when the Federal Reserve set reserve requirements at 0% for all depository institutions, it had been decades since the central bank last adjusted reserve requirements.

Lastly, the Federal Reserve acquired an additional tool of monetary policy shortly before the onset of the Great Recession. In 2006, Congress authorized the Federal Reserve to pay interest on reserve balances held in an account with a Federal Reserve bank. This new mechanism was to take effect in 2011, but Congress accelerated implementation in the fall of 2008 as a way to combat the financial crisis. Banks and other depository institutions now earn interest on both required reserves and excess reserves. The law technically allows the Federal Reserve to pay different rates on bank reserve balances: one for required reserves and one for excess reserves. In practice, however, the Federal Reserve has applied the same rate to both balances since the crisis. And since the Federal Reserve suspended reserve requirements in 2020, there is no distinction in the composition of bank reserves and thereby the interest rates paid by the central bank. A higher interest rate raises the rate of return on reserve balances. This encourages banks to hold more reserves, and essentially lend to the Federal Reserve, which reduces their ability to lend to households and businesses. A lower interest rate, on the other hand, decreases the rate of return on reserve balances but encourages banks to issue more loans to households and businesses. While this policy instrument is not relevant to the conduct of monetary policy prior to the Great Recession, the interest rate on reserve balances became a central tool of monetary policy in the post-crisis context of *relatively abundant* reserves.

Structure of the US Federal Reserve System

One of the distinctive aspects of the Federal Reserve is its decentralized organizational structure. As opposed to a single, national monetary authority, three major units comprise a system of central banking: the Board of Governors, the Federal Reserve banks, and the Federal Open Market Committee (FOMC). Table 7.2 presents the respective duties of each entity. The Board of Governors develops and implements the national agenda for monetary policy. Each governor—one of whom serves as chair—is appointed by the president of the United States and confirmed by the Senate for a single 14-year term. The Board determines reserve requirements and the interest rate on reserve balances. It also sets the discount rate in consultation with the Federal Reserve banks. All seven governors serve on the FOMC, which sets the agenda for open market operations and the federal funds

TABLE 7.2 Structure of the US Federal Reserve System

Entity	*Duties*
Board of Governors	- Develops the national agenda for monetary policy - Sets reserve requirements and the interest rate on reserve balances - Sets the discount rate in consultation with the Federal Reserve banks - Regulates individuals financial firms and the Federal Reserve Banks - Reports to the federal government and consults with foreign central banks - Located in Washington, DC
Federal Reserve Banks	- Carry out the day-to-day operations of monetary policy - Divided into twelve regional districts - Lend to member banks, manage the payments system, regulate individual financial firms, collect data, and represent the economic and financial interests of their regions
Federal Open Market Committee	- Sets the agenda for open market operations and the federal funds rate target - Comprised of all Federal Reserve Board Governors, the President of the New York Federal Reserve Bank, and four Federal Bank Presidents on a rotating basis - Conducts operations in foreign exchange markets - Meets at least eight times per year

rate target. Furthermore, the Board holds significant regulatory and oversight authorities over individual financial firms and the Federal Reserve banks. The Board regularly reports to the federal government, and consults with foreign central banks. Given its important functions in relation to the national and international economic systems, the Board of Governors is located in Washington, DC.

The Federal Reserve banks carry out the day-to-day operations of monetary policy according to the agenda developed by the Board of Governors. Due to regional variations in the sectoral composition of output and commerce, the original Federal Reserve Act divided the territory of the US into 12 districts, each with a Federal Reserve bank. The purpose of this structure was to limit the power of a national central bank. Moreover, the US economy at the time was much more regionalized and not yet an integrated, national market. The responsibilities of the Federal Reserve banks include lending to banks and other depository institutions through the discount window, managing the payments system, regulating individual financial firms, collecting data, and representing the economic and financial interests of their respective regions on the FOMC.

The FOMC establishes the agenda for open market operations and the federal funds rate target. All seven governors of the Federal Reserve Board are voting members of the FOMC. The president of the New York Federal Reserve Bank is a permanent, voting member of the FOMC. Although the remaining Federal Reserve bank presidents attend FOMC meetings, only four presidents hold voting rights, which they rotate each year. In addition to developing the direction and volume of open market operations, the FOMC conducts operations in foreign exchange markets in order to influence the value of the US dollar relative to foreign currencies. The FOMC meets at least eight times per year in order to discuss these policies.

The structure of the Federal Reserve System is unique in that it shares features of private organizations as well as government agencies; yet it differs from both. The Federal Reserve is similar to a government agency, in that its purpose is to serve the public interest as mandated by an Act of Congress. Like traditional government agencies, the president of the United States appoints the Board of Governors with the advice and consent of the Senate. Unlike traditional government agencies, the Federal Reserve does not rely upon funding by Congress. The central bank relies upon the interest earned on its asset holdings, and fees charged to banks and other depository institutions. However, the Federal Reserve does not earn a profit, as it must hold any net earnings with the US Treasury. This principle is known as central bank independence: although the central bank reports to and consults with the federal government, it develops and conducts monetary policy independent of government oversight. This feature has allowed the Federal Reserve to alter the conduct of monetary policy and develop new policy instruments, while fulfilling its legal mandates to maximize employment, maintain price stability, and manage interest rates.

Transmission Mechanisms and Macroeconomic Effects of Monetary Policy

This analysis has thus far investigated the effects of monetary policy on bank lending, short-term interest rates, and the availability of credit to households and businesses. But how does monetary policy affect the US money supply and market interest rates? For example, how does monetary policy affect long-term interest rates on auto loans, business loans, credit cards, and home mortgages? Furthermore, how does monetary policy affect the health and performance of the national economic system as measured by the growth rate of real gross domestic product (GDP), the rate of unemployment, and the rate of inflation?

During periods of recession or economic stagnation, the Federal Reserve conducts expansionary monetary policies. In an expansionary monetary policy—or monetary stimulus—the Federal Reserve seeks to increase the US money supply and lower market interest rates. Prior to the Great Recession, it accomplished these objectives using one or more of the following policies (usually the first two): an open market purchase, a reduction in the discount rate, or a reduction in reserve requirements. Albeit in different ways, each option expands the availability of credit for the reasons discussed earlier. However, the increase in the money supply occurs through a complex process known as multiple deposit creation. In order to understand this process, it's important to note that the official measures of the US money supply consist of two components: currency in circulation (cash and coins) and bank deposits (e.g., checking accounts, savings accounts, certificates of deposit, and money market accounts). In terms of their respective shares, bank deposits comprise nearly 90% of the money supply. If the money supply consisted entirely of currency in circulation, then the Federal Reserve could conduct a monetary stimulus simply by printing more cash and coins. Therefore, the process of expanding the money supply essentially involves expanding the level of deposits. When the Federal Reserve indirectly increases the ability of banks and other depository institutions to create loans using its policy instruments, it initiates a multiplier process whereby the initial increase in lending leads to multiple increases in deposits (i.e., money) across the banking system. This happens because households and businesses use new lines of credit to buy goods and services, such as cars, homes, capital goods, and infrastructure. Once those transactions are complete, the sellers of goods and services deposit the proceeds with a bank, which restarts the process again: banks have new funds with which to create loans, which bank customers use to consume and invest, which again increases deposits elsewhere in the banking system. The process of multiple deposit creation does not continue indefinitely, though—there is a limit. With each new round of deposits, banks held required reserves. Banks may also prefer to hold more excess reserves, or invest in government bonds. Each of these factors limits the supply of new credit to households and businesses. On the other hand, weak demand for credit from bank customers, as well as a stronger preference for holding currency, could also limit lending and deposit creation. In the end, the total increase in deposits represents the total increase in the money supply.

Conventional models of monetary policy suggest that monetary stimulus puts downward pressure on market interest rates. In the money market, the price of money is the interest rate as it represents the return to lenders on the supply side and the cost to borrowers on the demand side. Assuming no change in the demand for money, a monetary stimulus increases the supply of money, which produces a market surplus at current equilibrium interest rates. The amount of money that banks are able and willing to lend will initially exceed the amount of money that bank customers are able and willing to borrow. In order to entice borrowers, banks will lower interest rates on new lines of credit until the market reaches equilibrium again.

A change in market interest rates serves as the critical link between the conduct of monetary policy and the health and performance of the national economic system. In the case of a monetary stimulus, lower long-term interest rates entail lower borrowing costs for households and businesses. Conventional models of monetary policy suggest that households will respond by increasing expenditures on cars and homes, for example, which raises consumption. Businesses will likewise respond by increasing expenditures on capital goods and infrastructure, which raises investment. One or both of these factors is sufficient to raise aggregate demand beyond current production levels. As a result, output as measured by real GDP will increase. Stronger economic growth is typically associated with a lower rate of unemployment, since firms will require more labor in order to produce more output. However, demand pressures across the economic system may raise prices, resulting in a higher rate of inflation. To sum up, the complete effects of expansionary monetary policy on the financial sector and the economic system include an increase in bank lending, an increase in the money supply, lower market interest rates, stronger aggregate demand, an increase in real GDP, lower unemployment, and higher inflation. Table 7.3 presents the full effects of expansionary monetary policy on the banking sector, the money market, and the macro economy.

During periods of inflation or accelerating economic growth, on the other hand, the Federal Reserve conducts contractionary monetary policies. In a

TABLE 7.3 Effects of Expansionary Monetary Policy

Policy Options	- Open market purchase - Lower discount rate - Lower required reserve ratio
Banking Sector	- Increase in bank lending - Lower effective federal funds rate
Money Market	- Increase in the money supply - Lower market interest rates
Macro Economy	- Increase in aggregate demand - Increase in real GDP - Lower unemployment - Higher inflation

contractionary monetary policy—or monetary restraint—the Federal Reserve now seeks to reduce the US money supply and raise market interest rates. In order to stabilize an overheating economic system, it will first restrain the ability of banks and other depository institutions to lend using one or more of the following instruments: an open market sale, an increase in the discount rate, or an increase in reserve requirements. However, reducing the money supply principally involves reducing the level of bank deposits. When the central bank indirectly restrains the ability of banks to create new lines of credit, it sets off a process in which an initial decrease in lending results in multiple decreases in deposits across the banking sector. If access to credit is restricted, bank customers will find it more difficult to purchase goods, services, and resources. As the level of transactions recedes, so too will the level of new deposits at other banks, which restarts the process again: those banks will see fewer funds with which to create loans on their balance sheets, which will further restrain the ability of households and businesses to consume and invest, which again will reduce deposits elsewhere in the banking system. The total decrease in deposits therefore represents the total decrease in the money supply.

In the money market, a monetary restraint puts upward pressure on market interest rates. Given the level of money demand, a monetary restraint reduces the money supply, which causes a market shortage at current equilibrium interest rates. The amount of money that banks are able and willing to lend will be less than the amount of money that bank customers are able and willing to borrow. Borrowers must then compete for a smaller amount of money available in the market. In order to clear the money market of excess demand, banks will raise interest rates on new lines of credit until the market returns to equilibrium.

According to conventional models of monetary policy, higher costs of borrowing restrain spending by households and businesses, especially spending on long-term durable goods and capital investments. Aggregate demand will consequently be insufficient to maintain current output levels, leading to a contraction in production, as measured by negative real GDP growth. Layoffs and a higher unemployment rate will follow, as firms adjust labor demand to meet lower output levels. However, weaker demand across the economic system may lower prices, resulting in a lower inflation rate (or in severe cases, deflation). These outcomes, however, are the necessary corrections in order to counterbalance an overheating

TABLE 7.4 Effects of Contractionary Monetary Policy

Policy Options	- Open market sale
	- Higher discount rate
	- Higher required reserve ratio
Banking Sector	- Decrease in bank lending
	- Higher effective federal funds rate
Money Market	- Decrease in the money supply
	- Higher market interest rates
Macro Economy	- Decrease in aggregate demand
	- Decrease in real GDP
	- Higher unemployment
	- Lower inflation

economic system and persistent inflation: a decrease in bank lending, a decrease in the money supply, higher market interest rates, weaker aggregate demand, a decrease in real GDP, higher unemployment, and lower inflation. Table 7.4 presents the full effects of contractionary monetary policy on the banking sector, the money market, and the macro economy.

LEADERSHIP OF THE FEDERAL RESERVE BOARD OF GOVERNORS DURING THE GREAT RECESSION: THE PHILOSOPHY OF BEN BERNANKE

In order to fully understand the Federal Reserve's responses to the 2008 financial crisis and the Great Recession, it is essential to examine the philosophical and theoretical underpinnings of policymakers at the time. Ben S. Bernanke was chair of the Board of Governors from 2006 until 2014. Like his previous two predecessors, Bernanke steered the central bank through a consequential period of economic and financial history. Paul Volcker conducted contractionary monetary policies in order to reduce double-digit rates of inflation during the transition to neoliberal capitalism. Alan Greenspan largely conducted expansionary monetary policies in order to support access to liquidity during the so-called Great Moderation. Ben Bernanke guided the Federal Reserve through the worst crisis of capitalism since the Great Depression and the initial years of the sluggish recovery that followed, using a massive increase in the US money supply and a series of controversial bailouts.

Prior to his service to the Board of Governors, Bernanke was a prominent scholar of macroeconomics, monetary economics, and economic history. Bernanke made significant contributions to the study of the Great Depression, especially the transmission of the Depression across the global economy. In *Essays on the Great Depression*, Bernanke wonders: "I don't know why there aren't more Depression buffs." Similar in perspective to this textbook, Bernanke viewed the Depression as a lens for understanding the functioning of the macroeconomy. He was fascinated with not only the lessons of the greatest economic collapse in modern history but its enduring influence on macroeconomic thought, policymaking, and research. His academic work also advanced the concept of the Great Moderation, the purported era of stable economic growth and inflation between the

1980s and 2000s. In addition to his prestigious faculty position at Princeton University, Bernanke was a policy advisor to the Federal Reserve banks and chaired the Council of Economic Advisers during the George W. Bush administration. After his initial appointment to the Board in 2002, President Bush nominated Bernanke for chair in 2006, shortly before the onset of the Great Recession. Bernanke's foremost legacy as chair rests upon an aggressive and sustained expansion of the US money supply using both traditional and non-traditional tools of monetary policy. His scholarly publications and public remarks prior to the crisis shed light on the theoretical framework that informed his decisions during the crisis.

Bernanke was an adherent of the monetarist account of the Great Depression advanced by Milton Friedman and Anna Jacobson Schwartz. According to Friedman and Schwartz, the Great Depression—or as they refer to it, the "Great Contraction"—resulted from a contraction of the US money supply caused by bad monetary policies. Herein lies yet another example of how economists continue to debate the relationship between agreed upon, observable economic phenomenon. During the 1930s, the conventional wisdom advanced by Keynesianism was that the quantity of money played a passive and insignificant role in the transmission of the Depression. Economists and policymakers believed that the contraction of the money supply was a consequence (i.e., not the cause) of the collapse in output and prices, and discounted the ability of monetary policy to maintain economic stability. Keynesian accounts of the Great Depression held that the level of aggregate spending (i.e., not the quantity of money) ultimately determines the level of output and prices, and attributed the economic collapse to insufficient spending on goods and services. Expansionary fiscal policies and direct government intervention in investment decisions are therefore the necessary tools to maintain economic stability. Monetarists, however, counter that money played an active and significant role in the transmission of the Depression. Far from being passive, the contraction of the US money supply was an exogenous shock that led to a collapse in production and severe deflation. Friedman and Schwartz argue that the central bank had the necessary tools to counteract the monetary contraction and bank runs of the early 1930s, but failed to do so due to leadership turmoil within the Federal Reserve, misaligned policy priorities, and an incomplete understanding of monetary forces. The failure of the Federal Reserve to expand liquidity in order to stem the bank runs increased the severity as well as the duration of the contraction. Capitalism is therefore inherently stable, making the expansion of government intervention following World War II both unnecessary and counterproductive. In 2002, on the occasion of Friedman's 90th birthday, Bernanke famously confessed to Friedman and Schwartz: "I would like to say to Milton and Anna: Regarding the Great Depression. You're right, we did it. We're very sorry. But thanks to you, we won't do it again.

Beyond his work on the Great Depression, Friedman's monetarist "counter-revolution"—a response to the Keynesian revolution in macroeconomics—continues to inform policymaking by central bankers. It was instrumental in the ideological realignment of the economics profession during the 1970s, from the principles of Keynesianism to neoclassical economics. However, Friedman's revolution was not complete as he states in *The Counter-Revolution in Monetary Theory*:

> A counter-revolution, whether in politics or in science, never restores the initial situation. It always produces a situation that has some similarity to the initial one but is also strongly influenced by the intervening revolution. That is certainly true of monetarism which has benefited much from Keynes's work. Indeed I may say, as have so many others since there is no way contradicting it, that if Keynes were alive today he would no doubt be at the forefront of the counter-revolution. You must never judge a master by his disciples.

For example, Friedman advanced the principle of long-run money neutrality: although expansionary monetary policy can stimulate output and lower unemployment in the short run, the only effect of monetary stimulus over the long run is inflation. This principle was a significant challenge to the conduct of monetary policy by central bankers during the regulated stage of US capitalism. The implication is that expansionary monetary policy is limited in its ability to maintain a full employment level of output. Monetarists, Bernanke included, argue that excessive monetary stimulus throughout regulated capitalism contributed to high rates of inflation by the 1970s.

For Friedman and the monetarist school of thought, history offers multiple lessons for theory and policymaking on the potentially volatile effects of monetary instability. On the one hand, monetary contraction due to a lack of policy intervention led to the Great Depression. On the other hand, monetary expansion due to excessive policy intervention eventually led to excessive inflation following World War II. What are central bankers to do in practice? Friedman argues that the conduct of monetary policy should maintain, and only maintain, a stable rate of inflation through stable growth in the money supply: "A steady rate of monetary growth at a moderate level can provide a framework under which a country can have little inflation and much growth."

Interestingly, Bernanke has interpreted this consequential policy recommendation to also mean that monetary stability fosters economic efficiency and growth. In 2007, Bernanke drew upon these lessons as the housing market bust and subprime mortgage meltdown spread throughout the financial sector and economic system. The next sections therefore examine the multitude of responses by the Federal Reserve during the Great Recession and the early years of the recovery.

MONETARY POLICY DURING THE GREAT RECESSION: QUANTITATIVE EASING AND THE EXPANSION OF RESERVES

During the 2008 financial crisis and the Great Recession, the Federal Reserve conducted expansionary monetary policies in order to reduce short-term interest rates using its conventional policy instruments. More notably, it also invoked its emergency authority under the Federal Reserve Act in order to reduce long-term interest rates using quantitative easing, prevent the failure of individual financial institutions, and support the anemic housing market. This section focuses on the traditional and non-traditional actions taken by the central bank between August

2007 and June 2010. The next section then describes the conduct of monetary policy following the announcement of the central bank's plan for policy normalization in September 2014.

Let's first examine the effects of monetary stimulus on short-term interest rates using the conventional tools of monetary policy presented earlier. Although the peak of the 2001–07 expansion did not occur until December 2007, the Federal Reserve initiated its response to rising economic and financial instability during the summer of that year. Beginning in August 2007, the Federal Reserve conducted open market purchases of US government bonds. According to Figure 7.1, the first stage of conventional open market operations brought the effective federal funds rate from roughly 5.25% to 2% by May 2008. As the financial crisis accelerated during the fall of 2008, however, the Federal Reserve effectively reduced the federal funds rate to 0% by December, where it remained until December 2015. At the same time, the central bank reduced the cost of borrowed reserves by aggressively lowering the discount rate. According to Figure 7.2, the Board of Governors cut the discount rate from 6.25% to 2.25% between August 2007 and May 2008. Further reductions followed until it reached 0.50% by December. The Board of Governors then raised the discount rate slightly to 0.75% in February 2010, where it remained until December 2015. Figure 7.3 demonstrates the combined effects of conventional monetary stimulus and the central bank's common practice of maintaining a constant spread between the discount rate and the effective federal funds rate. The original intent of these policies was to create a "soft landing," but escalating uncertainty due to the housing market bust and subprime mortgage meltdown proved to be too significant. Lower borrowing costs were simply unable to counter negative expectations by households and businesses.

FIGURE 7.1 Effective Federal Funds Rate 2002–20

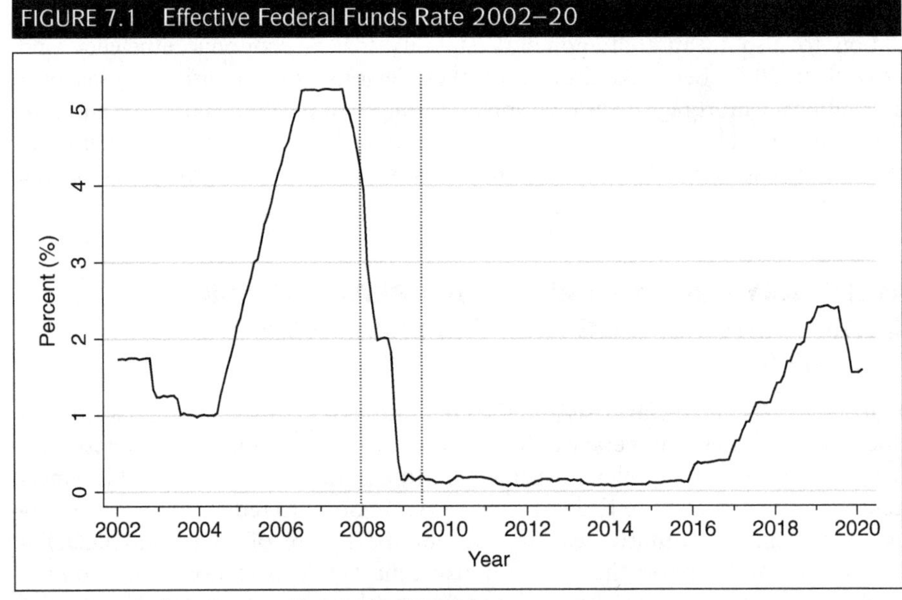

Units—percent | Not seasonally adjusted | Monthly.
Source: Federal Reserve Bank of St. Louis FRED economic data (https://fred.stlouisfed.org).

FIGURE 7.2 Discount Rate 2002–20

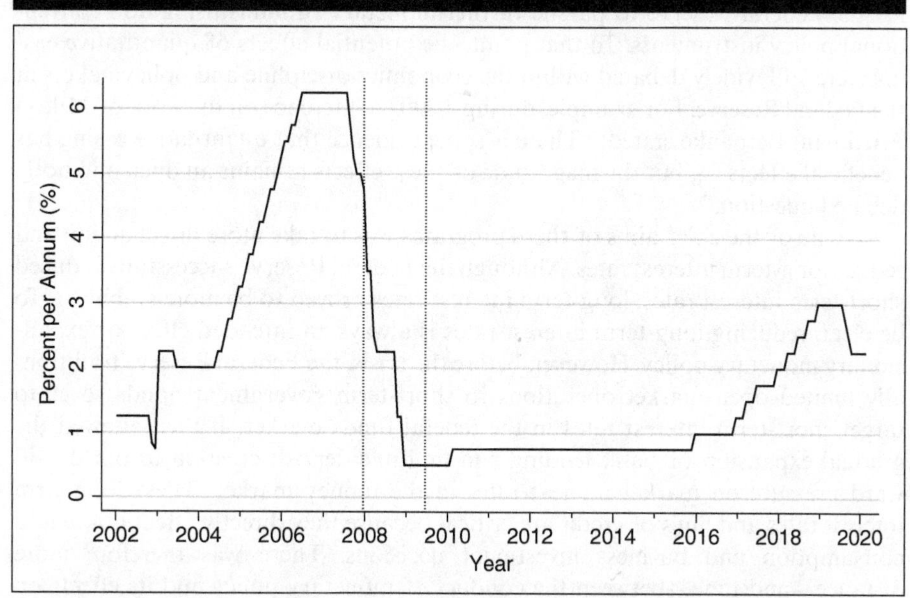

Units—percent per annum | Not seasonally adjusted | Monthly.
Source: Federal Reserve Bank of St. Louis FRED economic data (https://fred.stlouisfed.org).

FIGURE 7.3 Interest Rates 2002–20

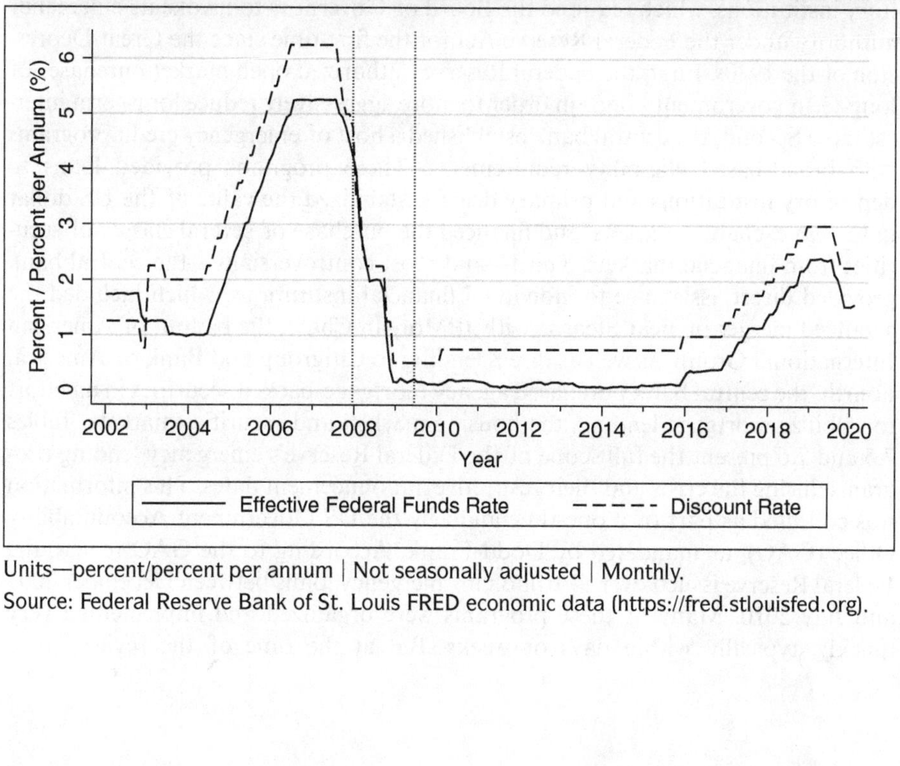

Units—percent/percent per annum | Not seasonally adjusted | Monthly.
Source: Federal Reserve Bank of St. Louis FRED economic data (https://fred.stlouisfed.org).

The historical severity of the financial meltdown and economic contraction led the Federal Reserve to pursue further monetary stimulus using non-conventional policy instruments. To that point, the potential effects of quantitative easing were still widely debated within the economics discipline and policymakers at the Federal Reserve. For example, during a 2003 conference on the work of Milton Friedman, Bernanke stated: "There is some evidence that quantitative easing has beneficial effects ..., but the magnitude of these effects remains an open and hotly debated question."

One of the chief aims of these programs was to take more direct action and reduce long-term interest rates. Although the Federal Reserve successfully reduced short-term interest rates, long-term interest rates proved to be more stubborn. To be clear, reducing long-term interest rates is always an intended effect of expansionary monetary policy. However, before the crisis, the Federal Reserve traditionally limited open market operations to short-term government bonds so as to target short-term interest rates in the federal funds market. It then allowed the gradual expansion of bank lending and multiple deposit creation to put downward pressure on market interest rates in the money market. These long-term interest rates and lines of credit are critical because they directly affect household consumption and business investment decisions. There was therefore more distance—and time—between the conduct of monetary policy and its effects on market interest rates and the real sector.

There were four major aspects of the Federal's Reserve strategy of quantitative easing. Taken together, the goal was not only to lower long-term interest rates but also to stabilize financial intermediation by non-bank financial institutions as well as financial markets. Many of these programs expanded the conduct of monetary policy beyond the traditional purview of commercial banks and other depository institutions, which required the Board of Governors to invoke its emergency authority under the Federal Reserve Act for the first time since the Great Depression of the 1930s. First, the Federal Reserve authorized open market purchases of long-term government bonds in order to more aggressively reduce long-term interest rates. Second, the central bank established a host of emergency credit programs with broad-based eligibility requirements. These programs provided loans to depository institutions and primary dealers, stabilized the value of the US dollar in foreign exchange markets, and financed the purchase of several classes of securities from financial markets. Third—and most controversially—the central bank provided direct assistance to individual financial institutions, which included the arranged merger of Bear Stearns with JPMorgan Chase, the bailout of American International Group, as well as direct lending to Citigroup and Bank of America. Fourth, the central bank purchased agency mortgage-backed securities in an effort to stabilize mortgage lending, the housing market, and securities markets. Tables 7.5 and 7.6 present the full scope of the Federal Reserve's emergency lending programs during the crisis and their respective announcement dates. This information was collected as part of a one-time audit by the US Government Accountability Office (GAO), as mandated by Dodd-Frank. According to the GAO review, the Federal Reserve issued over $1 trillion in emergency loans between December 2007 and July 2010. Many of these programs were organized and implemented very quickly, typically within days or weeks. But at the time of the review, most

TABLE 7.5 Government Accountability Office Audit of Federal Reserve Emergency Programs During the 2008 Financial Crisis: Broad-Based Programs and Support to Mortgage Lending and the Housing Market

Broad-Based Programs and Support to Mortgage Lending and the Housing Market		
Program	*Date*	*Description*
Broad-Based Programs		
Term Auction Facility	12/12/07	*Auctioned one-month and three-month discount window loans to eligible depository institutions*
Dollar Swap Lines	12/12/07	*Exchanged dollars with foreign central banks for foreign currency to help address disruptions in dollar funding markets abroad*
Term Securities Lending Facility	03/11/08	*Auctioned loans of U.S. Treasury securities to primary dealers against eligible collateral*
Primary Dealer Credit Facility	03/16/08	*Provided overnight cash loans to primary dealers against eligible collateral*
Asset-Backed Commercial Paper Money Market Mutual Fund Liquidity Facility	09/19/08	*Provided loans to depository institutions and their affiliates to finance purchases of eligible asset-backed commercial paper from money market mutual funds*
Commercial Paper Funding Facility	10/07/08	*Provided loans to a special-purpose vehicle to finance purchases of new issues of asset-backed commercial paper and unsecured commercial paper from eligible issuers*
Money Market Investor Funding Facility	10/21/08*	*Created to finance the purchase of eligible short-term debt obligations held by money market mutual funds*
Term Asset-Backed Securities Loan Facility	11/25/08	*Provided loans to eligible investors to finance purchases of eligible asset- backed securities*
Support to Mortgage Lending and the Housing Market		
Agency Mortgage-Backed Securities Purchase Program	11/25/08	*Purchased agency mortgage-backed securities to provide support to mortgage and housing markets and to foster improved conditions in the financial markets more generally*

Source: Brown (2011).

* Indicates that program was never used.

recipients had already repaid the loans. In fact, the Federal Reserve saw an increase in net earnings during this period in large part due to the interest earned through these programs—meaning, in the aggregate, the central bank did not incur losses on the loans. Nearly all programs concluded by July 2010.

The lasting legacy of the Federal Reserve's monetary stimulus is that it greatly expanded the level of reserves in the banking system. Between August 2007 and July 2010, total reserves of depository institutions increased from $39.2 billion to $995.6 billion. When the FOMC announced its plan for policy

TABLE 7.6 Government Accountability Office Audit of Federal Reserve Emergency Programs During the 2008 Financial Crisis: Assistance to Individual Financial Institutions

Assistance to Individual Financial Institutions		
Program	*Date*	*Description*
Bear Stearns		
Bridge Loan	03/14/08	*Overnight loan provided to JP Morgan Chase & Co. bank subsidiary, with which this subsidiary made a direct loan to Bear Stearns Companies, Inc.*
Maiden Lane	03/16/08	*Special purpose vehicle created to purchase approximately $30 billion of Bear Stearns's mortgage-related assets*
American International Group (AIG)		
Revolving Credit Facility	09/16/08	*Revolving loan for the general corporate purposes of AIG and its subsidiaries, and to pay obligations as they came due*
Securities Borrowing Facility	10/08/08	*Provided collateralized cash loans to reduce pressure on AIG to liquidate residential mortgage-backed securities (RMBS) in its securities lending portfolio*
Maiden Lane II	11/10/08	*Special purpose vehicle created to purchase residential mortgage-backed securities from the securities lending portfolios of AIG subsidiaries*
Maiden Lane III	11/10/08	*Special purpose vehicle created to purchase collateralized debt obligations on which AIG Financial Products had written credit default swaps*
Life Insurance Securitization	03/02/09*	*Authorized to provide credit to AIG that would be repaid with cash flows from its life insurance businesses*
Credit Extensions to Affiliates of Some Primary Dealers	09/21/08	*Loans provided to broker-dealer affiliates of four primary dealers on terms similar to those for Primary Dealer Credit Facility*
Citigroup Lending Commitment	11/23/08	*Commitment to provide nonrecourse loan to Citigroup against ring-fence assets if losses on asset pool reached $56.2 billion*
Bank of America Lending Commitment	01/16/09	*Commitment to provide nonrecourse loan facility to Bank of America if losses on ring- fence assets exceeded $18 billion (agreement never finalized)*

Source: Brown (2011).

* Indicates that program was never used.

normalization in September 2014, total reserves reached $2.8 trillion. Figure 7.4 presents this critical shift in the context of monetary policy, from one of *relatively scarce* reserves to one of *relatively abundant* reserves. As a result, the Federal Reserve developed and implemented new tools of monetary policy in order to adjust the US money supply, the availability of credit, and interest rates during the recovery.

FIGURE 7.4 Total Reserves of Depository Institutions 2002–20

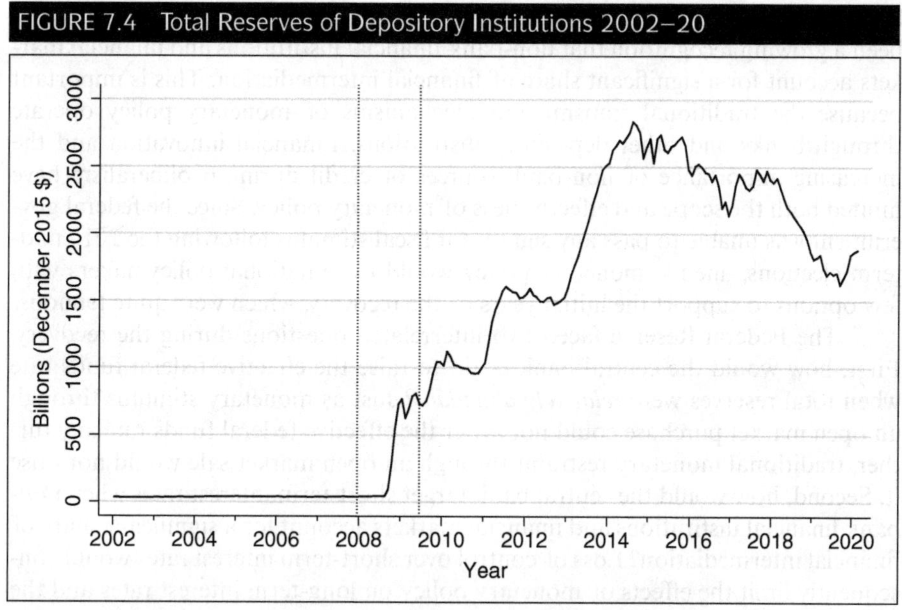

Units—$ billions (December 2015) | Not seasonally adjusted | Monthly.
Source: Federal Reserve Bank of St. Louis FRED economic data (https://fred.stlouisfed.org).

MONETARY POLICY FOLLOWING THE GREAT RECESSION: THE PIVOT TO POLICY NORMALIZATION

In the decades *prior* to the 2008 financial crisis and Great Recession, the Federal Reserve conducted monetary policy in a context of *relatively scarce* reserves. The FOMC used open market operations as the principal tool of monetary policy to adjust short-term interest rates. Furthermore, it authorized the buying or selling of short-term government bonds with banks and other depository institutions to adjust the availability of credit. The implication is that the FOMC could target the federal funds rate through small adjustments in the supply of bank reserves. Suppose, for example, that banks held $40 billion in total reserves. A $1 billion open market purchase would lead to a relatively significant increase in the supply of reserves and a lower effective federal funds rate. Traditional and non-traditional monetary stimulus *during* the crisis then led to a massive increase in total reserves held by depository institutions, and a much larger Federal Reserve balance sheet. The Federal Reserve acquired not only more short-term government bonds, as it usually does during a recession, but also long-term government bonds, mortgage-backed securities, and other toxic assets in order to increase liquidity, stabilize financial markets, and prevent individual financial institutions from failure. *Since* the Great Recession, the Federal Reserve has therefore conducted monetary policy in a context of *relatively abundant* reserves. This means that small changes in the supply of bank reserves will have little to no effect on the federal funds rate target. Suppose now that banks held $1 trillion in total reserves as opposed to the previous example of $40 billion. That same $1 billion open market purchase would lead to a relatively insignificant increase in the supply of reserves and do little to lower the effective federal funds rate. In the aftermath of the crisis, there has also been a growing recognition that non-bank financial institutions and financial markets account for a significant share of financial intermediation. This is important because the traditional transmission mechanisms of monetary policy operate through banks and other depository institutions. Financial innovation and the increasing importance of non-bank sources of credit during neoliberalism have limited both the scope and effectiveness of monetary policy. Since the federal government was unable to pass any significant fiscal stimulus following the 2010 midterm elections, anemic monetary policy would leave national policymakers with few options to support the initial years of the recovery, which were quite tenuous.

The Federal Reserve faced two interrelated questions during the recovery. First, how would the central bank begin to raise the effective federal funds rate when total reserves were *relatively abundant*? Just as monetary stimulus through an open market purchase could not lower the effective federal funds rate any further, traditional monetary restraint through an open market sale would not raise it. Second, how would the central bank target short-term interest rates when non-bank financial institutions and financial markets account for a significant share of financial intermediation? Loss of control over short-term interest rates would consequently limit the effects of monetary policy on long-term interest rates and the real sector. In order to address both of these critical issues, the Federal Reserve developed new tools of monetary policy and reoriented the use of its traditional policy instruments.

In September 2014, following Janet Yellen's appointment as chair of the Federal Reserve Board of Governors, the FOMC issued the first in a series of public announcements on the normalization of monetary policy. The stated goal of policy normalization was to return the effective federal funds rate and other short-term interest rates to customary levels, and eventually to decrease the size of the Federal Reserve balance sheet such that it would largely hold government bonds again. While the FOMC also stated that it would reduce bank reserves, it would not return to the levels seen prior to the Great Recession. The policy context of *relatively abundant* reserves would remain in place, and the use of open market operations to adjust the supply of bank reserves would no longer be the primary tool of monetary policy. Since the pivot to policy normalization, the FOMC has utilized two administered interest rates in order to move the effective federal funds rate into a *target range*: the interest rate on reserve balances, and an overnight reverse repurchase agreement facility. Implementation of this new process—which introduced two overnight, risk-free investment options to the financial sector—began in December 2015 once the national recovery was well underway. Let's examine each of these policy instruments and its effects on short-term interest rates.

The primary tool of monetary policy since the pivot to normalization has been the interest rate on reserve balances. The interest rate on reserve balances is the principal mechanism used by the FOMC to move the effective federal funds rate within the intended target range. In practice, the interest rate on reserve balances serves as the *upper* bound on the target range for the effective federal funds rate. Since lending to the central bank is a risk-free investment, commercial banks and other depository institutions should not lend reserves overnight in the federal funds market at a rate less than the interest rate on reserve balances. Suppose, though, that the effective federal funds rate fell below the interest rate on reserve balances. From the perspective of banks, this means that the rate of return on an overnight, risk-free loan to the Federal Reserve exceeds the cost of borrowed reserves in the federal funds market. Profit-motivated banks would borrow reserves at the effective federal funds rate, lend them to the Federal Reserve at the interest rate on reserve balances, and profit on the difference between the two. This process is known as arbitrage. But in doing so, the increase in demand for reserves would put upward pressure on the effective federal funds rate and bring it closer to the interest rate on reserve balances. Raising the interest rate on reserve balances therefore allows the FOMC to raise the effective federal funds rate without reducing bank reserves through an open market sale. Lowering the interest rate on reserve balances likewise allows the FOMC to lower the effective federal funds rate without increasing bank reserves through an open market purchase. For example, if the interest rate on reserve balances falls below the effective federal funds rate, the rate of return on an overnight loan in the federal funds market exceeds the rate of return on an overnight loan to the Federal Reserve. Profit-motivated banks would then withdraw their funds from the Federal Reserve and loan them in the federal funds market. But in doing so, the increase in the supply of reserves would put downward pressure on the effective federal funds rate and bring it closer to the interest rate on reserve balances.

Yet the effective federal funds rate is typically not equal to, but less than, the interest rate on reserve balances. The opportunity to lend to the Federal Reserve through interest on reserve balances applies only to banks and other depository institutions. The preponderance of non-bank financial institutions and financial markets in financial intermediation means that short-term interest rates might fall below the interest rate on reserve balances. In order to enhance its control over the effective federal funds rate, the FOMC implemented a supplementary tool of monetary policy: the overnight reverse repurchase agreement facility. In essence, this facility is an opportunity for non-bank financial intermediaries to lend to the Federal Reserve. Like the interest rate on reserve balances, the facility is another overnight, risk-free investment option for financial institutions. The overnight reverse repurchase agreement facility operates in two key steps. In the first step, a financial institution deposits funds with the Federal Reserve and receives government bonds as collateral. In the second step—the next day—the Federal Reserve repurchases the bonds and repays the financial institution with interest. In practice, the award rate on overnight reverse repurchase agreements serves as the *lower* bound on the target range for the effective federal funds rate. The reason is that when financial institutions lend to the Federal Reserve through this facility, the level of bank reserves falls. In the federal funds market, this temporarily reduces the supply of reserves, thereby raising the effective federal funds rate. And since lending to the central bank is a risk-free investment, financial institutions should not lend overnight in the federal funds market at a rate less than the award rate on overnight reverse repurchase agreements. The FOMC has publicly stated that it regards this mechanism as a supplementary monetary policy tool and will only utilize it as needed to control short-term interest rates.

Since implementation of this new process for conducting monetary policy, the FOMC has largely set a target range of 25 basis points for the effective federal funds rate. The FOMC utilizes the interest rate on reserve balances as the upper bound on the target range, and the award rate on overnight reverse repurchase agreements as a lower bound when necessary. Like the discount rate, the Federal Reserve exclusively controls both administered interest rates. This process has been successful in maintaining control over short-term interest rates in a context of *relatively abundant* reserves. Competition between multiple short-term investment options has kept short-term interest rates within the target range since the crisis.

In sum, the Federal Reserve now conducts expansionary monetary policy by lowering both the interest rate on reserve balances and the award rate on reverse repurchase agreements (i.e., by lowering the target range) to reduce the effective federal funds rate. It now conducts contractionary monetary policy by raising the interest rate on reserve balances and the award rate on reverse repurchase agreements (i.e., by raising the target range) to increase the effective federal funds rate. Figure 7.5 illustrates the conduct of US monetary policy following the pivot to normalization, and demonstrates FOMC control over the effective federal funds rate through changes in the interest rate on reserve balances (IORB) and the award rate on overnight reverse repurchase agreements (ONRRP).

What about the other conventional tools of monetary policy presented earlier? The FOMC continues to use open market operations, but not to target the federal funds rate. Instead, it utilizes open market operations to ensure that total reserves of depository institutions remain *relatively abundant*. The discount window remains in place to fulfill the Federal Reserve's function as a lender of last resort. As was the case prior to the crisis, the discount rate is still set above the effective federal funds rate in order to discourage banks and other depository institutions from relying upon central bank credit. Finally, although reserve

FIGURE 7.5 Conduct of US Monetary Policy Following Normalization

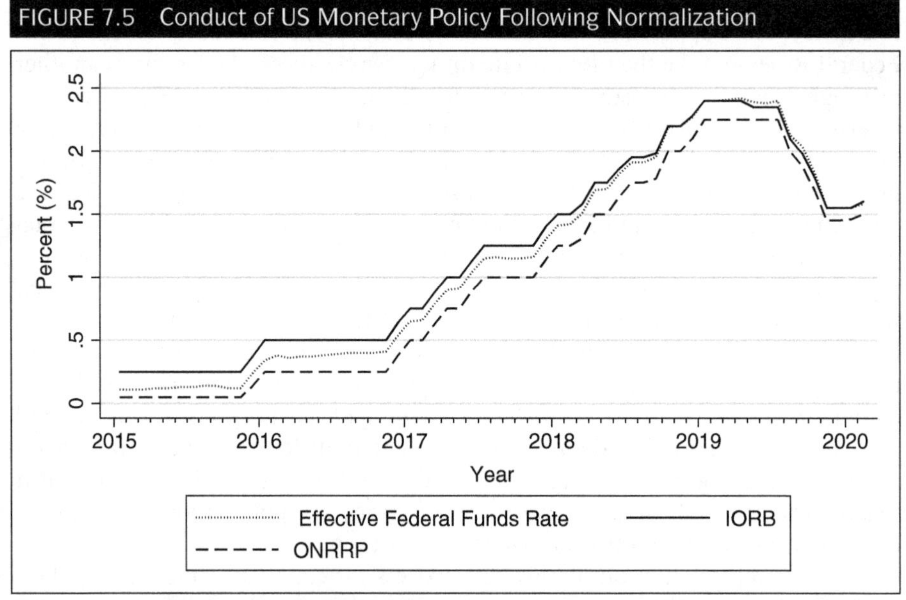

Units—percent | Not seasonally adjusted | Monthly average.

Source: Federal Reserve Bank of St. Louis FRED economic data (https://fred.stlouisfed.org).

TABLE 7.7 Tools of Monetary Policy since the 2008 Financial Crisis and Great Recession

Tool	Description
Interest Rate on Reserve Balances	- Rate of return on an account with a Federal Reserve bank - Available to banks and other depository institutions - Upper bound on target range for the effective federal funds rate - Primary tool of monetary policy since the crisis
Overnight Reverse Repurchase Agreement Facility	- Rate of return on an overnight investment in Treasury securities - Available to non-bank financial intermediaries - Lower bound on target range for the effective federal funds rate - Supplementary tool of monetary policy since the crisis
Open Market Operations	- Buying and selling of securities by the Federal Reserve - Used to maintain relatively abundant reserve balances
Discount Rate	- Interest rate on bank borrowings from the Federal Reserve - Set above the effective federal funds rate
Required Reserve Ratio	- Percentage of transaction accounts that must be held as reserves - Suspended during the Covid-19 pandemic recession in 2020

requirements remained in place during the recovery, they were suspended during the Covid-19 pandemic recession in 2020. Table 7.7 summarizes the Federal Reserve's monetary policy tools since the crisis.

A HETERODOX PERSPECTIVE ON MONETARY POLICY AND THE GREAT RECESSION

This chapter has analyzed the ability of the Federal Reserve to control short-term interest rates, and how the conduct of monetary policy evolved following the 2008 financial crisis and the Great Recession. While the Federal Reserve indeed regained control of short-term interest rates in a context of *relatively abundant* reserves, these new policy instruments are merely the *means* of monetary policy. The *effectiveness* of monetary policy depends upon the ability of the central bank to influence long-term interest rates and the real sector as intended. As the central bank, the Federal Reserve is under a legal mandate to maximize employment and maintain price stability. This aspect of monetary policy is much more complicated, uncertain, and protracted because it depends in part upon market forces in money markets and the spending decisions of private households and businesses. In the aftermath of the Great Recession, did the Federal Reserve successfully lower long-term interest rates? Did expansionary monetary policy lead to an increase in lending to households and businesses? Did expansionary monetary policy stimulate economic growth and lower unemployment? Put simply, did any of this actually work?

To answer these questions, let's turn again to an exemplar of heterodox research in the areas of financial regulation, monetary policy, and international finance: the work of Jane D'Arista. According to D'Arista, the answer to all of the aforementioned questions is no. Not only did monetary policy fail to produce its intended effects on long-term interest rates and the real sector after the Great Recession, it has failed for decades in both its expansionary and contractionary forms. In fact, D'Arista argues that monetary policy failures throughout the Great Moderation, combined with financial deregulation and financial innovation, contributed to the 2008 financial crisis. The chief failure of monetary policy has been the inability to produce *countercyclical* outcomes on the financial sector and the economic system, meaning outcomes that moderate the trajectory of financial markets and economic activity. The original intent of the Federal Reserve Act was to create transmission mechanisms that would stimulate the real sector during periods of economic stagnation by expanding the availability of credit, and restrain the real sector during periods of rapid growth or persistent inflation by restricting the availability of credit. These intended *countercyclical* transmission mechanisms were presented earlier in the primer section of this chapter. Since the transition to neoliberal capitalism, however, monetary policy has inadvertently produced *procyclical* outcomes, meaning outcomes that exacerbate or accelerate the trajectory of financial markets and economic activity. Monetary policy has expanded the availability of credit during periods of growth, and restricted the availability of credit during periods of stagnation. By the 2001–07 expansion, monetary policy contributed to a significant expansion of liquidity, and a rapid increase in debt that fueled a speculative housing market bubble, culminating in the financial crisis.

According to D'Arista, the primary mechanism that has weakened the effectiveness of monetary policy is countervailing capital flows between the United States and the rest of the world. While the Federal Reserve has successfully controlled short-term interest rates as intended, those changes have produced unintended capital flows that reverse the intended effect of monetary policy on the supply of credit. For example, the purpose of a monetary restraint is to restrict the supply of credit by raising short-term interest rates, usually during periods of excessive economic growth or inflation. However, higher short-term interest rates have led to capital inflows from abroad, which have expanded the supply of credit, and in turn lowered long-term interest rates. These market interest rates, which directly affect borrowing decisions by households and businesses, encourage more debt and more spending during periods of growth. Conversely, the purpose of a monetary stimulus is to expand the supply of credit by lowering short-term interest rates, usually during a recession. However, lower short-term interest rates have led to capital outflows from the United States, which have restrained the supply of credit, and in turn raised long-term interest rates. Higher long-term interest rates discourage consumption and investment when they are needed most. These developments not only extend the implementation lag of monetary policy, but also require the Federal Reserve to pursue more exaggerated changes in interest rates in order to influence the economic system.

D'Arista cites several examples of the failure of countercyclical monetary policy during the Great Moderation. First, during the 1990–91 recession, the

Federal Reserve conducted expansionary monetary policy and successfully lowered short-term interest rates. However, lower short-term interest rates in the United States implied lower rates of return on dollar assets relative to foreign assets. In a deregulated, globalized financial system, investors pursued the relatively higher rates of return on foreign assets, which led to capital outflows from the United States. The loss of capital led to a credit crunch in the US financial system that muted the effects of monetary stimulus on the real sector—the opposite of what should happen during a recession. Then, once the 1991–2001 recovery was underway, the Federal Reserve predictably raised short-term interest rates by conducting contractionary monetary policy. But as global investors sought the relatively higher rates of return on US assets, capital inflows led to a greater supply of credit in the United States that accelerated the recovery, but reversed the intended effects of monetary restraint on the real sector. Furthermore, US monetary policy during the 1990s destabilized emerging economies, especially Mexico. Monetary stimulus in the United States sent capital into Mexico, followed by massive capital outflows back to the United States in response to monetary restraint. A similar process occurred during the 2001 recession. Following a monetary stimulus during the downturn and the early years of the 2001–07 recovery, the Federal Reserve started raising the effective federal funds rate in 2004. Despite higher short-term interest rates, long-term interest rates were lower both in the United States and abroad for the reasons stated earlier: higher short-term interest rates led to capital inflows, which increased the supply of credit, and thereby lowered long-term interest rates. Lower long-term interest rates led to even more borrowing during the latter years of the recovery that fueled the housing market bubble.

D'Arista argues that the Federal Reserve's allegiance to free markets and deregulation ultimately weakened its own interactions with the financial sector and economic system. Instead of correcting the business cycle through countercyclical measures, the Federal Reserve inadvertently exacerbated economic and financial instability in the lead-up to the 2008 financial crisis. Mainstream economists overlook this point by celebrating the central bank's ability to maintain stable rates of inflation and economic growth after the 1980s. While both outcomes are technically true, they ignore the unprecedented spike in asset prices, especially in housing markets. Policymakers failed to understand how the transformation of the credit system—from one governed by depository institutions and central bank oversight to one governed by financial markets and unregulated institutional investors—weakened the traditional transmission mechanisms of monetary policy. The results have been a loss of control over the supply of credit, a loss of connection with the real sector, and—most importantly—a failure of monetary policy to substantively address the economic crisis in the wake of the Great Recession.

FINAL THOUGHTS

Although heterodox economics has produced substantive critiques of the Federal Reserve's actions during the 2008 financial crisis and Great Recession, mainstream economics has also criticized the conduct of monetary stimulus. One of the most telling assessments of Ben Bernanke's tenure came from Anna Jacobson Schwartz, who contributed to the development of the monetarist school of economic thought. In a 2009 op-ed published in the *New York Times*, Schwartz not only assails Bernanke's stewardship of the Federal Reserve during the crisis, but also argues against his reappointment as chair. She states: "As Federal Reserve chairman, Ben Bernanke has committed serious sins of commission and omission … Mr. Bernanke seems to know only two amounts: zero and trillions."

While Obama indeed reappointed Bernanke, this case further emphasizes the controversial nature of monetary policy across competing perspectives in economics, which endures today. The efficacy of monetary policy is once again being tested as the central bank responds to the financial and economic effects of the Covid-19 pandemic and persistent inflation.

The next chapter concludes this analysis of policy responses to the Great Recession. This chapter has demonstrated that, despite trillions of dollars in stimulus and 0% interest rates, monetary policy can still fail to resolve economic and financial instability. However, national policymakers hold yet another set of tools as a way to more directly address the economic crisis: expansionary fiscal policy.

Sources

Bernanke, B.S. (2000). *Essays on the Great Depression*. Princeton, NJ: Princeton University Press.

Bernanke, B.S. (2002, November 8). On Milton Friedman's Ninetieth Birthday [Transcript]. Remarks by Governor Ben S. Bernanke at The Conference to Honor Milton Friedman, University of Chicago, Chicago, IL. Retrieved from https://www.federalreserve.gov.

Bernanke, B.S. (2003, October 24). Remarks by Governor Ben S. Bernanke at the Federal Reserve Bank of Dallas Conference on the Legacy of Milton and Rose Friedman's *Free to Choose*, Dallas, TX [Transcript]. Retrieved from https://www.federalreserve.gov.

Blinder, A.S. & Zandi, M. (2010, July 27). *How the Great Recession was brought to an end*. Moody's Analytics.

Blinder, A.S. & Zandi, M. (2015, October 15). *The financial crisis: Lessons for the next one*. Center on Budget and Policy Priorities.

Board of Governors of the Federal Reserve System. (n.d.-a). *Ben S. Bernanke*. Retrieved from http://www.federalreservehistory.org.

Board of Governors of the Federal Reserve System. (n.d.-b). *Policy tools*. Retrieved from http://www.federalreserve.gov.

Board of Governors of the Federal Reserve System. (n.d.-c). *Structure of the Federal Reserve System*. Retrieved from http://www.federalreserve.gov.

Brown, O.W. (2011). *Federal Reserve System: Opportunities exist to strengthen policies and processes for managing emergency assistance* (GAO-12-122T). U.S. Government Accountability Office.

D'Arista, J. (2009). *Setting an agenda for monetary reform* (Working Paper #190). Amherst, MA: Political Economy Research Institute.

Federal Open Market Committee. (2014, September 17). *Federal Reserve issues FOMC statement on policy normalization principles and plans* [Press release]. Retrieved from http://www.federalreserve.gov.

Federal Open Market Committee. (2015a, March 18). *Addendum to the policy normalization principles and plans*. Retrieved from http://www.federalreserve.gov.

Federal Open Market Committee. (2015b, December 16). *Federal Reserve issues FOMC statement* [Press release]. Retrieved from http://www.federalreserve.gov.

Federal Open Market Committee. (2017, June 13). *Addendum to the policy normalization principles and plans*.

Retrieved from http://www.federalreserve.gov.
Federal Open Market Committee. (2019, January 30). *Statement regarding monetary policy implementation and balance sheet normalization* [Press release]. Retrieved from http://www.federalreserve.gov.
Federal Reserve Act, 12 U.S.C. § 226 (1913).
Federal Reserve Bank of St. Louis. (n.d.). FRED economic data [Data file and codebook]. Retrieved from https://fred.stlouisfed.org.
Friedman, M. & Schwartz, A.J. (1963). *A monetary history of the United States, 1867–1960*. Princeton, NJ: Princeton University Press.
Friedman, M. & Schwartz, A.J. (1965). *The Great Contraction, 1929–1933*. Princeton, NJ: Princeton University Press.
Friedman, M. (1970). The counter-revolution in monetary theory [Transcript]. Retrieved from http://www.hoover.org.
Schwartz, A.J. (2009, July 25). Man without a plan. *The New York Times*. Retrieved from http://www.nytimes.com.

Further Reading

D'Arista, J. (1994). *The evolution of U.S. finance, volume I: Federal Reserve monetary policy, 1915–1935*. New York, NY: Routledge.
D'Arista, J. (2008). U.S. debt and global imbalances. *International Journal of Political Economy*, *36*(4), 12–35. doi: 10.2753/IJP0891-1916360402
Epstein, G. (2019). *The political economy of central banking: Contested control and the power of finance, Selected essays of Gerald Epstein*. Northampton, MA: Edward Elgar Publishing.
Palley, T. (2014). *Monetary policy after quantitative easing: The case for asset based reserve requirements (ABRR)* (Working Paper #350). Amherst, MA: Political Economy Research Institute.
Palley, T. (2014). The politics of paying interest on bank reserves: A criticism of Bernanke's exit strategy. *Challenge*, *53*(3), 49–65. doi: 10.2753/0577-5132530303

CHAPTER 8

Fiscal Policy Responses to the Great Recession

This chapter concludes an investigation into the far-reaching policy responses to the Great Recession. This three-chapter part divides the emergency policy measures into the following categories: those that addressed financial structure and the 2008 financial crisis; those that addressed the economic crisis in the real sector; and those that addressed both. The Dodd-Frank financial reform (Chapter 6) altered financial structure, regulation and oversight of the financial sector, and the conduct of future bailouts by the government. The US Federal Reserve (Chapter 7) used traditional and non-traditional tools of monetary policy in order to combat the economic and financial aspects of the crisis. The central bank provided traditional monetary stimulus in order to boost economic growth and reduce unemployment. It also invoked its emergency authority, provided by the Federal Reserve Act, in order to stabilize financial markets and directly assist individual financial institutions. Chapter 8 therefore examines the ways in which the federal government—meaning the president and Congress—combated the economic crisis using the tools of fiscal policy. Between 2008 and 2012, the government spent nearly $1.5 trillion on expansionary fiscal policies that raised government spending, cut taxes, and increased income transfers. Although the total price tag for the fiscal stimulus was much smaller than the monetary stimulus, it was instrumental in stabilizing output and employment through the multiplier process.

Consistent with the pluralist approach of this textbook, this chapter uses the fiscal policy responses to the economic crisis as a case study for understanding the conduct of fiscal policy as well as the ongoing theoretical debate related to this topic. This chapter highlights the various points and turns in that debate, ranging from the revolutionary work of John Maynard Keynes during the early twentieth century, to more recent assessments of the stimulus packages during the Great Recession. To this day, the stimulus packages during the Great Recession remain controversial across the political spectrum. For example, critics on the Right argue that the fiscal stimulus was an excessive expansion of government into the economic system; that the spending provisions were politically motivated; and that it did not rely enough on tax cuts. Critics on the Left, on the other hand, argue that

DOI: 10.4324/9780429461316-11

the fiscal stimulus lacked an overarching progressive vision; that it was too small to close the enormous output gap; and that it relied too much on tax cuts. In either case, the conduct of fiscal policy during this period informed the economic agendas of subsequent administrations, and how the federal government has responded to subsequent crises, such as the Covid-19 pandemic.

The first section introduces readers to the three tools of fiscal policy: government spending, taxes, and income transfers. It explains the transmission mechanisms of each policy tool, the presence of automatic stabilizers within the federal budget, and the important differences between federal fiscal policy and state or local fiscal policy. The second section presents the concrete fiscal policies enacted during and after the Great Recession. It also highlights the critical work of economists Alan Blinder and Mark Zandi, who estimated the multiplier effects of specific measures on US output and employment. The next section then discusses the range of competing perspectives in economics on the conduct of fiscal policy. Significant theoretical differences exist not only between mainstream and heterodox economics, but also within mainstream economics. The final section poses a simple but complex question: what ultimately brought the Great Recession to an end in June 2009? At two points during the recovery, Blinder and Zandi examined this question by estimating the effects of multiple counterfactual policy scenarios on US macroeconomic performance. Which policy (or policies) stabilized real output, total payroll employment, the unemployment rate, and the inflation rate? What would have happened had the US government not intervened during the crisis? The results of these inquiries provide a compelling conclusion to this chapter as well as this unit on the policy responses to the Great Recession.

PRIMER ON THE CONDUCT OF FISCAL POLICY

Fiscal policy uses the tax and spending powers of the government in order to manage the health and performance of the economic system. Fiscal policy is conducted at *all* levels of government in the United States—that is, the federal, state, county, and municipal levels. At each level of government, there are multiple, and sometimes different, social and economic goals of the budgetary process. Governments raise revenues and make appropriations in order to provide public services to their communities, fund social welfare programs, promote national defense, redistribute income, and service debt, among other priorities. The primary focus of this chapter is the conduct of fiscal policy at the federal level, as enacted by the president and Congress, and the effects of fiscal policy on the national economic system during the Great Recession. The theoretical basis for fiscal policy presented here was developed by Keynesian economists during the 1930s and has informed macroeconomic policymaking since World War II. In this context, the purpose of fiscal policy is to manage the level of aggregate demand in order to minimize short-run volatility in the business cycle. In *A Tract on Monetary Reform*, Keynes explains the importance of the short run in economic analysis while de-emphasizing the long run:

> This *long run* is a misleading guide to current affairs. *In the long run* we are all dead. Economists set themselves too easy, too useless a task if in tempestuous seasons they can only tell us that when the storm is long past the ocean is flat again.

When successful, national fiscal policy produces countercyclical outcomes on output, unemployment, and inflation. An expansionary fiscal policy stimulates aggregate demand during a recession, while a contractionary fiscal policy restrains aggregate demand during periods of excessive economic growth or persistent inflation. However, this chapter also examines the conduct of fiscal policy at the state and local levels; how this differs from the federal level; and the important connection between federal fiscal stimulus and the economic stability of US states during the crisis.

Tools of Fiscal Policy

There are three major tools of fiscal policy: government spending, taxes, and income transfers. Each instrument, either directly or indirectly, affects aggregate demand in accordance with the government's economic priorities. Let's examine each tool in more detail. Although the term "government spending" appears general, it is actually quite specific. Government spending refers only to *direct* purchases of goods and services by the government. It does *not* refer to the total outlays of the government in a particular budget cycle, which include other types of payments besides direct purchases of output. The National Income and Product Accounts of the United States officially classify government spending as a component of gross domestic product (GDP) in addition to household consumption, business investment, and net exports. In order to understand why, consider the following example: suppose an auto company sells a new car that was produced in the United States. National income accounting records the purchase according to the sector of the economic system that claims the output. If an individual household in the United States purchases the car: "consumption." If an insurance company purchases that same car for its adjusters: "investment." If a household or business in Germany buys the car: "export." And if the US State Department buys the car: "government spending."

With regard to taxes, three tax codes comprise the vast majority of federal tax receipts. The individual income tax is a levy on wages and salaries, investment income, and other income sources. The corporation income tax is a levy on the profits of large corporations. The social insurance and retirement tax is a levy on payrolls that funds the Social Security program. Both employers and employees contribute to payroll taxes. Although the federal tax structure also includes a number of smaller tax codes, the government uses these three taxes to conduct fiscal policy.

Lastly, income transfers refer to transfer payments from the government to households or firms. In this case, the government itself does not purchase goods and services, but provides income to individuals or businesses in order to do so. Moreover, income transfers are not loans since recipients are not obligated to repay the government. Examples of transfer payments from the federal government include Social Security, unemployment insurance, disability insurance, Temporary Assistance for Needy Families and other welfare programs, Medicare and Medicaid, food stamps, business subsidies for investment or hiring, etc. Many income transfers are jointly funded by the states and the federal government. Table 8.1 summarizes the tools of fiscal policy at the national level as conducted by the federal government.

TABLE 8.1 Tools of Fiscal Policy*

Government Spending	- Direct purchases of goods and services by the government - Can be consumption or gross investment expenditures - Directly affects aggregate demand
Taxes	- Contributions to government receipts by the private sector - Levied on individual incomes, corporate profits, and payrolls - Directly affects disposable income - Indirectly affects aggregate demand through changes in consumption
Income Transfers	- Transfer payments from the government to individuals - Available to both households and firms - Directly affects disposable income - Indirectly affects aggregate demand through changes in consumption

* Refers to fiscal policy at the national level as conducted by the federal government.

A few stylized facts about the conduct of fiscal policy in the United States are important to note. These are oft-misunderstood points, especially in the popular press and among politicians:

- The fiscal policies enacted during the Great Recession are distinct from the various financial policies and bailouts, although the two certainly interacted in their effects. Whereas financial reform addressed financial structure and the 2008 financial crisis, fiscal policy addressed the economic crisis in the real sector, meaning the severe recession, high rates of unemployment, and potential for persistent deflation. Monetary policy addressed both the financial crisis and the economic crisis.
- Although President Obama signed the bulk of the fiscal stimulus measures during the crisis, the federal government's response actually began during the W. Bush administration. The W. Bush administration also initiated several emergency measures during the transition that were later signed by Obama.
- The Great Recession is by no means the first instance of expansionary fiscal policy. In fact, the federal government has used fiscal policy to combat *every* downturn since the Great Depression of the 1930s.
- The use of fiscal policy to minimize economic volatility is *not* exclusive to either Democratic or Republican administrations. Depending on the balance of power between the White House and Congress, as well as within Congress, many measures have been bipartisan in scope.
- Most fiscal policies combine the three policy instruments presented earlier. However, the major political parties in the United States place differing degrees of emphasis on the specific policy instruments. They absolutely differ as to the beneficiaries of such measures.
- In practice, the federal government has typically enacted fiscal policy in order to boost economic growth. The use of fiscal policy in order to reduce inflation is less common, but not unprecedented.
- Once benchmark interest rates are near 0%, and quantitative easing fails to provide any further stimulus to the economic system, expansionary fiscal policy is the *only* tool available to national policymakers during a recession.

- Although fiscal policy can be *discretionary* in nature, meaning Congress passes specific legislation designed to address an economic crisis, aggregate demand management is also *automatically* built into the structure of the federal budget, the federal tax code, and federal income transfers.
- The purpose of fiscal policy is to reset *short-run* economic activity. It is not an instrument of long-run economic growth; nor does it fundamentally restructure the economic system.

The Conduct of Discretionary Fiscal Policy

Let's first examine the conduct of *discretionary* fiscal policy using each policy instrument. In a discretionary fiscal policy, the president and Congress agree on legislation that actively manages aggregate demand in order to counteract volatility in the business cycle. The response by the federal government is purposeful and specific to the nature of economic instability, whether it be a recession or high inflation. The following analysis explains the conduct of an expansionary fiscal policy (or a fiscal stimulus), since that was the context of fiscal policy during the Great Recession. The government typically conducts fiscal stimulus during recessions or periods of economic stagnation, when aggregate demand is insufficient to maintain the current level of output. Albeit in different ways, each policy tool stimulates aggregate demand. If the government is successful in raising aggregate demand beyond current output levels, output will increase, unemployment will fall, and inflation will rise. The converse will occur during a contractionary fiscal policy (or a fiscal restraint), when the government actively reduces aggregate demand in order to restrain excessive inflation.

The first option during a recession is to *increase government spending*. Many policymakers and economists favor this option because it directly and unambiguously injects spending into the economic system. Since government spending is, by definition, a component of GDP, the government can increase aggregate demand simply by increasing its own demand for goods and services. For example, the federal government could award new defense contracts, a state government could invest in highway improvements, or a municipal government could order new fire trucks. In order to fulfill orders or contracts with the government, output and employment will rise in the sectors that produce such goods and services. However, the government does not need to spend the entire output gap during a recession. Expansionary fiscal policy initiates a multiplier process whereby the initial increase in government spending (G) leads to *multiple* increases in income and spending across the economic system. This happens because the initial increase in output and employment raises household income, which then facilitates more spending in the form of consumption (as well as some saving). This secondary increase in consumption (C) further stimulates output and employment, leading to more income and consumption again. The multiplier process does not continue indefinitely, however, since households typically save some portion of the income earned during each cycle. The process is therefore as follows:

$$\textit{Initial increase in } G \rightarrow \textit{Increase in Output} \rightarrow \textit{Increase in } C$$
$$\rightarrow \textit{Increase in Output} \rightarrow \textit{Increase in } C \ldots$$

According to Keynesian economists, the total increase in output across all cycles should exceed the initial increase in government spending. Mathematically, the total increase in output relative to the initial increase in government spending is known as the "multiplier." For example, a multiplier value of 2 means that output increases by $2 for every $1 initial increase in government spending. The multiplier value depends upon two factors: the amount of the initial increase in government spending; and the proportion of new household income that is consumed during each cycle. The multiplier value will be stronger in a more consumer-driven environment, since consumers spend a substantial portion of new income earned during each cycle. The multiplier value will be weaker in a thriftier environment, when households save a substantial portion of new income earned. Alternatively, a multiplier value of 2 means that the government must increase spending by half of the output gap. For example, if the economic system is mired in a $1 trillion output gap, then government spending must increase by $500 billion. The size of any stimulus package is therefore proportional to the magnitude of the recession: higher during longer, severe downturns and lower during shorter, mild downturns.

The second option available to the government is to *lower taxes*. Similar to government spending, the goal of a tax cut is to initiate a multiplier process. Unlike government spending, a tax cut does not directly raise aggregate demand. Rather, a tax cut first increases disposable income (*DI*), defined as gross household income less taxes plus transfer payments. Disposable income measures the amount of money that is actually available to households for either consumption or saving. For example, although a $250 billion tax cut increases *disposable income* by $250 billion, it does not necessarily increase *aggregate demand* by $250 billion. The critical question is: how much of this tax cut will households consume? This is the ambiguous aspect of expansionary fiscal policy using a tax cut, because it is up to the recipients to decide what to do with their new after-tax earnings. If households spend most of their tax cut, then a multiplier process will commence. The economic system will see an initial injection of consumption, which will increase output and employment, which will facilitate more spending again. The multiplier process in this case is as follows:

$$\textit{Tax Cut} \rightarrow \textit{Increase in DI} \rightarrow \textit{Initial increase in C} \rightarrow \textit{Increase in Output}$$
$$\rightarrow \textit{Increase in C} \rightarrow \textit{Increase in Output} \rightarrow \textit{Increase in C}\ldots$$

The multiplier value for a tax cut measures the total increase in output relative to the initial increase in consumption. The success of this policy therefore depends upon the size of the tax cut, the initial increase in consumption, and the share of new disposable income that households are willing to spend during each subsequent cycle. If households spend most of their new disposable income, the tax cut will generate a significant multiplier effect. If households save most of their new disposable income, or use it to pay down debt, the multiplier effect will be much weaker.

The third option is to *increase income transfers*. For example, the government could expand the provision of unemployment benefits by $100 billion. The effects and caveats of an increase in income transfers are the same as a tax cut. Once again, the objective is to generate a multiplier process that will close a significant output gap. However, this policy does not directly raise aggregate demand by $100 billion. Rather, an increase in income transfers first increases disposable income by $100 billion. The success of the fiscal stimulus, and the strength of the multiplier effect, ultimately depend upon how much of this new disposable income is initially spent. As was the case with a tax cut, the multiplier value measures the total increase in output relative to the initial increase in consumption. If households save most or all of their new after-tax earnings, the multiplier effect will be much weaker, and make it more difficult for the government to close the output gap. An expansionary fiscal policy using income transfers is as follows:

Increase in Transfers → Increase in DI → Initial increase in C
→ Increase in Output → Increase in C
→ Increase in Output…

Understanding Automatic Stabilizers

Although expansionary fiscal policy can be discretionary in nature, it can also occur without new legislation by the federal government. This is important because political gridlock often weakens or scuttles a discretionary policy response to instability in the business cycle. The term "automatic stabilizer" refers to measures within the federal budget that automatically produce countercyclical outcomes on aggregate demand and the business cycle. These measures stimulate aggregate demand during recessionary periods and restrain aggregate demand during inflationary periods. Automatic stabilizers apply to taxes and income transfers, but they do not apply to government spending—meaning government spending does not increase or decrease systematically with the business cycle. The federal tax code features automatic stabilizers because the United States has a largely progressive tax system, which applies higher tax rates to high-income individuals and lower tax rates to low-income individuals. Federal income transfers also feature automatic stabilizers because they are entitlement programs. By law, individuals have the right to access benefits, like unemployment insurance and food stamps, when they experience a loss of income or economic insecurity.

During a recession, these measures automatically reduce federal tax receipts and increase federal outlays. Tax revenues decrease as employment and income losses push individuals toward lower tax brackets. At the same time, spending on income transfers increases as more individuals qualify for entitlements. The combined effect of lower taxes and higher income transfers supports disposable income, and allows households to maintain a minimum level of consumption that would not be possible without such measures. That is the purpose of such mechanisms. Automatic stabilizers therefore support aggregate demand during periods of economic instability, and mitigate further reductions in output and employment.

During an expansion, these mechanisms automatically increase federal tax receipts and reduce federal outlays. As employment and income recover, individuals will move into higher tax brackets. With greater economic security and a stronger labor market, fewer individuals will qualify for entitlement programs. The combined effect of higher taxes and lower income transfers restrains disposable income and thereby household consumption. Why would the government pursue this option? The purpose of automatic stabilizers in this context is to limit the growth of aggregate demand in order to prevent excessive inflationary pressures during an economic expansion.

The Conduct of Fiscal Policy in Cities and States

This primer has largely focused on the conduct of fiscal policy at the federal level. While the tools of fiscal policy are the same at all levels of government, the conduct of fiscal policy by state and local governments differs from the federal government in two important ways. First, state and local governments are subject to *balanced budget requirements*, while the federal government is not. During a particular budget cycle, state and local outlays cannot exceed tax receipts. Second, federal fiscal policy therefore produces countercyclical outcomes on aggregate demand and the business cycle, while state and local fiscal policy produces *procyclical* outcomes. "Procyclical" means that cities and states conduct fiscal restraint during recessions and fiscal stimulus during expansions. These policy measures exacerbate the trajectory of the business cycle by reducing aggregate demand further during downturns, and raising aggregate demand further during recoveries. This distinction played a significant role in not only the transmission of the Great Recession nationwide, but also the fiscal policy responses to it.

Whether by discretionary policy or automatic stabilizers, the federal government engages in expansionary fiscal policy during a recession. In order to counteract economic stagnation, federal tax receipts decrease while federal outlays increase. An excess of outlays relative to receipts means that the federal government will run a budget deficit, and must borrow in order to cover the difference. While a higher public debt burden is not an insignificant issue, the absence of a balanced budget requirement is what allows the federal government to produce countercyclical outcomes on aggregate demand and the business cycle.

Cities and states, however, are unable to counteract recessions through the budgetary process. Since they face balanced budget requirements, cities and states must raise tax revenues and reduce expenditures when a deficit emerges. Households and businesses could then see higher tax bills and less access to social services during periods of significant economic distress. The enactment of contractionary fiscal policy during a recession implies that state and local fiscal policy produces procyclical outcomes on aggregate demand and the business cycle. Instead of counteracting economic stagnation, state and local fiscal policy reinforces it. Likewise, instead of restraining economic growth, state and local fiscal policy fuels it.

FISCAL POLICY DURING THE GREAT RECESSION

This section presents the concrete fiscal policy responses to the Great Recession. In 2010 and 2015, economists Alan Blinder and Mark Zandi conducted a full accounting of the fiscal stimulus packages enacted by the federal government. Taken together, the W. Bush and Obama administrations spent nearly $1.5 trillion on expansionary fiscal policies, or 10% of GDP, between 2008 and 2012. While economists continue to debate the effectiveness of individual measures, few would classify the total price tag as anything other than enormous. The fiscal stimulus delivered during the Great Recession was, up to that point, the largest since the Great Depression. This section comprehensively analyzes the major provisions of the government's response according to the three tools of fiscal policy: government spending, tax cuts, and income transfers.

Table 8.2 presents Blinder and Zandi's detailed accounting of expansionary fiscal policies throughout the crisis and the initial years of the recovery. In total, the federal government granted $701 billion in tax cuts to households and businesses. The $783 billion in increased expenditures, which includes both government spending and income transfers in this accounting, comprised slightly more

TABLE 8.2 Expansionary Fiscal Policies During the Great Recession

	Cost (Billions of US $)
Economic Stimulus Act of 2008	***170***
American Recovery and Reinvestment Act of 2009	***832***
Infrastructure and Other Spending	147
-Traditional infrastructure	38
-Nontraditional infrastructure	109
Transfers to State and Local Governments	188
-Medicaid	93
-Education	95
Transfers to Persons	307
-Social Security	13
-Unemployment Assistance	224
-Food Stamps	46
-COBRA Payments	24
Tax Cuts	190
-Businesses & Other Tax Incentives	40
-Making Work Pay	64
--First-Time Homebuyer Tax Credit	14
-Individuals Excluding Increase in AMT Exemption	72
--Cash for Appliances	0.3
Cash for Clunkers	***3***
HIRE Act (Job Tax Credit)	***17***
Worker, Homeownership, and Business Assistance Act of 2009	***91***
Extended Unemployment Insurance Benefits	55
Extended/Expanded Net Operating Loss Provisions of ARRA	33
Extended/Expanded Homebuyer Tax Credit	3
Department of Defense Appropriations Act of 2010	***2***
Extended Guarantees and Fee Waivers for SBA loans	1
Expanded COBRA Premium Subsidy	1
Education Jobs and Medicaid Assistance Act	***26***
Tax Relief, Unemployment Insurance Reauthorization, and Job Creation Act of 2010	***189***
Temporary Extension of UI Benefits (Outlay)	56
Temporary Extension of Investment Incentives	22
Temporary Payroll Tax Holiday (Change in Revenue)	112

(*Continued*)

TABLE 8.2 (Continued)

	Cost (Billions of US $)
Temporary Payroll Tax Cut Continuation Act of 2011	***29***
Middle Class Tax Relief and Job Creation Act of 2012	***125***
Total	**1,484**
Expenditures (Government Spending and Income Transfers)	**783**
Tax Cuts	**701**

Source: Blinder and Zandi (2015).
This material was created by the Center on Budget and Policy Priorities (www.cbpp.org).

than half of the total price tag. The government's response began with the Economic Stimulus Act of 2008, which was signed by George W. Bush. By far the largest and most controversial individual package was the American Recovery and Reinvestment Act of 2009 (ARRA), which was signed by Barack Obama. With a price tag of $832 billion, the ARRA alone accounts for well over half of the total fiscal stimulus. Congress also authorized several smaller measures during Obama's first term, which range between $2 billion and $189 billion.

Let's begin with the first instrument of fiscal policy: government spending. Increased government spending was a central priority of the ARRA. Although it included numerous provisions that funded direct purchases of output by the government, infrastructure spending was the largest category. Moreover, the stimulus package increased government spending on traditional infrastructure (i.e., roads, bridges, and utilities) as well as non-traditional infrastructure (i.e., childcare, education, healthcare, and housing). Infrastructure investment has been a classic weapon against severe economic crises since the Great Depression, and early 2009 was no different. The contraction in the real sector was still very much in full swing. The trajectory of US capitalism was tenuous and uncertain, leading policymakers to seek the most direct and unambiguous injection of spending. Some of the well-known government spending provisions of the ARRA include:

- grants to expand broadband and wireless service in rural communities;
- funding for education programs for disadvantaged children;
- grants for special education programs;
- grants to state and local governments for energy-efficiency improvements;
- grants to low-income families for home weatherization;
- funding to modernize the electric grid;
- funding for research and development of renewable energy technology;
- energy-efficiency and other improvements to federal buildings and facilities, including national defense;
- funding for biomedical research;
- grants to states for childcare services for low-income families;
- energy-efficiency and other improvements to public housing projects;
- funding to purchase foreclosed and vacant properties;
- grants to state and local governments for law enforcement;
- loans to improve wastewater treatment facilities;

- funding for the National Science Foundation; and
- investments in highway improvements, public transit, and high-speed rail.

However, as the popularity of the ARRA waned among both Congress and the public, subsequent stimulus packages deemphasized government spending, and largely extended tax cuts and unemployment benefits.

Nearly all of the individual stimulus measures lowered taxes for both households and businesses, which included tax rebate checks, tax credits, and traditional tax cuts. While most of the tax cuts were temporary, some were made permanent by Congress during the recovery. Tax rebates—a policy instrument historically favored by Republican lawmakers—were the first intervention against the recession in early 2008. The Economic Stimulus Act sent tax rebate checks to individuals in order to promote spending and stem negative expectations. One of the key provisions of the ARRA was the Making Work Pay tax credit, which was a payroll tax credit for workers. The ARRA also expanded eligibility for child tax credits, increased the earned income tax credit, and granted tax credits for college tuition and expenses. A series of household tax credits targeted consumer spending on long-term durable goods. The most famous example of this strategy was "Cash for Clunkers" during the summer of 2009. The program offered cash rebates to consumers to trade in old, fuel-inefficient cars and purchase new, fuel-efficient cars. Although short-lived, and a relatively small share of the total fiscal stimulus, the program stimulated demand for motor vehicles during an extremely uncertain period for the US auto industry. A similar provision within the ARRA encouraged consumer spending on household appliances. In order to prevent the ongoing collapse in housing prices, the government offered a significant tax credit to new homeowners through the ARRA, which it later extended. One of the few measures that Democrats and Republicans could agree on was a payroll tax cut, which applied to both employees and employers. The tax cut temporarily raised household disposable income and freed up capital for business investment. The payroll tax holiday became a key component of the smaller fiscal stimulus packages that followed the ARRA. However, businesses also received billions in both temporary and permanent tax cuts during the economic crisis. The ARRA included traditional business tax cuts and investment incentives, many of which were extended by subsequent stimulus packages during the recovery. In particular, the ARRA featured a net operating loss rebate, while the accelerated depreciation provision allowed businesses to quickly deduct plant and equipment costs. The HIRE Act offered businesses a payroll tax credit as an incentive to hire new workers. Lastly, many of the Bush-era tax cuts for both households and businesses were made permanent by the fiscal stimulus packages following the recession.

A significant increase in income transfers was central to the government's strategy of fiscal policy. These measures not only supported household disposable income but also alleviated economic insecurity in key areas, such as education, food, healthcare, and housing. Furthermore, the federal government provided aid to both individuals and state budgets in order to maintain a basic level of household consumption. Similar to the tax clauses, the income transfer measures were discretionary in that they temporarily expanded an entitlement program beyond its function as an automatic stabilizer. The government often extended the duration of benefits, expanded eligibility for benefits, paid more in benefits, or some combination thereof. The most important policy instrument in this area was the expansion of unemployment insurance. The ARRA extended the duration, and raised the amount, of weekly unemployment benefits. Unemployment insurance directly addressed income security during a period of significant employment and income losses. In fact, fears of a double-dip recession during the early years of the recovery led Congress to reauthorize these benefits multiple times. The ARRA also promoted individual access to education by increasing Pell grants and other forms of student aid. It addressed food insecurity by raising food stamp benefits. It addressed housing insecurity by providing grants for rent and the relocation of the homeless. In order to maintain access to healthcare, the COBRA subsidy allowed unemployed workers to pay the premiums for their previous employer's health benefits. Some of the most consequential provisions of the ARRA increased federal aid to the states, especially for entitlement programs that are jointly funded by states and the federal government. The foreclosure crisis, the financial meltdown, and the contraction of output and employment devastated state and local budgets across the United States. Balanced budget requirements would have forced state and local governments to raise taxes, cut spending, and lay off workers, which would have reinforced economic instability. Although severe economic and financial conditions forced many states to pursue such measures anyway, the ARRA lessened the pro-cyclical effects of fiscal policy by at least delaying further spending cuts and higher taxes. The stimulus package supplemented state funding for education, the Medicaid program, Temporary Assistance for Needy Families, public safety, and other direct services to communities.

But to what extent were these actions effective? Keynesian economists evaluate the efficacy of expansionary fiscal policy according to the strength of the multiplier process. A successful fiscal stimulus produces a multiplier value greater than one, meaning the total increase in output exceeds the initial increase in spending. In short, the government gets the biggest "bang for its buck." The policy increases economic activity to a greater degree than the initial investment. The expansion of the tax base essentially allows the government to repay itself once the recovery is entrenched. A multiplier value less than one does not imply that a fiscal stimulus reduces output. If the multiplier value is still positive, it simply means that the total increase in output is less than the initial increase in spending. Moreover, the strength of the multiplier varies by policy instrument and specific measure. For example, did government spending during the Great Recession produce stronger multipliers than income transfers (or tax cuts)? Did the housing tax credit stimulate output and employment more than the job tax credit? Was the increase in food stamp benefits more effective than the extension of unemployment insurance? To answer these questions, Table 8.3 presents Blinder and Zandi's multiplier estimates for the major provisions discussed in this section. Each figure indicates the one-year increase in output for every $1 increase in federal expenditures (or $1 decrease in federal taxes). Blinder and Zandi conducted this analysis at two key points: the first quarter of 2009 and the first quarter of 2015. The former corresponds to the recession while the latter corresponds to the recovery.

TABLE 8.3 Selected Multipliers Expansionary Fiscal Policies During the Great Recession

Government Spending	*2009 (I)*	*2015 (I)*
Increase in Infrastructure Spending	1.57	0.86
Increase in Defense Spending	1.53	0.87
Taxes - Households		
Making Work Pay	1.30	1.03
Child Tax Credit - ARRA Parameters	1.38	1.17
Earned Income Tax Credit - ARRA Parameters	1.24	0.87
Housing Tax Credit	0.90	0.61
Payroll Tax Holiday - Employees	1.27	0.94
Taxes - Businesses		
Payroll Tax Holiday - Employers	1.05	0.79
Loss Carryback	0.25	0.09
Accelerated Depreciation	0.29	0.23
Job Tax Credit	1.20	0.85
Income Transfers		
Extension of Unemployment Insurance	1.61	1.01
Increase in Food Stamps	1.74	1.22
Aid to States	1.41	0.58

Source: Blinder and Zandi (2015).
Figures indicate the one-year increase in output relative to a $1 increase in federal expenditures (or $1 decrease in federal taxes).
This material was created by the Center on Budget and Policy Priorities (www.cbpp.org).

In early 2009, the greater provision of income transfers produced significant multiplier effects, particularly the increase in food stamp benefits and the extensions of unemployment benefits. The strong multipliers for both programs meant that recipients largely allocated their new disposable income toward consumer spending. For example, for every $1 increase in federal expenditures on food stamps, output increased by $1.74. General aid to states was also very effective at alleviating the economic crisis in the states. The multipliers for government spending were strong for the reasons economists expect. It provided a direct and unambiguous injection of spending into the economic system, during a time when household consumption and business investment were extremely volatile. Interestingly, both infrastructure spending (typically a liberal mainstay) and defense spending (typically a conservative mainstay) generated strong multipliers. Blinder and Zandi note that, although infrastructure spending takes time to implement, it was an important source of job creation. The discretionary tax cuts during the crisis were largely effective at stimulating output and employment. Household tax cuts generally produced stronger multiplier effects than business tax cuts, with one exception: the housing tax credit. However, this analysis only measures the macroeconomic effects of the housing tax credit—that is, its ability to stimulate output and employment. Its effect on the housing market crash was nonetheless important and productive. The housing tax credit was instrumental in stabilizing the housing market because it encouraged first-time buyers to initiate a contract, and reversed market expectations that home prices would drop further. The payroll tax holiday for businesses as well as the job tax credit likely stimulated investment—and most importantly hiring—during a period when business expectations were low, and access to credit was limited due to the credit freeze.

According to Table 8.3, all of the multiplier estimates in early 2015 were lower, which is typical for most recoveries. By that point, the national recovery was entrenched, and the output gap was much smaller. The federal government therefore did not need to stimulate output as much, since the economic system moved back toward full employment. Yet several expansionary fiscal policies retained multiplier values greater than one: Making Work Pay, the child tax credit, food stamps, and unemployment. Blinder and Zandi's results demonstrate that these programs are consistently effective at stabilizing the business cycle and supporting economic growth.

CRITICAL PERSPECTIVES ON FISCAL POLICY DURING THE GREAT RECESSION

To this day, the fiscal policy responses to the Great Recession remain the subject of intense debate. This is due in part to the size, scope, and duration of the stimulus measures, all of which were historically significant. Debate and criticism of the fiscal stimulus packages have occurred within multiple circles, including the field of economics, other academic disciplines such as political science, public policy think tanks, and the media. Furthermore, distinct critiques have emerged on both the Left and the Right. Although the Right opposed most policy interventions from the beginning, many on the Left were underwhelmed by the size and composition of the ARRA, albeit for very different reasons. Criticism on the Right eventually informed the conduct of fiscal policy during the Trump administration, while dissatisfaction on the Left informed the fiscal responses of the Biden administration to the Covid-19 pandemic. In keeping with the pluralist theme of this textbook, this section presents the major assessments of expansionary fiscal policies during the crisis from competing perspectives in economics.

Let's begin with the *theoretical* arguments surrounding the conduct of expansionary fiscal policy. There is widespread agreement within the field of economics as to what happens *during* a recession: recessions occur when household saving exceeds business investment. The practical effect of this imbalance is that withdrawals of spending exceed additions of spending. As a result, aggregate demand will be insufficient to maintain current output levels. Firms will then see unexpected surges in inventories, which will lead them to reduce output and employment. In severe cases, the contraction of output and employment leads to deflation. Yet there are several areas where economists fundamentally disagree. First, there is widespread debate over the potential causes of recessionary gaps. For example, *why* does saving exceed investment? Why did businesses lose confidence and reduce investment? Or, why did households lose confidence and reduce consumption? Are the motivating factors *external* to capitalist production—that is, are they non-economic in nature? Or are the motivating factors *internal* to capitalist production—that is, are they economic in nature? Second, once a recessionary gap emerges, there is widespread debate over what happens next—or should happen next. Does capitalism feature self-adjusting mechanisms that automatically adjust aggregate demand and maintain full employment? If so, the government should maintain little to no intervention during a recession. But if not, the solution requires a policy intervention that manages aggregate demand in order to restore full employment.

Neoclassical economists subscribe to the conventional adjustment process presented in Chapter 5. According to that model, recessions are caused by external shocks to capitalism—meaning they are not caused by the internal operation of capitalism itself. Aggregate demand is inherently stable, and naturally gravitates toward full employment. If a recessionary gap arises, the economic system features self-adjusting mechanisms that increase aggregate demand and maintain full employment. When aggregate demand is insufficient, surpluses will emerge in markets for goods and services, capital goods, raw materials, labor, and credit. As those markets adjust to new points of equilibrium, consumer prices, factor prices, wages, and interest rates will fall. Lower prices will then stimulate consumption, investment, hiring, and production. Free markets therefore automatically correct volatility in the economic system—without an expansionary fiscal policy by the government.

During the Great Recession, the 2008 presidential campaign of John McCain was a strong proponent of this view. Shortly before the election, and at the height of the financial crisis, McCain famously stated that: "… the fundamentals of our economy are strong." McCain, along with most Republican candidates that year, viewed economic and financial instability as transitory, and largely rejected the use of comprehensive fiscal stimulus to stabilize aggregate demand. Markets simply needed to adjust prices in order to correct economic and financial volatility.

Keynesian economists, on the other hand, subscribe to the multiplier process presented in this chapter. In *The General Theory of Employment, Interest, and Money*, John Maynard Keynes was careful to emphasize that the multiplier model is not diametrically opposed to the conventional adjustment model. The conventional adjustment process is certainly possible, but merely a limited case that does not generally describe the real experience of capitalist crises:

> I shall argue that the postulates of the classical theory are applicable to a special case only and not to the general case, the situation which it assumes being a limiting point of the possible positions of equilibrium. Moreover, the characteristics of the special case assumed by the classical theory happen not to be those of the economic society which we actually live, with the result that its teaching is misleading and disastrous if we attempt to apply it to the facts of experience.

Keynesian economists reject the notion that lower market prices alone can stimulate aggregate demand for several reasons. Despite lower market prices, mass unemployment further suppresses demand for goods and services. Individuals will be unable to take advantage of lower prices simply because they lack the income. Consequently, market prices might never reach bottom during severe crises. Even if households and businesses are able to spend, they may be unwilling to spend due to negative expectations about the future direction of capitalism. Lower prices during a recession may also perpetuate a deflationary mindset, whereby individuals withhold spending simply because they expect prices to drop further: why buy now when there might be a better deal tomorrow? During the Great Recession, this mentality was absolutely present and perpetuated the collapse in housing prices. Keynesian economists therefore promote the use of expansionary fiscal policies that stimulate aggregate demand. Fiscal stimulus can enable spending by the unemployed, and reverse negative expectations about the trajectory of capitalist production as well as individual market prices. Without it, capitalist production could operate well below full employment output levels, with extremely high rates of unemployment and excess capacity. The most notable example of this outcome, of course, was the Great Depression. However, Keynesian economists view discretionary fiscal policy as a short-run solution to a recession—not a long-run source of economic growth. Keynes promoted greater government intervention during a crisis, but his views are actually quite nuanced. The government need not *generally* perform the activities of the private sector; but it *must* perform such activities if the private sector fails to do so. In *The End of Laissez Faire*, Keynes states: "The important thing for Government is not to do things which individuals are doing already, and to do them a little better or a little worse; but to do those things which at present are not done at all." In other words, if private consumption and investment are not forthcoming, then the government has a legitimate interest in pursuing deficit spending.

During the Great Recession, the Keynesian perspective informed the policy responses of the W. Bush and Obama administrations. Bush was much more cautious in early 2008. He recognized that fiscal stimulus was necessary, but sought to avoid an overextension of government in the decision making of individuals:

> Helping our economy requires us to take action. It is equally important that we not overreact. Our economic success is not the result of the wisdom of politicians in Washington, DC, but of the collective wisdom of the American people.

Bush favored indirect policy interventions that left spending decisions to individuals. For this reason, Republicans typically favor tax cuts as the instrument of fiscal policy. But as the crisis accelerated into early 2009, President Obama sought more immediate and comprehensive policy solutions:

> The situation we face could not be more serious. We have inherited an economic crisis as deep and as dire as any since the Great Depression. Economists from across the spectrum have warned that failure to act quickly would lead to the disappearance of millions of more jobs and national unemployment rates that could be in the double digits.

The Obama administration placed much more emphasis on direct action by the government through greater expenditures. For this reason, Democrats typically favor government spending and income transfers as the instruments of fiscal policy.

Since the Great Depression, and since the publication of *The General Theory*, neoclassical economists have developed several critiques of the Keynesian multiplier model. The most prominent retort is the concept of "crowding out." According to this model, short-run fiscal stimulus will ultimately suppress—or crowd out—private sector spending in the long run. Attempts by the government to raise aggregate demand through deficit spending will eventually be met with lower household consumption and business investment, thus negating the very purpose of the stimulus. The logic is as follows: when the government conducts an expansionary fiscal policy, whether by discretionary policy or automatic stabilizer, the government must run a budget deficit. Tax cuts by definition reduce revenues, while increases in government spending and/or income transfers raise expenditures. But in order to finance the budget deficit, the government must increase public borrowing by selling bonds. In the loanable funds market, this results in a significant increase in the demand for loanable funds, which creates a shortage at current interest rates. In order to clear the shortage, market interest rates must rise. Households and businesses will find it more difficult to access credit, which suppresses long-term consumption and investment, which therefore reduces aggregate demand. An expansion of the public sector, even when the intervention is well intended, ultimately leads to a contraction of the private sector.

Mainstream economists have pivoted away from Keynesian orthodoxy in still other ways. Prior to the Great Recession, Robert Lucas praised the field of macroeconomics for essentially answering its original challenge of crisis prevention. While he endorsed the use of fiscal policy, he favored long-run policies that encourage work and saving, not short-run policies that correct aggregate demand:

> Macroeconomics was born as a distinct field in the 1940's, as a part of the intellectual response to the Great Depression. The term then referred to the body of knowledge and expertise that we hoped would prevent the recurrence of that economic disaster. My thesis ... is that macroeconomics in this original sense has succeeded: Its central problem of depression prevention has been solved, for all practical purposes, and has in fact been solved for many decades. There remain important gains in welfare from better fiscal policies, but I argue that these are gains from providing people with better incentives to work and to save, not from better fine-tuning of spending flows. Taking U.S. performance over the past 50 years as a benchmark, the potential for welfare gains from better long-run, supply-side policies exceeds *by far* the potential from further improvements in short-run demand management."

During the recovery, he argued that two major policy initiatives of the Obama administration—the repeal of the Bush tax cuts, and the increase in medical costs associated with the Affordable Care Act—would limit long-term economic growth for this reason. Milton Friedman, of course, favored monetary policy as the preferred policy intervention, and discounted the use of fiscal policy. In a famous (and often misquoted) interview with *Time*, Friedman stated: "In one sense, we are all Keynesians now; in another, nobody is any longer a Keynesian."

Just as insufficient spending is not the cause of recessions, expansionary fiscal policy is not the solution. In his long-run study of monetary forces, Friedman found no example where fiscal policy had a larger effect on output and prices than monetary policy:

> One of the things I have tried to do over the years is to find cases where fiscal policy is going in one direction and monetary policy is going in the opposite. In every case the actual course of events follows monetary policy. I have never found a case in which fiscal policy dominated monetary policy and I suggest to you as a test to find a counter-example.

Fiscal policy was always passive to monetary policy—not the opposite. Recessions were associated with contractions of the money supply, while recoveries were associated with expansions of the money supply.

While this debate often takes place between mainstream microeconomics and macroeconomics, heterodox schools of thought have also formulated distinct and compelling critiques of expansionary fiscal policies, even when they reject the premise of crowding out, supply-side theory, or monetarism. For example, radical institutionalists argue that the combined policy responses to the Great Recession, fiscal stimulus included, failed to expand the joint stock of knowledge. While they were indeed successful at stabilizing aggregate demand, they failed to foster abundance. In fact, the traditional Keynesian emphasis on full employment is insufficient to achieve abundance. While full employment eliminates cyclical unemployment, it does not eliminate frictional, seasonal, and especially structural unemployment. These persistent forms of unemployment represent significant limits on society's joint stock of knowledge. Radical institutionalists therefore advocate for universal employment programs that expand access to the stock of knowledge, such as an employer-of-last-resort, living wage laws, and greater collective bargaining rights. Marxists, on the other hand, would argue that fiscal stimulus in no way resolves the crisis problematic of capitalism. Since the Great Recession, capitalism continues to relocate the centers of crisis formation to new spaces and new sectors. The economic system still requires the creation of profitable reinvestment opportunities in order to maintain compound growth. Yet the economic system faces real limits on the ability to do so. Despite cries of socialism and authoritarianism from the far Right, the Obama administration had no intention of restructuring class power, either through financial reform or the ARRA, for a simple reason: financial capitalists wielded significant influence within the Obama administration, and only got wealthier during the recovery. The transition away from neoliberalism is therefore not inevitable, and not to be solved by expansionary fiscal policies. Although the crisis appears as a problem of insufficient demand, the solution to capitalist crises requires political control of the working class, social control of money and wealth, and the dismantling of capitalist class relations and property rights.

Many of the theoretical arguments within the economics discipline informed *specific* critiques of the concrete fiscal policies enacted during the Great Recession. These assessments have been presented and debated by politicians, commentators, and the popular press. While they span the political spectrum, there are also some interesting areas of consensus. Conservatives view the fiscal stimulus measures, but especially the ARRA, as unnecessary expansions of government intervention. They argue that the sizable budget deficits during the crisis would inevitably crowd out the private sector, through either higher interest rates, higher taxes, or both. Republicans and conservative media outlets also branded the fiscal policies of the Obama administration as "pork barrel spending"—that is, spending that serves no legitimate economic purpose, and only funds political projects in Democratic districts. Conversely, progressives claim that the enormous output gap during the crisis required an even larger fiscal stimulus. Negative expectations suppressed private spending well into the recovery, even when the government provided the means to do so. They also argue that the fiscal policies during the Great Recession relied too much on tax cuts, most of which went toward household debt reduction, and not new spending. In this respect, they also questioned the political motivation of Obama's fiscal policies. Many political commentators agree that Obama included significant tax provisions as a way to find common ground with Republicans, even when they had no intention of giving him credit, let alone votes. But the most consistent criticism from the Left is that the ARRA lacked focus and a clear motivation. It lacked the focus of the fiscal, financial, and regulatory policies enacted during the Great Depression, which zeroed in on issues like collective bargaining rights, financial restructuring, homeownership, and income security. The ARRA appears indecisive in its dual focus on short-run economic stability and long-term structural issues. It invests in both problems, but does not fully commit to either. Despite the enduring controversy over these measures, there is common ground to be found. First, most analysts agree that the expansionary fiscal policies were based upon the expectation of a quick recovery, when in fact it was much more sluggish and uneven. Second, the fiscal stimulus did not address the root causes of the Great Recession in homeownership and mortgage lending. Third, analysts widely agree that the Obama administration did a poor job at marketing its policy proposals to both Congress and the public.

Critics and proponents agree that the fiscal stimulus was largely unpopular—but was it *effective*? Did it have a positive effect on the performance of the economic system? Most importantly, did it contribute to ending the economic crisis and jumpstarting the recovery? Aside from the theoretical debate over the conduct of fiscal policy, what does empirical research say about the contributions of the fiscal stimulus and the policy responses to the Great Recession at large? To answer these questions, the concluding section of this chapter returns to the critical work of Blinder and Zandi in this area.

THE END OF THE GREAT RECESSION

On September 20, 2010, the Business Cycle Dating Committee of the National Bureau of Economic Research (NBER) formally announced that the Great Recession had come to an end. The NBER designated June 2009 as the official trough of the recession, and the beginning of the next expansion. For many observers, the announcement came as a surprise, considering the severity of both the 2008 financial crisis and the economic crisis. It was only six months prior to June 2009 that economists openly debated the possibility of a second Great Depression. However, the Committee was measured in its statement. By no means had the US economic system regained its capacity prior to the crisis. In fact, many health and performance indicators would remain weak during the early years of the recovery. But the recovery was strong enough such that any subsequent deterioration of economic activity would not be part of the Great Recession.

The primary charge of the Committee is to determine the official dates of the US business cycle using a wide range of economic data, including employment, industrial production, real income, real output, and wholesale-retail sales. It determines the *chronology* of expansions and recessions—but it does not determine their *causes*. For example, the Committee does not assess whether free markets or government intervention determine the peaks and troughs of the US business cycle. The answer as to what brought the Great Recession to an end, which is a far more complex inquiry, was left to economists and the tools of statistical forecasting.

In their dual, landmark studies published during the recovery, Blinder and Zandi take up this charge by estimating the macroeconomic effects of the comprehensive policy responses to the Great Recession. They do so under multiple alternative scenarios using Moody's model of the US macroeconomy. As they carefully note, their results are only *estimates*. There is no scientific way to definitively determine what would have happened had the government not enacted certain policies (or any policies). Unfortunately, social scientists cannot perform the equivalent of controlled lab experiments when testing the empirical effects of policy interventions on the real world. Blinder and Zandi also provide a full accounting of the total cost of the wide-ranging policy measures, which were developed and implemented by both Democratic and Republican administrations, Congress under multiple changes in leadership, the Federal Reserve, the Federal Deposit Insurance Corporation (FDIC), the Federal Housing Administration (FHA), and the US Treasury Department. This section, which presents the results of their 2015 study, concludes this chapter on fiscal policy—and this three-chapter part on the policy responses to the crisis.

Table 8.4 presents Blinder and Zandi's full accounting of the policy responses to the Great Recession. The table itemizes both the original commitment by the

TABLE 8.4 Total Cost of Policy Responses to the Great Recession

	Original Commitment	*Ultimate Cost*
Federal Reserve System	*6,699*	*15*
Term Auction Credit	900	0
Other Loans	Unlimited	3
-Discount Lending (Primary, Secondary, and Seasonal)	Unlimited	0
-Primary Dealer Credit Facility	Unlimited	0
-Asset Backed Commercial Paper Money Market Mutual Fund	Unlimited	0
-AIG	26	2
-AIG (for SPV's)	9	0
-AIG (for ALICO, AIA)	26	1
Rescue of Bear Sterns (Maiden Lane)	27	4
AIG-RMBS Purchase Program (Maiden Lane II)	23	1
AIG-CDO Purchase Program (Maiden Lane III)	30	4
Term Securities Lending Facility	200	0
Commercial Paper Funding Facility	1,800	0
TALF	1,000	0
Money Market Investor Funding Facility	540	0
Currency Swap Lines	Unlimited	0
Purchase of GSE Debt and MBS	1,425	0
-Guarantee of Citigroup Assets	286	0
-Guarantee of Bank of America Assets	108	0
Purchase of Long-Term Treasuries	300	0
Treasury Department	*1,160*	*40*
TARP	600	40

(*Continued*)

TABLE 8.4 (Continued)

	Original Commitment	*Ultimate Cost*
Fed Supplementary Financing Account	560	0
Fannie Mae and Freddie Mac	Unlimited	0
Federal Deposit Insurance Corporation (FDIC)	***2,913***	***75***
Guarantee of U.S. Banks' Debt	1,400	4
-Guarantee of Citigroup Debt	10	0
-Guarantee of Bank of America Debt	3	0
Transaction Deposit Accounts	500	0
Public-Private Investment Fund Guarantee	1,000	0
Bank Resolutions	Unlimited	71
Federal Housing Administration (FHA)	***100***	***26***
Refinancing of Mortgages, Hope for Homeowners	100	0
Expanded Mortgage Lending	Unlimited	26
Congress	***1,460***	***1,484***
Economic Stimulus Act of 2008	170	170
American Recovery and Reinvestment Act of 2009	808	832
Cash for Clunkers	3	3
Additional Emergency UI Benefits	90	90
Education Jobs and Medicaid Assistance Act	26	26
Other Stimulus	20	20
Tax Relief, Unemployment Insurance Reauthorization, and Job Creation Act of 2010	189	189
Temporary Payroll Tax Cut Continuation Act of 2011	29	29
Middle Class Tax Relief and Job Creation Act of 2012	125	125
Total	**12,332**	**1,640**

Source: Blinder and Zandi (2015).
Unit - Billions of US $
This material was created by the Center on Budget and Policy Priorities (www.cbpp.org).

government and the ultimate cost of the emergency measures as of 2015. In total, the US government originally committed $12.3 trillion at the height of the 2008 financial crisis and the Great Recession. The Federal Reserve alone committed over half of that total toward purchases of long-term Treasury securities, multiple emergency lending facilities, direct assistance to individual financial institutions, and purchases of agency mortgage-backed securities. The FDIC committed $2.9 trillion to various debt guarantees and the increase in deposit insurance coverage. Congress committed $1.5 trillion to the expansionary fiscal policies presented in this chapter. The Treasury Department committed $1.1 trillion to the Troubled Asset Relief Program (TARP) and the receivership of Fannie Mae and Freddie Mac. The FHA committed $100 billion toward the subprime mortgage meltdown and foreclosure crisis.

In the end, Blinder and Zandi estimate that the ultimate cost to US taxpayers was $1.6 trillion—a small fraction of the original commitment. Why are most of the ultimate costs substantially lower than the original commitments? In some cases (e.g., the emergency credit facilities), borrowers eventually repaid the Federal Reserve with interest. In other cases (e.g., TARP), the federal government later resold toxic assets at higher market prices, and earned a profit. The fiscal stimulus packages account for most of the ultimate cost, while the remaining agencies lost between $15 billion and $75 billion. For example, the Federal Reserve only lost $15 billion of its massive commitment, principally from the AIG and Bear Stearns bailouts. The Treasury Department only lost $40 billion of the original $600 billion committed to TARP. The FDIC was unable to recover $75 billion in debt guarantees and bank resolutions, but otherwise recouped its original commitment. Although the FHA lost over one-quarter of its investment in home mortgage lending, this accounting does not include the positive effects of those programs on home values, housing market expectations, and the voluntary foreclosure crisis. Similarly, although Congress was not technically repaid for the fiscal stimulus, many measures generated positive multiplier effects on output and employment, which is not captured by this accounting. Lastly, it's worth noting that some of these programs are still in place as of this publication. For example, Fannie Mae and Freddie Mac are still under receivership; while the Federal Reserve still holds many securities acquired during the crisis on its balance sheet.

The most compelling aspect of the Blinder and Zandi studies is their estimates of the effects of alternative policy scenarios on macroeconomic performance. Before reviewing their results, a few caveats are important to note. First, Blinder and Zandi conducted a comprehensive analysis by largely examining two broad categories of policies: fiscal policy and financial policy. They did not investigate the contribution of most individual measures, which they acknowledge could range widely in terms of effectiveness. Second, regarding fiscal policy, they estimate the effects of discretionary fiscal stimulus on macroeconomic performance. In all scenarios, they assume that automatic stabilizers are at work. Third, regarding financial policy, they estimate the effects of the numerous emergency measures, such as quantitative easing and the Wall Street bailouts. In all scenarios, they assume that the Federal Reserve conducts a traditional monetary stimulus that lowers short-term interest rates.

They considered four possible scenarios. Using Moody's model of the US macroeconomy, Blinder and Zandi estimate the effects of each scenario on four measures of economic health and performance—real GDP, total payroll employment, the unemployment rate, and the inflation rate:

- The "Baseline" scenario is what actually happened, meaning it reports the actual trend in the performance measure between the first quarter of 2008 and the second quarter of 2015. It therefore includes the effects of all concrete fiscal and financial policy responses to the crisis.
- The "No Policy" scenario considers a nearly free market response to the crisis: no Wall Street bailouts, no quantitative easing, and no discretionary fiscal stimulus. This scenario essentially estimates the effects of a neoclassical adjustment process on US macroeconomic performance. The only policy mechanisms at work are automatic stabilizers and traditional monetary stimulus.
- "No Fiscal Stimulus" considers a scenario in which the government conducts financial policy but does not conduct discretionary fiscal stimulus.

- "No Financial Policy" considers the opposite scenario: the government conducts discretionary fiscal stimulus but does not conduct the Wall Street bailouts or quantitative easing.

Figure 8.1 presents the estimated effects of each scenario on real GDP. Without the fiscal policy, the trough of the Great Recession emerges during the fourth quarter of 2009—approximately six months after the actual trough. Relative to the Baseline scenario, the United States then experiences a quarterly output gap of roughly $500 billion, which largely closes between 2013 and 2015. Without the financial policy, the model again predicts a trough sometime in late 2009 or early 2010. However, the quarterly output gap is both significantly larger and more persistent throughout the recovery. Without any policy, the trough of the Great Recession does not occur until the first quarter of 2011—nearly two years later than the official trough—following an even deeper contraction of output. For several years during the recovery, the United States experiences a quarterly output gap of $2 trillion, which remains sizable well into 2015. Furthermore, the comprehensive policy responses accelerate the return of capitalist production to pre-recession output levels. According to the Baseline data, real GDP returns to its pre-crisis level ($14.9 trillion) in the fourth quarter of 2010. Without the fiscal policy, it takes until the second quarter of 2012. Without the financial policy, it takes until the fourth quarter of 2013. Without any policy, it takes until the third quarter of 2014.

Figure 8.2 presents the estimated effects of each scenario on total payroll employment. In the No Fiscal Policy scenario, quarterly payroll employment is roughly 2 million workers lower than the Baseline. Similar to the projection for real

FIGURE 8.1 Estimated Effects of Policy Responses on Real GDP

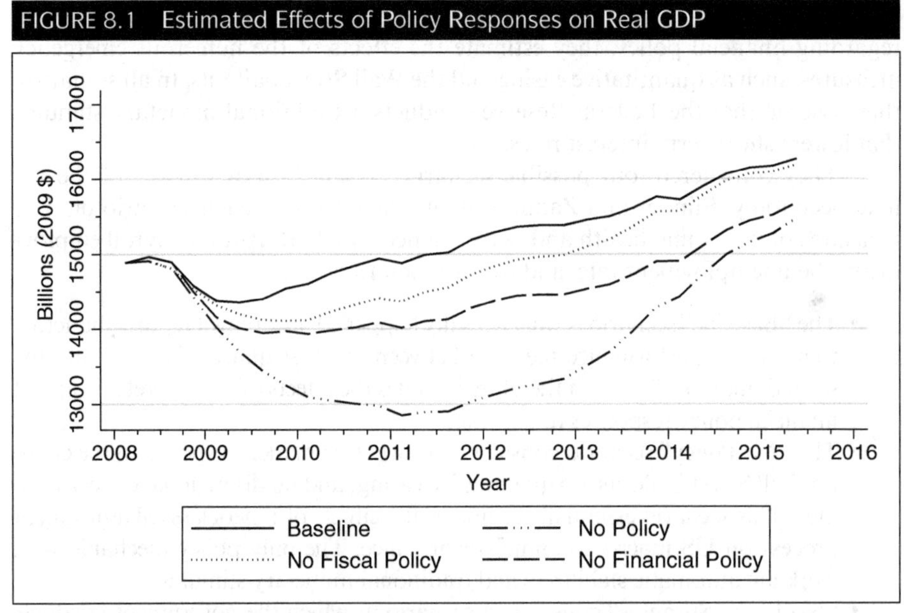

Units—$ billions (2009) | Seasonally adjusted annualized rate | Quarterly.
Source: Blinder and Zandi (2015).

FIGURE 8.2 Estimated Effects of Policy Responses on Total Payroll Employment

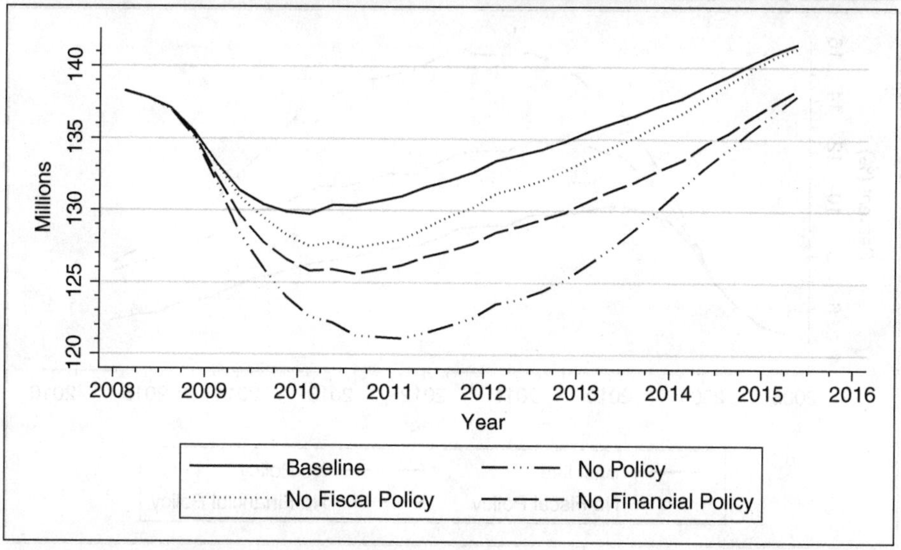

Units—millions | Seasonally adjusted | Quarterly.
Source: Blinder and Zandi (2015).

GDP, payroll employment eventually converges with the Baseline between 2013 and 2015. In the No Financial Policy scenario, job losses are more severe and show little convergence throughout the recovery. In the second quarter of 2015, for example, payroll employment is over 3 million workers short of the Baseline. In the No Policy scenario, US capitalism experiences even steeper job losses which don't begin to correct until the second quarter of 2011. Although recovery takes place thereafter, payroll employment remains millions of workers short of the Baseline. In all scenarios, including the Baseline, a jobless recovery is clearly present, as has been the case for most recoveries during the neoliberal stage of US capitalism. It took until the second quarter of 2014 for total payroll employment to return to its pre-crisis level (138.3 million workers). The model predicts a similar outcome without the fiscal policy. Without the financial policy, it takes until the second quarter of 2015. Without any policy, the jobless recovery continues into late 2015.

Figure 8.3 presents the projected impact of each scenario on the national unemployment rate—the ratio of total unemployed workers to the labor force. The actual unemployment rate peaked at 9.9% during the third quarter of 2009. The No Fiscal Policy model predicts a peak unemployment rate of 10.9% during the fourth quarter of 2010. Quarterly unemployment rates exceed 10% well into 2011, but gradually fall during the recovery. The No Financial Policy model predicts a maximum unemployment rate of 12.4% during the second quarter of 2010. Despite a gradual decline, it remains several percentage points higher than the Baseline scenario in early 2015. The No Policy model projects the grimmest counterfactual for the US labor market. In that case, the unemployment rate quickly exceeds 10% during the second quarter of 2009, and then 15% during the third quarter of 2010. Double-digit unemployment rates then plague US capitalism until the second quarter of 2014.

FIGURE 8.3 Estimated Effects of Policy Responses on the Unemployment Rate

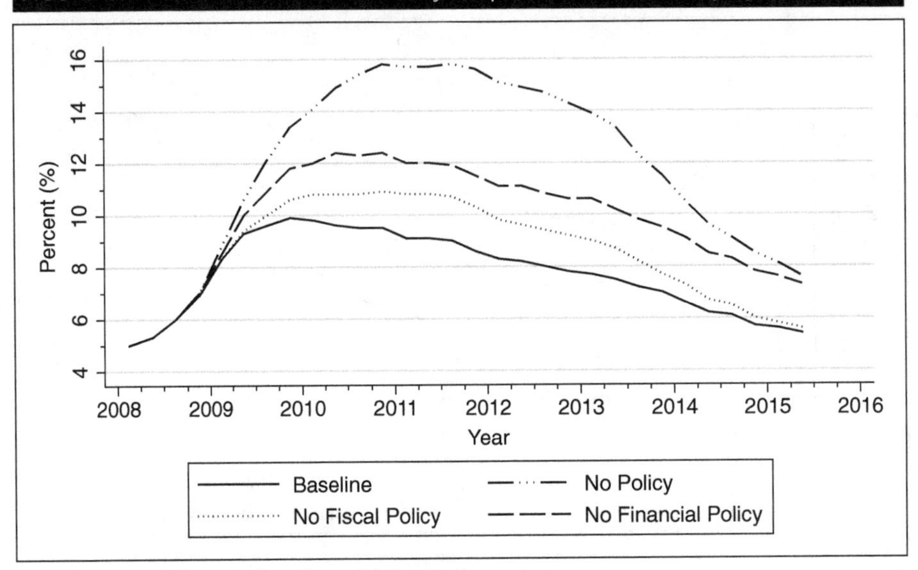

Units—percent | Seasonally adjusted | Quarterly.
Source: Blinder and Zandi (2015).

FIGURE 8.4 Estimated Effects of Policy Responses on the Inflation Rate

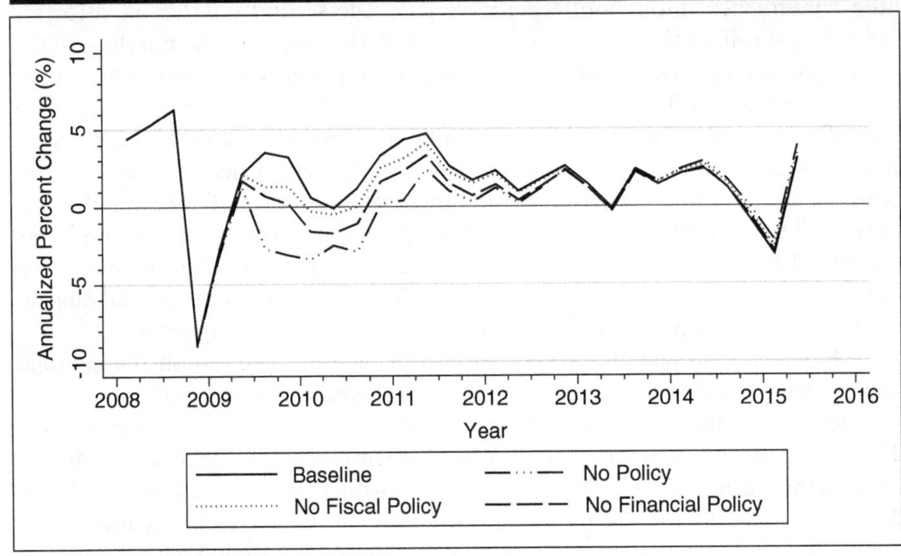

Units—annualized percent change | Seasonally adjusted | Quarterly.
Source: Blinder and Zandi (2015).

Figure 8.4 presents the projected impact of each scenario on the inflation rate. At the depth of the Great Recession, US capitalism experienced deflation during late 2008 and early 2009. Without the fiscal policy, the United States experiences weaker rates of inflation as well as several quarters of deflation in 2010. Without the financial policy, inflation rates are even weaker, and deflation is more persistent. Without any policy, the United States experiences a depression-like, deflationary cycle through most of 2010.

The ultimate test is whether these comprehensive policy responses prevented a depression. According to Blinder and Zandi, the answer is a definitive yes. Without the combined effect of the emergency policies, the ultimate costs to US taxpayers would have been far higher. The contraction would have been longer, and the recovery would have been more difficult. In each case, the combined effect of the two policy categories was always greater than their individual effects because they reinforced each other. Looking more closely at the results pertaining to this chapter, the fiscal stimulus alone had significant effects on output, employment, unemployment, and inflation. The fiscal stimulus stabilized the real sector and was one of the few sources of aggregate demand in 2009. In particular, the stimulus closed state and local budget shortfalls, thus preventing dire spending cuts, tax increases, job losses, and further economic stagnation. Expansionary fiscal policy therefore fulfilled its intended purpose according to Keynesian theory. However, the financial policies alone were more effective at stimulating the real sector across all four macroeconomic performance measures. Without the financial policies, US capitalism would have been in a much weaker position well into 2015. This does not mean that every individual fiscal or financial policy was effective, however. The political costs of the emergency measures were certainly real; as is their enduring controversy. According to Blinder and Zandi, the total price tag of the response—the most common complaint by critics—only speaks to the severity of the crisis and the challenges of monetary stimulus once interest rates reach 0%. Proposals to allow free markets to adjust without government intervention were simply not legitimate, and would have likely plunged US capitalism into another depression:

> When all is said and done, the financial and fiscal policies will have cost taxpayers a substantial sum, but not nearly as much as most had feared and not nearly as much as if policymakers had not acted at all. If the comprehensive policy responses saved the economy from another depression, as we estimate, they were well worth their cost.

FINAL THOUGHTS

Similar to financial reform, President Obama's fiscal policy agenda would be limited to his first term. During the economic crisis, many analysts viewed the fiscal stimulus as the first step in moving federal tax and spending priorities in a more liberal direction. In 2009, even Nobel Laureate Paul Samuelson, who served as an advisor to Presidents Kennedy and Johnson, acknowledged this point:

> Everyone understands now … that there can be no solution without government. The Keynesian idea is once again accepted that fiscal policy and deficit spending has a major role to play in guiding a market economy. I wish Friedman were still alive so he could witness how his extremism led to the defeat of his own ideas.

However, Republicans seized upon voter dissatisfaction with the policy responses to the Great Recession, leading to the conservative Tea Party movement during the 2010 midterm elections. The Tea Party flipped not only the leadership of the US House of Representatives but also many state legislatures and governorships. The pushback against government intervention was significant. After the 2010 elections, and throughout Obama's second term, restraint—not stimulus—became the priority for fiscal policy. State and local governments slashed budgets and attacked collective bargaining rights for public sector workers. Political brinksmanship over raising the debt ceiling nearly caused the United States to default. In response, the credit rating agencies downgraded US government debt. The inability to find consensus over the federal budget also led to fiscal sequestration as well as a government shutdown.

The conduct of fiscal policy during the Great Recession continues to inform the conduct of fiscal policy following the Great Recession. Although specific conditions change and evolve, the debate over fiscal policy has not. As a rebuttal to President Obama's domestic economic agenda, President Trump signed the Tax Cuts and Jobs Act in 2017, which included traditional supply-side tax cuts and tax reform. On the other hand, a more progressive Democratic agenda emerged during the recovery, which included proposals for a Green New Deal, Medicare for All, student loan forgiveness, and an expansion of the social safety net (e.g., greater access to childcare and healthcare, paid family leave, and tuition-free community college). The fiscal stimulus packages during the Great Recession also informed the federal government's response to the Covid-19 pandemic, which was enacted by both President Trump and President Biden. While most of those measures provided fiscal stimulus as a way to boost economic growth and reduce unemployment, subsequent measures provided fiscal restraint as a way to reduce inflation. In order to understand these policies further, and their relationship to the evolution of US capitalism following the Great Recession, the final chapter of this textbook examines the recovery in greater detail.

Sources

Blinder, A.S. & Zandi, M. (2010, July 27). *How the Great Recession was brought to an end*. Moody's Analytics.

Blinder, A.S. & Zandi, M. (2015, October 15). *The financial crisis: Lessons for the next one*. Center on Budget and Policy Priorities.

Business Cycle Dating Committee. (2010, September 20). Announcement of June 2009 business cycle trough/end of last recession [Press release]. Retrieved from http://www.nber.org.

Bush, G.W. (2008, February 13). Remarks on signing the Economic Stimulus Act of 2008 [Transcript]. Retrieved from https://www.presidency.ucsb.edu.

Friedman, M. (1966, February 4). Friedman & Keynes. *Time, 87*(5). Retrieved from http://www.time.com

Gross, D. (2008, September 17). "The fundamentals of our economy are strong." Slate. Retrieved from http://www.slate.com.

Keynes, J.M. (1923). *A tract on monetary reform*. London, UK: Macmillan.

Keynes, J.M. (1932). The end of laissez-faire. In J.M. Keynes, *Essays in persuasion* (pp. 312–22). New York, NY: Harcourt.

Keynes, J.M. (1964). *The general theory of employment, interest, and money*. San Diego, CA: Harcourt.

Lucas, R.E. (2003). Macroeconomic priorities. *American Economic Review, 93*(1), 1–14. Doi: 10.1257/000282803321455188

Obama, B.H. (2009, February 17). Statement on signing the American Recovery and Reinvestment Act of 2009 [Transcript]. Retrieved from https://www.presidency.ucsb.edu

Samuelson, P. (2009). The resurrection of Keynes. *New Perspectives Quarterly, 26*(2), 42 – 44. doi: 10.1111/j.1540-5842.2009.01088.x

Snowdon, B. & Vane, H.R. (2005). Interview with Milton Friedman. In B. Snowdon & H.R. Vane, *Modern macroeconomics: Its origins, development and current state* (pp. 198 – 218). Cheltenham, UK: Edward Elgar Publishing.

Wall Street Journal. (2009, February 17). Getting to $787 billion. Retrieved from http://www.wsj.com.

Further Reading

Galbraith, J.K. & Darity, W. (1994). *Macroeconomics*. Boston, MA: Houghton Mifflin.

Meeropol, M. (1998). *Surrender: How the Clinton administration completed the Reagan Revolution*. Ann Arbor, MI: The University of Michigan Press.

Piketty, T. (2015). *The economics of inequality*. Cambridge, MA: The Belknap Press of the Harvard University Press.

Pollin, R. (2003). *Contours of descent: U.S. economic fractures and the landscape of global austerity*. London, UK: Verso.

Snowdon, B. & Vane, H.R. (eds.). (1997). *A macroeconomics reader*. New York, NY: Routledge.

Research Institutes and Think Tanks Specializing in Fiscal Policy

Center on Budget and Policy Priorities	https://www.cbpp.org/
Economic Policy Institute	https://www.epi.org/
Levy Economics Institute of Bard College	https://www.levyinstitute.org
Roosevelt Institute	https://rooseveltinstitute.org
Tax Foundation	https://taxfoundation.org/

PART IV

The Recovery from the Great Recession

CHAPTER 9

Inequality, Populism, and the Arc to Covid-19

On February 19, 2009, CNBC editor Rick Santelli reported from his usual post on the floor of the Chicago Mercantile Exchange. The Obama administration had recently implemented the Homeowner Affordability and Stability Plan (HASP), one of several anti-foreclosure initiatives during the Great Recession. As compared to the industry-wide Wall Street bailouts, HASP was modest in both scope and price tag. It created incentives (not requirements) for mortgage lenders to reduce monthly payments to a sustainable share of borrower income, and provided funding to share the costs of repayment modifications with lenders. Moreover, like the other anti-foreclosure initiatives of the new Obama administration, HASP essentially continued the policies of the W. Bush administration. When CNBC's on-air contributors brought up the latest plan for struggling homeowners, Santelli delivered a historic five-minute rant on government bailouts and stimulus packages. He lambasted the administration for encouraging bad behavior by bailing out irresponsible homeowners: "This is America! How many of you people want to pay for your neighbor's mortgage that has an extra bathroom and can't pay their bills, raise your hand? President Obama, are you listening?"

He assailed expansionary fiscal policies for relying upon government spending and unrealistic multipliers in order to rebuild the economic system. He lamented Cuba's prosperity and wealth before its communist revolution and move toward collectivization. As his anger grew, traders on the floor began applauding and whistling in support. Santelli turned to the floor and said: "These guys are pretty straightforward, and my guess is, a pretty good statistical cross-section of America. The silent majority!"

Most famously, Santelli called for a modern-day Tea Party of capitalists as a counter to liberal bailouts and stimulus plans: "… We're thinking of having a Chicago Tea Party in July. All you capitalists that want to show up to Lake Michigan, I'm going to start organizing."

Those words—"Tea Party"—almost immediately became a rallying cry for opponents to Obama's domestic economic agenda. Although there was certainly opposition to Obama's policy proposals both before and during the 2008 US

DOI: 10.4324/9780429461316-13

presidential election, the Santelli rant ignited a new wave of conservative push-back. The Tea Party movement seized upon popular anger and dissatisfaction toward an overextended federal government, and the establishment economists in Washington, DC that enabled it. The Tea Party formulated an ideological challenge to the policy responses to the Great Recession, which supporters viewed as unconstitutional, un-American, and socialistic. In this sense, the movement went beyond the typical conservative arguments against government intervention in the business cycle. The advent of the Tea Party marked a more populist shift in right-wing political rhetoric and the Republican Party itself. As the recovery from the Great Recession progressed, right-wing populists seized upon cultural anxieties over diversity and demographic change. Many of these developments are directly related to the crisis itself and the policy responses to it. For example, readers will recall from Chapter 5 the "Great Mancession" narrative that emerged in conservative media circles during the recovery.

However, dissatisfaction with the policy responses to the Great Recession was not exclusive to the Right. A new wave of progressive social movements and policy proposals also emerged on the political Left. Progressive proposals went beyond the standard liberal arguments in favor of government intervention in the business cycle, especially during the neoliberal stage of US capitalism. Progressive activists and politicians seized upon popular anger and dissatisfaction—not toward an overextended federal government, but toward overextended corporate power and ongoing structural imbalances in the US economic system. As the recovery from the crisis took hold, progressives rallied against the disparity in the treatment of homeowners versus capitalists, the formation of even larger banks, insufficient fiscal stimulus, the intensification of income inequality, as well as long-standing issues of racial and gender stratification. These movements therefore marked a more populist shift in left-wing political rhetoric and the platform of the Democratic Party.

Unlike the Great Depression of the 1930s as well as the crisis of the 1970s, the Great Recession did not usher in a new social structure of accumulation. Neoliberalism is still in place, but without the bipartisan consensus that characterized previous recoveries from economic downturns during this period. Instead, sharp divisions over the direction of the economic system and social upheaval have occurred against the backdrop of weak economic performance and unresolved structural imbalances. As a consequence, intense disagreement over the nature and causes of pressing economic problems have led to polarization, gridlock, and brinksmanship in policymaking since the Great Recession.

Chapter 9 concludes this textbook with an investigation of the recovery from the Great Recession. Although the 2009–20 recovery was the longest US expansion to date, it was also one of the most turbulent. This investigation examines the complex and intersecting economic, political, and social issues that arose in the aftermath of the Great Recession, until the onset of the Covid-19 pandemic in early 2020. The first section opens with a data-driven analysis of the 2009–20 recovery. This section extends many of the data series presented in earlier chapters related to macroeconomic performance, income and wealth distribution, as well as economic trends and changes over the course of the recovery. The second section examines the pronounced growth of populism during the recovery, in both the United States and around the world. While right-wing and left-wing populists share an anti-establishment perspective, they fundamentally differ on the causes and solutions to economic challenges since the crisis. The final section of this chapter then discusses the ways in which economic performance and the surge in populist rhetoric combined to affect policymaking during the 2009–20 recovery. This section discusses Obama's domestic economic agenda following the Tea Party wave in 2010 as well as the major policy developments during the Trump administration.

THE 2009–20 RECOVERY IN PERSPECTIVE

According to the Business Cycle Dating Committee of the National Bureau of Economic Research (NBER), the recovery from the Great Recession is now the longest economic expansion to date. Between June 2009 and February 2020, US capitalism sustained positive economic growth for 128 consecutive months. In terms of length, the recovery exceeded several postwar expansions, including the celebrated 1991–2001 expansion (by eight months), the 1961–69 expansion (by 22 months), the 1982–90 expansion (by 36 months), and the 2001–07 expansion (by 47 months). This point is particularly noteworthy considering that many economists feared a "double-dip" recession during the early 2010s, similar to what transpired following the crisis of the 1970s. Yet the recovery from the crisis remains controversial and contested. Unlike the Great Depression as well as the crisis of the 1970s, the policy responses to the Great Recession did not lead to a new social structure of accumulation. National policymakers successfully halted the financial meltdown and reset economic growth, but they did not restructure the institutional setting of profit making and investment. Nor did they redress the preponderance of rising inequality, financial insecurity, and jobless recoveries during the capitalist growth process. Furthermore, intense dissatisfaction with the government's emergency measures eventually fueled populist movements on both the Left and the Right, initiating a new period of economic and social upheaval as US capitalism entered the Covid-19 pandemic recession in early 2020. In order to understand these developments, this section opens this final chapter with a data-driven investigation of the 2009–20 recovery. This presentation extends many of the data series and analysis presented in Chapters 2 through 4 of this textbook.

The 2009–20 Recovery: The Standard Measures

Table 9.1 first places the recovery from the Great Recession in historical context using the national income accounting and macroeconomic performance measures introduced in Chapter 2. Table 9.1 compares the 2009–20 recovery to the three preceding recoveries during the neoliberal stage of capitalism: 1982–90, 1991–2001, and 2001–07. Since Table 9.1 presents quarterly averages for each expansion, it is important to note that the NBER determined the fourth quarter of 2019 as the next *quarterly* peak in economic activity, which differs slightly from the *monthly* peak (February 2020).

In terms of the composition of US output, there was a decline in both the business investment and government spending shares of gross domestic product (GDP) as compared to the 2001–07 expansion. Gross private domestic investment averaged 16.6% of GDP during the 2009–20 recovery, while government

TABLE 9.1 Four US Recoveries During Neoliberal Capitalism

	[1]	*[2]*	*[3]*	***[4]***
	1982(IV)– 1990(III)	*1991(I)– 2001(I)*	*2001(IV)– 2007(IV)*	***2009(II)– 2019(IV)****
Shares of Gross Domestic Product (%)				
Personal Consumption Expenditures (C)	63.0	64.9	67.3	**67.8**
Gross Private Domestic Investment (I)	18.3	17.7	18.6	**16.6**
Government Consumption Expenditures and Gross Investment (G)	20.9	18.9	19.1	**18.6**
Net Exports of Goods and Services (NX)	−2.2	−1.6	−5.0	**−3.0**
Growth Rate of Real Gross Domestic Product	4.3	3.6	2.9	**2.3**
Civilian Unemployment Rate	6.7	5.5	5.3	**6.4**
Civilian Employment-Population Ratio	60.9	63.1	62.7	**59.3**
Rate of Inflation (Consumer Price Index)	3.9	2.7	2.9	**1.8**
Capacity Utilization Rate (Manufacturing)	79.9	81.1	76.7	**74.6**
Nonfarm Business Sector: Real Output per Hour of All Persons	2.0	2.3	2.5	**1.2**

Source: Federal Reserve Bank of St. Louis, FRED economic data: https://fred.stlouisfed.org.
All figures are quarterly averages. Figures in the lower half of the table are seasonally adjusted. Units for Growth Rate of Real Gross Domestic Product and Rate of Inflation (CPI) are compounded annual rates of change. Unit for Real Output per Hour of All Persons is percent change at annual rate.
*According to the National Bureau of Economic Research, the quarterly peak in economic activity occurred during the fourth quarter of 2019.

consumption expenditures and gross investment averaged 18.6% of GDP. Both results were all-time lows during the neoliberal era, but the drop in the share of business investment was particularly sharp. An increase in the household consumption share of GDP largely made up for this shortfall, continuing a steady upward trend since the 1980s, as well as a smaller trade deficit. On average, personal consumption expenditures accounted for 67.8% of GDP, while the trade deficit dropped to 3% of GDP. Interestingly, the business investment share of GDP during the 2009–20 recovery (16.6%) was precisely the quarterly average throughout the regulated stage of US capitalism. Notice, however, the very different composition of output presented in Column [1] of Table 2.2: the household consumption share was significantly smaller (60.6%), the government spending share was significantly higher (22.3%), and the United States was a net exporter (0.5%).

In terms of macroeconomic performance, the 2009–20 recovery extended the long-term decline in real GDP growth rates. For perspective, the average quarterly growth rate during the 2009–20 recovery (2.3%) was nearly half what it was during the 1982–90 recovery. The average national unemployment rate of 6.4% was particularly high; but similar to the 1982–90 expansion, there was obviously significant slack in the labor market following the crisis in the real sector, which continued well into the 2010s. The surge in unemployment is explained in part by an actual decrease in the employment-to-population ratio (59.3%), which was the lowest of the neoliberal era. Sluggish economic growth and a weak labor market kept the rate of inflation in check, which averaged less than 2%. The capacity utilization rate in manufacturing (74.6%) as well as labor productivity were also notably weaker than previous recoveries.

How are these results connected? Normally, an increase in business investment during an expansion leads to a higher capacity utilization rate as firms purchase more plant and equipment, technology, and infrastructure. Technological advancements in the production process then lead to higher labor productivity as well as stronger economic growth. The key point is that higher labor productivity allows real wages to increase as the economic system grows, which reduces income inequality between owners of capital and labor. Following World War II, a much higher unionization rate combined with a more regulated labor market also ensured that workers were compensated for productivity gains. This process has stagnated since the 1980s, however, and was noticeably weaker during the 2009–20 recovery. The sharp decline in business investment relative to GDP is associated with a much lower capacity utilization rate, markedly lower labor productivity, and thereby a weaker growth rate. Without substantive investment in job creation and overall economic capacity, lower labor productivity has continued to suppress real wages—an outcome that has been present in the US labor market since the early 1970s. Deregulation of the labor market and de-unionization have also contributed to the uncoupling of real wages from labor productivity. So, despite sluggish growth rates, owners of capital can claim a larger share of what meager economic growth there is. Income inequality now increases as the economic system expands. Moreover, economic expansion continues to require greater reliance on household debt in order to facilitate a greater share of consumer expenditures under stagnant earnings.

Structural Imbalances During the 2009–20 Recovery

Let's look more closely at how workers and households fared following the Great Recession in terms of job creation, debt overhang, and the distribution of wealth. First, according to Table 9.2, a jobless recovery clearly weighed down the 2009–20 expansion for nearly five years. A jobless recovery occurs when the economic system expands but without a substantial increase in labor demand, resulting in a persistently high unemployment rate. Although the economic system contracted between December 2007 and June 2009, it took until May 2014 for total non-farm payroll employment to reach pre-recession levels. Total non-farm payroll employment simply measures the total number of employed workers in the United States at a given time. On the one hand, the jobless recovery following the Great Recession is by no means unprecedented. This phenomenon has been a common feature of US expansions since the 1990–91 recession. On the other hand, the extent of the jobless recovery following the Great Recession is indeed unprecedented. Since

TABLE 9.2 Non-Farm Payroll Employment Recoveries, 1948–2014

Peak	*Trough*	*Duration of Recession (Months)*	*Number of Months to Reach Peak Employment*	*Date of Employment Recovery*
November 1948	October 1949	11	20	July 1950
July 1953	May 1954	10	23	June 1955
August 1957	April 1958	8	20	April 1959
April 1960	February 1961	10	20	December 1961
December 1969	November 1970	11	17	May 1971
November 1973	March 1975	16	25	December 1975
January 1980	July 1980	6	11	December 1980
July 1981	November 1982	16	28	November 1983
July 1990	March 1991	8	31	February 1993
March 2001	November 2001	8	46	January 2005
December 2007	**June 2009***	**18**	**77**	**May 2014**

Source - Federal Reserve Bank of St. Louis, FRED economic data: https://fred.stlouisfed.org

* According to the National Bureau of Economic Research, the next monthly peak in economic activity occurred in February of 2020.

the end of World War II, no period of expansion has seen such sluggish employment growth. Granted, the job losses during the crisis were severe, so there was significant ground to make up in order to reach pre-recession employment levels. That process undoubtedly takes time. In fact, the NBER cautioned in 2010 that labor market conditions would continue to deteriorate once the recovery began. Looking more closely at Table 9.2, notice the difference between the Great Recession and the 1973–75 and 1981–82 recessions. Both the 1973–75 and the 1981–82 recessions were 16 months in length—roughly the equivalent of the Great Recession—and reached similar rates of unemployment. Following those downturns, however, it only took between 25 and 28 months for total employment to fully recover—far less than the *77 months* following the Great Recession. For example, the US economic system reached a trough in March 1975 but returned to peak employment levels in December that year. Similarly, following a trough in November 1982, it took one year for total employment to fully recover.

Second, the housing market bust and 2008 financial crisis lessened, but did not completely eliminate, the household debt bonanza that emerged during the 1980s. Figure 9.1 presents the ratio of household debt to GDP since 1949. The vertical reference lines mark the official duration of the economic crisis—that is, the peak of the 2001–07 expansion to the trough of the Great Recession. Following a record peak in 2008, household debt relative to GDP steadily dropped throughout the 2010s, from 99.4% to roughly 80%. But 80% is historically very high and still exceeds the household debt ratio prior to the housing market bubble. Furthermore, the downward shift in the household debt ratio is largely due to deleveraging, and not higher interest rates. As discussed in Chapter 7, quantitative easing continued well into the recovery. Despite the US Federal Reserve's policy normalization announcement in 2014, monetary policy continues to operate in a context of relatively abundant reserves. Figure 9.2 presents the effect of this monetary policy stance on long-term government bond rates, which continued to decline during the 2009–20 recovery.

FIGURE 9.1 Household Debt as a Percent of Gross Domestic Product 1949–2020

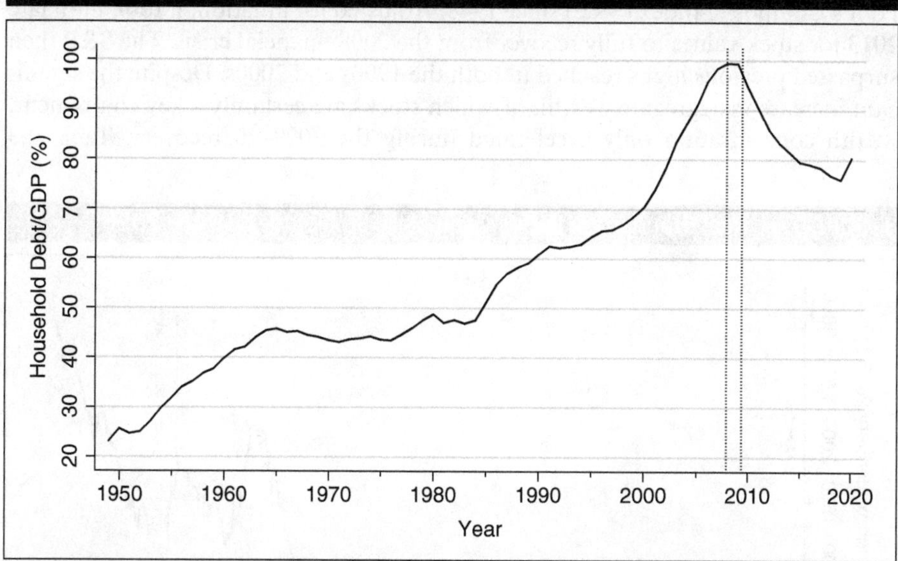

Note: The most recent monthly peak in economic activity occurred in February 2020.
Source: Federal Reserve Bank of St. Louis FRED economic data (https://fred.stlouisfed.org).

FIGURE 9.2 Long-Term US Government Bond Rates 1948–2020

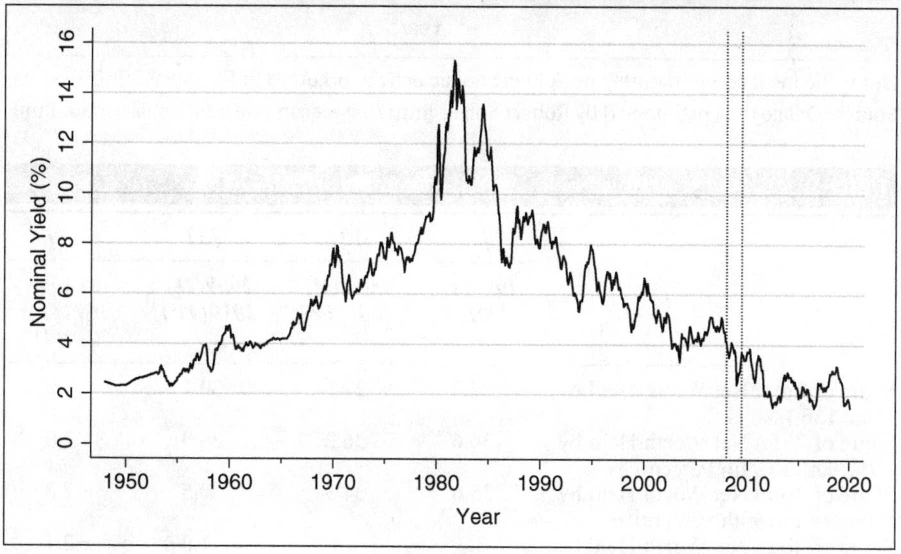

Note: The most recent monthly peak in economic activity occurred in February of 2020.
Source: Online data maintained by Robert Shiller (http://www.econ.yale.edu/~shiller/data.htm).

Third, following the stock market crash throughout the crisis, stock prices surged throughout the 2009–20 recovery. Figure 9.3 presents the real Standard & Poor's Composite Index (S&P) since 1948. Adjusted for inflation, it took until late 2013 for stock values to fully recover from the 2008 financial crisis. The S&P then surpassed previous highs reached in both the 1990s and 2000s. Despite the significant increase in aggregate wealth, of which stocks are certainly a key component, wealth concentration only accelerated during the 2009–20 recovery. Table 9.3

FIGURE 9.3 Real Standard & Poor's Composite Stock Index 1948–2020

Note: The most recent monthly peak in economic activity occurred in February 2020.
Source: Online data maintained by Robert Shiller (http://www.econ.yale.edu/~shiller/data.htm).

TABLE 9.3 Changes in Household Wealth Inequality, 1991–2019

	[1]	*[2]*	***[3]***	*[4]*
	1991(I)–2001(I)	*2001(IV)–2007(IV)*	***2009(II)–2019(IV)****	*Change, 1991(I)–2019(IV)*
Share of Total Net Worth Held by the Top 1%	27.0	27.5	**30.1**	7.0
Share of Total Net Worth Held by the 90th to 99th Percentiles	34.6	36.2	**38.9**	2.0
Share of Total Net Worth Held by the 50th to 90th Percentiles	35.6	34.3	**30.5**	−7.8
Share of Total Net Worth Held by the Bottom 50%	3.7	2.4	**1.0**	−2.1

Source: Federal Reserve Bank of St. Louis, FRED economic data: https://fred.stlouisfed.org.

The unit of measurement is the percentage of aggregate net worth. All figures in Columns [1] through [3] are quarterly averages for each wealth percentile.

*According to the National Bureau of Economic Research, the quarterly peak in economic activity occurred during the fourth quarter of 2019.

documents shifts in household wealth inequality during the last three recoveries. Similar to Table 9.1, Columns 1 through 3 report the average quarterly share of aggregate net worth for each wealth percentile. Column 4 then reports the net change in each wealth percentile's share between the first quarter of 1991 and the fourth quarter of 2019. Following the Great Recession, the top 10% combined held 69% of aggregate net worth, which extended a steady increase since the 1991–2001 expansion. The top 1% saw its average share grow to 30.1% of aggregate net worth, while the 90th to 99th percentiles saw their average shares grow to 38.9%. Further, between 1991 and 2019, the top 1% saw a 7 percentage point increase in its share of household wealth; while the 90th to 99th percentiles saw a 2 percentage point increase. In contrast, the average share held by the 50th to 90th percentiles sharply decreased during the recovery from the crisis. This result is again the most striking of this analysis and this period: the redistribution of household wealth continues to dispossess large swaths of the US middle class and even the upper-middle class. Relative to 1991, the 50th to 90th percentiles saw a 7.8 percentage point loss in household wealth. The bottom 50% of the household wealth distribution, which had very little net worth to begin with, saw their average share drop to a meager 1% during the 2009–20 recovery.

These results further emphasize the unevenness of the capitalist growth process since the early 1980s. Although the 2009–20 recovery was lengthy, there was a noticeable retraction of business investment that government spending did not supplant. In fact, government spending itself also retracted. Sluggish business investment contributed to a reduction in capacity utilization, labor productivity, and economic growth. As a result, the 2009–20 recovery did not mitigate the structural imbalances that emerged during the neoliberal stage of capitalism. Real wages continued to stagnate while job creation was historically sluggish and weak. Although the household debt overhang eased, it continues to be necessary in order for consumers to claim an increasing share of economic output. And despite the stock market recovery, wealth inequality only intensified. In *Capital in the Twenty-First Century*, perhaps the most significant economic work published during the 2009–20 recovery, Thomas Piketty emphasizes this key point:

> … A market economy based on private property, if left to itself, contains powerful forces of convergence, associated in particular with the diffusion of knowledge and skills; but it also contains powerful forces of divergence, which are potentially threatening to democratic societies and to the values of social justice on which they are based.

Trends and Changes During the 2009–20 Recovery

The next data series looks more closely at trends in the principal measures of US economic activity during the 2009–20 recovery. Much of the empirical analysis thus far has focused on averages, but averages can hide extreme data points, variations, volatility, and trends over time. Each figure in this series also compares the 2009–20 recovery to the 2001–07 recovery. Taken together, the data point to a weakening US economic system during the latter years of the recovery—before the onset of the Covid-19 pandemic in late 2019 and early 2020.

FIGURE 9.4 Growth Rate of Real Personal Consumption Expenditures 2002–19

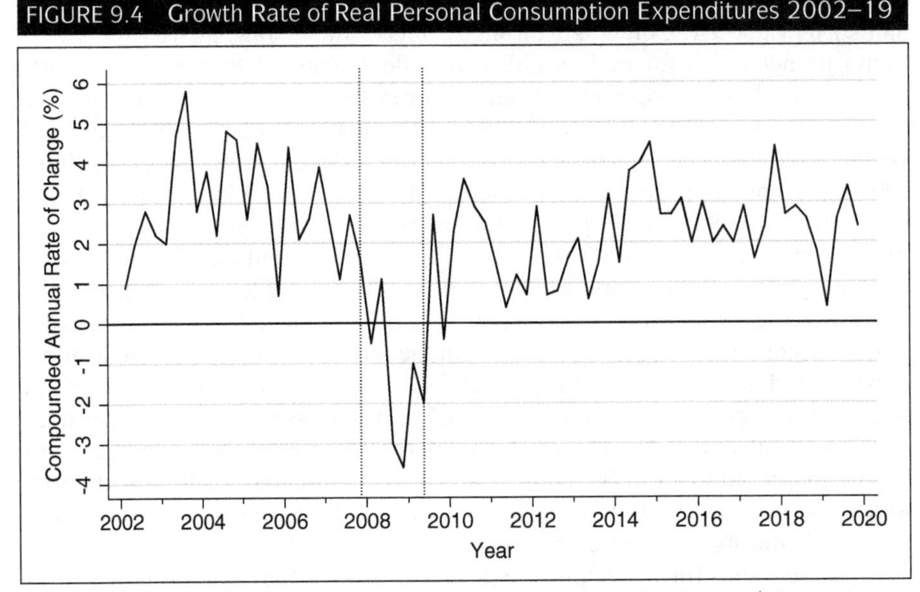

Units—compounded annual rate of change | Seasonally adjusted annual rate | Quarterly.
Source: Federal Reserve Bank of St. Louis FRED economic data (https://fred.stlouisfed.org).

Let's begin with the largest contributor of economic activity: consumption. As discussed in Chapter 4, the housing market bust and the 2008 financial crisis caused a massive cutback in consumption that plunged the real sector into crisis. Following a period that saw enormous losses of wealth, deleveraging, and negative expectations, how quickly did consumers rebound? Figure 9.4 reports the growth rate of real personal consumption expenditures between the first quarter of 2002 and the fourth quarter of 2019. Real personal consumption expenditures measure new spending by US residents on goods and services, after adjusting for inflation. Since the frequency of the data is quarterly, the unit of measurement is the compounded annual rate of change, or what the annual growth rate would be if the economic system sustained the quarterly growth rate for one year. Similar to most recoveries, consumption was stable throughout the 2009–20 recovery. Except for the fourth quarter of 2009, which saw a 0.4% rate of contraction, consumption grew consistently at positive growth rates. Although the average growth rates of each recovery are comparable, there appear to be two distinct phases during the recovery from the Great Recession. The first phase occurs until late 2014, where consumption slowly rebounds as it attains the growth rates seen during the 2001–07 recovery. The second phase occurs after late 2014, where consumption slowly weakens again. The key point is that the strength of US consumer spending was diminishing even prior to the massive economic disruptions caused by the Covid-19 pandemic.

In addition to the cutback in consumption, the 2008 financial crisis led to a significant reduction in business investment. How quickly did business investment in the production process return to normal during the 2009–20 recovery? Figure 9.5 presents the growth rate of real gross private domestic investment. Real gross private domestic investment measures business spending on durable capital goods

FIGURE 9.5 Growth Rate of Real Gross Private Domestic Investment 2002–19

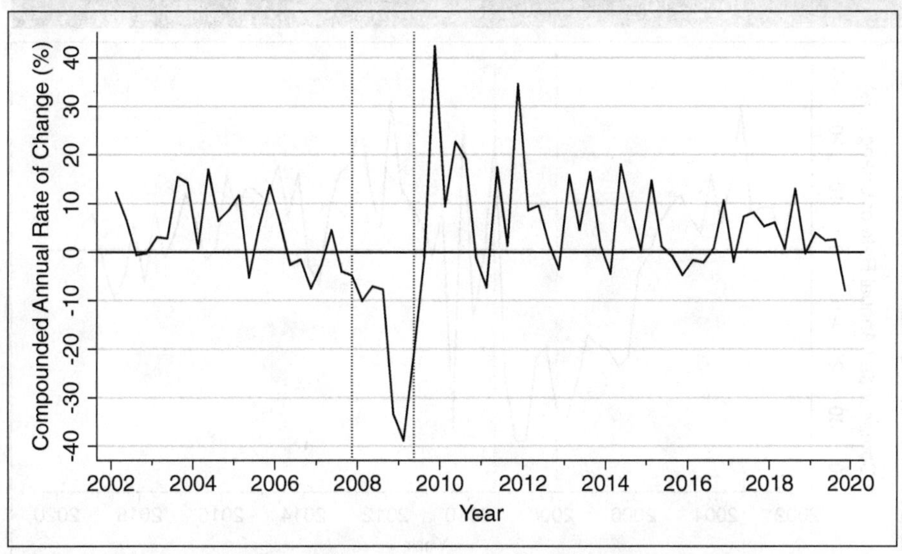

Units—compounded annual rate of change | Seasonally adjusted annual rate | Quarterly.
Source: Federal Reserve Bank of St. Louis FRED economic data (https://fred.stlouisfed.org).

and fixed assets—such as equipment, furniture, machines, software, structures, and vehicles—after adjusting for inflation. Similar to most recoveries, business investment was volatile throughout the 2009–20 recovery, regularly oscillating between periods of expansion and contraction. However, growth rates were markedly more volatile during the early years of the recovery. After returning to expected tendencies in 2012, there was a noticeable period of contraction in 2015 and 2016, after which growth rates were lower. Similar to consumer spending, US business investment clearly weakened prior to the Covid-19 pandemic.

Why was business investment sluggish during the 2009–20 recovery? Figure 9.6 examines a critical component of gross private domestic investment: private residential fixed investment. Figure 9.6 tracks the growth rate of spending on residential structures and equipment in real terms. Not surprisingly, in the aftermath of the housing market bust, US residential investment was extremely volatile until 2013—sometimes growing by over 20%, sometimes decreasing by 30%. After stabilizing, there is a downward trajectory in the strength of residential investment until late 2019, with some periods of contraction again. This finding further stresses both the significant contribution of residential investment to economic growth during the housing market bubble, and its lag on economic growth following the housing market bust. However, this data stops at the onset of the Covid-19 pandemic, which saw a very strong housing market.

Turning now to the mainstream performance measures of the US business cycle, Figure 9.7 documents the growth rate of real GDP between 2002 and 2019. Following sharp contractions of US output, especially at the height of the Great Recession in 2008, trends in economic growth essentially returned to those seen during the 2001–07 recovery. On average, economic growth ranged between 2% and 4%, although such growth rates are historically weak. The average growth rate

FIGURE 9.6 Growth Rate of Real Private Residential Fixed Investment 2002–19

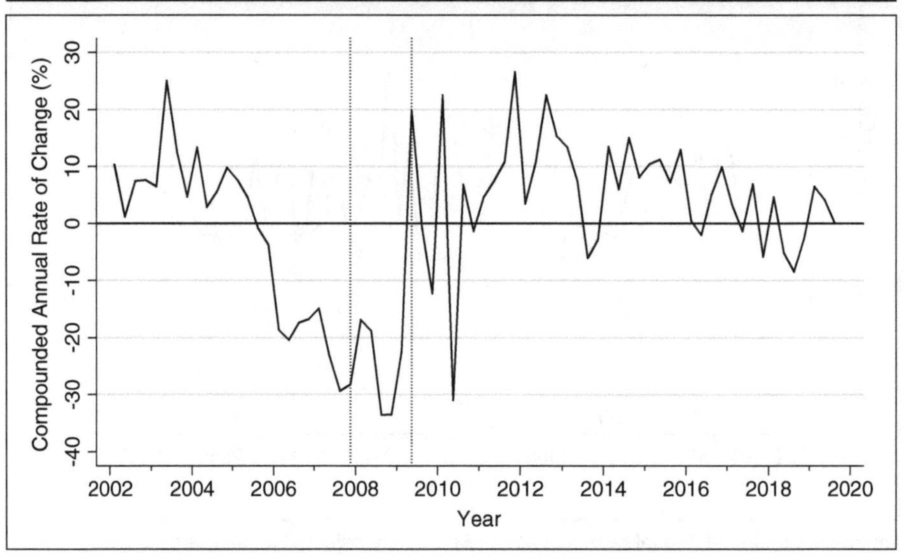

Units—compounded annual rate of change | Seasonally adjusted annual rate | Quarterly.
Source: Federal Reserve Bank of St. Louis FRED economic data (https://fred.stlouisfed.org).

FIGURE 9.7 Growth Rate of Real Gross Domestic Product 2002–19

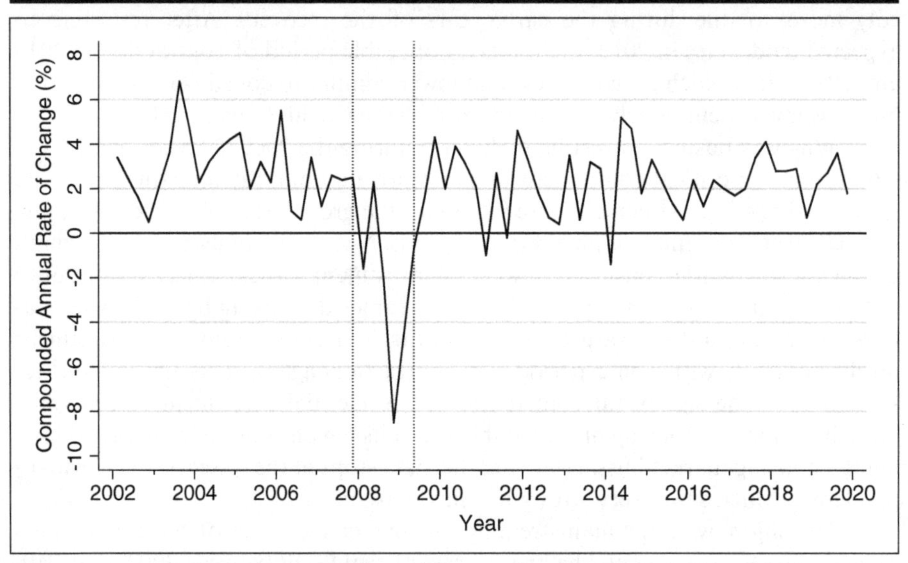

Units—compounded annual rate of change | Seasonally adjusted annual rate | Quarterly.
Source: Federal Reserve Bank of St. Louis FRED economic data (https://fred.stlouisfed.org).

during the 2001–07 recovery is indeed slightly higher, but that is largely due to the one-time surge during the third quarter of 2003.

Stable economic growth does not capture the significant challenges that US workers faced following the Great Recession. As predicted by the NBER, the national rate of unemployment continued to climb following the official trough of the downturn. Figure 9.8 presents the principal unemployment rate reported by the US Bureau of Labor Statistics: the ratio of the total number of unemployed persons to the total labor force. After peaking at 9.9% during the fourth quarter of 2009, the unemployment rate began a long but steady descent throughout the 2009–20 recovery. This is another example of how economists frame agreed-upon, observable phenomena in different ways. Some economists, especially those within the Obama administration, emphasized the consistently downward trend in the unemployment rate beginning in 2010, which never levelled off or increased again during the recovery. Other economists stressed the excessively high unemployment rates for much of the recovery. For perspective, unemployment peaked at 6.1% following the 2001 recession. Yet the 2009–20 recovery proceeded with unemployment rates in excess of 6.1% until the fourth quarter of 2014. Unemployment did not fall below pre-recession rates until 2017, but eventually reached 3.6% before the onset of the Covid-19 pandemic recession.

The next figures underline the weak labor market following the Great Recession with regard to employment and income growth. Figure 9.9 documents the growth rate of total non-farm payroll employment. Following a series of sharp job losses at the height of the crisis, total employment returned to positive growth fairly quickly. Moreover, employment returned to positive growth much sooner than the 2001–07 recovery. Similar to both components of private sector

FIGURE 9.8 Rate of Unemployment 2002–19

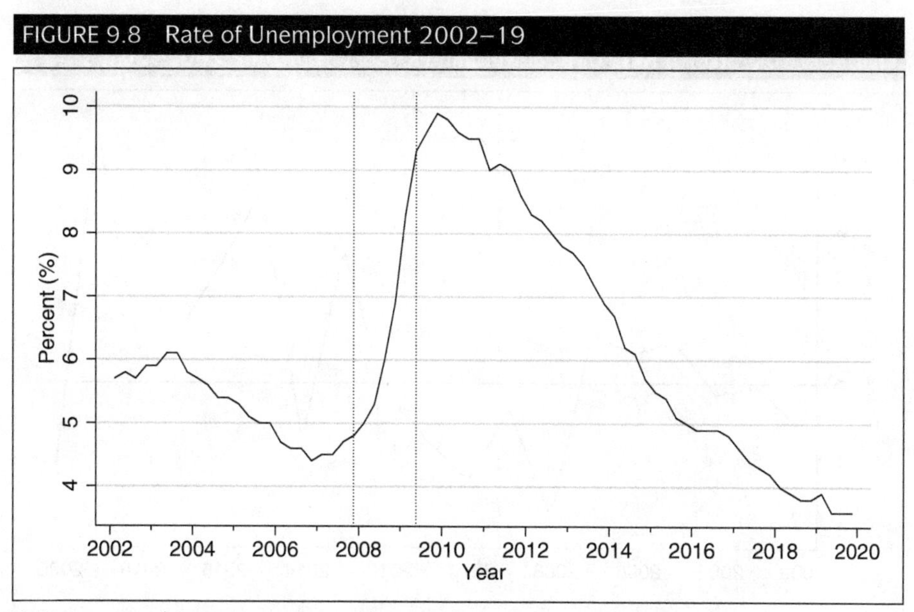

Units—percent | Seasonally adjusted | Quarterly average.

Source: Federal Reserve Bank of St. Louis FRED economic data (https://fred.stlouisfed.org).

FIGURE 9.9 Growth Rate of Total Non-Farm Payroll Employment 2002–19

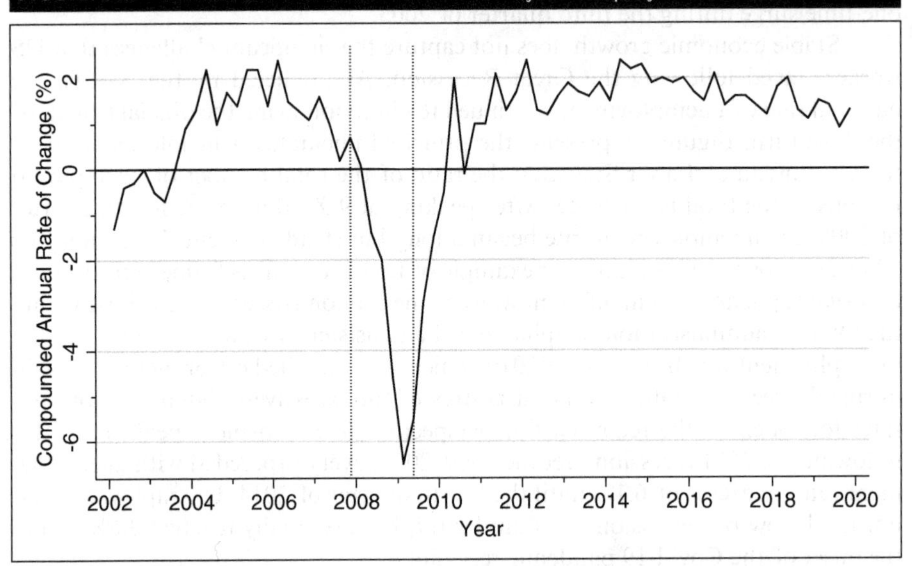

Units—compounded annual rate of change | Seasonally adjusted annual rate | Quarterly average.

Source: Federal Reserve Bank of St. Louis FRED economic data (https://fred.stlouisfed.org).

spending, there appear to be two distinct phases during the 2009–20 recovery. The first phase occurs until 2014, where job creation slowly rebounds as it attains the growth rates seen during the 2001–07 recovery. The second phase occurs after 2014, where job creation slowly weakens. Figure 9.10 then documents the annual

FIGURE 9.10 Growth Rate of Real Median Household Income 2002–20

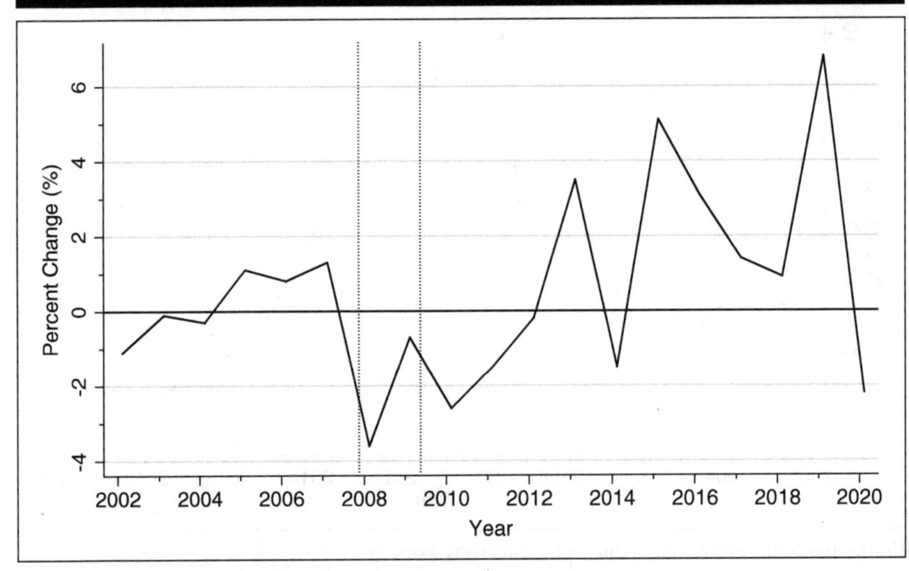

Units—percent change | Not seasonally adjusted | Annual.

Source: Federal Reserve Bank of St. Louis FRED economic data (https://fred.stlouisfed.org).

growth rate of real median household income between 2002 and 2020. Household income clearly struggled to grow following the Great Recession. Although several of the annual growth rates are higher than the 2001–07 recovery, it took until 2015 for household income to reach stables rates of growth. By January 2020, however, real household income once again contracted by over 2%, which had not happened since 2010.

Given the extent of weak economic growth, high unemployment, sluggish job creation, and stagnant incomes, demand pressures on consumer prices were relatively weak throughout the 2009–20 recovery. Figure 9.11 presents the rate of inflation according to the Consumer Price Index. As compared to the 2001–07 recovery, there was an evident downward shift in quarterly inflation rates following the Great Recession, including multiple periods of deflation. One of the important implications of lower inflation is that it raises real debt burdens, which remained substantial during the recovery, despite significant deleveraging by households.

The last figure in this analysis returns to the genesis of the 2008 financial crisis and Great Recession: the residential housing market. Figure 9.12 extends the Case-Shiller Home Price Index to January 2020. After reaching an unprecedented peak in 2006, real home prices in the United States plummeted well into 2012. In constant dollars, the National Home Price Index shows a roughly 35% correction in home values following the housing market bust. However, real home values eventually recovered by early 2020—not returning to the peak seen during the housing bubble, but surpassing the stable levels observed between the end of World War II and the late 1990s.

FIGURE 9.11 Rate of Inflation 2002–19

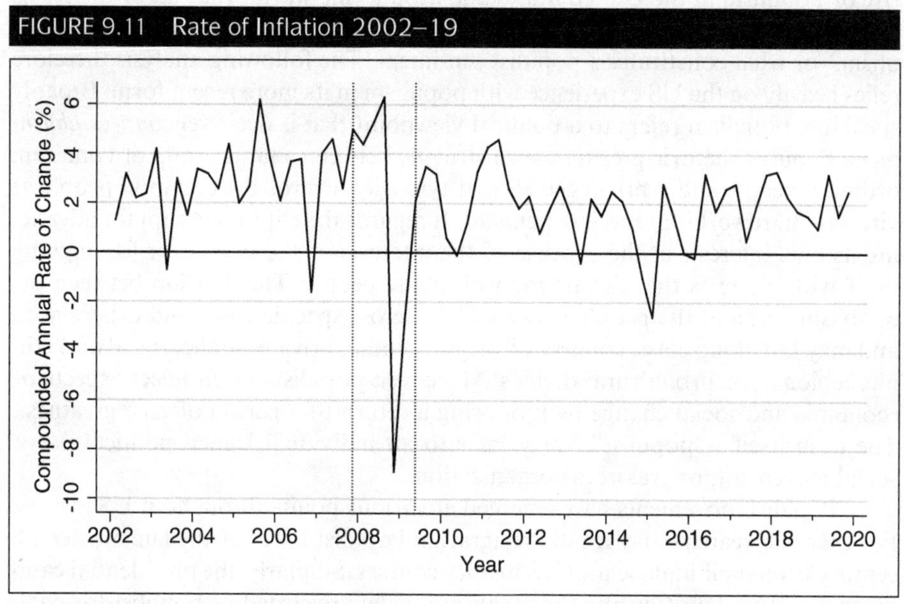

Units—compounded annual rate of change | Seasonally adjusted annual rate | Quarterly average.

Source: Federal Reserve Bank of St. Louis FRED economic data (https://fred.stlouisfed.org).

FIGURE 9.12 Real US Home Price Index 1890–2020

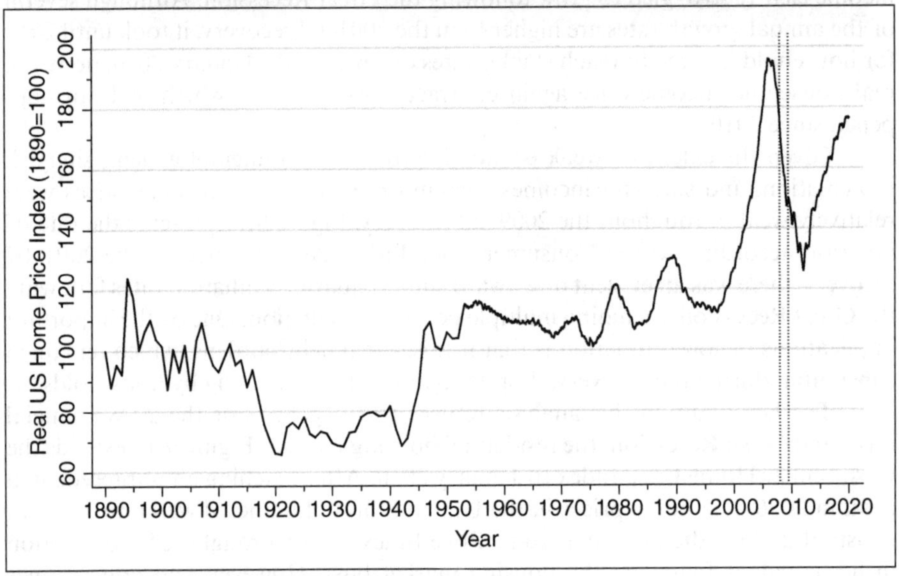

Source: Online data maintained by Robert Shiller (http://www.econ.yale.edu/~shiller/data.htm).

THE GROWTH OF POPULISM

One of the unique and critical aspects of the 2009–20 recovery is the pronounced rise of populism in the United States and around the world. Like all of the terms presented in this textbook, considerable debate exists over the meaning of "populism," or what constitutes a populist sentiment. The following analysis therefore relies heavily on the US experience with populism in its more recent form. Broadly speaking, populism refers to a political viewpoint that is decisively *anti-establishment*. Populist rhetoric presupposes a struggle between a large group of common, ordinary people and a privileged elite. It typically regards the common people as virtuous, hardworking, and independent. It regards the elite as corrupt for advancing its own interests at the expense of the interests of the people, or for aligning itself with interests that thwart the will of the people. The division between the establishment and the people varies widely across specific cases and experiences, and may fall along class, country of origin, gender, private-public, racial and ethnic, regional, or urban-rural divides. Moreover, populists often reject aspects of economic and social change by proposing a return to a period of past greatness. The term itself—"populist"—may refer to an individual leader, political party, social movement, or grassroots organization.

Populist movements have emerged at various points throughout US history. For example, readers may recall the agrarian Populist Party of the late nineteenth century from their high-school US history courses. Similarly, the presidential campaigns of Ross Perot during the 1990s are widely regarded as populist for challenging the mainstream party establishments, and assailing the effects of the national debt and free trade on the middle class. Considerable debate may exist over the meaning of "populism," but few would disagree that *this* wave of populism is a response to economic and cultural changes following the Great Recession. Moreover, the growth of populism has occurred on both the Left and the Right (although the extent of that growth is not necessarily equal). It has led to the creation of influential grassroots organizations and social movements. It has fueled upstart political campaigns that challenge existing economic, political, and social norms at virtually all levels of government. It has also dramatically shifted the policy platforms of the Democratic and Republican parties. To be clear, both major political parties have always featured populist elements or figures. The difference now is that those elements and figures are far more influential. While the growth of populism has influenced both sides of the political spectrum, that does not mean that they have found consensus. In fact, the opposite has largely occurred. Since each side of the political spectrum defines the conflict between the people and the establishment in different ways, and often *opposing* ways, they have reached fundamentally different conclusions about the nature of economic and social problems. At various points since the crisis, this has led to political brinksmanship, polarization, and uncompromising stances on policy making and power sharing.

Since the 2008 financial crisis and the Great Recession, populists within both political parties have rejected many of the central tenets of neoliberal capitalism—such as deregulation, financialization, globalization, and technological change—as well as the myth of the "Great Moderation." The bipartisan consensus over these features that emerged during the 1990s is long gone. Populists have challenged existing power structures within government and the economic system that favor the elite over the common people. But more specifically, discontent over the federal government and the Federal Reserve's responses to the crisis has fueled both left-wing and right-wing populism in the United States. For example, populist stances during the early years of the recovery often highlighted the dichotomy between "Main Street" and "Wall Street." "Main Street" usually refers to the interests of small businesses and the middle class, while "Wall Street" refers to corporate interests aligned with the government or global institutions. Right-wing populists have blasted the overextension of government resulting from the Wall Street bailouts, the Dodd-Frank financial reform, the expansion of the Federal Reserve's emergency authority, and the wave of expansionary fiscal policies. Left-wing populists have seized upon the overextension of corporate power, the lack of capitalist restructuring, the lack of significant legal punishment on the financial sector, and the ongoing intensification of income and wealth inequality. Diversity, demographic change, and other culture war issues—such as immigration, LGBTQ+ rights, reproductive rights, and diversity education—have also become major points of contention. All of these issues have led to sharp divisions not only between the major parties but also within each party. All of these issues have been articulated by captivating leaders that give voice to such anxieties and grievances.

Right-wing Populism

Let's look more closely at the growth of right-wing populism and left-wing populism in the United States. Although the presidency of Donald Trump is closely associated with the ascendance of right-wing populism, the Trump administration essentially sits on a long-term trajectory that has transformed the Republican Party, and pushed it further to the right. Trump advanced the growth of right-wing populism in fundamental ways, but it began before his presidential campaign in 2016, and has evolved further following his electoral defeat in 2020. During the early twenty-first century, right-wing populists have centered their attacks on academics, coastal elitism, free trade, immigration, infringements on religious freedom, the media, the postwar alliances of the United States and North Atlantic Treaty Organization (NATO), as well as urban crime. Returning to the broad definition of "populism" presented at the beginning of this section, right-wing populists allege that the federal government has aligned itself with leftist colleges and universities, Democratically controlled states on the East and West Coasts, China's dominance of the global economy, immigrants, secular interests, a leftist media establishment, the European Union's open borders, and progressive city leaders who refuse to impose "law and order."

Alaska Governor Sarah Palin, who was John McCain's running mate during the 2008 presidential campaign, was one of the first right-wing populists to emerge during the Great Recession. Palin's campaign speeches famously combined small-town, maverick charm with visceral attacks on the liberal media, environmentalists, gun control, secularization, big government, and even establishment Republicans. During the 2010 midterm elections, the nascent Tea Party movement mounted the first successful electoral campaign from the new populist Right. Although the Tea Party was a network of grassroots affiliates, it received significant financial backing from large donors such as the Koch brothers. The Tea Party principally attacked the expansion of government resulting from the Wall Street bailouts, expansionary fiscal policies, heightened financial regulations, and the growth of the national debt. The movement also vociferously opposed environmental regulations and national healthcare reform, especially the Affordable Care Act's individual insurance mandate. In general, the Tea Party called for a massive reduction in the size of government through lower taxes, significant cuts to the federal budget, and a lower national debt. The Tea Party organized nationwide protests against any public policy initiative ranging from healthcare reform to local library budgets. While the Obama administration was the principal target, Tea Party candidates aggressively campaigned against incumbent Republicans that either supported the policy responses to the Great Recession, the policies of the Obama administration, or both. The Tea Party contributed greatly to Republican victories at the federal, state, and local levels over several election cycles. At the national level, Republicans regained control of the US House of Representatives in 2010, and eventually the US Senate in 2014. More consequentially, Republicans won a wave of governorships and legislative majorities (sometimes super-majorities) at the state level. Many victories occurred in traditionally Democratic states of the industrial Midwest, such as Michigan, Ohio, and Wisconsin. At the federal level, the policy agenda of the Tea Party was limited due to President Obama's veto power and, until 2014, a Democratic majority in the Senate. At the state level, however, Republicans were able to pursue conservative fiscal agendas that cut taxes and aggressively cut public spending with little to no opposition from Democrats. The most controversial pieces of legislation altered longstanding labor laws and worker benefits. Republicans enacted right-to-work laws in union-dominated states, slashed the healthcare and retirement benefits of public employees, and eliminated public sector collective bargaining rights. Once an exemplar of bipartisanship, Wisconsin passed a divisive bill that stripped public employees of collective bargaining rights in 2011. Once a blue-collar, union stronghold, Michigan passed a right-to-work law in 2012.

Despite the ascendance of the Tea Party in 2010, Republicans nominated an establishment candidate for president in 2012. Following Mitt Romney's loss to President Obama in the general election, as well as their continued minority status in the US Senate, the Republican National Committee conducted an "autopsy" on its recent election losses. One of the chief goals of the Growth and Opportunity Project was to translate Republican successes at the state level, which were indeed substantial, to Republican successes at the federal level, especially the presidency:

> The Republican Party needs to stop talking to itself. We have become expert in how to provide ideological reinforcement to like-minded people, but devastatingly we have lost the ability to be persuasive with, or welcoming to, those who do not agree with us on every issue. Instead of driving around in circles on an ideological cul-de-sac, we need a Party whose brand of conservatism invites and inspires new people to visit us. We need to remain America's conservative alternative to big-government, redistribution-to-extremes liberalism, while building a route into our Party that a non-traditional Republican will want to travel. Our standard should not be universal purity; it should be a more welcoming conservatism.

The Project recommended greater outreach to racial and ethnic minority voters. It encouraged Republicans to support comprehensive immigration reform as a way to attract more Hispanic voters. It also encouraged greater inclusivity on social issues as a way to attract younger voters and women voters. In the end, Republican primary voters, and eventually the Party leadership, would spurn the recommendations of the Growth and Opportunity Project during the 2016 election cycle.

Donald Trump's candidacy (and then presidency) combined right-wing populism with traditional conservatism, as well as non-traditional policy positions for a Republican candidate. Trump pledged to fix a broken federal government and redress the plight of working people, who were left behind by globalization and liberal economic policies. His populist views centered on three areas: immigration, trade, and China. On immigration, Trump assailed US immigration law for being lax on terrorists, suppressing wages in the labor market, and contributing to urban crime. The open borders of the European Union were a frequent target of his attacks. His most famous pledge, of course, was the construction of a physical wall along the US-Mexico border. During his administration, Trump imposed a travel ban on several Muslim-majority countries, implemented a family separation policy at the southern border, and enacted stricter immigration enforcement by executive order. On free trade, Trump committed to renegotiating the North American Free Trade Agreement and withdrawing from the Trans-Pacific Partnership, a proposed trade agreement between 12 countries across North America, South America, Asia, and Oceania. On China, Trump promised a more aggressive stance against China's growing influence on the global economic system. In office, he imposed trade restrictions and tariffs in order to protect American industry and workers. Trump also embraced several traditionally conservative positions, especially on social issues and other culture war issues. He courted evangelical voters by opposing abortion, barring transgendered individuals from serving in the military, and championing religious freedom. He promised to nominate Supreme Court justices that would overturn the constitutional right to abortion, and support Second Amendment rights. On race and civil rights, he lambasted professional football players for protesting the National Anthem, and the removal of Confederate statues from public spaces. Across these issues he fueled outrage over "wokeness" and "cancel culture." On foreign affairs, however, he deviated from the Republican Party platform in important ways. His "America First" foreign policy was much more isolationist than his predecessors by opposing American exceptionalism, multilateral agreements, and the postwar alliances of the United States, while also fostering relations with autocrats, dictators, and rogue states. Trump publicly criticized NATO members, especially Germany, for not spending enough on national defense. He eventually withdrew from two of President Obama's signature foreign policy achievements: the Iran Nuclear Deal and the Paris Climate Agreement. He also deviated from the Republican Party platform on fiscal policy and the federal budget. He supported the provision of unemployment insurance for displaced US farmers during his trade war with China. He pledged to retain Social Security and Medicare. He supported greater federal investments in infrastructure. On healthcare, he gave voice to the devastating effects of the opioid epidemic on rural areas.

Despite Trump's election loss in 2020, populism continues to be enormously influential on the Right. The House Freedom Caucus is now the most organized and recognizable faction of right-wing populists at the national level. The Caucus is a group of far-right Republicans in the House of Representatives. It was formed by a group of former Tea Party members in 2015, who were frustrated with the current leadership of the House under Speaker John Boehner, and sought to push the party even further to the right. The Caucus combines many of the former Tea Party's conservative positions on fiscal issues and the federal budget with social conservatism. This is one area where the House Freedom Caucus differs from the Tea Party, which had placed greater emphasis on the federal budget and the economy over social issues. The Caucus is also strongly aligned with the positions and policies of Donald Trump.

Left-wing Populism

Like right-wing populism, the growth of left-wing populism has also been motivated by vehement opposition to the policy responses to the Great Recession. However, left-wing populists frame the struggle between the people and the establishment in different ways. As a result, they have reached different conclusions about the nature of economic and social problems since the Great Recession, and especially the potential solutions to those problems. Right-wing populists frame the policy responses to the crisis as a massive overextension of *government*. They view the government as a separate entity with its own interests, which it imposes on the people. Any action by the government is an intervention in the economic system. Right-wing populist rhetoric therefore emphasizes a conflict between the government and the people. Left-wing populists, however, argue that the policy responses to the crisis only further consolidated corporate power, especially that of financial corporations. Rather than being a separate entity with its own interests, the government is an instrument of corporate interests. The problem is not government intervention in the economic system, but *corporate* intervention in the activities of the government. Left-wing populist rhetoric therefore emphasizes the conflict resulting from massive income inequality, such as between the "1%" and the "99%." A good example of this distinction is their opposing views of the Federal Reserve. Neither right-wing nor left-wing populists view the central bank as truly independent. Both view the central bank as an instrument of external influences. They simply differ on the nature and source of those influences. Whereas right-wing populists view the Federal Reserve as an instrument of the federal government, left-wing populists view the Federal Reserve as an instrument of the financial sector.

Since the 2008 financial crisis and the Great Recession, left-wing populists have centered their attacks on several economic, political, and social developments. Many on the Left were dissatisfied with the disparate treatment of homeowners as compared to financial capitalists by the federal government, especially the lack of legal accountability for financial capitalists, despite the fact that Democrats held the presidency and a majority in both Houses of Congress. That difference in treatment contributed in part to the growth of income and wealth inequality during the 2009–20 recovery. Moreover, the wave of bankruptcies and arranged mergers during this crisis led to the formation of even larger banks and financial institutions. Left-wing populists frequently point to the differing experiences of owners of capital and workers during the recovery. Whereas owners of capital benefited from the stabilization of financial institutions, the recovery of financial markets, the return of corporate profits, and a surge in cash reserves, workers continued to face a jobless recovery, stagnant earnings, underemployment, and declining labor force participation. Fiscal austerity and attacks on labor rights at the state level have only intensified inequality. Left-wing populists have also organized around diversity and embraced demographic change, such as the growing participation of women, immigrants, and racial and ethnic minorities in the labor market.

Like right-wing populism, there is a trajectory from the grassroots to electoral campaigns and successes. Occupy Wall Street (OWS) was the first major social movement from the new populist Left following the Great Recession. OWS organized around several issues, but income and wealth inequality as well as the undue influence of corporate lobbying were the biggest. The OWS movement began during the fall of 2011 with the occupation of Zuccotti Park in lower Manhattan. Following the clearing of Zuccotti Park in November that year, it evolved into a national and global campaign against inequality. OWS protestors typically organized through general assemblies and slogans, such as "We are the 99%" and "Banks got bailed out, and we got sold out."

Following OWS, the next major social movement on the Left was Fight for $15. Fight for $15 began in 2012 when fast food workers in New York City went on strike. It became a campaign for workers in the low-wage service sector, such as fast food, healthcare, and retail. Fight for $15 calls for a living wage of $15 per hour and collective bargaining rights over working conditions. It has also rallied against the reliance on food stamps by low-wage workers, wage theft by corporate employers, unsafe working conditions, and sexual harassment on the job. Although

Fight for $15 began as a relatively small protest, it eventually led to nationwide strikes across the United States and around the world. Fight for $15 has been successful at raising the minimum wage at the state and local level, and continues to be a major presence in the labor movement.

The 2009–20 recovery has also seen the marked growth of social movements against racial and gender stratification—for example, Black Lives Matter, #MeToo, and the transgender rights movement. Black Lives Matter was formed in 2013 following the death of Trayvon Martin. It seeks to eliminate the systematic, violent oppression of Black communities by the government and white supremacists. #MeToo, which was originally formed in 2006, became a global campaign for survivors of sexual violence in 2017. These movements have not only galvanized the Left around economic justice and social justice, but also provoked the ire of the Right for spreading "wokeness" and "cancel culture."

Left-wing populism has fueled a number of serious political campaigns and victories that have pushed the Democratic policy platform further to the left. The most significant figure in this regard has been Vermont Senator Bernie Sanders, who ran for president twice as a democratic socialist. Sanders has been a long-time advocate for environmental justice, racial equality, social justice, and workers' rights. His presidential campaigns in 2016 and 2020 included concrete proposals for the cancellation of medical debt and student loan debt; a Green New Deal that would restructure US energy consumption toward renewable energy sources and away from fossil fuels; Medicare for All, which would expand the current retiree healthcare benefit to cover the uninsured; the expansion of Social Security benefits; tuition-free higher education; as well as universal childcare and housing. These programs would be financed by a new wealth tax, a new financial speculation tax, lifting the cap on the Social Security tax, and other measures that would place a higher tax burden on the top 1% of the income and wealth distributions. Massachusetts Senator Elizabeth Warren, who also ran for president in 2020, has expressed left-wing populist sentiments. Warren has been a longtime advocate for consumer financial protection, student loan forgiveness, financial restructuring, and the prosecution of corporate executives whose actions led to the 2008 financial crisis. Several left-wing populists were elected to the US House of Representatives in 2018—most notably "The Squad," a group of young, progressive, women of color: Alexandria Ocasio-Cortez of New York, Ilhan Omar of Minnesota, Ayanna Pressley of Massachusetts, and Rashida Tlaib of Michigan. At the state level, activists on the Left have successfully organized ballot referendums on criminal justice reform, environmental protection, minimum wages, reproductive rights, and the legalization of recreational marijuana. Following the 2018 and 2022 midterm elections, Democrats have reclaimed many governorships and state legislative majorities in the Midwest from Tea Party Republicans.

The United States is by no means exceptional in this regard. Throughout the world, economic and social upheaval as well as the growth of populism have led to major political shifts during the early twenty-first century. Like the United States, many countries have seen the growth of both right-wing and left-wing populism. For example, in 2015, Great Britain voted to withdraw from the European Union in a narrow popular referendum. At the same time, democratic socialist Jeremy Corbyn became leader of the British Labour Party. Brazil elected right-wing populist Jair Bolsonaro in 2018, only to return left-wing populist and former President Luiz Inácio Lula da Silva to power in 2022. In Europe, right-wing populist parties have grown in influence since the Great Recession, such as the Law and Justice Party in Poland and the far-right Alternative for Germany (AfD). Right-wing populist parties and leaders, such as Viktor Orbán in Hungary, have pushed back against European integration, immigration, and LGBTQ+ rights. On several continents, right-wing populist autocrats have consolidated power during this period, such as Vladmir Putin in Russia, Recep Tayyip Erdoğan in Turkey, Narendra Modi in India, and Rodrigo Duterte in the Philippines.

However, the US experience does emphasize a key point of the social structure of accumulation theory presented in Chapter 2: during a period of economic and social upheaval, the transition to a new stage of capitalism is *not* inevitable. Rather, it requires a unique set of historical conditions, conflicts, or struggles. At the height of the Great Recession, many economists (including many within the mainstream) expected another wave of capitalist restructuring, similar to what transpired during the Great Depression. But that clearly did not happen. Restructuring never happened because restructuring was never the goal of the Obama administration or the Federal Reserve. The goal—which they accomplished successfully—was to stop the financial contagion and restart economic growth. David Harvey, who has applied the Marxian tradition to neoliberalism and the Great Recession, argues that capitalist restructuring results from shifts in class power. Regulated capitalism emerged in the aftermath of the Great Depression because workers consolidated class power. Likewise, neoliberal capitalism emerged in the aftermath of the crisis of the 1970s because capitalists consolidated class power. Neither restructuring was inevitable. The aftermath of the 2008 financial crisis and the Great Recession did not give way to a new stage of capitalism, for two reasons. First, a significant share of Obama's 2008 presidential campaign donations came from financial corporations, particularly Goldman Sachs. Unlike the Great Depression, advocates for the financial industry were involved with the reform process from the beginning. Second, the growth of populism has exacerbated divisions and competition between workers—not consolidation. This quote by Karl Marx and Friedrich Engels in *Manifesto of the Communist Party* is telling in this regard: "This organisation of the proletarians into a class, and, consequently into a political party, is continually being upset again by the competition between the workers themselves."

When workers compete against each other, and are more concerned with the race, gender, or country of origin of other workers, it limits the consolidation of political power that could transform their common sources of exploitation. This is why neoliberalism remains in place despite enormous economic and social upheaval since the Great Recession, and the opposing visions of right-wing and left-wing populists. The next section therefore examines the concrete effects of this important transformation on policymaking during the 2009–20 recovery.

POLICY RESPONSES DURING THE 2009–20 RECOVERY

The final section of this chapter analyzes the major policy developments during the 2009–20 recovery. In addition to its unprecedented length, the recovery from the Great Recession is notable for a further reason: two diametrically different presidential administrations conducted fiscal and financial policies. This characteristic stands in contrast to some of the other notable US expansions following World War II. For example, the 1961–69 expansion largely fell under the liberal

Kennedy and Johnson administrations. The 1982–90 expansion fell exclusively under the conservative Reagan and H.W. Bush administrations. The lengthy 1991–2001 expansion is largely associated with the Clinton administration, while the short 2001–07 expansion is associated with the W. Bush administration. The 2009–20 recovery, however, fell under the administrations of Barack Obama and Donald Trump, who clearly had very different policy priorities and positions. In fact, the latter ran on a campaign that sought to undo the accomplishments of the former. This section therefore discusses the ways in which national economic performance during the recovery (as presented in the first section of this chapter) as well as the surge in populist rhetoric (as presented in the second section) combined to affect policymaking. This analysis largely focuses on the policy mechanisms discussed earlier in this textbook—that is, fiscal policies and financial policies—against the backdrop of continued expansionary monetary policy under relatively abundant reserves by the Federal Reserve.

Policymaking During the Latter Obama Years: Gridlock, Brinksmanship, and Austerity

The conduct of fiscal policy responses to the Great Recession was a major point of contention throughout the 2008 presidential election. John McCain argued that "the fundamentals of our economy are strong," and rejected the use of expansionary fiscal policy to mitigate the crisis in the real sector. Barack Obama, on the other hand, countered that jumpstarting the economic system required direct fiscal stimulus through increased expenditures, far beyond the scope of the indirect policy instruments deployed by the W. Bush administration, which focused primarily on tax cuts and incentives. Obama won the general election by carrying 365 electoral votes to McCain's 173 electoral votes. In doing so, Obama flipped several states that had voted for George W. Bush, including the traditionally Republican strongholds of Indiana and North Carolina. Although fiscal stimulus was the priority in 2008, condemnation from the nascent populist Right and concerns over the deficit began to set in with both voters and lawmakers—including many Democrats. During the 2010 midterm elections, Democrats lost several seats in the US Senate and majority control of the US House of Representatives to the Tea Party rebuke. To be clear, the goal of the Tea Party movement was not to bring pragmatism and compromise to policymaking. It was first and foremost to build ideological opposition to Obama's domestic economic agenda, and bring it to a halt. As a result, the conduct of fiscal policy at the federal level shifted from stimulus to restraint—or "austerity"—for the remainder of Obama's tenure. The prime example of this shift was the debt ceiling standoff during the summer of 2011.

The "debt ceiling" refers to the maximum amount of money that the Treasury is legally permitted to borrow. The debt ceiling itself does not permit Congress to increase expenditures, or even increase the deficit. It simply allows the Treasury to continue servicing the debt obligations issued during previous budget cycles. The reasons or sources of such debt obligations do not matter. The Treasury issues bonds in order to cover any excess of expenditures over revenues, whether the deficit was due to tax cuts for corporations and the wealthy, an increase in government purchases of goods and services, an expansion of income transfers, or simply a bad economy that triggered automatic stabilizers. Prior to 2011, there was little to no controversy, partisan debate, or especially concessions related to increasing the statutory debt ceiling. Treasury bonds were regarded as the safest debt instruments in the world, as they are backed by the full faith and credit of the US government. Regardless of the strength of the economic system in the short run, the Treasury has the largest economic system in the world from which to raise funds and finance the obligations of the United States. For this reason, Treasury securities consistently received AAA status from the major credit rating agencies. The consequences of not raising the debt ceiling would be devastating for financial stability, the health of the economic system, as well as national security. First, it would lead to an unprecedented default by the US government, which would send shockwaves through global financial markets, and likely trigger a global financial crisis. Second, it would force an immediate halt to legally mandated spending in several critical areas of the federal budget, such as Social Security, Medicare, and national defense.

But in 2011, Tea Party Republicans used the pending breach of the debt ceiling to extract concessions from Obama and Senate Democrats. In exchange for raising the debt ceiling, they demanded a wide range of spending cuts to reduce the deficit, but without any increase in taxes. After tense negotiations over numerous proposals from both sides, including a failed "Grand Bargain," all sides reached an agreement at the eleventh hour: the Budget Control Act. The Budget Control Act included the following measures:

- an immediate increase in the debt ceiling;
- a series of spending cuts, which in total exceeded the increase in the debt ceiling, over the next ten years;
- no tax increases;
- an agreement to hold a vote on a balanced budget amendment to the US Constitution; and
- automatic budget sequestration.

The automatic budget sequestration measure was particularly important. The Budget Control Act called for the formation of a joint committee that would propose over $1 trillion in more comprehensive measures to further reduce the deficit. If the committee did not reach an agreement, Congress would be permitted to raise the debt ceiling again, but automatic cuts in both mandatory and discretionary spending would ensue. The automatic budget sequestration was an incentive for both sides to avoid measures that each found abhorrent. Partisan gridlock once again prevented the committee from finding compromise, however, which indeed triggered the sequestration for the next several fiscal years. Upon signing the Budget Control Act, President Obama delivered these pragmatic remarks:

> Congress has now approved a compromise to reduce the deficit and avert a default that would have devastated our economy … This compromise guarantees more than $2 trillion in deficit reduction. It's an important first step to ensuring that as a nation we live within our means. Yet it also allows us to keep making key investments in things like education and research that lead to new jobs and assures that we're not cutting too abruptly while the economy is still fragile.

Although the Budget Control Act resolved the debt ceiling crisis, it would not prevent an unprecedent shift in outlook on US government debt. On August 5, 2011, Standard & Poor's downgraded its credit rating on long-term Treasury securities from AAA to AA+. In its press release, S&P expressed concerns over not only the national debt burden of the United States but especially the extent of political gridlock and brinksmanship:

> the downgrade reflects our view that the effectiveness, stability, and predictability of American policymaking and political institutions have weakened at a time of ongoing fiscal and economic challenges … we have changed our view of the difficulties in bridging the gulf between the political parties over fiscal policy, which makes us pessimistic about the capacity of Congress and the Administration to be able to leverage their agreement this week into a broader fiscal consolidation plan that stabilizes the government's debt dynamics any time soon … The political brinksmanship of recent months highlights what we see as America's governance and policymaking becoming less stable, less effective, and less predictable than what we previously believed. The statutory debt ceiling and the threat of default have become political bargaining chips in the debate over fiscal policy. Despite this year's wide-ranging debate, in our view, the differences between political parties have proven to be extraordinarily difficult to bridge, and, as we see it, the resulting agreement fell well short of the comprehensive fiscal consolidation program that some proponents had envisaged until quite recently.

Obama's decisive re-election in 2012 did nothing to stem partisan gridlock. In fact, it became even more entrenched following the 2014 midterm elections, when Democrats lost majority control of the US Senate. For the remainder of his second term, Obama therefore focused on priorities and measures that did not require Congressional approval, such as foreign policy achievements, multilateral agreements on trade and climate change, as well as executive orders on immigration. In 2012, the Obama administration established the Deferred Action for Childhood Arrivals (DACA) immigration policy. DACA established legal employment for undocumented immigrants who were brought to the United States as children, and a reprieve from deportation. In 2014, Obama and Raúl Castro normalized relations between the United States and Cuba. In 2015, the United States joined the Iran Nuclear Deal, a multilateral agreement that limited Iran's nuclear program in exchange for the easing of economic sanctions. The United States also joined the Paris Climate Accords that year—an international agreement to limit greenhouse gases and other contributors to climate change. In 2016, the United States signed (but did not ratify) the Trans-Pacific Partnership, a controversial trade agreement among several countries of the Pacific Rim. But Obama was ultimately unable to move forward on the biggest domestic priority of his second term: a comprehensive infrastructure investment bill. In the end, his principal second-term achievements would become fodder for right-wing populists during the 2016 election cycle, who viewed them as constraints on American sovereignty and stature.

Fiscal Policy and Financial Reform During the Trump Administration

Donald Trump's domestic economic agenda was, in large part, a direct response to the measures enacted against the 2008 financial crisis and the Great Recession, by both the W. Bush and Obama administrations. Put simply, Trump believed that Obama and the Democrats got it all wrong on fiscal policy and financial reform. While Trump's populist rhetoric and unique brand of Republicanism informed his major economic policies, those policies also retained classic conservative prescriptions for fiscal policy and financial policy, such as supply-side tax incentives and deregulation. With Republican majorities in both Houses of Congress during his first two years in office, Trump was able to sign two major pieces of domestic economic legislation: the Tax Cuts and Jobs Act in 2017; and the Economic Growth, Regulatory Relief, and Consumer Protection Act in 2018.

Throughout his tenure, the Right as a whole assailed Obama for conducting expansionary fiscal policies and increasing the deficit. Yet Trump enacted two policies that exacerbated the deficit. First, Trump moved to end sequestration, the mandatory and discretionary spending caps implemented following the debt ceiling standoff in 2011. Second, Trump signed the Tax Cuts and Jobs Act in late 2017. The Tax Cuts and Jobs Act included a package of standard tax cuts advocated by Republicans. However, it also included several tax reform measures—that is, changes to the structure of tax deductions, credits, and penalties in order to broaden the tax base. Analysts regard it as a major piece of tax legislation, and the largest since President Reagan's tax cuts in 1986. While some provisions of the Tax Cuts and Jobs Act were made permanent, many are set to expire in 2025.

The major provisions of the Tax Cuts and Jobs Act include the following:

- across-the-board reductions in individual income tax rates;
- a significant cut in the corporation income tax rate, from 35% to 21%;
- a significant increase in the standard deduction for both individuals and couples that file jointly;
- a $10,000 limit on state and local tax deductions;
- a reduction in the limits on tax deductions for home mortgage interest and home equity;
- the elimination of tax deductions for work-related expenses;
- an increase in the child tax credit; and
- the elimination of the individual insurance mandate from the Affordable Care Act.

By far the largest tax benefit of the Act was the reduction in the corporation income tax rate. The most noteworthy permanent provision was the elimination of the individual insurance mandate, long the scourge of Tea Party Republicans.

The second major piece of domestic economic legislation signed by President Trump was a partial repeal of Dodd-Frank. Analysts use the term "partial" repeal because, although the Economic Growth, Regulatory Relief, and Consumer Protection Act alters Dodd-Frank, its original structure remains intact. The Economic Growth Act reduces the strength of Dodd-Frank's regulations and reforms, but it does not repeal and replace them. For example, the long title of the law states that the purpose is to "provide *tailored* regulatory relief, and *enhanced* consumer protection" (emphasis added). Such language demonstrates at least tacit recognition that a full repeal would have been challenging and disruptive to financial intermediation.

Like Dodd-Frank itself, the Economic Growth Act includes an array of new measures. However, the most consequential changes to the measures presented in

Chapter 6 are as follows. First, the Economic Growth Act alters Federal Reserve oversight of large banks and depository institutions. According to Dodd-Frank, systemically important banks were automatically subject to heightened oversight by the Federal Reserve if they held more than $50 billion in total assets. The Economic Growth Act alters this mechanism by raising the total assets threshold from $50 billion to $250 billion. Furthermore, on an individual basis, the Federal Reserve can apply heightened oversight to banks with $100 billion to $250 billion in assets. The partial repeal then eliminates automatic heightened oversight to banks with $50 billion to $100 billion in assets. Second, the Economic Growth Act alters the frequency of mandatory stress tests for large banks, and eliminates them entirely for banks with less than $100 billion in total assets. Third, the Economic Growth Act repeals the Volcker Rule for smaller, community banks—that is, banks with less than $10 billion in total assets. The Volcker Rule refers to the limitations on risky, proprietary trading by banks set forth in Dodd-Frank.

EPILOGUE: THE ARC TO COVID-19

By 2019, many economists predicted that the US economic system was heading toward a recession. The fact that the recovery from the Great Recession was approaching the ten-year mark, which had only happened once in US history, was evidence alone. In fact, many of the economic performance measures presented in this chapter support that projection. No one knows for sure if (or when) US capitalism would have entered a downturn on its own. The decisive blow to the capitalist growth process was the onset of the Covid-19 pandemic, which triggered a peak in February 2020. However, despite economic and financial stabilization in the United States, the crisis would continue to spread across the world. For example, Iceland experienced its own housing market crash and economic crisis. The European Monetary Union faced a sovereign debt crisis in 2009. Brazil also experienced a major economic crisis in 2014.

The Covid-19 pandemic recession was much shorter than the Great Recession, of course. But like the Great Recession, the pandemic recession is yet another complex and fascinating case study for understanding debates over human behavior, the conduct of policymaking, and competing schools of economic thought. For that reason, this is an appropriate point to conclude this investigation of the 2008 financial crisis and the Great Recession. Throughout US history, recoveries are in large part conditioned by the recessions that preceded them. So, while economists have shifted their focus from capitalism post-2008 financial crisis to capitalism post-pandemic, many economic, political, and social developments between 2007 and 2009 continue to shape the trajectory of US capitalism. As of this writing, Fannie Mae and Freddie Mac are still under the conservatorship of the federal government. Despite the partial repeal in 2018, the Dodd-Frank financial reforms remain in place, which include a new federal agency devoted toward consumer financial protection. Those reforms (and the partial repeal) are being tested with the wave of regional bank failures in Silicon Valley. The Federal Reserve continues to conduct monetary policy under relatively abundant reserves. Lessons learned during the Great Recession informed the fiscal stimulus packages of both political parties during the pandemic. Certainly, the influence of populism continues to affect political debate and the conduct of policymaking. As always, the goal of this textbook has been to understand not only how these developments arose, but the ways in which they influence the evolution of capitalism—in still untold ways.

Sources

Barbour, H., Bradshaw, S., Fleischer, A., Fonelledas, Z., & McCall, G. (2013). *Growth and opportunity project*. Republican National Committee.

Black Lives Matter. (n.d.). http://www.blacklivesmatter.com

Business Cycle Dating Committee. (2010, September 20). *June 2009 business cycle trough/end of last recession* [Press release]. Retrieved from http://www.nber.org.

Dube, A. & Kaplan, E. (2012). *Occupy Wall Street and the political economy of inequality*. Amherst, MA: University of Massachusetts.

Economic Growth, Regulatory Relief, and Consumer Protection Act, 15 U.S.C. § 1601 (2018).

Federal Reserve Bank of St. Louis. (n.d.). *FRED economic data* [Data file and codebook]. Retrieved from https://fred.stlouisfed.org.

Fight for $15. (n.d.). http://www.fightfor15.org

Gross, D. (2008, September 17). "The fundamentals of our economy are strong." *Slate*. Retrieved from http://www.slate.com.

Harvey, D. (2011). *The enigma of capital: and the crises of capitalism*. New York, NY: Oxford University Press.

The Heritage Foundation. (2009, February 19). *CNBC's Rick Santelli's Chicago Tea Party* [Video]. YouTube. https://youtu.be/zp-Jw-5Kx8k

Marx, K. and Engels, F. (1978). Manifesto of the Communist Party. In R.C. Tucker (ed.), *The Marx-Engels reader* (pp. 469 – 500). New York, NY: W.W. Norton & Company.

me too. Movement. (n.d.). http://metoomvmnt.org

National Bureau of Economic Research. (n.d.). US business cycle expansions and contractions. Retrieved from http://www.nber.org.

Obama, B. (2011, August 2). Remarks on the federal budget [Transcript]. Retrieved from https://www.presidency.ucsb.edu.

Piketty, T. (2017). *Capital in the twenty-first century*. Cambridge, MA: The Belknap Press of Harvard University Press.

Sanders, B. (n.d.). *How does Bernie pay for his major plans?* http://www.berniesanders.com

Savitz, E. (2011, August 5). S&P downgrades U.S. debt. *Forbes*. Retrieved from http://www.forbes.com.

Shiller, R.J. (n.d.). *Online data – Robert Shiller* [Data file and codebook]. Retrieved from http://www.econ.yale.edu/~shiller/data.htm.

Tax Cuts and Jobs Act, 26 U.S.C. § 1 (2017).

US Bureau of Economic Analysis. (n.d.). *A guide to the National Income and Product Accounts of the United States*. Author.

Further Reading

Byrne, J. (ed.). (2012). *The Occupy handbook*. New York, NY: Back Bay Books.

Eichacker, N. (2017). *Financial underpinnings of Europe's financial crisis: liberalization, integration, and asymmetric state power*. Cheltenham, UK: Edward Elgar Publishing.

Foster, J.B. & McChesney, R.W. (2012). *The endless crisis: how monopoly-finance capital produces stagnation and upheaval from the USA to China*. New York, NY: Monthly Review Press.

Gordon, D.M. (1978). Up and down the long roller coaster. In Union for Radical

Political Economics (Ed.), *US capitalism in crisis* (pp. 22–34). New York, NY: Union for Radical Political Economics.

McDonough, T., Reich, M., & Kotz, D.M. (eds.). (2010). *Contemporary capitalism and its crises: social structure of accumulation theory for the 21st century*. New York, NY: Cambridge University Press.

Piketty, T. (2015). *The economics of inequality*. Cambridge, MA: The Belknap Press of Harvard University Press.

Piketty, T. (2020). *Capital and ideology*. Cambridge, MA: The Belknap Press of Harvard University Press.

Sapolsky, R. (2017). *Behave: the biology of humans at our best and worst*. London, UK: Vintage.

INDEX

Please note that page references to Figures will be in **bold**, while references to Tables are in *italics*

E

G

I

J

K

L

M

P

Q

R

S

T

U